Mozart and the Mediation of Childhood

NEW
MATERIAL
HISTORIES
of
MUSIC

———

a series edited by
James Q. Davies *and*
Nicholas Mathew

Also published in the series:

Musical Vitalities: Ventures in a Biotic Aesthetics of Music
Holly Watkins

Sex, Death, and Minuets: Anna Magdalena Bach and Her Musical Notebooks
David Yearsley

The Voice as Something More: Essays toward Materiality
Edited by Martha Feldman and Judith T. Zeitlin

Listening to China: Sound and the Sino-Western Encounter, 1770–1839
Thomas Irvine

The Search for Medieval Music in Africa and Germany, 1891–1961: Scholars, Singers, Missionaries
Anna Maria Busse Berger

An Unnatural Attitude: Phenomenology in Weimar Musical Thought
Benjamin Steege

Mozart and the Mediation of Childhood

Adeline Mueller

The University of Chicago Press   CHICAGO AND LONDON

The University of Chicago Press, Chicago 60637
The University of Chicago Press, Ltd., London
© 2021 by The University of Chicago
Published 2021
Printed in the United States of America

30 29 28 27 26 25 24 23 22 21   1 2 3 4 5

ISBN-13: 978-0-226-62966-7 (cloth)
ISBN-13: 978-0-226-78729-9 (e-book)
DOI: https://doi.org/10.7208/chicago/9780226787299.001.0001

This book has been supported by the AMS 75 PAYS Fund of the American
Musicological Society, funded in part by the National Endowment
for the Humanities and the Andrew W. Mellon Foundation.

Library of Congress Cataloging-in-Publication Data

Names: Mueller, Adeline, author.
Title: Mozart and the mediation of childhood / Adeline Mueller.
Other titles: New material histories of music.
Description: Chicago ; London : The University of Chicago Press, 2021. |
Series: New material histories of music | Includes bibliographical
references and index.
Identifiers: LCCN 2020051370 | ISBN 9780226629667 (cloth) |
ISBN 9780226787299 (ebook)
Subjects: LCSH: Mozart, Wolfgang Amadeus, 1756–1791. | Mozart,
Wolfgang Amadeus, 1756–1791—Influence. | Children—Austria—
History. | Music and children—Austria—History.
Classification: LCC ML410.M9 M89 2021 | DDC 780.92—dc23
LC record available at https://lccn.loc.gov/2020051370

♾ This paper meets the requirements of ANSI/NISO Z39.48-1992
(Permanence of Paper).

for Nora

Contents

Abbreviations

Abert   Hermann Abert, *W. A. Mozart*, trans. Stewart Spencer, ed.
               Cliff Eisen (New Haven, CT: Yale University Press, 2007
               [1919–1921])

AmZ   *Allgemeine musikalische Zeitung* (Leipzig, 1798–1848)

Anderson   Emily Anderson, trans. and ed., *The Letters of Mozart and His
               Family*, 2nd ed., prepared by A. Hyatt King and Monica Caro-
               lan (London: Macmillan, 1966 [1938]), 2 vols.

Documents   Otto Erich Deutsch, *Mozart: A Documentary Biography*, trans.
               Eric Blom, Peter Branscombe, and Jeremy Noble (Stanford,
               CA: Stanford University Press, 1965)

Dokumente   Otto Erich Deutsch, *Mozart: Die Dokumente seines Lebens*
               (Kassel: Bärenreiter, 1961)

Edge/Black   *Mozart: New Documents*, ed. Dexter Edge and David Black,
               first published June 12, 2014, https://sites.google.com/site
               /mozartdocuments/

Halliwell   Ruth Halliwell, *The Mozart Family: Four Lives in a Social Con-
               text* (Oxford: Clarendon Press, 1998)

Köchel 6   Ludwig Ritter von Köchel, *Chronologisch-thematisches Ver-
               zeichnis sämtlicher Tonwerke Wolfgang Amadé Mozarts*, 6th
               ed., ed. Franz Giegling, Alexander Weinmann, and Gerd
               Sievers (Wiesbaden: Breitkopf & Härtel, 1964 [1862])

MBA   W. A. Bauer, Otto Erich Deutsch, and Joseph Heinz Eibl,
               eds., *Mozart: Briefe und Aufzeichnungen, Gesamtausgabe*, rev.
               ed. (Kassel: Bärenreiter, 2005 [1962–1975]), 7 vols. [refer-
               ences are to letter number and line]

NMA	W. A. Mozart, *Neue Ausgabe sämtlicher Werke* (Kassel: Bären-reiter, 1955–2010)
NMD	Cliff Eisen, *New Mozart Documents: A Supplement to O. E. Deutsch's Documentary Biography* (London: Macmillan, 1991)
OMO	*Oxford Music Online*, http://www.oxfordmusiconline.com

Figures and Musical Examples

FIGURE 0.1. Jean-Baptiste Delafosse, engraving of Louis Carmontelle's portrait of the Mozarts (1764). © The Trustees of the British Museum, shelfmark 1864,0611.50.

Leopold would not let go of the print. Years earlier, when the family was in Paris in 1764 on their European tour, their friend and assistant Friedrich Melchior von Grimm had commissioned a portrait of Leopold and his two children, engraved to be sold alongside prints of Wolfgang's accompanied sonatas Opus 1–4 (fig. 0.1). The print identifies Nannerl as "virtuoso, age eleven," Wolfgang as "composer and master of music, age seven."[1] The family sold or consigned copies of the print at every major city along their tour. Ten years later, Leopold wrote to his wife from Mannheim to ask her to send him five or six of the prints for him to give away to friends and associates.[2] A year after that, he was still trying to find out whether Grimm had sold the remainder of his copies.[3] In 1778, on the eve of Mozart's twenty-second birthday, fourteen years after the portrait was first printed, Leopold reported that he had written to music sellers in Amsterdam, Zurich, Winterthur, Bern, Geneva, and Lyon with whom he had left copies of the portrait and sonatas, hoping to recover any profit or remaining prints—apparently, he heard nothing back.[4] Leopold was only trying to maximize the return on his investment; but it was long past the time when the portrait was an accurate likeness of his son and daughter.

The print's youngest subject, meanwhile, chafed at this discrepancy between past and present. In a letter home from Paris later that year, just after his mother had died, Wolfgang complained to his father about his reception in France: "What annoys me most of all here is that these stupid Frenchmen seem to think I am still seven years old, because that was my age when they first saw me."[5] Although he did not mention the portrait, it doubtless had some hand in arresting Mozart at age seven in the European imagination. The biographical sketch of Mozart in Forkel's 1784 *Musical Almanac for Germany*, for instance, erroneously stated that during their Paris sojourn, "the father and the children were engraved in copper in the actual performance of a concert."[6]

Meanwhile, the sonatas that had been printed alongside the portrait and that had so astonished Europe had in Mozart's adulthood also become something of a liability: in an unsuccessful effort to persuade Breitkopf & Härtel to publish Wolfgang's music, Leopold wrote to the publisher somewhat sheepishly, "Surely you will not judge him by the clavier sonatas which he wrote as a child?"[7] What had been an asset for young Mozart became, in his maturity, something of an albatross. Years after Mozart's death, Nannerl again revived the portrait: when arranging with Breitkopf to publish his works in 1799, she sent the firm a copy, saying that it proved how adorable he was before being permanently scarred from smallpox. "He was a small but well-proportioned child," Nannerl added, sounding an oddly defensive note.[8]

The portrait is anything but well-proportioned, as one can see at a glance. Seated at the harpsichord, Wolfgang's legs are shortened out of scale with the rest of his body. This makes the figure into a hybrid. His top half is that of the "composer and master of music" who has mastered the codes and conventions of adult musical expression. His dangling, stunted legs, however, are those of the seven-year-old boy who, as eyewitnesses described, could in one moment accompany himself improvising an operatic aria, and in the next play marbles or chase after a cat. The portrait is a representation not so much of what Mozart looked like as what it was like to look *at* him, to attempt to reconcile his stunning talent with his miniscule frame. At once grotesque and endearingly vulnerable, the image might have inspired in viewers a complicated reaction: the impulse to shelter the small body, and at the same time an uneasy awareness that this child was far more self-sufficient than his diminutive legs might at first suggest. The print both symbolized and enacted the capture, commodification, and monumentalization of Mozart's own childhood.

As we look back on the so-called "pädagogisches Jahrhundert" (pedagogical century), Mozart stands out as the quintessential mediated child, in an age that saw increasingly strenuous, comprehensive, public, and commercial interventions in the lives of children. He was by no means the first child performer to scrape together a living on the public stages of Europe. Neither was he the first prodigy to be invited to perform at court, nor the first child genius to publish before puberty. He was, however, the first to do all of those things, at such a young age, across such a wide area of Europe, and to such near-universal acclaim. As a result, his influence stretched beyond music, even the arts. He was cited in an imperial court case as evidence of the potential reasoning capacity of children younger than seven. He became a footnote in the revised edition of Rousseau's *Emile, or On Education*. He lent his name and talents to several child philanthropic programs and reforms. And in communicating directly to children in music for and about them, he contributed to the genre of juvenile literature through which children were first constructed as consumers and readers. Even after his death—in biographies for young readers, excerpts in piano tutors, spurious musical works of a playful nature, and other Mozart trifles—"child-friendly" Mozart helped enshrine the childlike itself as an aesthetic. These are the conditions that helped give rise to the sentimentalized child of the nineteenth century, a notion that arguably dominates attitudes toward childhood to this day.

"Enlightenment is an event in the history of mediation," assert Clifford Siskin and Alan Warner in their book *This Is Enlightenment*.[9] The premise of the present book is that Mozart is an event in the history of the mediated child. He was arguably the first commoner to grow up, year by year, in the public eye, the first whose persona was mediated from childhood onward primarily through the marketplace, and the first to be mythologized and packaged directly to children through print. This meant that Mozart could be leveraged as no child had before in a host of initiatives that were being promoted and debated in late Enlightenment Europe. During and after his own childhood, he either forced or reinforced changes in attitudes toward children's agency, their intellectual capacity, their political and economic value, the outlines of their work, school, and leisure time, and their relationships with each other and with the adults around them. Were it not for his celebrity, someone of his professional status—neither an aristocrat, nor a bureaucrat, nor a man of letters—would never have influenced these aspects of children's lives in the ways he did.

But if the present book makes more of Mozart than previous scholarship has done—in arguing for him as a pivotal figure in the history of childhood, and not just of music—it also makes less of him, in that his influence cannot be explained solely, or even primarily, through the brilliance of his music. Rather, Mozart's influence on the history of childhood had at least as much to do with his presence in the marketplace, circulating in music, literature, criticism, and images—his "brand," in other words. Moreover, his influence appears somewhat inadvertent. While he helped shape conversations around childhood and its meanings, he was also shaped by them. He may have surfed the waves, but he was also carried along by the tide.

One of the principal tidal forces, and a condition of possibility for Mozart as an event in the history of the mediated child, is print. The proliferation of print—a major focus of the contributors to Siskin and Warner's collection—allowed for a figure like Mozart to have as notable a presence in pedagogy and aesthetics as a Basedow or a Gottsched. As Siskin and Warner explain, "mediation is the condition of possibility for Enlightenment—and Enlightenment mediations become the condition of possibility for the many other discursive, material, and intellectual transformations that often become the focus of Enlightenment studies."[10] To adapt this for the present book, Mozart's mediation through printed music became "the condition of possibility" for the mediation of childhood itself.

The phenomenon of the Mozart family portrait, and the uses to which it was put in the decades after it was introduced into circulation, suggest three affordances of print that bring the various historiographical and disciplinary strands of this book into conversation with one another:

Print lingers. The printing of Mozart's likeness and music allowed his childhood to be separated from him both temporally and geographically. He became both a public exceptional child, and an exceptionally *public* child, a figure who embodied much of what pedagogues and philosophers prized in children as symbols of Enlightenment perfectibility. At the same time, the preserving of Mozart's childhood well into his adult years, and beyond his lifetime, coincided with the Romantic preoccupation with sequestering and prolonging childhood. No other figure embodies this threshold moment so fully. This is what Mozart can offer to the history of childhood.

Print misleads. Much of what we have come to accept as self-evident in Mozart historiography are accidents of availability, contingent on what was reproduced (and reproducible) in print. At the same time, certain strands of early Mozart reception overlap with debates in the German-language press about the moral functions of music and theater. These moral debates echoed much of the pedagogical rhetoric of the period, often by the same authors. Contextualizing the reception of Mozart within these other discourses shows just how pedagogical in intent Austrian Enlightenment music was. This is what the history of childhood can offer to Mozart studies.

Print is unfinished. The meanings and effects of music in print are notoriously difficult to pin down, even—as we shall see—when they are attached to explicitly didactic texts in explicitly didactic children's periodicals. Music is therefore ideally positioned to provide what historians of childhood have been calling for since the 1990s: an acknowledgment of the unfinished, emergent nature of constructions of childhood, and a greater attention to children as agents rather than mere screens for the projection of adult fantasies. After all, as mediators between composers and listeners, performers introduce a note of unpredictability and mutual interdependence into those encounters, one we may productively map onto encounters between adults and children.[11] Young and old meet in the zone where adults remember and children project. Print and performance alike offer pretexts, and at least a limited set of instructions, for navigating that zone of encounter. Music, in particular, offers opportunities for children to be heard, and for adults to fall silent and listen. This is what music can offer to the histories of print and childhood.

As is by now apparent, the present study is transdisciplinary in both its approach and its conclusions, drawing from recent work in musicology, Enlightenment studies, childhood studies, and histories of print. Each of these disciplines has come into closer contact with the others in recent years, their encounters raising questions. What role did music play in the emergent juvenile print market? How did developments in child welfare, education, and the reception of precocious children affect one another? How did printed music shape the Austrian Enlightenment, and vice versa? Scholars such as Hugh Cunningham, James van Horn Melton, and David Thomas Cook have shown how policy, pedagogy, and the marketplace intersected in the modern history of childhood.[12] And several historians of the Austrian Enlightenment—most notably Tim Blanning, Derek Beales, and Heather Morrison—have demonstrated how central music and print were to Habsburg politics.[13] My book complements these efforts by offering a musicologist's perspective on how Mozart and his music shaped the reevaluation of childhood during the Austrian Enlightenment. When the archive allows it, I also identify the effects those changes had on the lived experiences of historical children—not least, on Mozart himself.

Mozart came of age at the same time as the modern cult of the child, and he remains to this day one of its chief exemplars. Yet the clichéd image of Mozart the *Wunderkind* remains undertheorized and underhistoricized. It is all too easy to dwell on his symbolic status as a prodigy, particularly his posthumous reputation as the ultimate Romantic savant. Even to treat the changing construction of childhood in this period as merely a facet of intellectual or cultural history is to ignore its effects on the everyday lives of real children. In this book, I argue that Mozart's direct engagement throughout his life with children—as performers, reader-consumers, and subjects of musical performance—had concrete effects. Thousands of real children across the Habsburg Monarchy were affected by the Salzburg phenom and the idea he personified: that childhood itself could be packaged, consumed, negotiated, circumscribed, deployed, performed—in short, mediated. Drawing on a range of evidence, from double concertos and Benedictine school operas to Habsburg court edicts and children's periodicals, I show that, while we need the Enlightenment to help us understand Mozart, we also need Mozart to help us understand the Enlightenment, as well as the mediations of childhood unfolding in our own time.

The pragmatic, reformist orientation of the Habsburg Monarchy, and the proliferation of print, were relative constants of the Austrian Enlightenment, and both shaped discourses of childhood. Domestic reforms regarding child welfare, labor, education, and criminal justice were increasingly circulated, debated, and defended in print, alongside a new genre of literature aimed directly at the child reader. Working across national, confessional, and even certain class boundaries, print mediated between policies, ideologies, and lived realities—between those who wished to change the way children were viewed and treated, and those whose attitudes they sought to transform. As changes in policy coincided with a rise in naturalistic and sentimental representations of children in popular theater, music, and literature, Habsburg subjects encountered the notion of childhood as a phase of life worthy of increased care and oversight. Music, with its vaunted emotional immediacy and cachet of sociability, was a powerful way to reach both children and the parents and educators who came under increasing scrutiny in print (and who were, after all, the ultimate consumers of children's print).

Mozart's engagement with children was ad hoc, driven largely by opportunities in an unpredictable marketplace. He agreed to an appearance here, contributed to a periodical or song collection there. His (and his father's) business decisions placed him at the center of many collisions between ideal and actual children—whether directly, as when he composed songs for a children's periodical printed for the benefit of Vienna's Taubstummeninstitut (Deaf-Mute Institute, an outdated and offensive term), or indirectly, as when a collection of moralizing tales for children used one of his four-hand keyboard sonatas to epitomize sisterly affection. Throughout and immediately after his life, Mozart prompted reevaluations of the responsibilities adults and children had to one another, and how children might be made profitable in new ways.

The standard historiographical narrative about childhood tends to skip from early Enlightenment models of the child as a *tabula rasa* for the civilizing process, to the nineteenth-century image of childhood as doomed, distant, and inherently angelic.[14] This narrative has traditionally leaned on top-down sources such as pedagogical philosophy, children's literature, and visual culture. For a few decades in late eighteenth-century Austria, Mozart exemplified a messier, more contingent, bottom-up picture of the child as a sophisticated, socially embedded subject. Paternalistic concern was tempered with sincere rapprochement, even companionship, a model of childhood that has begun to make a comeback in policy, pedagogy, and historiography over the past forty years or so.[15] Its acknowledgment of children's agency has affinities with the agency now attributed in the humanities to the consumer, the reader, and the performer. The time is right, therefore, to examine the eighteenth-century precedent for this notion of agency, in a moment in which childhood, print, the marketplace, and the performing arts met and influenced one another in unprecedented and far-reaching ways.

Each chapter of the book identifies an aspect of childhood mediated by a particular institution or corpus of music to which Mozart contributed. The six chapters cover the following themes: reason, industriousness, virtue, work and play, familial affection, and the childlike. These themes often overlap, with certain threads emerging across and between chapters: for example, the interaction between print and performance, the negotiation of public and private, and the redrawing of the boundaries of childhood as a stage in the life course. Chapter 1 considers the emergence of Mozart as a published composer at age seven. Commentators imputed the astonishing quality of his first sonatas not (as later generations would assert) to a productive deficit of reason on the part of their prepubescent composer, but to his having attained mature reason preternaturally early. Accordingly, Mozart was understood by critics, court chroniclers, and philosophers not as the latest or most exceptional in a long line of child virtuosos, but rather as a prodigy of languages and letters—a *puer doctus* (child scholar). That the proofs of Mozart's genius, his compositions, appeared in print gave them an authority and a permanence that eyewitness accounts of his performances could not equal. This geographical and temporal extension of the encounter with the child composer fed into ideas about identificatory reading, and changed the terms by which children's capacity to reason was adjudicated. When he served as evidence in an imperial court case and its later reversal, Mozart was made to stand for the potential reasoning capacity of all children. The import of this episode cannot be overstated: central assumptions about childhood autonomy, aesthetic and moral judgment, and music as a rational art were all being reevaluated in the wake of Mozart's success, with real consequences for children and families across the Monarchy.

Chapter 2 looks at Mozart's role in the Austrian Enlightenment reforms of state-sponsored child welfare and education. Mozart was a poster child for one such reform, when at age twelve he appeared as the featured composer and conductor in a ceremony consecrating the new church at Vienna's Waisenhaus (Orphanage), which had recently come under Habsburg control. The Waisenhaus was known for eliding musical with military discipline; Mozart's appearance was thus part of a wider effort to refashion Austrian orphanages from privately run factory-worker training facilities into public charities aimed at the molding of ideal Habsburg subjects. Years later, Mozart contributed several Lieder to a periodical benefiting Vienna's Taubstummeninstitut, and to a collection published by the Prague Normalschule (Teacher Training Institute). In both of these cases, Mozart and his music promoted music as a branch of *Industrial-Unterricht* (industrial education) and as a promotional tool for Maria Theresa's and Joseph's reform policies. This dual public-relations function marks a period of transition in the role of the music-making child as an agent of political spectacle: from an ideal of power and continuity to one of service and progress.

Mozart's first opera, *Apollo et Hyacinthus* (K. 38, 1767), was part of a long tradition of *Schuldramen* performed by young students at the Benedictine University in Salzburg. By the time of *Apollo et Hyacinthus*'s premiere, however, a pamphlet war over Schuldramen was in progress, a debate that hinged on the question of whether youth were susceptible to moral suggestion through theater. Meanwhile, *Kindertruppen*—wandering troupes of professional child actors—were crisscrossing the Habsburg lands, performing skilled and often bawdy adaptations of adult plays, operas, ballets, and pantomimes. One Kindertruppe Singspiel, *Das Serail*, formed the basis for Mozart's unfinished Singspiel of 1779, *Zaide* (K. 344/336b), and the timing and personnel involved suggest that it may even have been undertaken with Vienna's Theatralpflanzschule (Theatrical Nursery), a youth training institution for the National Singspiel, in mind. In chapter 3, I show how Mozart's encounters with and contributions to these genres and institutions intersected with broader debates about the compatibility of theatrical entertainment and moral instruction. The spectacle of the performing child was particularly vexing to reform-minded pedagogues, as innocence and naturalness were increasingly essentialized in children and posited as vulnerable to external threats from consumer culture. As Schuldramen and their music made room for the harlequinade and Volksstück, and Kindertruppen sought a more literate and morally elevated repertoire, both addressed the uneasy relation between sexuality and commerce in the theater.

Whereas the first three chapters of this book focus on policy and the

public experience of childhood, chapters 4, 5, and 6 turn to domestic en-
tanglements between children and adults. Chapter 4 surveys music's role
in the emergence of a self-consciously differentiated literature for children in German. With philosopher-reformers supplanting clergy as the
chief architects of the German-language educational agenda, pedagogues
sought out new ways to market education and entertainment, developing
a corpus of periodicals, miscellanies, and anthologies that purported for
the first time to be age-appropriate. The Kinderlieder published in these
readers alongside moralizing stories, dialogues, and plays drew on the
same qualities prized in Lieder more generally, among them accessibility
and "noble simplicity." They often figured play as a kind of work, in the
sense of rehearsing adult gender roles around labor. Mozart's Kinderlieder for a more general commercial readership are addressed here: the two
Lieder included in the 1768 *Neue Sammlung zum Vergnügen und Unterricht* (K. 52 and 53), and the three included in the 1791 *Liedersammlung für
Kinder und Kinderfreunde* (K. 596–98), whose texts came from Mozart's
own copy of a children's reader. Mozart's Kinderlieder exemplify this disciplining strain in play, but occasionally, utilitarian Enlightenment *Bildung* gives way to a more mischievous or world-wise child's voice. We
will also find the rhetoric of an authentic *Kinderton* influencing the more
familiar notion of the *Volkston*.

Chapter 5 moves from vocal to instrumental music, bringing together
Mozart's instrumental works that perform the family: music for four
hands dedicated to and performed by siblings (including Mozart and his
sister), and two concertos commissioned by specific parents and children: the concerto for three keyboards (K. 242, 1776) and the concerto
for flute and harp (K. 299, 1778). I interpret this music as a form of family
portrait—much as portraits, novels, sentimental plays, and juvenile literature ennobled middle-class family relationships—and also as a kind of
scenario for encounters between family members. The music stages compromise, turn-taking, and autonomy in ways that invited identification on
the part of dedicatees, performers, and listeners, and that suggest allegorical readings in terms of the new ideal of the affectionate family. Chamber
music thus ritualized a newly prized intimacy between siblings, parents,
and children, one that the Mozarts themselves had long been understood
to represent.

Chapter 6 explains how Mozart became child-friendly. Toward the
end of his life and for some years afterward, he was characterized by
many as an eccentric composer of difficult and artificial music. Another
strain of Mozart reception, however, emphasized the elegant, light, and
simple qualities in his music, and it is this version of Mozart that dom-

inates his popular reception to this day. Some clues as to how "child-friendly Mozart" took hold in the popular imagination can be found in the forms of print through which he was marketed to youth in the first decades after his death: biographies and biographical sketches for young readers; youth-oriented works spuriously attributed to Mozart (including a minuet dice game, a musical alphabet, and a lullaby); and finally, the print debut of Mozart's earliest compositional sketches. These publications helped smooth out Mozart's perceived eccentricities and make him more accessible. They also completed the process that Leopold had first set in motion when he printed Mozart's Opus 1–4: the merging of the juvenile and the monumental. When a spurious lullaby was included among Mozart's works due to its "Mozartisch" qualities, the circular logic affirmed what the previous thirty years had helped establish: the essentializing of qualities such as the naïve, whimsical, and pleasing as fundamentally Mozartian. Ultimately, then, I explore the rebranding of the term *Mozartisch*, from difficult to delightful—a semantic shift, I argue, that epitomizes Mozart's legacy to the modern child.

Much work still needs to be done in correcting music's peripheral status in both childhood studies and Enlightenment studies. Social history is also crucial for combating the tendency for childhood in the Enlightenment to be understood as something to be "fashioned," "invented," or "imagined" (to quote from three recent titles in childhood studies).[16] While my study is still rooted in print evidence, and in narratives originating from positions of official and unofficial power, I look at Mozart's engagement with children and childhood as mediated in reciprocal, often unpredictable ways: whether in a concerto for a father and daughter, a sonata by an eight-year-old boy, a musical dice game, or a Mass for the consecration of an orphanage church. In foregrounding music, the book's broader project is to advance a new understanding of the history of childhood as a dynamic, lived, *performed* experience, rather than (as more commonly understood) solely as theory, projection, or fantasy—in other words, as something mediated not just through texts or objects, but also through actions.

CHAPTER 1

Precocious in Print

From alphabet blocks to swaddling bands, from "A sound mind in a sound body" to "We know nothing of childhood," John Locke's *Some Thoughts concerning Education* (1693) and Jean-Jacques Rousseau's *Emile, ou De l'éducation* (1762) represent for many the alpha and omega of the Enlightenment reevaluation of the child. The narrative originates with Locke, who pioneered a child-centered system of individualized education based on the principle of natural reason and the developmental benefits of play, and established a discourse of the rights of children.[1] Seventy years later, Rousseau expanded on Locke, valorizing children's innate virtue.[2] Through a carefully choreographed "negative education," Rousseau argued, parents and educators could mitigate or even bypass the corrupting effects of inadequate and oppressive social systems.[3]

For all their differences, Locke and Rousseau were united by their faith in experiential learning, in benevolent guardianship as the motivating principle of education, and in education as the cornerstone of social reform at large. They also shared a new view of children as thinking, feeling beings, possessed of legitimate needs and perspectives. Despite this, theirs were still essentially top-down approaches to childrearing, presenting the child as a largely passive beneficiary of learning—whether as a *tabula rasa* or "empty cabinet," in Locke's formulation, or as a special kind of "noble savage," in Rousseau's.[4] Their paternalistic orientation is reflected in the format they both chose to promulgate their approaches: the extended essay-treatise, addressed to parents and tutors.[5] What Locke and Rousseau shared, and what their works enshrined, was a construction of the child as recipient.

In this chapter, I draw on an alternative conception of Enlightenment childhood, one that treated children not so much as "passive parrots" but rather as "artful collaborators," to use Marah Gubar's description of child characters in Golden Age literature.[6] This reversal or at least softening of the top-down orientation saw adults begin to engage directly with children as readers, consumers, performers, and even authors—participants in their own self-fashioning. Principal among the agents of this reorientation, I argue, was Mozart. And it was not primarily as a musician that he influenced the Enlightenment conception of childhood. Mozart's status as a publishing composer had the more significant and lasting effect.

Opus 1–4 (1764–1766), the accompanied sonatas for keyboard and violin that Mozart's father had printed and sold throughout the family's first European tour, along with their initial reception, are well accounted for in Otto Erich Deutsch's documentary biography and its various addenda, and excerpts from this literature are staples of Mozart biography.[7] But the sonatas are generally treated only as evidence of the extent of Mozart's astonishing talents, rather than scrutinized for their broader historical import. Of all the aspects of Mozart historiography to which overfamiliarity risks blinding expert and non-expert alike, his precocity is perhaps the most glaring. Mozart's sensational achievements before reaching adolescence are now so well known that we take them for granted, and we begin to think of him in a category of childhood all by himself. But treating him as an anomaly minimizes his impact.

I revisit this evidence, along with some lesser-known material, in order to recover Mozart's place at the heart of late eighteenth-century debates about children and childhood. Like the Victorian-era child literary characters Gubar writes about, the professional child Mozart was a "highly acculturated" and "fully socialized subject."[8] In reevaluating the early reception of his first printed works, and situating him among the other precocious children to whom he was compared, I identify the assumptions about childhood that rulers, pedagogues, and men of letters had to adjust in the wake of his success. Chief among those assumptions was the minimum age of reason, whose revision down and then back up again—both times with Mozart as the standard-bearer—had repercussions not just in print culture, but in policies that affected children across the Habsburg Monarchy.

The word "reason" and its semantic neighbors—knowledge, intelligence, ability, skill, talent, genius—appear again and again in the early reception of Opus 1–4. But what did these terms mean in the 1760s? Some might see the reasoning child as merely an affirmation of Locke's and Rousseau's Enlightenment faith in experiential learning; the incremental process by which children acquire the capacity to reason (i.e., make informed choices, recognize truth) speeds up in those children more favorably disposed to its acquisition. But, as I hope to show, Mozart's juvenile compositions suggested to many that children were capable of indepen-

dent, creative thought, and could produce works of art and learning that
were worthy of serious appraisal by adults. This was something different
in kind: it went beyond the child's successful absorption of knowledge
or internalization of principles of reason to encompass a more autonomous exercise of one's intellect and imagination. To put it another way:
if childhood was defined by Locke and Rousseau largely as a time of defi-
ciency of (or freedom from) reason—"an age," as the historian Anthony
Krupp puts it, "under the sign of 'not yet'"—Mozart embodied a childhood under the sign of "yes, now."[9]

This "yes, now" view of the child was mediated through print, but a
different kind of print than *Some Thoughts* or *Emile*—not a treatise, but
popular music, aimed at a broad readership and intended for domestic
performance. Mozart was a child himself, one who embodied precocity and whose music enabled consumers to reenact that precocity. But
this was not a precocity that can be read backwards from Romanticism,
as so many scholars of Mozart's prodigy years have done. Commentators like Peter Kivy, Maynard Solomon, Gloria Flaherty, and Peter Pesic
have tended to privilege nineteenth-century constructions of Mozart
as an eternal child or demigod, mistaking his early mastery of a highly
conventional style for transcendent originality or divine "lack of experience."[10] Reading up to and around the years of Mozart's prominence as
a child composer, and sampling a range of responses to his emergence
in the 1760s, yields a different picture. Whereas nineteenth- and many
twentieth-century commentators frequently imputed Mozart's genius to
a productive deficit of reason, those attempting to account for Mozart in
his own time seemed more inclined to understand him as having attained
mature reason preternaturally early.

In order to ground this idea of Mozart as a thinking, reasoning child,
I begin by reassessing the cultural currency of Opus 1–4. These prints
were commodities, like all printed music.[11] But as music, they invited a
sustained, intimate, repeatable identification with their composer, imply-
ing a different notion of readership than that in a circulating image, book,
or periodical.[12] As texts, they were agents of legitimization, preservation,
and immortalization. Imagining their performance as "acts" generates
another, perhaps more evanescent, set of meanings to do with sympathy
with the child author, and recognition of children's reasoning power.[13]
Mozart's importance to Enlightenment childhood originates in his status
not as an anomaly, but as an exemplar—a fact that is often missed when
looking at Mozartiana solely as biographical evidence.

Unlike Locke or Rousseau, Mozart did not set out to alter Enlightenment notions of children's reasoning capacity. Nor was his influence per-

manent. Nevertheless, reactions to his precocity fed back into the top-down discourses of pedagogy, philosophy, and policy, discourses that to this day constitute the main themes of childhood historiography. The imperial court case I discuss later in the chapter, in which Mozart was "Exhibit A" in a debate about children's capacity to reason, had real import for thousands of children, not just child geniuses. It is for this reason that his early career warrants reevaluation from within the historical norms to which his precocity represented a challenge.

To Be a Reasoning Child

"Picture to yourself the furore which they will make in the world when people read on the title-page that they have been composed by a seven-year-old child." So wrote Leopold Mozart in 1764 to the wife of his friend and landlord Lorenz Hagenauer, referring to Wolfgang's keyboard sonatas with optional violin accompaniment, Opus 1 (K. 6–7) and 2 (K. 8–9), which Leopold was preparing for publication in Paris (fig. 1.1).[14] While Wolfgang had composed the sonatas when he was seven, by the time they appeared in print he was eight. So began a pattern of downward revision of Mozart's age by one to two years, an innocuous but (for the Mozarts) advantageous slippage that became a common feature in the promotion of child prodigies.[15]

Wolfgang and his sister Nannerl were less than a year into their first European tour, and while the two children's public concerts and court appearances had brought them great acclaim, child virtuosos were nothing new.[16] Since the seventeenth century, precocious musicians had been familiar ornaments of the courts of Europe, and by the middle of the eighteenth century, exceptional child musicians and singers had become fixtures of public concert life in cities like London, Paris, and Amsterdam. Child composers, on the other hand, were a genuine rarity. Prodigies sometimes performed (or claimed to perform) their own music, but they appear almost never to have printed these works, and the few isolated instances of printed music by composers under twenty either did not mention the composer's age or were later disclaimed as juvenilia.[17] For instance, Andrea Stefano Fiorè described his *Sinfonie da chiesa* (Modena, 1699) as "the last squalls of my infancy [*infanzia*], and the first expressions of my boyhood [*puerizia*], having just turned thirteen."[18]

That division of childhood into two phases, *infantia* and *pueritia*, goes back to antiquity, and it still held in the mid-eighteenth century. The concept informs Charles Burney's observation in 1771 that Mozart's "premature and almost supernatural talents astonished us in London a few years

FIGURE 1.1. Title page, Mozart, *Sonates pour le clavecin . . . Oeuvre premiere* (K. 6–7, Paris, 1764). Courtesy of Österreichische Nationalbibliothek, shelfmark SA.86.C.12/1.

ago, when he had scarce quitted his infant state."[19] However, the duration and meaning of each phase was somewhat in flux. The familiar biological rites of passage in youth—the loss of one's baby teeth and the onset of puberty—were interpreted differently in different periods, and even by different writers within the same period.[20] Most writers seem to have agreed that, up until at least age seven, children were not capable of rational thought, particularly moral reasoning. This is why from the early modern period, seven tended to be the minimum age of (limited) criminal responsibility, and of one's first communion in the Catholic rite. Both criminal and Canon law followed the ancient Romans in presuming children under seven unable to distinguish between right and wrong: they were in the same category of *doli incapax* (incapable of evil intent) as the insane.[21] It may also explain the double meaning of *infantia* as both the first phase of life and "inability to speak" or "want of eloquence."[22] In the 1741 German-Latin dictionary owned by Leopold Mozart, "infans" was defined as a child who could not yet speak, "puer" as a child of either sex up to age ten.[23] *Pueritia* had since the early modern period often been lumped together with infancy as an "age of ignorance" or *infirmitas* preceding puberty.[24] Criminal law followed this assumption too, usually granting some measure of leniency between age seven and twelve or fourteen.[25] This dual age limit for criminal responsibility was current in the Habsburg Monarchy during Mozart's time, being upheld by Maria Theresa in the *Constitutio Criminalis Theresiana* of 1768.[26]

Locke and Rousseau both concurred with the notion that prepubescent children possessed at best a limited capacity to reason, and that intellectual precocity in children was something to treat with caution, even skepticism. As Rousseau warned:

> Nature wants children to be children before being men. If we want to pervert this order, we shall produce precocious fruits which will be immature and insipid and will not be long in rotting. . . . I would like as little to insist that a ten-year-old be five feet tall as that he possess judgment. Actually, what would reason do for him at that age? . . .
>
> The most dangerous period of human life is that from birth to the age of twelve. This is the time when errors and vices germinate without one's yet having any instrument for destroying them.[27]

Although Rousseau often positioned himself in opposition to Locke, his image of "rotting fruit" owed much to Locke's own organicist metaphors for child development. Here is Locke:

> No Body can think a Boy of Three or Seven Years old should be argued with, as a grown Man . . . *Pertness*, that appears sometimes so early, proceeds from a Principle, that seldom accompanies a strong Constitution of Body, or ripens into a strong Judgment of Mind. . . . There is not so much pleasure to have a Child prattle agreeably, as to reason well.[28]

As one might expect, Locke and Rousseau meant different things by the words "reason" (*la raison*), "reasoning" (*raisonner*), and "judgment" (*le jugement*). Locke's concept of reason was still essentially a moral, religious understanding, while Rousseau defined it as informed *amour-propre*.[29] They also differed in their assigning of a minimum age to the ability to reason and the capacity for deliberate vice—seven for Locke, twelve for Rousseau.[30] Nevertheless, they agreed on the dangers of transgressing those age limits.

As wary as they were of child precocity, both pedagogues were even more suspicious of music as a subject for study by boys. Locke sniffed that music "wastes so much of a young Man's time, to gain but a moderate Skill in it, and engages often in such odd Company, that many think it much better spared"; while Rousseau lumped it together with "tennis, croquet, billiards, the bow [and football]" as a "game of skill."[31] Indulging his natural inclination toward music theory, Rousseau began to outline an elementary music literacy curriculum, emphasizing the composition of simple melodies, but then cut himself off with "But this is too much about music. Teach it as you wish, provided that it is never anything but play."[32] Music returns later on in the book only as an accomplishment for Emile's intended, Sophie, and as an agent of their courtship. Music's value for young men was as a form of recreation or sport, a rest for the mind, but musical composition in the young—like other forms of artistic invention such as writing or painting—appears not to have even entered Locke's or Rousseau's minds.

By 1763, when the Mozarts embarked on their European tour, Locke was still the primary authority on childrearing for most readers across Europe, and *Emile* had just been published and was creating a sensation.[33] The idea, then, that a seven-year-old boy could produce intelligent music worth preserving in print—and, by implication, music worth being performed by adults, for there was as yet no separate corpus of music for children—would have struck many as peculiar at best. For all these reasons, Leopold had to have been certain that Opus 1–4 would be a success. And he doubtless had no small hand in ensuring that outcome: we know that he closely supervised and edited Wolfgang's first efforts as a composer. But if this music managed to distinguish itself, it might in so doing reflect poorly on the style, exposing *galant* music to critique as mere triviality. Good composition was presumed to demand years of study and apprenticeship. The seven-year-old had only been at it for, at most, four years; if it was this easy, where was the art?

In the end, Opus 1–4 made an even greater "furore" than Leopold had predicted. Critics who encountered the sonatas either enthusiastically proclaimed, or grudgingly admitted, that not only did they corroborate eyewitness accounts of the boy's talents as a performer and improviser—they constituted a sensation in their own right. Father Beda Hübner wrote in his diary, "The boy is an accomplished composer who, during the time he was in Paris, himself composed such beautiful, artful and precious music . . . that not only the whole Parisian Court but the whole world was amazed thereat, the more so as all the music at once appeared in public print in Paris."[34] A commentator in Hamburg asked with incredulity, "Is it conceivable that a child of 7 should, thanks to an adroit dedication, appear in public print?"[35]

In skeptical, novelty-weary London, some critics apparently could only make sense of Wolfgang's talents by assuming him to be a grown man in disguise. A letter from a "Recto Rectior" to the *Public Advertiser* (probably written or at least requested by Leopold himself) claimed that Wolfgang's detractors

> assert it is not the Performance of a Child—a Child Eight Years of Age, but of a Man—a Man reduced by some Defect of Nature to an Insignificancy of Person, which conceals from the careless Observer his more advanced Age.—That he is now in his fifteenth, his twentieth or his thirtieth Year, according as the Spirit of his Opponents think fit to place him.[36]

Leopold's "Opponents" may well have been real, or simply a fabrication to drum up publicity. Nevertheless, "Recto Rectior" claimed that Leopold was prepared to produce "ample Testimony of the Child's Nativity" to anyone still in doubt. The provocation of Wolfgang's age in the Opus 1–4 prints was thus prolonged, as the music was understood both to "prove" Wolfgang's talent, and to necessitate further (written) "proofs" of Wolfgang's age.[37]

As Ilias Chrissochoidis observes in his discussion of this letter, the precise verification of Mozart's age would continue to be a major sticking point in early Mozart reception, culminating in Daines Barrington's 1769 report to the Royal Society, "Account of a Very Remarkable Young Musician," in which he reproduced verbatim the certification of the date, and even time, of Mozart's birth from the archbishop of Salzburg's chaplain.[38] Of course, age could only be a sticking point once it had become standard practice to record it. This is equally true of the minimum age of criminal responsibility, which as several historians have noted only became attached to a specific number once birth registries had become commonplace.[39] Mozart thus benefited from and bolstered a growing concern for pinpointing, and universalizing, stages of development.

From the beginning, reason was implicated in the debates and disbelief over Mozart's age. The Bohemian violinist Antonín Kammel, living in London in 1765, described Mozart as one who "plays the instrument like a virtuoso, composes like an angel, plays even the most difficult pieces prima vista and thereby possesses the reason that only a man of 40–50 can have."[40] Charles Burney echoed this reaction, writing that at age eight, Mozart's "invention, taste, modulation, and execution in extemporary playing, were such as few professors are possessed of at forty years of age."[41] There is a distinct unease to these accounts, a rhetoric of "age inversion" that would, in the nineteenth century, take on more uncanny overtones.[42] In the eighteenth century, however, a perplexing figure like Mozart was less an aberration than a challenge: he must either be reconciled to existing systems of knowledge, or force a new explanation altogether.

Selling the Child Composer: The Rhetoric of the Opus 1–4 Prints

Opus 1–4 were billed as "sonatas for the clavier which can be performed with the accompaniment of the violin" (violin or transverse flute, in the case of Opus 3). Accompanied sonatas were in vogue in Paris at the time, and Mozart had studied other works in the genre.[43] Despite its popularity, the accompanied sonata was a curious genre for Mozart's debut: fashionable, to be sure, but not necessarily accorded a great deal of esteem. Yet Leopold was a shrewd promoter, and the very modishness, accessibility, and flexibility of instrumentation of these accompanied sonatas suggests that he knew how to cultivate public as well as aristocratic patronage.

In addition to their obvious function as instructions for performance, Opus 1–4 were souvenirs, artifacts of celebrity that—like biographies, portraits, and other forms of print media—helped construct the public persona of the artist.[44] That Mozart's first opus numbers were equated with other forms of souvenir is clear from the way they were advertised in the Paris and London press. In Paris, the music was offered for sale alongside Jean-Baptiste Delafosse's engraving of the famous portrait of the Mozarts by Louis Carmontelle (see introduction, fig. 0.1). The advertisement in the *Mercure de France* read "Those who would like to join to these sonatas the portrait of the little author [*petit auteur*] will find it at the same address."[45] In London, Opus 1 and 2 functioned even more blatantly as a unit of currency: they could take the place of a ticket in granting a member of the public an audience with the Mozarts.[46]

Promotional broadsheets like the Delafosse engraving had long been a common feature of advertising campaigns for all manner of touring human and animal curiosities, from "wild men" and conjoined twins to elephants and rhinoceroses.[47] Such broadsheets served a triple function: as advertisements for future viewings, tie-ins to a viewing in progress, and souvenirs thereafter.[48] The Mozarts appear to be the first, however, to have sold a portrait of a musical prodigy while on tour, and the first to sell such a portrait alongside original music by the prodigy, in a cross-promotional marketing effort.[49]

Portrait and score may well have been intended to be read as a unit: the Delafosse engraving seems at least in part to depict a performance of one of the accompanied sonatas. Taking another look at this portrait, we see Leopold, author of the renowned violin treatise *Versuch einer gründlichen Violinschule* (Augsburg, 1756), casually taking the expendable violin part, feet crossed and instrument tipped in a pose of ease as he cedes pride of place to his son. The sharply outlined body of the harpsichord draws the viewer's eye across the center of the image, forcing a comparison between the heft of Leopold's white-stockinged calves and Wolfgang's exaggeratedly small feet, which hover at a considerable distance above the tiled floor.[50] That it is the smallest member of the family who takes the largest, lead instrument seems at first burlesque, but it reinforces the fact that Wolfgang was the composer of the works. In the image, he becomes Leopold's equal, the "father" of the sonatas with which the portrait was paired. Such an image seems to coach adult consumers in engaging directly with, and even subordinating themselves to, the "little author." And encountering the image every day as it hung in the owner's parlor wall or joined a bound collection of prints would have normalized this role reversal.

My interpretation so far has not accounted for the presence of Nannerl in the portrait: these accompanied sonatas of course had no vocal part, so her presence in the background of the image is vestigial. But then, Nannerl was always the odd one out: highly regarded for her keyboard playing but without much of a chance at a career in composition, her depiction here as a singer seems designed to discourage any comparison of the two children on the same instrument. The caption to the engraving reinforces the blunt and inevitably gendered distinction, identifying Nannerl as "virtuoso," while Wolfgang is "composer and master of music." Many of the eyewitness accounts reproduced this distinction—Wolfgang was "ein Tonkünstler," Nannerl "seine Schwester," or, as in the Hamburg periodical, the sister played "with more art and fluency than her little brother, but the boy with far more refinement and with more original ideas."[51]

In a way, Leopold could not have asked for a better foil for Wolfgang than Nannerl. She grounded her brother in a tradition of cultivated musical virtuosos, while at the same time highlighting what made him unprecedented, just as the image highlights the difference in their stature. Her feminine accomplishment set off his masculine mastery, just as the diagonal leading lines with her father draw the eye toward the diminutive center of the image. The engraving might therefore be read as a composite or idealized portrait, rather than a snapshot of a single moment in time—a choreographed representation of domestic nonchalance, revealing the hierarchies of authorship and talent that underpinned the outwardly harmonious family unit.[52]

Just as the portrait fixed the children's age, Opus 1–4 also promised to preserve Wolfgang's childhood composerly voice well past the point at which he was no longer a child. In London, Leopold had copies of the already-published sonatas deposited at the British Museum, along with a copy of the Delafosse engraving and an original work in manuscript, the English-language motet "God is Our Refuge" (K. 20, 1765). This was the first instance of sheet music being recorded in the Museum's "Book of Presents."[53] Storing music alongside the Museum's animal specimens, globes, and ancient and exotic artifacts ensured that Mozart's juvenilia would forever be items of public record, monumentalized as relics of the "Prodigy of Nature."[54] And, as we shall see, the trope of the "seven-year-old boy" froze Mozart at his most youthful, and therefore most exotic.

If the prints were associated with conservation, monumentalization, and posterity, there was also a sense in which they might have been seen to confer authenticity on young Mozart's claims to authorship, to corroborate the extravagant claims of eyewitnesses to Mozart's talent. There are numerous stories of Wolfgang's compositional facility being put to the test in theatrically staged "examinations" that involved his being sequestered while completing compositional exercises. Opus 1–4 were not executed under such circumstances, but they served much the same function, multiplying *ad infinitum* the number of potential adjudicators who could, like Charles Burney, be "convinced of [Mozart's] great knowledge in composition by his writings."[55] Even their infelicities were welcome proof of Wolfgang's authorship. While preparing Opus 2 for publication, Leopold had corrected a series of parallel fifths in the first menuet of the second sonata (K. 9). It was a common novice's mistake. But despite Leopold's efforts, the fifths were erroneously left in for the final engraving. Leopold half-rejoiced at this oversight on the part of the printer, because, as he put it, "they are a proof that our little Wolfgang composed them himself, which, perhaps quite naturally, not everyone will believe."[56] While the mistake would eventually be corrected in later impressions, its initial appearance was a kind of blessing to Leopold, because it carried the stamp of authenticity.

Opus 1–4 were more than just conversation pieces, souvenirs, or monuments. As musical scores, they were living documents, meant to be reanimated—as James Davies reminds us in the context of another musical souvenir—through "the intimate space of the possessor's physique."[57] A member of Paris, London, or Amsterdam's upper middle class might have purchased one of the prints to commemorate a private audience with the Mozarts or attendance at one of their public concerts, or to demonstrate to their acquaintances their fashionability in keeping abreast of the latest novelties. But a different kind of encounter was implied when that consumer, or perhaps another member of his or her household, then sat down at the keyboard and played through Mozart's music, reenacting that public image of "private" music-making represented in the Delafosse engraving. What would it mean to play and replay music composed by a child, to commune with that child's composerly invention through the hands and mind of another child, or those of an adult?

We might consider, for example, the Theme and Variations movement that concludes the last sonata in the Opus 4 set (K. 31/ii). One of Wolf-gang's special strengths was his ability to improvise at length upon a given theme. Improvisational feats were a part of nearly every one of his public and private concerts from his earliest days as a performer, and they were frequently mentioned in accounts of those concerts. If, as commentators have noted, theme and variations sets seem more than other forms to preserve something of the evanescence of live performance, they argu-ably also allow the performer to identify more closely with the compos-er's free flow of invention, to assume (if only vicariously) the role of the talented improviser.[58] To play through a set of Wolfgang's variations was thus to recreate—via the fixed medium of a score—something of the sensation not just of hearing the boy improvise a set of variations, but of actually taking on the improvising boy's persona.

Music treatises of the period regularly enjoined performers to identify with the composer of the music they played. Leopold's own 1756 violin treatise, for which he was still celebrated throughout the Mozarts' Euro-pean tour, had asserted that "in practising every care must be taken to find and to render the affect *which the composer wished to have brought out.*"[59] Leopold's phrasing is almost identical to that found in Carl Philipp Emanuel Bach's 1753 *Essay on the True Art of Playing Keyboard Instruments,* which asserts that in performing a piece, a musician "must make certain that he assumes the emotion which the composer intended in writing it."[60] Applying this to the Theme and Variations movement of Opus 4 would require the performer to identify with a child who was himself emulating an adult. Might this sympathetic ideal of performance have produced something else in addition to a reinscription of celebrity, something profoundly unsettling to received notions of child develop-ment, childhood creativity, and child-adult rapport?[61] Susan Stewart has written of the charged nature of tactile encounters, whether with souve-nirs or objects in a museum; touch, she observes, "is a threshold activity" that prompts bodily change in both subject and object.[62] Through touch, those who owned and played Mozart's Opus 1–4 achieved an unprece-dented (and infinitely repeatable) physical proximity with a boy who dis-played the intellectual maturity of a man. The resulting intimacy transcended any written account of Mozart, precisely because it was not just visual, but kinesthetic.

Discourses of Natural Genius

As the paratexts to Opus 1–4 make clear, Leopold and his circle recognized the importance of this readerly-performerly identification with a precociously creative child, and the questions it would inevitably raise about child genius. In the dedication to his Opus 1, Wolfgang—via his ghostwriter, the family's patron Friedrich Melchior von Grimm—claimed that "Nature has made me a Musician as she makes the nightingales."[63] The association of composers and nightingales was a familiar one; in fact, many readers would have recognized this as a reference to Augustine, who in the *De Musica* (387–391 CE) famously used the nightingale as a figure for natural as opposed to artificial music.[64] Nightingales, Augustine asserted, are unable to perceive the *ratio* of the universe, or even of their own song; the pleasing sounds they make are accidental, for "an irrational animal does not use reason; therefore, it does not possess an art."[65] Were readers of the dedication to Opus 1, then, meant to view Mozart as a nightingale himself, imitating and even taking pleasure in pleasing sounds, but having no faculty to understand what he was doing? Or was this just another instance of the "rhetoric of humility" common to many dedications and prefaces?[66] The dedication also indicates an instability around the concept of genius at this time, which might help explain the often conflicting terms within which Mozart's Opus 1–4 were received.

At one end of the ontology of genius was the discourse on "natural genius," which goes back to Bacon, Addison, and Pope but gained particular momentum in the 1750s.[67] In his 1759 *Conjectures on Original Composition*, Edward Young argued that inspiration could precede or transcend "the rules of the learned."[68] Young even distinguished between "Infantine" and "Adult" genius, the former requiring some measure of education and nurturing, the latter springing "out of Nature's hand, as *Pallas* out of *Jove's* head, at full growth, and mature."[69] While Young's *Conjectures* were translated into German as early as 1760, he had been preceded in many of his conclusions by Gotthold Ephraim Lessing, who wrote in 1752 that a man of exemplary spirit could become "great without rules," acting as "his own school and books."[70] By the 1770s, the idea of natural genius would be normalized in German circles through works like Johann Georg Sulzer's *Allgemeine Theorie der Schönen Künste* (1771–1774). Sulzer affirmed Lessing's and Young's assertions that those who are "the founders of their art" are "endowed [by nature] with all that was necessary for this purpose."[71]

The idea of "natural genius" was fashionable in England when the Mozarts arrived there in 1764, and was inevitably exploited by the canny Leopold as a marketing tool. In the dedication to Opus 3, published while the Mozarts were in London and probably ghostwritten this time by Leopold, Wolfgang engages in an extended imaginary conversation with his muse, the "capricious" Spirit (*Génie*) of Music, telling him: "When the Queen [Charlotte, Opus 3's dedicatee] deigns to listen to me, I surrender myself to thee and I become sublime."[72] This sentimentalist vocabulary—"surrender," "sublime"—helped bolster the claim, stated earlier in the dedication, that genius could be at work even in as lowly a genre as the sonata. But the rhetorical swerve from the Opus 1 dedication is noteworthy: instead of nightingales and direct apologias to the dedicatee, we have a witty, self-deprecating dialogue to which the dedicatee is now merely a bystander. And in spite of intermittent praise for the Queen, the "Mozart" of this dedication attributes all that is admirable in the sonatas not to her, nor to his biological father, but to another father ("mon père"): the Spirit of Music, whose children are "as free as the British people."[73] The change in tone from the Paris to the London dedication signals the extent to which Leopold understood how best to flatter each of his target audiences.

An equally strong and long-lived current of thought resisted associations of genius with the spontaneous, immediate, and original.[74] Many continued to argue that art required learning, practice, and "artifice" in the earlier sense of the word—particularly for music, which has always been as much a physical and mechanical as a mental and artistic discipline.[75] Take for instance Johann Joachim Quantz's 1752 treatise on flute playing, which registered the growing traction of the concept of natural genius even as he cast doubts on its application to musical composition:

> If no knowledge [*Wissenschaft*] were necessary, and pure natural ability [*das pure Naturell*] were sufficient, then why do the pieces of experienced composers make a stronger impression, gain a wider dissemination, and remain in vogue longer than those of untutored instinctive writers; and why do the finished products of every good composer show a great improvement over his first sketches? Is this to be attributed to pure natural ability, or to ability and knowledge combined? Natural ability is innate, while knowledge is acquired through good instruction and diligent inquiry, and both are necessary to a good composer.[76]

The valorization of knowledge acquired, or genius enhanced, through diligent instruction dominates the early reception of Mozart; this might come as a surprise, given later generations' tendency to romanticize him as a mysterious, spontaneous, even untutored genius.[77] In his *Correspondance littéraire* of 1766, Grimm listed all the genres in which the ten-year-old had already distinguished himself as a composer, concluding: "what is most incomprehensible is this profound knowledge [*science*] of harmony and its most hidden passages, which he possesses to the supreme degree."[78] In the same year, Johann Adam Hiller addressed the Mozart children in an issue of his Leipzig music journal, observing that "Such precocious virtuosi certainly do much honour to their father, since they have attained to all this through his instruction."[79] What Grimm and Hiller heard in Wolfgang's compositions, in other words, was not wild, untutored, or eccentric creativity, not "*das pure Naturell*," but rather refined mastery, remarkable proficiency, "*Wissenschaft.*"

Mozart *as* puer doctus

Because composition and performance were evaluated so differently at the time (despite their frequent conflation in practice), Mozart's rapid acquisition of compositional skill could not be explained through comparison with other child virtuosos, still less his music's appearance in print. From the 1730s, composer life-writing in German was increasingly emphasizing the early manifestation of musical talent, with Telemann and Handel prominent examples; but there was still almost no immediate precedent for Mozart's audaciously young entry into the marketplace as a *petit auteur*.[80]

Another category of "little author," however, already had a presence in eighteenth-century print culture: the intellectual prodigy, or *puer doctus*.[81] The humanists' answer to the hagiographical trope of the *puer senex* (literally, "young old one"), these child scholars earned their fame through precocious achievements in the fields of language, philology, and mathematics. Two such *pueri docti*, both born in 1721, appeared more than once in the early reception of Mozart: Christian Heinrich Heineken of Lübeck, who died at age four, and Jean Philippe Baratier, of Schwabach and Halle, who lived to age nineteen (fig. 1.2).

As Johannes Traudes and Ingrid Bodsch have shown, Heineken and Baratier were well known throughout the eighteenth century.[82] They, and the tradition of child scholars to which they belonged, provide an important context for remarks like the one that opens Hiller's 1766 ar-

FIGURE 1.2. (a) Christian Fritsch, illustration, in Schöneich, *Merkwürdiges Ehren-Gedächtnis von . . . Christian Henrich Heineken* (Hamburg, 1726). Courtesy of SLUB Dresden, http://digital.slub-dresden.de/id346366224/7. (b) Johann Georg Wolffgang, after Antoine Pesne, *Baratier présenté par Minerve* (Paris, 1735). Courtesy of Smithsonian Libraries, Image ID SIL-SIL14-B2-01.

ticle on the Mozart children: "In the sciences, there have been precocious scholars [*Gelehrte*] who were rightly regarded as miracles of nature.
Music has likewise boasted such precocious scholars, or *virtuosi* [*Gelehrten, oder* Virtuosen] as they have to be named in musical terminology."[83]
The terminological frustration evident in Hiller's phrase "have to be
named" indicates his preference for the more scholarly term *Gelehrte* to
describe what Mozart was achieving; and behind it, an abiding discom-
fort with the artisanal trappings of music. "Virtuoso" was apparently an
inadequate term for what Mozart was.

Publications by prodigies of letters and sciences can be found throughout Western history, from the legal philosopher Hugo Grotius to the
mathematician Gottfried Wilhelm Leibniz.[84] Some eighty-nine prodigies were profiled in a 515-page tome, *Des enfans devenus célèbres par leurs
etudes ou par leurs ecrits* (Children Who Became Famous Through Their
Studies or Through Their Writings), which was published in Paris in
1688, five years before the publication of Locke's *Some Thoughts concerning Education*.[85] The book's author, the biographer and librarian Adrien
Baillet, claimed that *Des enfans* originated in a didactic game of "guess the
author" that he used to play with his young charge, the twelve-year-old
son of the advocate general of France. But Baillet's main goal was to prove
to skeptical readers that "children are capable of more than just playing
and guarding the sheep."[86] Ever since the Middle Ages, it had been common to fear that the appearance or encouragement of precocious intelligence in a child presaged his or her early death.[87] In the preface to *Des
enfans*, Baillet argued that even weighty subjects such as philosophy,
mathematics, law, and theology can be introduced to children without
harm to their health.[88] Baillet concluded his preface with this provocative statement: "what has been found to occur in every century before
ours has not become impossible in our own, and will not merely be an
event of history."[89] Baillet was here challenging not just the advocate general's son, but his readership at large, to take their place in the pantheon
of learned children.[90]

These two intellectual prodigies to whom Mozart was compared in the
early reception, Heineken and Baratier, were the most renowned in the
German-speaking lands, and in both cases, observers claimed that their
achievements exceeded anything in Baillet's *Des enfans*.[91] We have no evidence that Leopold was personally acquainted with Heineken or Baratier, although he did know one of Baratier's biographers, Samuel Formey
(the *Encyclopédiste* and secretary to the Berlin Academy), through their
mutual friend, the poet and philosopher Christian Fürchtegott Gellert.[92]
It is likely, though, that the Mozarts were aware of Heineken and Baratier.

After all, their fame lasted well past Mozart's lifetime: they appear together in Immanuel Kant's 1798 *Die Anthropologie in pragmatischer Hinsicht* (Anthropology from a Pragmatic Point of View), serving as a caution on the limits of natural genius. Kant draws again on the same imagery of "ripening fruit" that served Locke and Rousseau:

> [A] prematurely clever prodigy (*ingenium praecox*), like *Heinecke* in Lübeck, or *Baratier* in Halle, of ephemeral existence, are deviations of Nature from her rule, rarities for a natural history collection. And while their premature ripening arouses admiration, it is also often cause for repentance on the part of those who promoted it.[93]

Kant's cautionary take on the two prodigies is a throwback to the kind of superstition Baillet sought to combat. Regardless, the passage indicates that Heineken and Baratier were still familiar figures some seventy years after their heyday.

The younger of the two, Heineken—the so-called Lübecker Wunderkind—appears to have been the first for whom the term "Wunderkind" was used in connection with someone other than the Christ child.[94] Heineken died too early to have published any works, but was reputed to have been able to read the Old and New Testament in Latin by age three, and to be learned in geography and genealogy; he even underwent a successful examination by no less a person than the king of Denmark. Heineken was also known to Georg Philipp Telemann, who later penned two elegies for him (one of which is shown in fig. 1.2a).[95] Nearly forty years later, Heineken was referenced in the first poem known to have been written in Mozart's honor, the 1762 "Auf den Kleinen Sechsjährigen Clavieristen aus Salzburg" (To the Little Six-Year-Old Keyboard Player from Salzburg). Addressing Mozart directly, the poem concludes by taking up that familiar anxiety about a premature death:

> I only hope that your body can withstand the strength of your soul,
> And that you do not, *like the Lübeck child*, go too early to the grave.[96]

The association between Mozart and Heineken was particularly apt in 1762, because at this point Mozart had not published anything, but had only given in-person proofs of his extraordinary aptitude.

Unlike Heineken, the other prodigy born in 1721—Baratier, a master of languages and philology—managed to publish extensively in his relatively short life, beginning when he was thirteen. And it was Baratier to whom Daines Barrington drew a comparison in his 1769 report on

Mozart to the Royal Society. After describing the various compositional tests he had set Mozart, and making note of his Opus 3 sonatas, Barrington wrote:

> Having stated the above mentioned proofs of Mozart's genius, when of almost an infantine age, it may not be improper perhaps to compare them with what hath been well attested with regard to other instances of the same sort. Amongst these, John Barratier hath been most particularly distinguished, who is said to have understood Latin when he was but four years old, Hebrew when six, and three other languages at the age of nine.[97]

It was only after three more paragraphs on Baratier that Barrington turned to an example from music: Handel. Barrington noted that Handel "is said to have composed some church services when he was only nine years old, as also the opera of Almeria, when he did not exceed fourteen."[98] In reality, *Almira* premiered in 1705, when Handel was twenty, and the earliest church music to survive dates to 1707. Baratier's much earlier forays into print made him arguably a closer precedent for Mozart.[99]

The use of the word "proof" in Barrington's Mozart article also begs comparison with the reception of *pueri docti* like Baratier. One review of Baratier's first book, a 247-page translation and commentary on the medieval Hebrew *Voyages of Rabbi Benjamin of Tudela*, read: "We have already seen proofs of his knowledge in this journal . . . the book that we announce here contains [further proofs] more varied and in greater number."[100] For both Heineken and Baratier, and for Mozart after him, original works by these children and printed eyewitness accounts and biographies each conferred authority on one another. Hiller's aforementioned 1766 article, to take another example, identified Wolfgang as "already so adept in composition that in Paris half a dozen clavier sonatas of his have been engraved."[101] The fact of the print itself therefore served as a proof of Mozart's genius.

For his part, Barrington may have been prompted to associate Mozart with Baratier by another man of letters, the physician Samuel-Auguste Tissot. In 1766, Tissot published a letter in the Swiss periodical *Aristide ou le citoyen* explaining Mozart's gifts via comparison with such "born" geniuses as Ovid and Molière, and speculating about the neurological characteristics common to child prodigies.[102] That same year, Tissot gave his inaugural lecture as professor of medicine at the University of Lausanne (published in 1768 as *De la santé des gens de lettres*) on the same topic, using, among others, the example of Baratier.[103] In an Enlightenment revival of the old superstition about prodigies dying early, Tissot reckoned that mental and physical development were essentially a zero-sum game, and that speeding up one half of the child's constitution would weaken the other. According to the earlier publication, Wolfgang had escaped this fate because his work did not fatigue him, and because he was allowed a degree of balance and freedom, as opposed to the hothouse environment more commonly associated with prodigies. Tissot concluded by hoping that "fathers whose children show outstanding talents should emulate M. Mozard [*sic*], who, far from pressing his son, has always been careful to moderate his fire and to prevent him from giving way to it."[104] The article ended up being as much about Leopold as Wolfgang, and Tissot seemed to argue for treating the Mozarts as a model family.[105]

The same year that Tissot's article on the Mozarts appeared in *Aristide*, another man of letters made a similarly universalizing remark about Mozart. Pierre-Michel Hennin, the French ambassador in Geneva, wrote that

> The little Mozart's talents remind me of those of a young Frenchman whom I saw draw with all possible force and truth. If things continue in this way, soon one will become a painter or musician before reaching the age of reason, and what we have admired as incredible will be so common that our praise will appear absurd.[106]

Here, Mozart has been compared not to a musician, but to a visual artist, one whose creations—like those of Baratier and Heineken—would outlast the ephemeral moment of performance. Furthermore, Hennin believed that Mozart was not just an exceptional child, but the harbinger of an age of exceptional children. This represents an about-face from the medieval and early modern figure of the *puer senex*, which, as Michael Witmore argues, had always been interpreted "in the spirit of inversion," as the exception that proved the rule. Witmore continues: "what made these precocious saints admirable is the fact that they did *not* bear out the usual assumptions about the absorption and irrationality of children."[107] Unlike child saints, Heineken, Mozart, and other secular Enlightenment *Wunderkinder* were presented as imitable, models as opposed to marvels.

Hennin's prediction turned out to be truer than he knew, at least in one sense. For increasingly over the eighteenth century, intellectual prodigies were no longer automatically treated as mere freaks of nature, "prodigies" in the original sense of the word as monstrous singularities. Rather, they were often viewed as subjects for emulation, with lengthy, detailed accounts of their courses of instruction appearing in frequent reprints throughout the century. One rector and pedagogical reformer even issued a *Methodus Lockio-Baratieriana* (or *Lockeian-Baratierian Method*) in 1735. This play-based course of instruction introduced children as young as four to foreign languages and sophisticated reasoning, because, as the author argued (echoing Baillet), young children are far more capable of exercising their "*judicium*" than was often acknowledged.[108]

Revising the Age of Reason

That notion of *judicium* in the young was where Mozart had perhaps the most direct influence on children across the Monarchy. The context was a Habsburg legal case challenging the age at which Jewish children could be baptized Catholic without their parents' consent. This episode, as with the references to Heineken and Baratier in the early reception of Mozart, has been noted in Otto Erich Deutsch's 1961 anthology of Mozart documents. But Deutsch presents the episode with the utmost brevity, and in doing so downplays its significance. The excerpt in Deutsch reads as follows:

> Proposal of the Vienna Court Chancery, 19 January 1765
> (concerning the earliest age at which Jewish
> children should be allowed to be baptized)
>
> . . . as only in the past year certain children, born at Salzburg, were conducted round the world under the seventh year of their age, who are so experienced in music as even to compose, which calls for more than a *iudicium discretivum* [discretionary judgment].[109]

Deutsch gives three citations, and includes an addendum that "Maria Theresa decided on 15 February 1765 that Jewish children should not be baptized before completion of their seventh year."

The episode as Deutsch presents it certainly demonstrates the scale of Mozart's renown. That the Chancery coyly sidestepped the boy's name only reinforced his celebrity through its absence (Maria Theresa knew Mozart personally from his well-received appearances at court in 1762). The appellation "seven-year-old" was already a part of Mozart's identity, almost a sobriquet, thanks in large part to the title page of Opus 1.[110] And the phrase "so experienced in music as even to compose" affirmed again that Mozart's genius was proven primarily through his compositions. The Chancery could have described Mozart in terms of his imperial approbation. Instead, they referred to his "round-the-world" tour, and to his compositions. The arbiter of his reasoning capacity, in other words, was not his Empress, but the international public, a fact that Maria Theresa's closest counsel already knew to exploit.[111]

What is arguably most noteworthy about this episode, however, is the use to which Mozart was put. The debate about the age at which one was deemed mature enough to embrace Catholicism shows that it was an important marker of maturity—as important, perhaps, as the age of minimum and full criminal responsibility, sexual consent, or matrimonial autonomy. The intersection of childhood and religious identification was key in the Habsburg Monarchy, where Catholic identity was fundamental to political and philosophical notions of selfhood.[112] In Maria Theresa's forced-baptism ruling and its later revision by Joseph II, Mozart was the central case in debates about prepubescent children as competent, productive, and above all, rational.

The significance of this episode becomes clear once one goes beyond Deutsch's abbreviated account to rediscover the context of the Court Chancery's opinion. It originated in two incidents that were all too common across Catholic Europe, involving the kidnapping and forced baptism of Jewish children. The first, in 1756, was committed by a nanny in Moravia, and the second, in 1763, by the cellmate of a nursing mother in Prague; both cases were appealed all the way to Maria Theresa. The Papal Consistorium that Maria Theresa consulted on these cases concluded that both forced baptisms were illegal, but nevertheless valid, for to reverse a baptism after it had been performed would profane a sacrament. Therefore, the Consistorium concluded, the children should not be returned to their parents, but brought up in the Catholic orphanages to which they had been turned over by their kidnappers.

Many issues besides childhood were at work in these cases: the rights of families and civil law versus the *favor fidei* (the Catholic dictum that "favored the faith" over all other law), the rights of mothers versus fathers, of parents in the criminal justice system, and behind it all, religious intolerance and anti-Semitism. But when it came to the question of the *anni discretionis*—literally, "years of discretion," or the age of reason—this was where the Papal Consistorium disagreed, and it was here that Mozart's name was invoked.

The Council of Trent had not specified the exact age that constituted the *anni discretionis*. The theory and practice of both baptism and first communion could vary widely, and it was generally left up to the parents and confessor of the child in question to decide when a child was capable of understanding the gravity of the latter sacrament—usually seven to twelve, but different in each case depending on the circumstances.[113] In

1747, however, Pope Benedict XIV fixed the age at which Jewish children could "choose" baptism against the will of their parents at seven.[114] Benedict stated that a child of seven could be baptized without his parents' consent if an ecclesiastical authority deemed him to be "of sufficient reason" (*sufficientis discretionis*).[115]

Benedict's papal bull was cited in the Court Chancery's 1765 opinion on the two forced-baptism cases. And while Deutsch is right that Maria Theresa's Currenda (ruling) held to Benedict's identification of seven as the *anni discretionis*, in the next sentence of the Currenda (which Deutsch omits) she allowed for even younger children to be admitted to the Catholic faith without their parents' permission:

> For those Jewish children who have not yet reached their seventh year, but desire to be baptized, an investigation will in each case be made by spiritual and secular authorities, so as to make an accurate test of whether they possess the necessary light of reason [*Licht der Vernunft*] for this great undertaking.[116]

It appears that the Chancery's citation of Mozart was at least partly responsible for convincing Maria Theresa that children even younger than seven might be deemed to "possess the necessary light of reason" for conversion. After all, Mozart was, according to the Chancery, possessed of *judicium discretivum*, and he was presented not as exceptional, but as paradigmatic. Or, to put it another way: his exceptionality was understood as indicative of the potential exceptionality of all children.[117] The anti-Semitic ends to which this conclusion was marshalled are shameful enough. But Mozart was also a model for an equally insidious kind of anti-Semitism, for the Chancellors read his creative precocity as evidence of an equal degree of moral precocity.[118]

The conflation of musical and religious judgment drew on late Enlightenment and proto-Romantic associations of genius with struggle and rebellion. In early composer biographies such as Johann Mattheson's *Grundlage einer Ehrenpforte* (1740) and Mainwaring's *Memoirs of Handel* (1760), the formulaic presentation of an obstinate, self-taught child doggedly pursuing music against parental opposition helps establish a sense of inevitability to the blossoming of genius: what begins as a passionate interest develops naturally as the child innocently pursues that interest. Mainwaring even likened Handel to the mathematician and inventor Blaise Pascal: both "pursued their respective studies not only without any assistance, but against the consent of their parents, and in spite of all the

opposition they contrived to give them."[119] Although this assertion mis-
represented Pascal's early life, the way Mainwaring harnessed Pascal to
Handel shows the biographical privileging of youthful talent and tenacity
overcoming adult resistance.[120] Stephen Rose has identified these tropes
as part of a wider goal to jettison music's artisanal associations and shore
up its respectability as a gentleman's profession, a true "liberal art."[121] For
Maria Theresa's Chancery, it also allowed Catholicism itself to be elided
with visionary foresight. The child who supposedly wished to pursue
baptism against his parents' wishes, like the child who wished to pursue
music against his parents' wishes, was not to be regarded as disobedient
and ill informed, but rather as wise beyond his years.

Such self-serving elisions of creative and spiritual autonomy were
short-lived, however. Maria Theresa's ruling was reversed by Joseph II in
1782, less than two years after he assumed sole rule following his mother's death. It is worth dwelling for a moment on the circumstances of this
reversal, because Mozart is mentioned once again (although no record
of this later episode appears in Deutsch's *Documents* volume, or its later
addenda). This is therefore not only an important and hitherto overlooked document of Mozart reception; it also represents a turning point
in the institutional history of Austrian childhood, one in which religious
affiliation and moral reasoning were decoupled, and religious choice was
made both morally neutral and off-limits to children.

Joseph and his mother had argued bitterly over the question of toleration throughout the 1770s, and as soon as Joseph took over as sole
emperor and regent, he moved swiftly to reverse his mother's policies.[122]
In October 1781, he issued the Patent of Toleration, which granted religious freedom to Protestants and Greek Orthodox Christians. In January of the following year, Joseph extended religious freedom to Jews
with the Edict of Tolerance, which expanded certain rights while cur-
tailing others in the name of assimilation.[123] Just two months after that,
the new Court Chancery issued a Votum reversing Maria Theresa's 1765
Currenda on the illicit baptism of Jewish children. As a logical conse-
quence of the legitimization of Judaism, they declared that it took more
than a basic knowledge of right and wrong to decide between religions.
They suggested that the *anni discretionis* should be reset to the surprisingly advanced age of eighteen, arguing that even fourteen—the age of
full criminal responsibility—did not guarantee the maturity of mind for
such a decision.[124]

Among the reasons the Chancery gave for this proposed change was
"today's education," which in its greater sophistication demands "more
time than usual" for a youth to understand the strengths and weaknesses

of different religions.[125] The Chancellors also cited legal precedent from a number of challenges to the 1765 ruling by Jewish families, as well as the pragmatic wish to prevent baptized Jews from having second thoughts and rescinding their baptism. But the Chancellors also revisited their predecessors' exemplars, the Mozarts. "The children from Salzburg who had been brought to Vienna," they wrote, "do not fit here as an example."[126] As before, while they initially referred to "children" in the plural, it soon becomes apparent that they were thinking more of Wolfgang the *Gelehrter* than Nannerl the *virtuose*. The Chancellors now found that Wolfgang's compositional gifts did not afford him the necessary degree of "*judicium discretivum*":

> A natural ability for an art (*Genie*) can from time to time break out and thereby, for example in music, achieve something quite decent by following the rules and making a mere effort of memory; but it will remain a mere plaything even to a ripe old age and after much experience, without textured and powerful thought. If the Salzburg children had had to decide which of two high-quality compositions was the best, and to give the correct reasons, the seven-year-old would have had just as immature a judgment [*Urtheil*], and it is mature judgment [*Urtheil*] alone that is relevant to the adoption of another religion.[127]

Once both religions were recognized as equally valid, it seems, there was less at stake, and a more subtle form of discernment was required, in an individual's free choice between them. It became as much a matter of aesthetics, of taste, as of morality. And while that conflation of aesthetic judgment and moral judgment is a thorny issue in its own right—one that would be further parsed by philosophers from Kant onward—neither aesthetic judgment nor moral judgment were believed to be vouchsafed by compositional talent, even genius.

Joseph upheld the Chancery's proposed new age limit of eighteen in cases throughout the 1780s, although it was 1789 before he would legislate it explicitly.[128] Like his mother, though, he left himself a loophole: he would accept the conversion of children "of any age" without their parents' consent, on the condition that their knowledge of Catholicism was entirely self-taught.[129] This was of a piece with Rousseau's philosophy of negative education, where tutors crafted environments within which their students might explore independently and learn with minimal intervention; it even recalls the aforementioned biographies that romanticized child autodidacts like Handel and Pascal.

There was a knock-on effect for Mozart reception in Joseph's protection of children's "right to immaturity." In making a case for an expanded period of adolescence, the authors of the new Votum downgraded the conventional wisdom about the nature of Mozart's child genius, reinterpreting his *iudicium discretivum* as "mere" rule-following and memorization. This might have been due in part to the new, adult Mozart with whom Vienna was becoming acquainted in 1782. Mozart had just settled in the city the previous year, and was known to all as, significantly, an *ex*-prodigy. Despite his popular acclaim, he had left the service of the archbishop of Salzburg under notorious circumstances and had defied both his father's professional legacy and advice, all in the year he turned twenty-five (the age at which, according to Roman law, a person reached full majority).[130]

Whatever the motivations for the Chancery's backpedaling on the young Mozart, it is clear that the discourse of the reasoning child no longer held the rhetorical force that it had before.[131] Even as discourses of natural genius were on the rise, creative precocity among children was now, at least in one circumstance, read simply as mimicry, a form of *executio*. And Mozart was no longer a *Gelehrter* but merely another kind of *virtuose*. It was as though after the intervening eighteen years, that dedication to Opus 1, with its ambivalent reference to the nightingale, had been retroactively settled in favor of the boy Mozart as Augustine's "irrational animal."

Mozart might have been a pawn in both 1765 and 1782, but he was part of a serious legislative debate regarding religious freedom, one with actual consequences for thousands of Jewish and Protestant children and families across the Habsburg Monarchy.[132] Far from just theorizing about the implications of Mozart's childhood production, the Austrian court put those implications into practice. This recalls the misguided efforts of some late eighteenth-century progressive parents to raise their children exactly according to Rousseau's *Emile*: as Julia Douthwaite concludes, these mostly failed experiments "forced the would-be pedagogues to rethink their concept of perfectibility."[133] In a similar fashion, the experiment of treating all would-be Catholic converts as potential Mozarts—and the legal challenges to that antisemitic policy by many Jewish families—forced the Court to rethink what it meant to attain the "age of reason." Finally, whereas Mozart's published music had since the beginning been treated as proof of his own genius, he eventually became himself an item of evidence: first in favor of the reasoning seven-year-old, and then against it. That the argument still rested on the autonomy of children as thinking subjects, rather than on restoring their previous status as generic members of a household or extensions of their fathers, shows just how far the rhetoric of the independent child had come.

The 1782 decision was part of a tide of legislation extending the upper age limit for the category "child." Maria Theresa had already established compulsory education for children ages six to twelve with the 1774 *Allgemeine Schulordnung*, which cemented state takeover of educational administration following the 1773 papal suppression of the Jesuit orders.[134] In 1787, the Court Chancery ruled that factories could not employ children until age nine, so that they might be able to attend school full-time for at least three years beginning at age six.[135] This was not just the first child labor law in Austrian history; it was the first worker protection law of any kind, predating England's Health and Morals of Apprentices Act by fifteen years. And finally, the age of minimum criminal responsibility was raised by Joseph in 1787 from seven to twelve.[136] Joseph's decree equated childhood with other conditions in which free will is lacking, such as temporary or permanent insanity. There is no clearer indication of an expanded ontology of childhood than the extension of the *doli incapax* defense by five years.[137]

The discrepancies and shifts in the boundaries of childhood were lexicographical as well as legal, as a comparison of two major German-language dictionaries shows. While in 1744, Zedler's *Universal-Lexicon* asserted that childhood lasted only until age seven, by 1775 Adelung's *Versuch eines grammatisch-kritischen Wörterbuches* had raised its age limit to ten.[138] Both dictionaries were published in Leipzig, but they circulated widely throughout German-speaking Europe, and they register the extension of childhood as a protected phase of life.

Next Mozarts

Despite this growing child protectionism, the generation of composers who came of age after Mozart were under increasing pressure to perform, and to produce, at younger and younger ages. We might begin with Mozart's own circle: he took on a protégé, Johann Nepomuk Hummel, who studied and lived with the Mozarts for two years (1786–1788) and went on an extended European tour at age ten at Mozart's urging. Hummel was often compared to Mozart, as was Mozart's own son, Franz Xaver, who debuted as a keyboardist at age six (at a 1797 memorial concert for his father) and published his first work at age eleven. Prodigies had for some time after Mozart been publishing music in their preadolescence. Elizabeth Weichsell's *Three Lessons for the Harpsichord or Piano*

Forte, printed in London in 1775, trumpeted her "eight Years of Age" on the title page.[139] Charles Burney—hoping no doubt to beat Barrington at his own game—submitted an "Account of an Infant Musician" to the Royal Society in 1779, detailing the skills of the Norwich-born William Crotch, who had begun to teach himself to play the organ at age two and performed at the Chapel Royal at age three. Burney eagerly put Crotch to the same sorts of tests to which Barrington had subjected Mozart ten years earlier, and although the boy's instincts are remarkable, his many mistakes led Burney to conclude—recalling Mozart's nightingale reference in the Opus 3 dedication—that "his voluntaries are little less wild than the native notes of a lark or a black-bird."[140] Despite this strong implication that the boy's reason was immature, "Reason" figured prominently in Burney's account from the first sentence—although he hastened to clarify that reason rarely develops consistently across the senses or identically for each child. Baillet's *Des enfants* even put in an appearance, if only to draw a distinction between Baillet's and Burney's categories of age and medium:

> notwithstanding the title of his work, [Baillet] speaks not of infants but adolescents, for the youngest wonder he celebrates in literature is at least seven years old; an age at which several students in music under my own eye have been able to perform difficult compositions on the harpsichord, with great neatness and precision.[141]

Barrington, too, published several more studies of musical prodigies, though each subject seemed younger, their demonstrable capacities murkier, than the model to which all seemed to aspire.[142] One of his prodigies, Samuel Wesley, was introduced to him as "an English Mozart" by William Boyce, and he even seemed to have taken a leaf from the Mozart playbook, "joining sonatas to a portrait of the little author":

> I can refer only to one printed proof of [Wesley's] abilities as a composer, which is a set of eight lessons for the harpsichord, and which appeared in 1777 [at age eleven], about the same time that he became so known to the musical world that his portrait was engraved, which is a very strong resemblance.[143]

In his enthusiasm, Barrington even began to supply these "printed proofs" himself: in his report on Wesley, he included an engraving of a "little ballad" by the boy, "Autumnus comes with sickly brow," a setting of a poetic text by a fellow prodigy, the child poet Thomas Percy.[144]

FIGURE 1.3. Chodowiecki[?], illustration to Georg Christoph Lichtenberg, "William Crotch, das musikalischer Wunderkind," *Taschenbuch zum Nutzen und Vergnügen fürs Jahr 1780* (Göttingen). Courtesy of ETH Bibliothek Zürich, shelfmark Rar-6528.

Barrington's fascination with prodigies landed on a third boy in 1778. In his report on William Crotch, published two years after Burney's, Barrington included a transcription of one of Crotch's "voluntaries, which was taken down whilst he was playing it. I told the child that it should be published as *Crotch's* composition."[145] Barrington seemed acutely aware of the implausibility of this appellation: after all, Crotch's four-bar "composition" resembles nothing more than a modulation exercise gone awry, a fact Barrington himself admitted. Nevertheless, Crotch's family astutely promoted his celebrity, touring with him nearly continuously from age three to nine (1778–1784) and advertising his appearances with prints and posters that magnified his exoticism.[146] His fame extended to the German press as well, with one engraving appearing in the Göttingen *Taschenbuch zum Nutzen und Vergnügen fürs Jahr 1780* (fig. 1.3).[147] In what could almost be a burlesque of the Mozart family portrait, Crotch is depicted in silhouette, "3 years, 7 months old," so young as to still be in his infant gown. His little foot rests on a stool, recalling Mozart's foreshortened legs in the

Delafosse engraving; but his body is larger than life, dwarfing the minia-
turized organ at which he sits.

As we will see in chapter 6, the extending of juvenilia further and further into composers' youths ended up feeding back into the initial wave
of posthumous Mozart mythification. In the first major biography of
Mozart, published in 1829, Mozart's earliest sketches and studies from the
Nannerl Notenbuch were reprinted in toto. They predate Opus 1 by several
years, but that they are to this day considered Mozart's K. 1–5—despite
the difficulty of disentangling Wolfgang's from Leopold's authorship—
indicates that they have been received into the composer's canon in a way
even his own father could not have likely foreseen.

Such precedents and proofs had their drawbacks for these "next
Mozarts." After his emergence as a published child composer, apprentice composers were no longer shielded from the public, under construction, as it were. On the contrary, if they showed talent, they might be dis-
played not just at court or in private salons but in public concerts and in
print, and thus be subject to critical scrutiny on a mass scale, with all the
risks that entailed. Grimm reported in the *Correspondance littéraire* that
the parents of François-Joseph Darcis hoped to write "la second tome
du jeune Mozart," but his "pitiable" music, published around age twelve,
showed him to have "not a shadow of talent."[148] Even Mozart himself
had already been vulnerable to criticism in the early press: a couple of
months after his *Aristide* article on Mozart, Tissot published a letter from
the pseudonymed "Barbophylax," who related a withering remark made
by "a young whipper-snapper of a doctor [who] here had the insolence
to assure us most definitely that with pages of Mozart's music alone, he
cured a case of insomnia that had resisted all other remedies."[149] Barbophylax's outrage by no means detracts from the fact that he, and Tissot,
were amplifying the doctor's joke (and, for all we know, Barbophylax or
even the doctor may have been Tissot himself).

Even as a policy of child protection began to emerge, then, the cult
of celebrity urged child composers into the limelight earlier and earlier.
How might we reconcile these two contrary directions? The history of
childhood is replete with similar paradoxes, particularly in the nineteenth century: Viviana Zelizer traces how, even as child labor became
taboo in early twentieth-century America, children's sentimental value
to their household was increasingly "monetized and commercialized."[150]
Jacqueline Rose writes that the figure of Peter Pan stands for the Golden
Age ideal of "innocence not as a property of childhood but as a portion
of adult desire," a move that James Kincaid interprets in more contro-
versially Freudian terms, as "erotic doublespeak."[151] The protectionism

that paradoxically infantilized children even as it established the conditions for their exploitation, that divested them of social agency even as it shielded some from labor, can trace at least part of its roots back to Mozart and his "progeny."[152]

Probably the most legendary of the "next Mozarts" was Beethoven. His first printed compositions at age eleven drew on many of the Opus 1–4 tropes: his young age was advertised on the title pages of both the Dressler Variations (WoO 63, 1782–1783, "agè de dix ans") and the "Kurfürstensonaten" (WoO 47, 1783, "alt eilf Jahr"). In his dedication to the "Kurfürstensonaten," Beethoven (or his ghostwriter) even borrowed from Mozart's Opus 3 the conceit of the conversation with one's Muse: "Eleven years, thought I, and how will the countenance of an author sit with me? and what will men of the arts say about it? I almost became timid. But my Muse willed it—I obeyed and wrote."[153]

Christian Gottlob Neefe's familiar introduction of Beethoven in the 1783 *Magazin der Musik* mentioned the publication of the Dressler variations, concluding that Beethoven "would surely become a second Wolfgang Amadeus Mozart were he to continue as he has begun."[154] Meanwhile, Beethoven continued to suffer by comparison with his predecessor. In 1783–1784, he contributed two Rondos and two Lieder to issues of a musical weekly, the *Blumenlese* (and *Neue Blumenlese*) *für Klavierliebhaber*, that was critiqued anonymously in Johann Nicolaus Forkel's *Musikalischer Almanach* of 1784. The review is notorious for having dismissed all of the music, including Beethoven's, as the effort of rank beginners.[155] But the critic (possibly Forkel himself) also drew some broader conclusions about post-Mozart prodigy mania. He observed sardonically that "we must have fallen back into the Ages of Wonders," because

> musical works that, in the Age of Light, would have perhaps been considered as the first efforts of a beginner in music, like a *Chreia* [entry-level rhetorical exercise] of a seventh- or eighth-grader in our schools, are now recognized as masterpieces of composition, and boys of twelve years are the greatest clavier players that man has ever heard, come close in musical knowledge and in familiarity with counterpoint to the most famous professors. . . . Marvelling and admiration have been with good cause held by many wise people as a sign of ignorance.[156]

While Beethoven was confronting the high standards set by Mozart, Mozart himself had already been absorbed into one of the foundational texts of Enlightenment child development: *Emile*, one of the two texts with which this chapter began. In the first edition of 1762, Rousseau had rattled off a list of exceptional child performers, including acrobats, Nicolini's troupe of child actors (about which more in chapter 3), and "the little English girl that all of Paris still remembers performing wonders on the clavecin at the age of ten."[157] Rousseau hastened to assure readers that he was advocating merely for a more advanced physical education. The 1780 Rousseau Complete Works edition, published posthumously and incorporating Rousseau's own changes and additions over the previous decade, includes a footnote to the sentence about the English girl. The footnote reads "A little boy of seven has since that time performed even more astonishing ones [wonders]."[158]

The "boy of seven" is obviously Mozart, a fact that is affirmed in most critical editions of *Emile* but that appears to have escaped the attention of Mozart scholars. This footnote probably originated with Rousseau himself, who supervised the 1780 revision of *Emile*. But even if it was the interpolation of an editor, what did it mean to equate Mozart with these prodigies of bodily performance—child acrobats, actors, and violinists? In some ways, this may at first glance appear an about-face: the *Gelehrte*, the "composer and master of music," has been reduced to a mere *virtuose*, setting precedent for Joseph's 1782 reversal of the baptism ruling. The quandaries raised by Mozart's emergence as a publishing boy composer seem to have been resolved. But the footnote described Mozart's feats as "even more astonishing" than those of the Nicolini troupe or the English girl. Were they more astonishing because they signaled as much a mental as a physical precocity, giving the lie to Rousseau's own skepticism regarding premature mental development? That Rousseau (or someone in his circle of editors) took notice of Mozart, tried to make sense of him, and added a footnote to a major pedagogical treatise because of him suggests the extent to which the child Mozart would continue to dominate conversations about childhood for years to come.

Mozart's emergence as a publishing boy composer thus stands as an emblem for a number of often contradictory ideas and agendas surrounding childhood in the late Enlightenment. His Opus 1–4 prints were commemorative and evidentiary. They were agents of an intimate identification with, or at least recognition of, the child as a creative agent, a thinking and creating being. And they struck many as closer to the scholarly works of intellectual prodigies than to the performances of musical virtuosos. This is in large part because, as printed compositions, they were indisputably texts, more lasting than improvisations or performances. Like Baratier's translations, they could be verified and critiqued by an anonymous mass of consumer-performers, rather than relying solely on ephemeral performance and eyewitness accounts. This geographical and temporal expansion of the encounter with the child composer changed the terms of the validation of children's claims to reason, to social engagement, and ultimately, to agency. And as the pendulum swung back and forth between candidates for the *anni discretionis*, the prints endured, preserving Mozart's childhood voice until well into his adulthood.[159]

The questions raised by Mozart's emergence as a thinking, creating child were by no means resolved later in his life. Nor was the range of ideologies to which he could be harnessed as an icon diminished. For better and for worse, Opus 1–4, and the variety of childhoods they inscribed, would continue to haunt Mozart and Mozart reception long after his feet had finally reached the floor.

✳ CHAPTER 2 ✳

Music, Philanthropy, and the Industrious Child

In August 1768, Leopold Mozart wrote at length to Lorenz Hagenauer from Vienna on a topic that was on many Austrians' minds at the time: smallpox.

> The Empress has installed the English inoculator [Jan Ingenhousz] in a house for children in Medling, near Schönbrunn. It accepts poor children, each of whom, or their parents, receives a ducat upon entry. Already over forty have been inoculated, and are doing well. . . . Almost all the medical men are going into a frenzy over it. Big surprise? This was just a certain disease, and a certain treatment that, whether it had worked or not, would have been very profitable for medical men. God be praised! *Our inoculator was the best.*[1]

What Leopold meant by "our inoculator" was the full-blown disease itself. Wolfgang and Nannerl had come down with smallpox less than a year earlier, and it had nearly killed them both. But for many parents like Leopold, waiting for a random infection still seemed safer than voluntarily submitting to inoculation. The procedure involved having live, human smallpox grafted onto a healthy individual, causing (one hoped) a less severe case of the disease. This process struck many as both a grave medical gamble and, as Leopold indicates, a dangerous flouting of God's will.[2]

Smallpox was one of the many factors contributing to an average child mortality rate of around 50 percent in Europe in the eighteenth century.[3] It claimed 400,000 European lives annually and as many as one in six children throughout the eighteenth century, and it had already struck tragically close to home for the imperial family.[4] When word reached Maria Theresa of Jan Ingenhousz's successful inoculation efforts in England, she invited him to inoculate her entire family. This was an extraordinary personal and political risk: inoculation still had an uneven success record, and it was opposed by most Austrian medical professionals. But the gamble paid off when the children survived. Immediately afterward, Maria Theresa launched the pilot program described by Leopold.

The Mozarts were doubtless aware of, and perhaps even attended, the celebrations that marked the program's success. As reported in the *Wienerisches Diarium*, a special thanksgiving service was held at the Schönbrunn Palace Chapel in September 1768, which included a singing of the *Te Deum*. That evening, the imperial family threw open the doors of Schönbrunn gardens to the city at large, lighting it for a celebration at which "different ensembles enlivened the general joy with the cheerful sound of their instruments."[5] Such musical performances and their published accounts augmented the spectacle of the philanthropic initiative, generating the "frenzy" that reached even skeptics like Leopold.

Wolfgang was a featured participant in several public ceremonies or publications associated with new child welfare initiatives during the period of 1765–1790. In this chapter, I will look at three such initiatives: the Vienna Waisenhaus (Orphanage), the Vienna Taubstummeninstitut (Deaf-Mute Institute), and the Vienna and Prague Normalschulen (Teacher Training Institutes). These three institutions overlapped in their methods and personnel. They also exemplified two enlightened absolutist ideals articulated by Otto Ulbricht: a concerted striving toward a more humane, compassionate society, and the increasing reach of state influence in matters of the family.[6] The institutions are also linked by Mozart's presence as a kind of "celebrity endorser," his fame boosting the profile of the event or publication and its underlying initiative. In the first two cases, the effort was on behalf of children at the margins of society—orphans, foundlings, and deaf children. In the third case, the reach was much broader: universal education, and its role in the reconciliation of the Monarchy's widely varying confessional, ethnic, and geopolitical affiliations. Circulating in print, Mozart's contributions helped further the Habsburg reform, and centralization, of child welfare initiatives.

For a musician like Mozart who was increasingly beholden to commercial patronage, benefit concerts and publications were a fail-safe way to appeal to a broad public—career advancement cloaked as beneficence. Leopold had already recognized this opportunity in London, where Wolfgang's boyhood appearance at a concert benefiting the Lying-In Hospital allowed him "to perform thereby the act of an English patriot who, as far as in him lies, endeavours to further the usefulness of this hospital which has been established *pro bono publico*. That is, you see, one way of winning the affection of this quite exceptional nation."[7] The charity appearance became as much a public-relations opportunity for the freelance musician as for the institution and its sponsors.

Mozart did not have as direct an influence on child welfare advocacy as he had on the imperial debate about conversion, as discussed in chapter 1. And he was by no means the only composer to be linked to Habsburg child welfare institutions. He was, however, by far the most famous one, and his status as a child prodigy (and later, an ex-prodigy) made him an attractive figure to attach to child welfare initiatives. His exceptionalism helped elevate orphans and disabled children, while his productivity became a model for the potential productivity of all children in the care of the state. Through the music he composed for these three institutions, and the mere fact of his presence, Mozart served as a standard-bearer for the industrious child, long after his own "industrious childhood" had ended.

Children and Habsburg Philanthropy

Once the Habsburg Monarchy embraced a reformist agenda, children were among the many underserved groups whose fortunes were at least in part improved. From the beginning of the co-regency of Maria Theresa and Joseph in 1765 to Joseph's death in 1790, the Monarchy undertook concerted, sustained, and multifaceted efforts to improve the lives of children, particularly children of middle- and low-income families, through public health programs like the smallpox inoculation, reforms of foundling hospitals and orphanages, improved teacher training, the standardization of education, and compulsory primary schooling.[8]

As with charity and philanthropy across Enlightenment Europe, child philanthropy encompassed a host of individual, local, and state efforts, religious and secular agendas, and activities ranging from the routine, to the preventative, to the interventionist.[9] Philanthropy in its broadest etymological sense, as "love of mankind," was a cornerstone of the leading pedagogical philosophy of the German Enlightenment, Philanthropinism (about which more in chapter 4).[10] But particularly as practiced in the Habsburg Monarchy, educational and child welfare reform were by no means charity for charity's sake. The stated goal of efforts to standardize and improve education — according to a 1771 pamphlet announcing the establishment of the Normalschule (Teacher Training Institute) — was to prepare children to become "good Christians, useful citizens, and productive members of society."[11] This mercantilist agenda was prioritized by Joseph as he assumed increasing control over domestic policy after 1765.[12] Step one — increasing the gross number of able-bodied subjects —

influenced efforts to lower infant and child mortality rates by mitigating smallpox, infanticide, abandonment, and other causes of death. This was asserted by Joseph in a 1765 memorandum defending population growth as a top priority: "It is from the maximum number of subjects that all the benefits of the state derive."[13] Step two—improving the economic productivity of those subjects—motivated the reforms to education and occupational training. This was the philosophy first expounded in Philip Wilhelm von Hörnigk's 1684 *Oesterreich über Alles, wann es nur will* (Austria Over All, If It So Wishes), in its fourteenth edition by 1764: that able-bodied, industrious men were as precious a commodity to the state as its natural resources.[14]

It was no great stretch to look to children as the most promising target of these efforts. As James van Horn Melton has shown, many saw state-sponsored school and child welfare programs as the best ways to encourage productivity and inculcate diligence and subservience among all Habsburg subjects.[15] Partnering with businesses, churches, and the military, child welfare institutions were conceived and promoted as labor nurseries, emphasizing what we now call "return on investment." Children were put to work, whether at spinning wheels, printing presses, or in military exercises, not just to generate immediate profit and increase the self-sufficiency of the institutions that harbored them, but also to inculcate them into a life of industrial productivity.[16]

For Maria Theresa and Joseph, child philanthropy also presented enticing public-relations opportunities, fulfilling the Enlightenment ideal of benevolent paternalism in absolute rule while giving the appearance of modernization. The term "public relations" is anachronistic, given that it did not emerge until the twentieth century. Nevertheless, Maria Theresa and Joseph were sensitive to, and interested in controlling, public opinion, as were other Enlightenment monarchs. Influenced by political writings out of Britain, France, and northern Germany, Habsburg enlightened absolutism relied on an identification of the ruler as benevolent mother or father, and also as servant, of the state and its subjects. The transmission of this message constituted a nascent form of what we now call public relations.[17]

As Hugh Cunningham has argued, charity itself could be a form of public relations: "Both at [the] civic and national level," he writes, "charity lent, or was intended to lend, legitimacy to what were, in a revolutionary age, often fragile structures of power."[18] This was particularly true in the Habsburg Monarchy, where Catholicism affected every aspect of state policy toward children, from the expropriation of Jesuit property for children's schools to the adaptation of north German pedagogical trends promulgated by Protestants.[19] Children were, as they have always been, particularly effective as the public face of any state initiative: increasingly viewed as innocent and vulnerable, representative of the promise of a nation and of humankind more generally, their welfare was an unassailable priority.

Children in performance were a particularly effective form of charity promotion, a stratagem dating back to the orphan choirs of Byzantium, where child singers served as symbols of imperial power and continuity.[20] But in late eighteenth-century Vienna, music could also be an agent of, and promotional tool for, imperial progress, reform, and service.[21] The music of child welfare initiatives afforded new ways for the Habsburgs to engage with their subjects, bringing the traditions of imperial and ecclesiastical spectacle into the modern age.

The Waisenhaus

In 1768, at the age of twelve, Mozart was the featured composer in a ceremony consecrating the new church at Vienna's Waisenhaus, which had recently come under Habsburg control and expansion. Mozart conducted the Waisenhaus choir and orchestra in works he had composed for the occasion, and, according to the report in the *Wienerisches Diarium*, even joined the choirboys in the singing of the motets. We know how significant Mozart's participation in this event was by how frequently it is mentioned, not just in biographies of Mozart from Nissen onward, but also in accounts of the history of the Waisenhaus throughout the nineteenth century.[22]

The plight of orphans and abandoned children had long been a concern of Maria Theresa. Her founding of the Waisenhaus was part of a move to separate orphan children from the adult populations of the poor, sick, and criminal with whom they were traditionally housed, and thereby to improve their living conditions. It was also, as with many such initiatives in the eighteenth century, a way to stem what was perceived to be an unacceptably high rate of infanticides; decriminalizing unwed mothers in crisis required offering them a viable alternative to infanticide or abandonment.[23] In 1742, just two years into her reign, Maria Theresa authorized the textile factory owner Johann Michael von Kienmayer to build an orphanage next to his factory in the Rennweg district, in which girls could be raised until they were of an age to work in the factory. When the orphanage was complete in 1745, Maria Theresa began a two-decade process of transferring children and consolidating existing orphanages. In 1762, she bought both the residence and the factory from Kienmayer out-

FIGURE 2.1. Philipp Jacob Gütl, frontispiece, *Vollkommener Bericht von der Beschaffenheit des Waisenhauses Unser lieben Frau auf dem Rennwege* (Vienna, 1774). Courtesy of bpk-Bildagentur / Staatsbibliothek zu Berlin, Stiftung Preussischer Kulturbesitz, shelfmark Fd 9842<3> / Art Resource, New York.

right, and established the Waisenhaus Unser Lieben Frau auf dem Rennweg, which went from an average annual population of 350 children in 1760, to 600 in 1767, and around 900 in 1780. In a 1767 engraving, the Virgin Mary—after whom both the Empress and the Orphanage were named—is shown watching over the children of the Waisenhaus (fig. 2.1).

One would think that such an initiative would meet with universal support from the general public. But many throughout Europe were suspicious of efforts to improve orphanages. Even the London Foundling Hospital came in for criticism from writers like the economist Joseph Massie, who feared it would have "ill effects . . . upon the religion, liberty, and domestic happiness of the people of Great Britain."[24] German critics also debated the utility of orphanages, in what has been called the "Waisenhausstreit."[25] And Vienna was no exception: the 1772 issue of the annual report of the Waisenhaus auf dem Rennweg referred to "violent attacks, slander, and invective" against the institution, and declared defensively that "Anyone who visits the orphanage at any time or hour and tests the children themselves will discover in only a few minutes that the . . . libelous writings are forged out of malicious, selfish, and willful intent."[26]

Maria Theresa and Joseph's strategy for the Waisenhaus was to brand it as a blend of technical school and military institution. In 1759, they hired as director Ignaz Parhamer [Parhammer], the Jesuit priest and confessor to Emperor Franz I who would helm the Waisenhaus for the remainder of its existence, even after the 1773 expulsion of the Jesuits. Parhamer quickly became known for military discipline at the Waisenhaus, earning the moniker "Kindergeneral," a fact to which Friedrich Nicolai, in the 1781 account of his journey through the German lands, bore somewhat skeptical witness. Nicolai described the children's Corpus Christi procession as a "geistlich-militarische Komödie" (spiritual-military comedy), and concluded, "After careful consideration, I was not convinced that such a forced, so-called military education is useful for children."[27] But Parhamer was no great outlier in his discipline-based approach to education: military orphanages had been around since at least the 1720s, and military training was a common justification for orphanages throughout the eighteenth century.

Martin Scheutz describes Austrian orphanages at this time as an amalgam of "workhouse, factory, school, monastery, and penitentiary."[28] In the case of the Vienna Waisenhaus, he might have added "conservatory." As Scheutz and David Black have shown, Parhamer developed a strong music program at the Waisenhaus, and not just military band music.[29] In a move that was probably inspired by other institutions like the London Foundling Hospital and the conservatories of Venice and Naples, Parhamer arranged for all Waisenhaus children to be instructed in music and drawing alongside reading, writing, and math.[30] In fact, of the six orphanages whose daily schedules Scheutz has studied, Vienna's Waisenhaus was the only one to mark out time for music instruction in its published timetable; and the instruction was "in different styles of music," not just musical rudiments for singing Psalms.[31] Particularly talented musicians could be admitted to the choir or instrumental ensembles, which performed at Mass, weekly academies, processions and feast days (especially the Feast of Saint Caecilia), and for special visitors to the orphanage.[32] As early as 1764, the Waisenhaus began publishing annual reports on the music program as a supplement to the general reports, identifying the instructors, schedule, program, and instruments, and summarizing the program's goals and objectives as "1. The greater glory of God; 2. The well-being of the children; 3. The benefit of the orphanage."[33] This indicates that the music program was exceptional enough to be considered an asset to the Waisenhaus's overall image.

The Mozarts probably experienced one of these Waisenhaus performances firsthand, or heard about it through the annual reports, or both, in 1768. Having just returned to Vienna after fleeing the latest smallpox outbreak (the one that almost killed the Mozart children), and eager to build on their successes and continue ingratiating themselves with the imperial family, the Mozarts attached themselves to the Waisenhaus project. They visited with Parhamer several times, joining him at a public display of the orphanage's military trainees and later at the laying of the foundation stone for the new Waisenhaus church.[34] At one or more of these events, they would have negotiated Wolfgang's participation in the church consecration ceremony, which took place that December.[35] Whether it was Parhamer's idea or one of the Mozarts', the partnership would surely have appealed to Leopold: as he wrote home to his friend and landlord Lorenz Hagenauer, here was an opportunity to triumph over the "enemies" who had prevented Wolfgang's *La finta semplice* from being produced in Vienna.[36] Leopold had already witnessed firsthand how successful a pro bono appearance could be for Mozart, having engineered his appearance at the Lying-In Hospital in London. Back in Austria and aging out of prodigy status, Leopold hoped Wolfgang would benefit from a repeat of the London strategy.

For the consecration of the new Waisenhaus church, Mozart supplied a Solemn Mass, an Offertory, and a trumpet concerto, the latter performed by one of the Waisenhaus's child trumpeters. This was an enormous amount of music to be commissioned from one composer, let alone a twelve-year-old. The account in the *Wienerisches Diarium* noted that the "extraordinarily talented" Mozart performed the music himself (which probably means he accompanied on organ), conducted the ensemble, and even sang along during the motets.[37] One 1824 account even describes Mozart as having conducted "like an orphan" ("als ein Waisenknabe"), which might indicate that he was dressed in the uniform or vestments of a member of the Waisenhaus Choir.[38] Though impossible to verify, this

EXAMPLE 2.1. Mozart, Missa Solemnis in C minor, K. 139, "Et resurrexit" (Allegro), mm. 128–33

detail suggests that nearly sixty years after the event, historians were still sensitive to the visual impact of Mozart standing with the orphans for whom he had composed so much music.

The spectacle of Mozart conducting his own score and joining in the singing would have only enhanced this impression of solidarity. As David Black notes, "for the first time, the orphans would perform music by a composer about the same age as themselves."[39] The offertory, trumpet concerto, and any motets composed by Mozart for this ceremony do not survive (*Benedictus sit Deus* K. 117 has been put forth as a possible candidate for the offertory, but scholars do not agree on this attribution). The Missa Solemnis K. 139, however, is thought to be the Mass Mozart composed for the event.[40] Its operatic sweep, and the gravitas of its C-minor sections, affirm the significance of the occasion, and how far Vienna had come since Maria Theresa had first taken steps to improve the plight of the city's orphans.

Knowing Mozart's abiding interest in composing for his performers, we might hear in K. 139 a tribute to the talent and discipline of the Waisenhaus singers and musicians.[41] The choral parts, with their many chromaticisms and modulations, are equally challenging to the solo parts. The extended trombone trio that opens the "Agnus Dei," with its long cantabile line for the alto trombone, suggests that the Waisenhaus lower brass were as talented as the soloist in Mozart's lost trumpet concerto.[42] And in one of the most striking moments of any Mass, the "Et resurrexit" of the Credo (ex. 2.1), a tritone motif that had first been presented in the basses in the Gloria is now reharmonized as a perfect fourth and given over to a single soprano soloist, while the orchestra drops out to highlight the "lark-like" solo flourish.[43]

That flashy bit of *a cappella* coloratura is by far the most exposed solo passage in the entire Mass, and would thus have been sung by the most talented soprano in the Waisenhaus choir.[44] Recalling the challenging concertos and oratorios composed by Vivaldi for the prodigies at the Ospedale della Pietà in Venice some fifty years earlier, Mozart's concerto-like flourishes in the Mass stage the spectacular soloist as a model orphan, just as Mozart's own participation positioned him as a model child.[45]

For several years afterward, the Waisenhaus musicians continued to be featured in other special events, though no composers of the stature of Mozart were involved. As in 1768, these events were reported in the *Wienerisches Diarium*. They included local canonization celebrations and the formal inauguration of the Waisenhauskirche in May 1770.[46] At this latter event, in addition to the choir, trumpets, and timpani that participated in the worship services, several Vespers and Litanies included "special concertos on clarinets, traversi (flutes), clarini (trumpets), and violins."[47] Two years later, in 1772, solo performances again figured prominently at a public evaluation of the Waisenhaus by the School Commission. After a day of rigorous examinations and demonstrations in various academic subjects, the Commission and the public were treated to "a performance of some musical pieces by the children on different instruments. One boy played a concerto on the violin with great skill; another played one on the oboe; a girl sang a foreign aria."[48] Solo performances by talented individuals stand out from the otherwise undifferentiated mass of orphans described as participating in public ceremonies. The notion of focusing attention on a single exceptional figure as a metonym for the promise of the institution as a whole appears to originate in 1768, when the ultimate exceptional child, Mozart, conspicuously participated in a ceremony honoring an institution devoted to the upbringing of the lowliest children.

No single member of the Waisenhaus music program appears to have gained musical fame later in life. Of the rank and file, we have only brief glimpses of some of their professional placements: as choirboys, cantors, or courtly or military musicians.[49] But there is more distant evidence of the Waisenhaus's influence. As will be discussed further in chapter 3, for a brief time in the late 1770s Joseph gave nominal support to a Theatralpflanzschule, or theatrical training institute, attached to the National Theater. The institute was the brainchild of Johann Heinrich Friedrich Müller, an actor, playwright, and family friend of Mozart's who had collaborated with him on the Singspiel *Bastien und Bastienne* in 1768. Müller's plan for the Theatralpflanzschule identified orphanages like the Waisenhaus auf dem Rennweg as sources of talent, and may well have recruited from them.[50] Furthermore, in his memoir, Müller wrote that Joseph was inspired to support the initiative after encountering "several boys and girls at Parhamer's, in whom he believed he had found genius and talent for the theater." In particular, a pair of young girls singing High Mass impressed him with their "exceptionally beautiful voice[s], bestowed by nature."[51] Once again, soloists at the Waisenhaus stood as symbols for the promise of all the orphans housed there. The theatricality and the practicality of child welfare initiatives had come full circle: now, thanks in part to Mozart's storied appearance at the Waisenhaus a decade earlier, even the lowliest orphans could, at least theoretically, attain the caliber of performers at the Monarchy's most prestigious theater.

The Taubstummeninstitut

Mozart does not appear to have performed in any other public events associated with child welfare institutions like the Waisenhaus. In print, however, he lent both his name and his talents to two such institutions, composing songs in 1787–1788 for publications by the Vienna Taubstummeninstitut and the Prague Normalschule. The circumstances in these cases were altogether different from his Waisenhaus appearance. As opposed to a one-time event, printed music allowed Mozart to reach a much wider, more dispersed, and more heterogeneous audience directly. The lofty, public genre of the Mass now gives way to the modest, domestic genre of the Lied; large combinations of vocal and instrumental forces are replaced by music for solo voice and keyboard. As we shall see, however, the performative subtexts found in the Waisenhaus Mass persist in these new contexts. In both cases, an attention to the literary contexts of Mozart's Lieder reveals the ways they ennobled juvenile industriousness and productivity, joining reform-minded child welfare initiatives to a broadly pleasing genre of home entertainment.

Founded in 1779, the Taubstummeninstitut was one of Joseph's legendary child welfare initiatives. It even earned special mention in the official *Trauerrede* (Eulogy) published at his funeral in 1790. In addition to his providing for soldiers, taking in unwed mothers, feeding and educating orphans, and sustaining the poor and sick, Joseph was lauded for dedicating himself to "forming even those most unfortunate and, until this eighteenth century, most neglected creatures, *die Taubstummen*, into human beings, citizens, and Christians."[52]

The author of the *Trauerrede* knew of what he spoke. In an age already notorious for its neglectful treatment of people with illnesses and disabilities, deaf people were among the most neglected. Ever since Aristotle declared, in his *De sensu et sensibili* of 350 BCE, that speech and hearing were essential for higher reasoning, deaf people were treated as little better than animals or monsters.[53] Absent a standardized method of communication between hearing and non-hearing people, deaf people could not contribute to a household economy; perhaps even more crucially in strenuously Catholic Austria, they were not allowed to receive the sacraments, because it was believed they were incapable of comprehending religious instruction. Believed to be condemned to eternal damnation, they were treated as social pariahs. Even well-meaning attempts to "cure" deafness often involved painful mutilations, surgeries, and quack medicines, and isolated attempts to educate them in the early modern period (such as the sixteenth-century school for deaf children established in Spain by a Benedictine monk) failed to take hold.[54]

But attitudes were changing by the mid-eighteenth century, particularly among the French *philosophes*. Denis Diderot's twin essays, *Letter on the Blind for the Use of Those Who See* (1749) and *Letter on the Deaf and Mute for the Use of Those Who Hear and Speak* (1751), argued convincingly for a reevaluation of the intellectual capacities of blind and deaf people.[55] In 1760, the Abbé Charles-Michel de l'Épée founded the world's first free school for the deaf in Paris, the *Institut des Sourds-Muets*.[56] L'Épée had developed a complex sign language for use in the school (complete with verb endings and gender of nouns), and the school gained fame across Europe. At the same time, rising literacy rates, the proliferation of print, and practices of silent reading initiated a "widespread shift from performance to text-based knowledge" that, as Lennard J. Davis has shown, opened a new space for deaf people in Europe's intellectual life.[57]

While visiting his sister Marie Antoinette in Paris in 1777, Joseph met with L'Épée and visited his famous school. He was so impressed that upon his return he charged the priest Friedrich Stork and the German-language instructor Joseph May with apprenticing to L'Épée, with the goal of establishing a similar institute in Vienna.[58] The Taubstummeninstitut opened in 1779 with twelve residential students, increased to twenty-seven the following year, and by 1789 had forty-eight students. The mission of the Institute was stated clearly by Stork in his 1786 publication, *Guide to the Instruction of Taubstummen, Following the Teaching Method of Abbé de l'Epée in Paris, with News of the Imperial Royal Taubstummeninstitut in Vienna*. Here was a place "where [those] who would otherwise have remained ignorant of religion, and useless to the state, are educated to be civilized people, good Christians, and useful citizens."[59] That trifecta of goals could almost be taken verbatim from the 1771 pamphlet about the Normalschule quoted earlier ("good Christians, useful citizens, and productive members of society").[60] Once again, in the charitable move to help deaf people, human rights and industrial productivity were inseparable. Nevertheless, the Institute acknowledged deaf children's equal claim to the Enlightenment ideology of perfectibility.[61] And while deaf children were not included in the compulsory primary education mandate of the 1774 *Allgemeine Schulordnung* (they would not be guaranteed an education until 1883), the founding of the Taubstummeninstitut was an important step toward normalizing deafness in Austrian society.[62]

A large part of the Institute's public-relations efforts were its regular examinations of the students, which were open to the general public. Taking a leaf from the Waisenhaus playbook, the Taubstummeninstitut held weekly examinations and annual public demonstrations, at which students would answer a series of catechistic questions about religious doctrine and carry out exercises in grammar and arithmetic. The question-and-answer session could involve any combination of writing, speaking, or signing, according to the student's preference. The *Wiener Zeitung* reported on each of these examinations, much the same as it had done for the Waisenhaus examinations a decade earlier, and the accounts made the examinations sound like performances. They were described as being extraordinarily well attended, with audiences giving "the loudest applause" and being "moved to tears" by the students' expression, "through written sentences and signs, [of] such correct and clear ideas as one can ever have from the most sublime secrets of our religion."[63] As a supplement to these exhibitions, the Taubstummeninstitut published annual updates (an echo of the Waisenhaus's annual reports), turning print itself into a kind of public performance.

Not all witnesses joined in the acclaim. Nicolai described a visit to the Taubstummeninstitut in the same 1781 volume in which he had voiced skepticism about the Waisenhaus. Here, his apprehension turned on the catechistic instruction at the Institute. Nicolai allowed that deaf children might be able to memorize complete answers to questions, but he remained unconvinced that "they also understood the meaning of the words," and "perhaps it would be best not to bother them with" such abstract concepts.[64] Johann Pezzl—a fellow Mason of Mozart's—was even more cynical. In a chapter on the Taubstummeninstitut in his 1786 *Sketches of Vienna*, Pezzl claimed that Stork and his teaching staff were wasting their time teaching their students such subjects as religion, natural science, and psychology, since deaf children, "squalid and neglected by Nature," would never have the insights and perfectibility of "completely well-organized [nondisabled] children." Pezzl even went on to argue that in offering such instruction to deaf children, the Institute was implicitly depriving hundreds of thousands of hearing children access to this kind of elite education. In Pezzl's view, all deaf children needed was enough moral instruction to know the difference from right and wrong, and enough training so they wouldn't be beggars.[65]

Despite the callous tone of Pezzl's remarks, in the very next paragraph he praised the Taubstummeninstitut for seeking another means of proving its worth to the general public: a printing press. The press was the brainchild of the Institute's third teacher, Johann Strommer, and initially funded by Joseph II. When the Institute first announced the press in the *Wiener Zeitung* in 1786, it was presented as an economic asset: the author of the announcement (probably Strommer) claimed that the press would provide important vocational training for the boys of the Institute, but would also enable the Institute itself to become more self-sufficient, thereby freeing up money for other needy subjects.[66] In another example of the business of charity, the press was presented as a fundraising tool.[67] And it is this printing press that would soon draw Mozart into the mission of the Taubstummeninstitut.

The press's first publication was a significant one: Stork's aforementioned *Guide*, which was accompanied with an engraving of the sign-language alphabet in use at the Institute, drawn by a "taubstummen Maler" and engraved by a "taubstummen Kupferstecher."[68] In both its content and its creators, the illustration forcefully underscored the point that deaf people possessed talents and skills that could be developed and made profitable. The press quickly built up a large catalogue, added a second and third machine in order to keep up with demand, and netted 150–200 florins each week in profit (for comparison, Mozart's annual imperial salary in 1787 was 800 florins).[69] The press also enabled the Institute to publish their own teaching method, the results of their popular public examinations, and job placements for their graduates.[70]

Alongside these publications, the Taubstummeninstitut printed a children's periodical, part of a growing literary genre that will be discussed further in chapter 4. The *Angenehme und lehrreiche Beschäftigung für Kinder in ihre Freistunden* (Pleasant and Instructive Pursuits for Children in their Free Time, 1787–1788) was not aimed solely at deaf children, but at the widest possible juvenile readership. And the readership was sizable: the list of subscribers in the first volume includes 246 names, from clergy, military, and government officials to educators and lesser aristocracy, while subsequent volumes included information about where to secure a subscription in twenty-five provincial capitals across the Monarchy, from Prague to Pest to Freiburg. When it was first advertised in the

Wiener Zeitung, May was listed as the editor, "together with some practical educators."[71] Yet his name does not appear in the issues themselves, nor does the periodical ever use the word "Taubstumme," except in identifying the publisher on the title page as the Taubstummeninstitut. Readers would have known, however, that this was one of the press's internal publications, and understood it to be identified with the broader aims of the Taubstummeninstitut.

In the preface to the first volume, the editors addressed their child readers directly. The periodical was meant for them to carry with them on walks and share with one another "when you have free time."[72] Its contents would help clarify "what you often see and don't understand."[73] Those loaded terms "sehen" und "verstehen" offered an implicit riposte to critiques of the Taubstummeninstitut such as Nicolai's, which had frequently questioned the children's capacity for understanding. Adulthood, the preface continued, was not simply a matter of being fully grown, but of understanding much, in an echo of Kant's 1784 definition of Enlightenment as "the emergence of man from his self-imposed immaturity."[74] The editors went on to describe the periodical's contents as "anything that can be made comprehensible to children in their childhood, help them in their knowledge, and provide the basis for making them useful citizens, until they reach their adolescence."[75]

Embodying this eclectic, didactic approach to the periodical's mission, May's *Beschäftigung* had the typical lineup of children's periodical offerings: stories, skits, poems, nonfiction, and riddles, nearly all with a clarification as to the intended moral. Opportunities were also often taken—or manufactured—to explain one or more of Joseph's decrees, always with an emphasis on the Emperor's fatherly concern for all his subjects—Joseph the "Landesvater" taking the place of his mother, the "Landesmutter." The periodical was meant to be shared by boys and girls, but boys were the principal readership: they were to use the periodical's contents to cultivate the "virtue," "understanding," and "cleverness" that would allow them to be "invited into the company of adults," whereas girls were offered "everything that can serve to increase your amiability, amuse you, and make you truly happy."[76] The contents were also often gendered, with "housekeeping" sections for girls and a long disquisition in volume two entitled "Modesty for Girls." Somewhat unusually for its time, the editors also published, and replied to, letters from its child readers, including critical ones such as complaints about the difficulty of the riddles. This will be important later when we come to Mozart's role in the periodical, but it also demonstrates that from the beginning, the *Beschäftigung* was presented as being in a reciprocal dialogue with its readers.

The text was enhanced by occasional tipped-in sheets, whether an engraved illustration, map, or song. These addenda were always connected to the topics explored in the periodical.[77] An article in volume 4 describing the various historical sieges of Belgrade, for instance, was accompanied by a detailed map of the region. And the first of the five songs that appeared in the periodical over its two-year run was appended to a short story about a boy with two canaries who neglects the one that doesn't sing. In what can only be read as a veiled plea for tolerance for deaf people, the boy's father chides him for his partiality. The episode ends with the father's words, sounding suspiciously Josephinian: "Fritzchen, mark my words: you have learned nothing, little son, if you persist in dividing."[78] In the song that follows, "Der Knabe beim Vogelfang" (The Boy as He Catches Birds), a boy expresses pity for a bird he has captured, promising to take care of it—a metaphor for Joseph's enlightened paternalism toward the children and youths benevolently confined at the Taubstummeninstitut and elsewhere.[79]

The *Beschäftigung*'s songs participated in a sublimated rapprochement between hearing authors, deaf typesetters and engravers, and an undifferentiated readership, newly mediated through print. As Lennard Davis argues, "given a written text, there is little difference between a hearing person and a deaf one . . . Writing is in effect sign language."[80] Printed music is a different case, but to encounter printed music in the Taubstummeninstitut's children's periodical arguably forced at least a reflection on ways of hearing, reinforcing the Institute's assimilationist goals. As May had his students recite in his *Erste Kenntnisse für Taubstumme*: "I am deaf-mute. / But I will not remain mute. I am learning how to speak at school. I will be unmuted. I am an ex-mute."[81] According to this catechism, muteness—not unlike childhood itself—was only a temporary disability, one that could and would be overcome. Including music in the Taubstummeninstitut's periodical performed a similar function, uniting deaf children with the hearing world through print—a quietly radical, and infinitely repeatable, act for the *Beschäftigung*'s readers, both hearing and deaf.

Mozart may not have been aware of all these layers of signification to his contributions to the *Beschäftigung*. But his "Die kleine Spinnerin" (The Little Spinner-Girl, K. 531, 1787) and "Lied beim Auszug in das Feld" (Song on Departure for the Battlefield, K. 552, 1788) worked the same way as the periodical's other engravings (both illustrations and songs), conversing intertextually with their surrounding content. It's unclear how Mozart came to be associated with the periodical, or how he came by the two poems, both of which are anonymous. Unlike the Waisenhaus appearance, Mozart had no need of the job for either income or publicity, especially given his recent successes with *Le nozze di Figaro* and *Don Giovanni* in 1786–1787. It therefore was more likely to have been a casual undertaking for an acquaintance. The strongest connection is through the engraver and publisher Ignaz Alberti, who illustrated the engraving in the *Beschäftigung* reproduced as figure 2.2. Alberti was a member of Mozart's Masonic lodge, and just four years later he published both the *Liedersammlung für Kinder und Kinderfreunde* (in which Mozart's last three Lieder, K. 596–98, appeared) and the first edition of the libretto to *Die Zauberflöte*.[82] Another possible connection is Christoph Torricella, the art and music dealer who engraved a number of Mozart's works from 1784 until 1786, and who was also the authorized dealer for the Taubstummeninstitut press.[83] We also know that another Institute publication, Amand Wilhelm Smith's *Philosophical Fragments on Practical Music* (1787), was in Mozart's library at the time of his death.[84]

Whatever the circumstances leading to Mozart's contributions to the *Beschäftigung*, he seems to have been well briefed on the thematic affiliation between the songs and their surrounding literary content in the periodical. As Derek Beales observes, Mozart's "Lied beim Auszug in das Feld"—composed on August 11, 1788, and published in volume 4—is bellicose and propagandistic, reinforcing the surrounding articles in propping up the controversial, ultimately ill-fated Austro-Turkish War (1787–1791).[85] As Matthew Head points out, the song's explanatory annotations "attest to the strategic deployment of the mode of derogatory stereotype represented by Osmin in *Die Entführung aus dem Serail*."[86] But there is more to this song than the propaganda and racism Beales and Head identify. It was introduced in the *Beschäftigung* as part of a plan to honor family members of the periodical's readership who had died in the war. The editors announced that they were starting a series called "Monuments to the Heroes of the League of Joseph and Catherine II," so that, "in order to sing into their sentimental souls the deeds of their deceased fathers or relatives, young readers might, from time to time, sing with full heart these songs accompanied with music."[87]

The editors stressed that these "written memorials" would not just be for the aristocracy, but for the common folk as well.[88] Readers were invited to submit the names of fallen loved ones for publication in subsequent issues; again, Strommer appears to have been the innovator here, as his was the name to which children were directed to address their letters. The quality of the songs, the editors wrote, would be assured by a survey of the previous Lieder published in the three existing volumes of the *Beschäftigung* (including, it hardly needed mentioning, Mozart's own previous contribution, "Die kleine Spinnerin").[89] "Lied beim Auszug in das Feld" was directly preceded by a "Foreword to Youth" in verse, addressed to those—especially boys—who had lost a father in the war. The poet claimed that Mozart's song would ensure that the readers' grandchildren would know what their fathers had sacrificed. "Dear son!" the poem ends. "Hear how your father earned his salvation . . . / See here the hero-fathers' image!"[90] The Lied immediately followed, its martial mode and meter under the tempo marking "With dignity."

Our fuller knowledge of the immediate print context for "Lied beim Auszug in das Feld" suggests additional layers of meaning in this most occasional of Mozart's compositions. Beales writes that "the text of the song perfectly illustrated the confusion and inconsistences—or complexities—in prevailing attitudes to the war and to government policy in general." Nevertheless, in setting it, Mozart "conspicuously associated himself with a highly specific and elaborate piece of war propaganda."[91] In the context of the periodical, however, the song emerges as both propaganda and a coping strategy for the children of military casualties. The grieving son is invited to ventriloquize his father, remembering him at his best and most heroic—"beim Auszug," at the moment of departure. Second, the Lied encourages the son to view Joseph as a worthy surrogate, "the father . . . / Who loves his children," and, behind him, a benevolent God "who takes Heathen and Turk, Jew and Christian / Unto him as his children."[92] Finally, the sore tritone in the codetta, unresolved, sounds a brief note of awkwardness, even ugliness, beyond the words of comfort and resolve.

If "Lied beim Auszug in das Feld" is primarily addressed to boys, the earlier song Mozart contributed to the *Beschäftigung*, "Die kleine Spinnerin"—composed on December 11, 1787—presents an ideal daughter. The connections between "Die kleine Spinnerin" and its surrounding text in volume 1, however, are more opaque. The song is not appended to an article on spinning. Instead, it comes immediately after a long dialogue, "Der Biber" (The Beaver), in which a father tells his son Karl and daughter Hanchen all about the beaver species: their morphology, their method of designing dams and raising their young, their methods of attacking and defending, their habitat, and their usefulness to humans (fig. 2.2). The conversation turns out to be about far more than just natural history, with the father indulging in frequent digressions on organicism, creation, the natural order, class, learning methods, and Emperor Joseph's fatherly concern for his subjects (with occasional interjections from, and corrections to, the children's mother).

FIGURE 2.2. I[gnaz] Alberti, illustration to "Der Biber," *Angenehme und lehrreiche Beschäftigung für Kinder*, vol. 1 (Vienna, 1787), after 81. Courtesy of Universitätsbibliothek Augsburg, shelfmark 02/VI.1.8.235-1.

This extended dialogue, which runs to sixty-one pages over multiple weekly issues, came in for some criticism in the letters to the editor. One young reader, identified only as "M. v. S." (which could be a cipher for "May und Stork"), complained that "It is really too long, and I can honestly confess that it did not entertain me in the least."[93] The editors printed a chastening five-page response to M. v. S. After acknowledging that there may have been others who were similarly bored, the editors cautioned all their readers that when they were grown, they would need to be able to set themselves to tasks for five, six, or seven hours at a time. They then affirmed the inseparability of the "lehrreich" from the "angenehm":

> Everything that we write is intended to entertain you, but mark well the difference; you should draw from our little newspaper not only entertainment [*Vergnügen*], but also usefulness [*Nutzen*]. May God in Heaven forbid that you should become accustomed in your tender youth to mere games, to mere entertainment, and never to some seriousness, some effort of your souls![94]

There follows an additional eighteen pages on beavers, as though the editors were almost daring their readers to abandon the topic. The father admonishes the children to "take beavers as your model," because "amongst colleagues there must be the same diligence [*Fleiß*] and mutual understanding [*Einverständnis*]."[95] At the end, the father tells his children, "And with that, my children, my story is ended; for your attention I give you this engraving."[96] The next page is "Die kleine Spinnerin," the song by Mozart, offered as a reward for practicing that diligence that would be so useful later in life (fig. 2.3).

1. What are you spinning? asked Fritz from next door,
When he visited us lately.
Your little wheel is turning like lightning!
What's the good of that?

2. Better to come out and join in our game!
"Herr Fritz, I shall do nothing of the kind,
If you must know, I have my own ways
Of passing the time.

3. What good is it? A silly question!
You have a lot to learn!
If you'd stop playing all day long
You wouldn't have to ask.

4. For my two little sisters
I'm spinning linen blouses:
As things grow dearer every year
Why shouldn't I mind my wheel?

FIGURE 2.3. Mozart, "Die kleine Spinnerin" (K. 531), in *Angenehme und lehrreiche Beschäftigung für Kinder*, vol. 1 (Vienna, 1787), after 178. Courtesy of Universitätsbibliothek Augsburg, shelfmark 02/VI.1.8.235-1.

5. And when I spin a sturdy band
That costs a pretty penny,
My mother weighs it pound by pound
Upon our pair of scales.

6. And what she would have paid for spinning
She notes down in chalk

And deducts it from our spinning costs
So I can have a dress.

7. When other maidens are untidy
I have a pretty skirt;
And people say, What a lovely child,
And she no longer plays with dolls!

8. My mother loves to hear such things
And they also do me honour:
That's what I would lose, my sirs,
If I were not hard-working.

9. So hum away, dear spinning wheel,
And fill my spool with thread;
Winter's nigh, it will be cold
On my sisters' way to school.

10. And if the people were to see them
Suffering from the cold,
How they would despise me!
No, I'd rather they would not."[97]

In "Die kleine Spinnerin," the unnamed protagonist's "neighbor Fritz" comes over to her house to try to coax her out to play. Fritz's entreaty takes up the first five of the song's forty lines, while the spinner-girl's refusal pours out in a single, uninterrupted, thirty-five-line sermon on the value and rewards of filial duty and household labor. The girl speaks of Fritz's urge to play as naïve, and she goes on to relate what her spinning contributes to the (struggling) family economy, to her sense of self-worth, and to the reputation of her mother. It is a point of pride for the girl to have exchanged her toys for the instruments of labor, but more than that, to be seen to have done so, to be considered by others too mature for such infantile play. Thus does the spinner-girl exemplify the "diligence," "obedience," and "orderliness" listed as prized qualities for children in a 1780 alphabet for children published in Vienna.[98]

The anonymous poet could have presented this dialogue as a real-time exchange between Fritz and the girl. Instead, it is introduced as a narrative of a past event, one being related after the fact by the girl herself (or even perhaps by another member of the household). A more salient audience is implied by the girl's parenthetical address to "my sirs" in verse 8.

This is reinforced by two other moments in which the girl refers to what people say or might say in response to her behavior. First, she imagines people admiring her pretty skirt (bought with the savings from her spinning) and remarking of her, "What a lovely child, / And she no longer plays with dolls!" The spinner-girl's second reference to external judgment comes in the last verse, when her final justification for industriousness is that she wishes to avoid the rebuke of those who might see her younger sisters walking to school in the winter, suffering in the cold for lack of proper clothing—the clothing that she herself could spin for them. "How the people would despise me!" she frets. "No, I'd rather they would not." The actual encounter between the girl and Fritz that first motivated the poem has now been overtaken by several hypothetical encounters between the girl and a diffuse crowd of imagined judges. Her final reasoning is a negative one: it is not the earning of approbation, but the avoidance of disapprobation, that acts as the final motivation for the girl's conscientious choice. "Die kleine Spinnerin" is suffused with a sober awareness of the true value of a daughter, learning to weigh her contribution to the household "pound for pound."

The spinner-girl's awareness that her youth is being lived out in public, subject to the approval of adults both near (her mother) and far ("die Leute"), is a familiar refrain in Enlightenment discussions of womanhood more generally. In describing Emile's intended, Sophie, Rousseau wrote that since "woman is made specially to please man,"

> it is important, then, not only that a woman be faithful, but that she be judged to be faithful by her husband, by those near her, by everyone. It is important that she be modest, attentive, reserved, and that she give evidence of her virtue to the eyes of others as well as to her own conscience. . . . These are the reasons which put even appearances among the duties of women, and make honor and reputation no less indispensable to them than chastity.[99]

Just as the spinner-girl is a representative of an ideal of self-conscious femininity, the encounter between Fritz and the girl could be read as an allegory of the conflict between the bored letter-writer and more dutiful readers of the periodical. Like the diligent spinner-girl, industrious readers—as industrious as beavers—are encouraged to see both household work and reading about natural history as superior to aimless play. The *lehrreich*, in other words, encompasses or supersedes the *angenehm*.

Mozart's setting also threads the needle between playful and industrious. The setting begins with a glancing reference to the pumping of a treadle in the opening motive, which toggles back and forth between dominant and tonic.[100] But Mozart tempers the pious text with a playful melody. In his typology of Mozart Lieder, Ernst August Ballin has categorized "Die kleine Spinnerin" as a Viennese Singspiellied, based on its lively eighth-note rhythm, the declamatory phrasing, and the leaping intervals.[101] The ascending major sixths at mm. 5–6 and 9–10, with their dotted rhythms, seem particularly jaunty, and a swooping gesture over the same interval marks the cadence at mm. 19–20. That swooping gesture establishes a mischievousness that contradicts the spinner-girl's staid maturity. For someone who is hard at work, she seems to be having an awfully good time doing so. If we hear the treadle beneath the spinner-girl's feet, then, we also hear the floorboards beneath the feet of the Singspiel heroine whose language the spinner-girl coopts: both are on stage, playing to their audiences' expectations. The combination of the extended auto-quotation (if the narrator is indeed the girl herself) and the jocular tone of the music results in a "to the *parterre*" quality to the Lied (one not unlike the provocative epilogues of the child actors discussed in chapter 3).

At another level, the spinner-girl's industriousness, however jaunty, is an allegory not just of the *Beschäftigung* periodical but of the Taubstummeninstitut's project as a whole. In her 1765 *Spinnschulen-Aufrichtungs-Patent* (Decree for the Establishment of Spinning Schools), Maria Theresa had decreed that all abandoned or poor children should be enrolled in spinning schools from ages seven to fifteen. The scarcity kept at bay by the spinner-girl's industriousness, then, was all too real a threat for many marginalized children.[102] As for the Taubstummeninstitut, its printing press was intended as vocational training for the boy students, while girl students were instructed in "the various styles of handiwork proper to their sex, such as sewing, knitting, and silk spinning."[103] In the annual reports, the Institute proudly reported on successfully placing male graduates at other printing presses, female graduates in domestic work. So Mozart's spinner-girl could also be read as a figure for the female student at the Institute, looking forward to giving back to her mother ("Unser lieben Frau") by fulfilling that promise in which the Institute had put its faith.

As the various child characters in the *Beschäftigung* modeled diligence and industriousness for their readership, the periodical as a whole participated in another project: the coopting of children's free time. David Gramit has shown how German singing manuals and lullaby collections "disciplined" private singing, standardizing and commercializing what once had been an unmonitored aspect of family life.[104] The Taubstummeninstitut's printing press was purportedly conceived as a way of turning the students' free time into a profit-generating trade.[105] And as we have already seen, the editors of the *Beschäftigung* urged their young readers to a heightened awareness of the labor economy within which they and their free time were implicated:

> You must listen to us gladly, remember with care our advice and our teaching, and diligently seek to put it all to work, dear children, otherwise we will surely have worked in vain, and your good parents will have spent the money for this our journal in vain for you; because even though something costs so little, you should not tempt your parents to submit to any expense that you will make useless through your non-use of the thing: your dear parents must purchase everything with effort, and would become angry with you if you used something without purpose that they could have made good use of in a different way.[106]

This is an extraordinarily candid expression of the "return on investment" philosophy of pedagogy underpinning the Taubstummeninstitut's investment in the printing press, and behind that, Joseph's investment in the Institute. Just like the spinner-girl, who has her own ways of "passing the time," and just like Vienna's deaf children, all young readers of the *Angenehme und lehrreiche Beschäftigung in ihre Freystunden* are urged to view those "Freystunden" as not free at all: rather, free time comes at a price, and can also be put to profit.[107]

Mozart's musical contributions to the *Beschäftigung* were clearly major selling points for the Institute. A November 1788 announcement listed the magazine's contents as "fables, stories, riddles, short correspondences, various inventions, illuminated engravings, [and] songs with music by the famous Mozart," as though no other composers had contributed settings (of course they had, but neither were anywhere near his level of celebrity).[108] And in the preface to the first issue of volume 2, the editors apologized profusely for some errors in the initial engraving of "Die kleine Spinnerin" when it had first appeared in the weekly format. They even offered to exchange readers' flawed copies for the corrected one wherever the subscription copy was sold, and they promised not to inflict such an inconvenience on their readers again.[109] Both Mozart and his father were sticklers for accuracy in engraving, so it could be that Mozart insisted the Taubstummeninstitut print the erratum. Regardless, that the editors of the periodical would print such an apology shows just how powerful Mozart was as a "celebrity endorser."[110]

The Normalschule

In this chapter's final case, Mozart's name and talents were once again marshalled for an ambitious initiative that affected all of the Monarchy's children. The Waisenhaus and Taubstummeninstitut were Viennese institutions that sought to draw marginalized children—orphans, foundlings, and deaf children—into the fold of society. Beyond these targeted projects in the capital, there existed a much more sweeping effort to standardize the education of both young children and their teachers across the Habsburg lands. In the first sentence of her 1774 *Allgemeine Schulordnung* (General School Ordinance), Maria Theresa proclaimed that "the education of youth of both sexes is the most important foundation for the true happiness of nations."[111] Joseph felt the same, but feared the consequences of a highly educated populace. Consequently, he raised fees on secondary schools, and made only primary education universal.[112] Joseph's anti-intellectual stance would earn him criticism from the Austrian intellegentsia, but he remained steadfast: education must always be *"standesmässig,"* appropriate to the child's class and social station, and that meant that only primary education would be universally accessible.[113]

In this as in so many aspects of statecraft, Austria looked to its nearest neighbor and rival, Prussia, as a model for the centralization of primary education. Frederick II had already enacted his *General-Landschul-Reglement* (General Rural School Regulation) in 1763, which mandated and standardized elementary education.[114] One of the most persistent obstacles to its successful implementation was a lack of teacher training institutes.[115] So after the dissolution of the Jesuit orders, when Maria Theresa set about drafting her *Allgemeine Schulordnung*, she turned to a man, Johann Ignaz von Felbiger, who in the 1760s had successfully helped improve Central European Catholic parish schools through a systematic establishment of *Normalschulen*, or teacher training schools.[116] Felbiger's method had already formed the basis for Parhamer's approach to education at the Waisenhaus.[117] And Felbiger's gift for reconciling the Catholic and cameralist interests of the state made him the ideal choice to both draft the *Allgemeine Schulordnung* and supervise its implementation.

Melton has argued that "In the eighteenth century . . . schools became a central target of state policy precisely because they offered an instrument for exacting obedience in a less coercive fashion."[118] In tandem with efforts to increase enrollment in primary school, the schools themselves became more child-friendly, and music played a key role in inculcating their values. Felbiger already knew this in the 1760s, when he was charged with reforming the parish schools in Silesia. In the preface to a 1766 collection of new *Catechistic Songs* for use in the schools in Sagan, Felbiger wrote: "The rhyme of songs, which aids in memorization, makes children retain the words of the songs much better than those which are in the ordinary Catechistic textbooks."[119] Two years later, in a circular to schoolteachers accompanying a revised edition of the *Catechistic Songs*, Felbiger argued that Lieder are "nothing other than prayers put into rhymes":

> It is therefore not enough to honor God only through singing with the lips, or with the tone of the voice: the heart must not be removed from the Almighty, but rather exalted to Him. Those who sing must, as Paul says, sing with the spirit and the entire being.[120]

When Felbiger took over imperial school reform for Maria Theresa, song collections again played a prominent role, even if music was mentioned only in passing in the *Allgemeine Schulordnung* itself. New Catholic and catechistic songbooks similar to those brought out by Felbiger in Silesia began to be published in Vienna (some under the auspices of the St. Anna Normalschule) and distributed for free.[121] To have such publications put out by the Normalschule also reinforced the mutual interdependence of school reforms and church reforms. As Joseph sought to rein in the power and profligacy of the Catholic Church, the promotion of a Protestant-informed style of congregational singing among children (the next generation of congregants) was an important aspect of his long-term strategy.

As it had for the Waisenhaus and Taubstummeninstitut, music also figured prominently in the examinations, graduations, anniversary celebrations, and other high-profile events through which the Normalschule demonstrated its value to the public. For example, the 1780 examination of thirty-one junior officers at the Vienna Normalschule concluded with a "Schlußgesang" composed by Hofklaviermeister Josef Antonín Štěpán (Steffan). The description in the *Wiener Zeitung* of the "very moving song with Turkish music" performed by the graduates, and the identification of Štěpán as the composer of the "thoroughly excellent piece," conveys the significance of music in eliciting public approval and legitimization for the institution.[122]

Given the importance of music, and particularly printed song collections, in the early history of the Vienna Normalschule, it stands to reason that subsequent Normalschulen established throughout the Habsburg lands would print their own music. And this is where Mozart enters the picture, in a song collection published by the Normalschule in Prague. Prague's first Normalschule was established there in 1775, and Bohemia

FIGURE 2.4. Ludwig Kohl, title page engraving, Aleš Pařízek, *Ausführliche Beschreibung der am 15. November 1800 gehaltenen Jubelfeyer der k. k. Normalschule in Prag* (Prague, 1801). Courtesy of Bayerische Staatsbibliothek München/Bildarchiv, shelfmark Paed.th.4294.

would be renowned as one of the most successful regions for Habsburg school reform, with 674 industrial schools opened between 1779 and 1798, and an overall attendance rate of two-thirds by 1790.[123] Like its predecessor, the Prague Normalschule soon began publishing books, having inherited the Jesuit printing press following the dissolution of the order. Many of the Normalschule publications appeared in dual editions, one German, one Czech, so as to reach the maximum number of readers in the Bohemian lands.[124]

From early on, music had figured prominently in the life of the Prague Normalschule. Franz Steinsky, a handwriting and natural history teacher there, led the students in singing at Mass beginning in 1778, rehearsing the songs during school hours.[125] As Steinsky wrote years later, choral instruction provided the only precedent for the kind of communal instruction favored by pedagogical reformers and implemented at the Normalschule.[126] This elision of "Zusammengesang" and "Zusammenunterricht" can be seen in the title page engraving to the twenty-fifth-anniversary account of the Normalschule (fig. 2.4). The group of boys receiving a volume from Athena looks almost indistinguishable from choirboys clustered around a score; even their mouths are open as though in song.

Bohemians had long been famed for the quality and extent of their music instruction. Eyewitnesses from Charles Burney to Christoph Willibald von Gluck confirmed that not just choirboys or courtiers, but ordinary children in the *Landschulen*, were given a strong foundation in music as part of their daily education.[127] As Melton points out, this was due in no small part to the prominent role long given to music in the earlier parish schools, as part of the emphasis on participatory and communal religious ritual.[128] Some reformers, however, saw the centrality of music in the provincial schools as a liability. Ferdinand Kindermann, the head of the Bohemian School Commission and thus in a sense the "Felbiger of Prague," wrote a critical report on education in the Bohemian town of Kaplitz in which he sniffed that, after "cramming" the students' heads with words and a rudimentary few questions out of the catechism, they learned "a little music, which the country schools were inclined to make one of their most important subjects."[129] The equivocal reception of the prominence of music in the image of Czech schooling was never just about classroom singing. At stake was the delicate balance of power between Vienna and the religious and linguistic heterogeneity of the hereditary lands.

The first song collection published by the Normalschule appeared in 1783, the *Lieder zur öffentlichen und häuslichen Andacht* (Songs for Public and Domestic Worship, 1783, hereafter *Andachtslieder*), edited by Steinsky with assistance from Kindermann. Other songbooks designated for "öffentlichen und häuslichen" use had already appeared in Lemgo, Gotha, Göttingen, Vienna, and Altona in the preceding decade.[130] But most of those previous collections included only the texts of hymns, with at most a reference to existing melodies to be found elsewhere. The 1783 Prague *Andachtslieder*, on the other hand, included an extended set of mostly original melodies. It was issued in two versions, a short edition of just 32 pages, and an expanded edition of 241 pages, subtitled *With Melodies Mostly from the Best Masters of Our Country*, which included five tipped-in sheets of 118 melodies.[131] As Steinsky indicated in a closing note to the expanded volume, the melodies were "engraved very small so as not to make the book too expensive," and would "need to be copied over into a special hymn book" in order that they could be used in a school or church setting.[132] Just seven of the 118 melodies were taken from preexisting collections. The rest, as Steinsky's preface asserted, were commissioned by "our most outstanding masters," such as Štěpán, Kozeluch (probably Leopold), and František Xaver Dušek.[133] Lieder indicated with three asterisks were composed by Steinsky himself.[134]

Why go to this trouble and expense commissioning new tunes from Czech composers? The opening epigraph of the *Andachtslieder* clarified the rationale: Psalm 149:1, "Sing to the Lord a new song." In the foreword, Steinsky affirmed the centrality of song to religious worship, but argued that the modern-day Christian's ears, "accustomed to noisy symphonies," would find the melancholy old church songs an affront.[135] He went on to ask rhetorically whether "there is no way to avoid the coarseness of modern church music as well as the distastefulness of the old choral songs?" The answer, of course, was this collection, many of whose settings Steinsky asserted had already been in use at the Prague Normalschule for several years.[136] Youth and reform schools were thus presented as centers of innovation in sung worship, and the collection itself was held up as responding to shifts in public taste.[137]

While children were not directly addressed as the principal readership, the book's mention of the Normalschule would have only reinforced public knowledge of Steinsky's position there. The collection was therefore understood to be intended for the domestic devotional practices of children and youth. A year after its publication, Joseph issued a decree establishing a new parish division and a new order of worship for Prague, for which many of the *Andachtslieder* were reprinted; the melodies in this new volume, called *Kirchengesänge und Gebete gemäß der Gottesdiensteinrichtung zu Prag* (Church Songs and Prayers Following the Prague Order of Worship), were keyed to the *Andachtslieder*.[138] The same year, a Czech translation of the *Andachtslieder* was published by the Normalschule press and distributed "to all pastors, school supervisors, and teachers throughout the Bohemian lands, to disseminate the edifying songs in churches and schools."[139] This collection was instrumental in Joseph's efforts to standardize Catholic singing across the Monarchy.

By the time the second, revised German-language edition appeared in 1788, the editors had persuaded Mozart to contribute two simple, strophic hymns: "O Gottes Lamm" (O Lamb of God) and "Als aus Ägypten" (When Out of Egypt) (K. 343a and b).[140] David Black and others who have studied these songs note that no copies of the third or fourth editions of the *Andachtslieder* appear to have survived.[141] The fifth edition, however, from 1805 (expanded to 332 pages), again included Mozart's songs, along with an extended preface (possibly by Steinsky, though it is not attributed) that suggested Mozart had originally composed them on the request of Johann Joseph Strobach, the director of the orchestra at the National Theatre who had conducted productions of *Figaro* and *Don Giovanni*, and the choir director at the church of St. Nicholas.[142]

Because the intervening third and fourth editions of the *Andachtslieder* appear not to have survived, it is uncertain whether Mozart's songs first appeared in the fifth edition or earlier. Nevertheless, the editors were clearly at pains to explain Mozart's presence in the *Andachtslieder*. He is mentioned in a fourteen-page subsection of the preface entitled "Public Judgments on Our Song Collection," an exhaustive refutation of the negative review of the first edition of *Andachtslieder* in the *Allgemeine deutsche Bibliothek*. Just as Mozart's presence in the *Beschäftigung* had added luster to the Taubstummeninstitut's project, his presence here in the *Andachtslieder* seemed intended to serve the same purpose.

Another song collection related to the Prague Normalschule used Mozart's music as an accompaniment to youthful industriousness. As mentioned before, despite Maria Theresa's concerted investment in teacher training and curricular standardization, Joseph inherited a situation in which on average only about 20–30 percent of eligible students attended school.[143] Employing both the carrot and the stick, Joseph enacted heavy fines for truancy, but also established *Industrieschulen*, or industrial schools, so that children might contribute to their family income while gaining basic literacy. The model for this was the Prague Normalschule, where Kindermann—the co-editor of the *Andachtslieder*—had introduced spinning classes in which girls would learn and practice the trade of spinning while engaging in moralizing storytelling and conversation with their instructors.[144] This program's success at drawing in families and raising the overall enrollment rate earned Kindermann the position of supervisor of Bohemian parish education in 1775. As Melton notes, "The relatively high attendance rate (75 percent) in schools with spinning classes points to Kindermann's success in linking elementary schooling with rural industry."[145]

In 1789, a year in which Mozart passed through Prague twice while traveling with Prince Lichnowsky, the Normalschulbuchdruckerey published a *Sammlung einiger Lieder für die Jugend bei Industrialarbeiten* (Collection of Some Songs for Youth at Industrial Work), edited by Franz Stiasny, a teacher in the girls' classes at the Normalschule. In the preface to the *Sammlung*, Stiasny wrote that he had already tried these songs out with his students while they learned sewing, spinning, and knitting.[146] Stiasny revealed that his students were much more excited to sing songs than to hear stories being read aloud. He wrote that he carefully observed their reactions to certain songs and selected only those that had pleased them the most. The collection includes an alternate setting of "Die kleine Spinnerin" to Mozart's in the *Beschäftigung*. But an even closer Lied to Mozart was identified in the collection by Paul Nettl: one of the songs, "Sey uns willkommen in blumigstem Kleide," is sung to the tune of "Se vuol ballare" from *Le nozze di Figaro* (fig. 2.5).[147] This contrafactum suggests that Stiasny and his female students were familiar enough with this tune to enjoy adapting it to new ends.

> Let us be welcome in the most flowery dresses
> Ornaments of the acres and country joy!
> Pick roses for children, as long as they bloom:
> Be merry, joyful; the years fly by!
>
> Let fops grumble, we children, we joke,
> We dance and jump and laugh heartily,
> Free from affliction, sorrow, and grievances,
> Faithful to God, to virtue, and to our Emperor!

It's a refreshingly mischievous choice, the sly minuet in which Figaro vows to "school" his master.[148] Stiasny retains Mozart's lopsided phrase structure of five four-bar phrases, though the final two phrases have been, for lack of a better word, domesticated: the syncopated exclamations on "sì!" are gone, rendering the final two phrases more parallel, in keeping with the revised text underlay with its full repetition of the last line.

We cannot know whether Mozart sanctioned this contrafactum—it appears to be the only explicit quotation of preexisting music in the *Sammlung*—but given his own tongue-in-cheek quotation of *Figaro* in *Don Giovanni*, he would doubtless have been amused to hear a room of "kleine Spinnerinnen" ventriloquizing Figaro. But while the girls may have sung the lines "we children, we joke, / Dance and jump and laugh full heartily" (in text that will be echoed in Mozart's 1791 song "Das Kinderspiel," to be discussed in chapter 4), they were sitting bent over their spinning wheels; and whereas for many families work time preempted school time, now even vocational training had to make room for moral education.

The songs in the *Sammlung*, Stiasny wrote, "give my students a lively mood and joyful feeling; excite their industriousness, multiply their profits, and at the same time enrich their hearts with beautiful sensations."[149] This was more than just an echo of Kindermann's rhetoric. In Friedrich Arnold's 1787 account of his travels in Prague, he described observing a class of singing spinning girls who had, in his words, managed to "turn industriousness into a game":

> The entire class was thus together, and now they began at once to sing an instructive song to a very cheerful melody, which made them work

FIGURE 2.5. "Frühlingsliedchen," in Stiasny, *Sammlung einiger Lieder für die Jugend bei Industrialarbeiten* (Prague, 1789), 174. Courtesy of Scripta Paedagogica Online, shelfmark AD5683.

even harder. Here, therefore, was employment and amusement bound together.[150]

Arnold went on to remark that there was ample precedent for singing in a Normalschule spinning class. In an essentializing account of Czech musicality, he wrote:

> The Bohemian workman is accustomed to singing a little song to himself as he works. If he does not do so, he is ill-humored. But to be sure, the songs he uses himself are not of the best type. . . . The majority of these girls will surely become workers themselves, and they will then impercep-tibly introduce this better genre of songs. This is the true way to abolish abuses, and he who wished to do something for humanity should donate his money to such institutions.[151]

Arnold seems to imagine these female students sitting in the Normal-schule at their spinning wheels as though they were stealth song reform-ers—or perhaps, to recall the inoculation program with which this chapter opened, as the musical equivalent of public health workers, "inoc-ulating" a new generation of Czech workers against a too-rough singing at work. So whereas publications like the *Beschäftigung* promulgated an ideal of the industrious, obedient child, collections like Stiasny's *Sammlung* held up child workers as the agents of social betterment across the generations. This shows just how far the business of charity, and the inter-twining of music and child welfare, had come since the twelve-year-old Mozart had lent his music and his image to the Waisenhaus.

CHAPTER 3

Acting Like Children

In the previous chapter, I showed how the Habsburg focus on industrial education can inform our understanding of Mozart's music for Vienna's Waisenhaus and Taubstummeninstitut, and Prague's Normalschule. These education and child welfare institutions were aimed at maximizing the industriousness of the Habsburg Monarchy's future subjects. Molding children into productive workers required disciplining their free time and making industriousness itself a virtue, as we saw in Mozart's Lied "Die kleine Spinnerin." At the same time, we could observe the theatrical wink with which Mozart's spinner-girl performed her industriousness.

In this chapter, I turn to another category of child performer, and child worker, with which Mozart was more closely linked, one that raised additional questions with respect to virtue: the child as theatrical performer. In Salzburg, Mozart came into contact with two types of child-oriented theater: *Schuldramen* (school dramas) performed by students at Salzburg's Benedictine University, and *Kindertruppen*—wandering troupes of professional child actors that crisscrossed Europe, performing adaptations and parodies of adult theatricals.[1] At first sight, these two institutions could not have been more different: sacred versus secular, lofty and learned as opposed to lively and commercial. The two institutions' repertoires overlapped surprisingly often, however, with *commedia dell'arte* pantomimes sharing the stage with Latin tragedies in the Schuldramen, and Kindertruppen staging Shakespeare and Lessing alongside the latest farces. Particularly in Salzburg, the two institutions were often in direct competition with one another. And Archbishop Schrattenbach (Mozart's first employer) was an enthusiastic patron of both.[2]

While growing up in Salzburg, Mozart participated in both of these institutions. His first public appearance, at age five, was dancing in one of the pantomime interludes for the university performance of the Latin play *Sigismundus Hungariae rex* (1761). And his first staged opera, the intermedium *Apollo et Hyacinthus* (K. 38, 1767), was performed at the university theater by students. The *licenza* that he composed and performed for the anniversary of the archbishop's consecration ("Or che il dover," K. 36, 1766) took place after an evening's entertainment by a wandering troupe of Italian comedians. The next evening, the Italian troupe's performance was followed by an appearance by the most renowned *Kindertruppe* to come through Salzburg, the Berner troupe. It is likely that Mozart attended at least one performance by the Berner troupe, and several of his later Singspiel collaborators were closely associated with children's troupes. One Berner troupe Singspiel, *Bastienne*, may have been the means by which Mozart undertook the Singspiel *Bastien und Bastienne* (K. 50, 1768), and another, *Das Serail*, formed the basis for Mozart's unfinished Singspiel *Zaide* (K. 344, 1779). The timing and personnel involved in *Zaide* suggest that it may even have been undertaken with the Theatralpflanzschule (Theatrical Nursery), a short-lived training institution for Vienna's National Singspiel, in mind.

These two theatrical institutions, Schuldrama and Kindertruppen, inspired debates about childhood, virtue, and the theater. Kindertruppen were particularly confounding to reform-minded pedagogues, as the spectacle of a dissembling child contravened the innocence and naturalness increasingly attributed to childhood. And even as troupes like Berner's cultivated a more literate and morally elevated repertoire and identity over the 1770s, persistent reports of exploitation and abuse led to efforts to develop unassailable alternatives. Meanwhile, a pamphlet war over Schuldramen was underway in the German-language press, hinging on the question of whether the young were vulnerable to moral suggestion through drama. This was playing out against the backdrop of imperial decrees considering the age of sexual consent and the regulation of child labor.[3] Both the university theater and the commercial theater thus operated within a broader "sexual system," the term used by the social historian Isabel Hull to identify "the patterned ways in which sexual behavior is shaped and given meaning through institutions."[4]

Mozart, then, was creating some of his earliest theatrical works at a time when philosophers and pedagogues argued about the compatibility of entertainment with moral instruction, and the propriety of children's participation in a profession with long-standing associations with prostitution. The three works through which I examine Mozart's engagement with Schuldramen and Kindertruppen are *Apollo et Hyacinthus*, *Bastien und Bastienne*, and *Zaide*. All three navigate the uneasy relation between sexuality and commerce in the theater, and all raise the same questions that preoccupied pedagogues and child welfare advocates: how to understand children and their place in the social order.

Benedictine *Schuldrama and* Apollo et Hyacinthus

Ever since the founding of Salzburg's university by the Benedictines in 1622, Schuldramen had constituted major events both in the university calendar and in the theatrical and political life of the city.[5] An outgrowth of Jesuit year-end and Lenten dramas, Schuldramen provided opportunities for students to improve and demonstrate their Latin-language proficiency, as well as to promulgate Benedictine values.[6] Performances took place during special occasions and at the end of the school year (*Finalkomödien*), with students playing in the orchestra and performing in the majority of the roles.[7] Schuldramen also fulfilled political and public relations functions, in keeping with Salzburg's status as an archbishopric whose ruler was also the head of the church. As Thomas Lederer summarizes, "The Salzburg university plays served to illustrate certain aspects of ecclesial doctrine and of political expedience and, of course, to extol the Prince-Archbishop as a paragon of orthodoxy and wise statesmanship."[8] Finally, the university was Salzburg's only permanent public theater—the remainder of Salzburg's theatrical life was confined to the archbishop's private court theater and the brief residencies of the wandering troupes. Lavish sets, machines, and props made the Schuldrama a must-see event in Salzburg.

The backbone of the Schuldrama was the five-act Latin tragedy, which from early on was performed with sung *intermedii* (usually in Latin) between the acts that often complemented the main plot. In the eighteenth century, afterpieces were added in the form of pantomimes or even separate Singspiels, broad comedies in German (often in Salzburg dialect).[9] The evening's entertainment was therefore similar to that of opera houses, where an opera seria would be performed with intermezzos and epilogues. For the *intermedii* and pantomimes, court composers like Michael Haydn and Anton Adlgasser collaborated with the university faculty, and student performers were joined by singers and musicians from the archbishop's chapel. Following the Jesuit practice, the Finalkomödie were performed twice: first for an all-female audience, then for an all-male audience.[10]

Schuldramen constituted young Mozart's introduction to the theater. His first documented public performance was among the *salii* (dancers) in the 1761 Finalkomödie *Sigismundus Hungariae Rex*. But he did not act in the tragedy itself, or sing in its *intermedium*, *Tobias*, with music by Kapellmeister Johann Ernst Eberlin. Instead, he danced in one or both

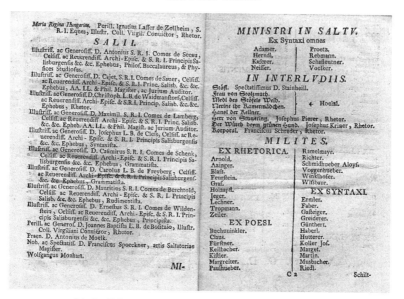

FIGURE 3.1. Marian Wimmer, *Sigismundus Hungariae Rex* (Salzburg, 1762). Courtesy of Universitätsbibliothek Salzburg, shelfmark R-4102-I.

of the two pantomimes or *interludii* identified in the *Perioche* (program) as *Stöfl und sein Weib* (Steve and His Wife) and *Der Würth beym grünen Hund* (The Landlord of the Green Dog Inn) (fig. 3.1).[11] These "Bauernschwänke" (farmer farces) were a popular form of *interludium* in Salzburg, with Stöfl/Steffl a Hanswurst type seen at the university theater since 1748.[12] According to the theater historian Otto Rommel, such folk elements in baroque school dramas played a large part in the development of the later Viennese "Volksstück."[13] While the context may have been elevated, then, young Mozart was clowning around.

By appearing in the 1761 *Finalkomödie*, Wolfgang was not only taking part in one of Salzburg's most popular theatrical traditions; he was also following in his father's footsteps. Leopold had sung in at least six Jesuit productions in Augsburg when he was young, beginning at age four.[14] He probably saw this as an ideal opportunity to introduce his son to the Salzburg court. He had already arranged for Mozart to apprentice to Haydn and Adlgasser on the *geistliche Singspiel, Die Schuldigkeit des ersten Gebots* (K. 35), which was performed at the archbishop's residence theater in March 1767. Two months later, Wolfgang "flew solo," composing the music for *Apollo et Hyacinthus*, the *intermedium* to the tragedy *Clementia Croesi*. The texts for both were written by Father Rufinus Widl, and the performance by his students, the third-year (Syntaxist) class at the university grammar school, took place in the Große Aula (Great Hall) in May.

Given the popularity of German-language pantomimes and Singspiels at the university theater, it seems at first surprising that Leopold would not have selected one of those genres for Wolfgang's debut. But the nobler, more conservative genre of the Latin *intermedium* probably seemed the prudent choice for the eleven-year-old boy's first contribution to the Benedictine University. And given that Wolfgang had already composed *Die Schuldigkeit des ersten Gebots*, perhaps Leopold felt it was important for him to distinguish himself in a Latinate genre if he were to secure a commission for an *opera buffa*, which was certainly next on their wish list.[15] Despite its loftier genre, however, Mozart's *intermedium* retained some elements of the pastoral style found in its neighbors, such as Michael Haydn's *Der Traum*, which had been the pantomime for the preceding play in the calendar, a Carnival performance of *Pietas in Hostem*.

Widl's *Apollo et Hyacinthus* is an adaptation from Ovid. In the *Metamorphoses*, Hyacinthus and Apollo are lovers, and Hyacinthus dies tragically by Apollo's hand in a discus-throwing accident. Other post-Ovid sources add a jealous foil, Zephyrus, who murders Hyacinthus by blowing the discus off-course. This was a somewhat risky plot to stage in a Benedictine boys' school. Widl softened the homoerotic overtones by changing the lovers' relationship into a platonic one and adding a love interest for Apollo, Hyacinthus's sister Melia.[16] On a more practical note, Melia provides the *intermedium* with a second soprano role and its lone female character, rounding out the cast of principals to five (two sopranos, two altos, and a tenor). The Latin *intermedii* for Schuldramen around this time tended to have five characters, one of whom was female (all were played, of course, by boy singers). Even though Zephyrus was now a rival of Apollo's for Melia, Widl still had him voice a passion for Hyacinthus that approaches idolatry and hints at the original myth's homoeroticism.

If Zephyrus serves as a lightning rod for all the "sins" portrayed in the *intermedium*, Melia performs the same function for its virtues. She worships the gods properly, recognizes Apollo's divinity, and immediately promises to accept his offer of marriage. Even her lone offence is committed out of an excess of virtue: she banishes Apollo when she believes him to be her brother's killer, in an extended duet that closes act 2. But Apollo forgives her blasphemy, because he recognizes that she was motivated by chaste filial devotion and naïve trust in Zephyrus. When all is put right at the end of the *intermedium*, Melia's father Oebalus affirms that she has earned mercy through her virtue: in one of the final lines before the closing terzett, Oebalus declares, "Thus an innocent does not forfeit his reward."[17]

Apollo et Hyacinthus is among the first examples of Mozart composing with specific voices in mind—in this case, young male voices. The casting of the *intermedium* was recorded in the Perioche, and a comparison of this one with others from the period shows that the same singers were recruited again and again for these Schuldramen, and that most were local choristers.[18] This suggests that at the time Mozart was composing *Apollo et Hyacinthus* he would have been familiar with these singers' voices, both by reputation and by firsthand experience. He drew on the singers' ages and voice types in depicting their characters. Melia and Hyacinthus are both soprano roles, while Apollo and Zephyrus are altos, and Oebalus a tenor. Mathias Stadler (Oebalus) was the oldest of the cast at twenty-three, and a student at the university who would soon join the court music as a tenor and later violinist.

Joseph Vonderthon (Zephyrus), aged seventeen, was a musician at St. Peter's and the son of a local choirmaster. Vonderthon's name does not appear in any Periochen before *Apollo et Hyacinthus*, and his age, along with the fact that his next two roles were dancing roles, suggests he was in the "grace period" that often followed a chorister's voice break.[19] If he was on the cusp of this break during *Apollo et Hyacinthus*, his voice might have helped convey something strained or "unnatural" about Zephyrus's character. In his aria, act 2's "En! duos conspicis" (Behold! You see two suitors), Zephyrus tries to convince Melia that she should marry him instead of Apollo. The aria, in A major, ranges from the A below the staff to the E a fifth above it, with several leaps across the *passagio* almost designed to highlight Vonderthon's break.

Apollo is a much higher alto role, and was portrayed by a much younger singer, the twelve-year-old chapel chorister Johann Ernst. Apollo's entrance aria, "Iam pastor Apollo" (I am the shepherd Apollo), in A major, is a fourth higher than Zephyrus's "En! duos conspicis." For the B section of this da capo aria, however, Mozart gave Ernst some challenging (and quite low) coloratura passages, which suggests Ernst's range, technique, and breath control were superior to Vonderthon's.[20]

Christian Enziger (Hyacinthus) was the same age as Ernst, and was a relative newcomer who only appears once more in the Salzburg Periochen. Felix Fuchs (Melia) was a fifteen-year-old soprano who often sang the first descant in oratorios in the Salzburg Cathedral and at court.[21] Fuchs and Ernst were Haydn's and Adlgasser's go-to soprano and alto from before, and long after, *Apollo et Hyacinthus*. They often played the lovers, whether in Latin *intermedii* or in vernacular German Singspiels, such as the roles of Damon and Amaryllis in Haydn's *Der Traum*. Their history portraying romantic leads would have been familiar to Mozart, and reinforced the fact that, despite the title *Apollo et Hyacinthus* referring to the original myth, the *intermedium's* "modern" protagonists are Apollo and Melia. The closing terzett for Melia, Apollo, and Oebalus, the G-major triple-meter "Tandem post turbida fulmina" (At last, after violent lightning), even recalls pastoral elements in Amaryllis and Damon's F-major triple-meter duet from *Der Traum*, "O Amaryllis, ich lebe vergnügt" (O Amaryllis, I live merrily).

At the same time as Mozart was making his mark in the Schuldrama, deftly navigating its generic vocabulary, moral codes, and sexual subtexts, the genre itself was under attack for those same codes and subtexts. In 1762, Johann Gotthelf Lindner published *Beitrag zu Schulhandlungen*, a set of four Schuldramen in German prefaced by a set of remarks on the genre.[22] Lindner was the rector of the Lutheran cathedral school in Riga at the time, and in his preface he argued (among other things) that children should not be given immoral characters to play. Errant behavior was acceptable as long as it was eventually corrected, but children should not be allowed to portray "beasts and monsters" or "complete villains."[23] Lindner also complained about the portrayal of female characters by boy students, and the representation of love scenes, which were in his mind appropriate only in the professional theater. "It is only fatherly and brotherly love [and] friendship (if they are absolutely guiltless and decent) . . . that even the fire of tenderness cannot instill with poison, arouse lusts, or mislead natural, irreproachable impulses."[24]

A dismissive critique of Lindner's plays triggered a spate of defenses and counterattacks to which even Johann Gottfried von Herder contributed in 1768. Herder's unpublished essay, which circulated in manuscript, questioned why, just as he and his fellow men of letters were beginning to study human life more closely, anyone would want to exclude youth and children from the stage.[25] To censor their theater, he argued, was to deny that young people's lives could be as dramatic as their elders, that they had passions and conflicts of their own.[26] Citing Horace, Rousseau, and Diderot, Herder advocated passionately for realism in the theater, including children's theater. If all students are meant to do is portray models, then, Herder feared, "we will have to show not natural, but Political men [the capitalization is Herder's], no longer men, but apes, on the stage."[27]

We might call this debate a *Schuldramenstreit*, as it overlapped with the *Hanswurststreit*, a pamphlet war about the functions and content of German theater that had begun in 1737 when Caroline Neuber symbolically banished Hanswurst from her troupe's performances, escalated when Empress Maria Theresa banned extemporized theater in 1752, and took off in the press in 1768 with Joseph von Sonnenfels's *Letters on Viennese Theater*.[28] Although the two debates focused on different repertoire, both shared a concern with the moral and didactic potential of theater. As Martin Nedbal has noted, proponents of moral didacticism in the theater made much of its wide appeal. In 1755, the actor and playwright Friedrich Wilhelm Weiskern—who would later collaborate with Mozart on *Bastien und Bastienne*—referred to didactic plays as "sugar-coated medicine for the soul," in a clear parallel to pedagogical language already encountered in chapter 2 vaunting "pleasant *and* instructive pursuits."[29]

In Salzburg, however, the Benedictine University was something of a holdout when it came to theater reforms. Even after the Austrian Studien-Hofkommission banned school performances in all Gymnasien in December 1768, performances continued in Salzburg for another eight years.[30] What finally brought the Schuldramen to an end in Salzburg, it seems, was not the moral question so much as the personal preferences of the archbishop. Schrattenbach's main objections to the Schuldramen had been their inordinate length, not their content, and his successor Colloredo objected primarily to their cost.[31] In 1775, Colloredo opened Salzburg's first public theater, with the stated goal of creating a "Bildungstheater."[32] A year later, he issued the *Schulordnung* "De publicis perorationibus," in which he ordered that fully staged Schuldramen be replaced by unstaged readings at the prize-giving ceremonies.[33] Finally, in 1778, Colloredo closed the university theater entirely. Throughout this final period in its history, Salzburg's composers and librettists were experimenting with the form and content of the Schuldrama, including replacing the Latin *intermedium* altogether with an elevated German *Zwischenspiel* (perhaps partly in an effort to forestall the genre's death). Salzburg thus represented both the trend toward secularization and commercialization in German theater, and the tenacity of its didactic aspirations, even after Schuldrama as a genre was disappearing.

Although Mozart never returned to this genre after *Apollo et Hyacinthus*, we know that he was aware of these theatrical debates. He even mentioned the *Hanswurststreit* in a 1781 letter to his father, when discussing plans for a Singspiel collaboration with Johann Gottlieb Stephanie the Younger (which would eventually become *Die Entführung aus dem Serail*), observing: "I do certainly find that in music the [Hanswurst] has not yet been banished, and in this respect the French are right."[34] If Mozart's characters Pedrillo, Papageno, and other comic sidekicks are anything to go by, he too remained partial to Hanswurst, and to the social subversion for which he stood, throughout his operatic career.[35] And the failure and closure of both the university theater and the public theater were likely contributing factors in Mozart's decision to leave Salzburg and the archbishop's service in favor of Vienna.

Kindertruppen and Bastien und Bastienne

Despite Schrattenbach's antipathy to long *Schuldramen* evenings, and Colloredo's shuttering of the university theater, Salzburg theater historians hasten to add that this in no way means that either archbishop was against all forms of theater. On the contrary, each in their time supported and attended the wandering troupes that came through Salzburg. Schrattenbach's love of farcical theater even earned him some criticism during his lifetime.[36] In February 1767, for instance, Schrattenbach declined to attend the Schuldrama produced in honor of his own birthday in favor of an Italian troupe's performance at his own *Residenztheater*. The no-show caused a minor scandal.[37]

Schrattenbach apparently had a particular fondness for children's troupes.[38] Virtually every adult wandering troupe had young actors, usually children of acting families apprenticing to their parents' profession. But troupes comprised entirely of children and young performers were a popular novelty, hearkening back to companies of Elizabethan boy choristers like the Children of St. Paul's and the Children of the Chapel Royal (immortalized as "little eyases" in Shakespeare's *Hamlet*).[39] The seventeenth- and eighteenth-century children's troupes traversed the same routes and performed much the same repertoire as their adult counterparts, mastering a staggering number of plays, operas, ballets, and pantomimes.[40] These troupes appeared everywhere from fairground shacks to imperial coronations, from Amsterdam to Paris, Vienna to Hamburg.

Enlightenment *philosophes* like Denis Diderot and Jean-Jacques Rousseau praised the talents of one of the earliest traveling children's troupes, the Piccoli Hollandesi, active in the 1740s.[41] In his 1749 *Abhandlung von den Pantomimen*, Johann Mattheson credited the Piccoli Hollandesi with single-handedly reviving the ancient Greek art of pantomime.[42] Other critics, however, such as Gotthold Ephraim Lessing, evinced a more skeptical, at times even squeamish attitude toward the precocity of child actors.[43] The same qualities that had sustained the popularity of the spectacle also unnerved moralists and theater reformers: chief among these qualities was the child actors' uncanny ability to impersonate the behavior of adults, including romance and violence. Children's troupes often specialized in the more risqué forms of comedy associated with the *com-*

media dell'arte and its descendants, long after Hanswurst was supposedly banished from the German stage. And even as children's and other wandering troupes helped circulate loftier, more literate dramas and operas across the German-speaking lands, from Shakespeare to bourgeois tragedy, they still preserved the extemporized physical comedy of their forebears.[44]

The most famous of the German children's troupes in the late 1760s was the one led by Felix Berner [Perner], active from 1761 to 1787, which came through Salzburg on at least two occasions in the 1760s. The troupe was known variously as "die jungen Schauspieler unter der Direction des Herrn Felix Berner," "die gelernten [or gelehrten] Kinder," and simply "die Pernerischen Kinder" or "die Bernerischen Jugend." Evidence of Berner's troupe survives in a sizable corpus of librettos, scenarios, and reviews in the contemporary press, as well as in a forty-odd-page chronicle of the troupe by company member Franz Xaver Garnier, the *Nachricht von der Bernerischen jungen Schauspieler-Gesellschaft*, which went through three editions (1782, 1784, and 1786).[45] Garnier's detailed account of the troupe's personnel and repertoire shows their extraordinary popularity. It also shows how the troupe evolved over the twenty-five years of its existence.

When the Berner troupe first visited Salzburg, in 1766, the performers ranged in age from six to seventeen, with an average age of eleven. Fifteen years later, in 1781, the upper age limit had risen from seventeen to twenty-one, with an average age of fourteen.[46] It is important to remember, though, that many actors in the so-called "adult" troupes debuted in their early to mid-teens, so there was a good deal of overlap in age between adult and children's troupes.[47] And as various contemporary accounts make clear, adult personnel in Berner's troupe often performed in the plays and operas alongside the youngsters, especially as the romantic leads in tragedies and serious operas.[48] While the main selling point, therefore—and the main issue for critics—was the uncanny spectacle of precocious children impersonating adults, there may also have been adolescents and young adults impersonating the child actors themselves. Age, it seems, was a fluid category like gender, and performers might occupy a negotiable space between young and old.[49]

Kindertruppen were criticized for one of two transgressions. On the one hand, they forced audiences, even in the age of naturalism, to acknowledge the fundamental unnaturalness of acting, as in this review in Vienna's main critical journal, the *Realzeitung*:

> It is either unclear or burlesque, when a boy in the role of an old man says things which only a man could know. If these plays are not expressly pro-

duced for children, if they are plays in which only grown people should act, then such a play remains most unnatural.[50]

Kindertruppen's other transgression had to do with boundaries around children and propriety. Take for instance Christian Felix Weisse (about whom more in chapter 4), the playwright, Singspiel librettist, and editor of the most influential children's periodical of the age, *Der Kinderfreund* (1775–1782). In a 1778 issue of *Der Kinderfreund*, Weisse had one of his fictional avatars lament the shocking performance of "a certain acting company of children" who had recently come through Leipzig:

> I could not stand it, as I heard them singing and saying the most amatory, I don't want to say, the most rude things, accompanied by the most brazen gestures. O how I pitied the poor innocent victims of cheap profit: for I saw what they will become before long, as already the shame of their first youth (many were still children) was killed, and they may have become this already, if the paternal eye of God is not watching over them, and has [not] wrested them from perdition in a miraculous way.[51]

Weisse's vehement opposition to the exploitation of these actors may have been motivated by more than just noble concern for children's welfare. After all, the domestic children's theatricals he published in the pages of *Der Kinderfreund* were just as much commercial products, just as much "for sale," as the performances of the troupes he sought to discredit.[52] Nevertheless, his condemnation registered the uncomfortable realities of the Kindertruppen's intersections with sexuality and commerce, as well as the continuing popularity of their enterprise even after protectionist discourses around childhood were underway.

Far from sidestepping these criticisms, the Berner troupe embraced and often thematized them, especially in the prologues, epilogues, dedications, and farewells that framed the troupe's performances. In 1775, on the occasion of the troupe's arrival in Schönbrunn gardens, an unnamed "little Thalia" addressed Empress Maria Theresa directly. "Oh, Empress," the actress pleaded,

> protect our play,
> We are still small, our chest is still too narrow,
> But our heart expands,
> It beats already in a flowing throng,
> Every drop of blood flows for you,
> Exalted ruler, Germany's ornament.[53]

The familiar trope of exaggerated modesty in theatrical paratexts, where the ostensible meagerness of the artistic offering is meant to amplify the greatness of the patron, is here embodied in the physical smallness of the performer herself, whose heart and body stand metonymically for the company as a whole.

The elevated tone of the encomium to Maria Theresa notwithstanding, the Berner troupe, like its predecessors, also drew on its performers' youth as a source of humor both satirical and bawdy.[54] In an epilogue "to the parterre" from 1779 following a performance of the suggestive *Das Milchmädchen und die beiden Jäger* (The Milkmaid and the Two Hunters), the lead actress Margaretha Liskin (who often delivered such epilogues, and may be the actress shown in fig. 3.2) extended the familiar erotic subtext of the broken milk jug into an allegory of her own commodification as a performer:

> "Now it's broken, the beautiful jug," as Geßner's fawn says, "there lie the
>   pieces." . . .
> I've now carried my milk to the stage, offered it for sale to all.
> Fancied myself a wife, and had the dearest, best husband
> That ever a maid could wish for.[55]

Liskin (or, more likely, Berner speaking through her) went on to allegorize the deflowering of young women in the troupe:

> Too small even for the stage, but we know how to be older,
> But then come the knights on their vigorous steeds.
> Charming us maidens and breaking the lances, . . .
> Taking us for wives into the knights' company, and paying for us with
>   pure gold.
> Is it not better?—Better, sirs, that we stay, and do not get older.
> And stay with you as a little choir, a delight for eye and ear.[56]

This epilogue bears local and autobiographical connotations, referring to the anticipated end of the troupe's residency, Liskin's inevitable loss of virginity, and the troupe members' eventual passage into adulthood. The appeal to arrested youth—please do not marry us, let us stay in the troupe and thus forever young—was double-edged. If anything, the clash between the perceived innocence and guilelessness of children, and the morally suspect profession of acting in which they were put on display, was good for business—Garnier claimed that in 1780 as many as 1,100 attended the troupe's performances in Bern, and 1,200 in Zurich.[57] In the

FIGURE 3.2. *Demithige Dancksagung von der kleinen gelerten pernerischen actrice und Tänzerin* (Humble Thanksgiving from the Little Learned Pernerish Actress and Dancer) [Margarethe Liskin?] (Salzburg, 1783). Courtesy of Stadtarchiv Salzburg, Bibliothek, shelfmark 015.799-Ü.

end, this combination of popularity and controversy should not necessarily surprise us: such disparities and subtexts continue to haunt the spectacle of young performers in our own time.

I spend so much time on the Berner troupe not just because they were the preeminent children's troupe of Mozart's time, and the one that left the greatest archival footprint. It is also because they traveled through

Salzburg at the same time the Mozarts were there, right around the time Wolfgang was composing *Die Schuldigkeit des ersten Gebots* and *Apollo et Hyacinthus* and seeking the commission for *La finta semplice* (K. 51/46a, 1769)—in other words, the earliest years in Mozart's apprenticeship as an opera composer. The troupe may have been indirectly responsible for Mozart's Singspiels *Bastien und Bastienne* and *Zaide*. Finally, the Berner family was also personally known to the Mozarts, as revealed in a 1785 letter by Leopold to which I will return at the end of this chapter.

The troupe's first documented sojourn in Salzburg began in December 1766, their debut taking place just one day after the ten-year-old Mozart's *licenza* K. 36 (the tenor concert aria "Or che il dover") was heard as part of the celebration of the anniversary of Archbishop Schrattenbach's ordination.[58] Information is lacking about what the Berner troupe performed at their debut—the court diarist Father Beda Hübner noted only that the troupe consisted of six girls and four boys, and that they would be in residence at the Rathaus following Advent.[59] The troupe stayed through Carnival, appearing before the court in February 1767, where the program included the Singspiel *Der Großsprechende Spanier* (The Boasting Spaniard; by Johann Joseph Felix Kurz, with music by troupe choral director Palma) and two ballets.[60]

Berner's troupe also had a *Bastienne* Singspiel in their repertoire, and it is thought that the version they were using had premiered at Vienna's Kärntnertortheater in 1764, with a libretto by Friedrich Wilhelm Weiskern (he who had called moral theater "sugar-coated medicine for the soul") and Johann Heinrich Friedrich Müller. The music, by Charles-Simon Favart, was from the original *opéra-comique Les amours de Bastien et Bastienne* (1753), with five new numbers by Johann Baptist Savio.[61] Commentators believe the Berner troupe's 1766–1767 sojourn was the means by which Mozart and the Salzburg court trumpeter Johann Andreas Schachtner, a family friend of the Mozarts, were exposed to *Bastien und Bastienne* and came to collaborate on their own version in 1768.[62]

Yet historians do not seem to have raised the inevitable question that follows: could Mozart's *Bastien und Bastienne* have been conceived with the Berner troupe in mind? It is unlikely that Mozart would have undertaken such an extensive compositional project without a commission, or at least a particular theater in mind, especially given his busy schedule and the family's aspirations. We know little about the circumstances of the Singspiel's origins, because the Mozarts were in Salzburg and Vienna at the time, so there is no family correspondence from this period. In addition, the manuscript paper used for *Bastien und Bastienne* suggests that Mozart began working on it after leaving Salzburg, whether in

Vienna or perhaps in Olmütz.[63] Georg Nikolaus von Nissen's assertion in the 1828 *Biographie* that the Singspiel was performed at the residence of Anton Mesmer in September or October of 1768 has not been confirmed, and regardless, it seems unlikely that Mesmer, a private citizen, would have commissioned the work.[64] Another possibility is that a second, through-sung version of *Bastien und Bastienne* was being prepared in early 1769, after Mozart had returned to Salzburg from Vienna. Among Schachtner's revisions to Weiskern and Müller's libretto was the resetting of the spoken dialogue as recitative, and Mozart's settings of the first four recitatives are on Salzburg paper.[65] This version remained unfinished, but it may have been undertaken for the Berner troupe. On their next sojourn in Salzburg in 1774, they performed a *Bastienne* Singspiel at court in November. Mozart and Schachtner were both employed in the court music by then, so they would likely have attended this performance.[66] Gabriella-Nóra Tar speculates that this version may have included some of Mozart's music, but if so, neither the Singspiel nor Mozart were mentioned in the review of the company's second stay in the short-lived periodical *Salzburger Theaterwochenblatt* (1775–1776), nor in any editions of Garnier's *Nachricht*.[67] For now, the evidence remains inconclusive.

Like *Apollo et Hyacinthus*, *Bastien und Bastienne* stages sexual desire and jealousy, and is shot through with cynicism about the sexual economy. In Bastienne and Colas's first scene together, she admits that she has no money with which to pay him for his assistance, and offers him her earrings instead, to which he replies, "With such a pretty child as you, I'd be content with a couple of kisses."[68] Bastienne's subsequent aria, "Wenn mein Bastien im Scherze" (When my Bastien, as a joke), describes how Bastien "stole a little flower" from her, and how she "felt in my heart the same pleasure that he felt from the theft," in an allegory as familiar as the broken milk jug.[69] Bastienne's subsequent aria, "Würd ich auch, wie manche Buhlerinnen" (If I, too, like many a coquette), indicates that she knows how easy it would be to attract the kind of admirers that her rival, the unnamed "Edelfrau" (noblewoman), seems to have; and she allows Colas to persuade her to feign interest in a rich urban suitor of her own in order to inflame Bastien's jealousy.[70]

In that same aria, however, Bastienne affirms her renunciation of the seductions of the city in favor of "the virtue / [that] still exists among shepherds' huts." Colas upholds this anti-urban bias, declaring:

> It would be hard for such innocence ever to be encountered anywhere other than in the country. In the city one is already cleverer when one is still in the cradle, and the daughter often knows more than the mother.[71]

Bastien's aria about Bastienne, "Meiner Liebsten schöne Wangen" (My beloved's lovely cheeks), continues this theme with a second verse that baldly indicts the sexual economy of the city:

Profiteers, who by proud inclinations
Are usually captivated only by rarities,
Would love her innocence, and would
Consider themselves fortunate through her.[72]

Here one finds parallels with Liskin's epilogue to *Das Milchmädchen*, both knowing and vulnerable; as Linda Tyler puts it, "Bastienne's musical persona emerges a hybrid character: mostly French *ingénue*, but part Italian servant and German Mädchen as well."[73] That no one thought twice about Mozart setting texts such as these suggests that, as with *Apollo et Hyacinthus*, it was perfectly acceptable for a boy of twelve to be familiar with operatic tropes of seduction and promiscuity.

Given its subject matter, it is somewhat surprising that "Meiner Liebsten schöne Wangen" is the aria from *Bastien und Bastienne* that was adapted for publication in a children's periodical in 1768 (alongside a second Lied by Mozart, "An die Freude," to be discussed in chapter 4). The periodical, *Neue Sammlung zum Vergnügen und Unterricht* (1768), was published in Vienna as a sequel to the children's magazine *Gesammelte Schriften zum Vergnügen und Unterricht* (1766–1767).[74] These appear to have been Vienna's first children's readers (the main center of German children's publishing being Leipzig), and like the *Beschäftigung* discussed in chapter 2, their contents included edifying plays, poems, songs, stories, and essays.[75] Although we know little of the circumstances that led Leopold to arrange to have the aria from *Bastien und Bastienne* adapted for publication in this periodical, we know that in March 1768 he had written to Hagenauer from Vienna that Maria Anna Mozart was requesting "the first part of the *Kinder Magazin*" from their mutual friend Schachtner.[76] Scholars have historically assumed that Maria Anna was referring to the *Lehrreiches Magazin für Kinder* (1758–1767), the German edition of the first children's magazine to appear in France, Madame Leprince Beaumont's *Magasin des enfans* (1756).[77] However, it seems more logical that what Maria Anna meant by "Kinder Magazin" was not the Leipzig *Lehrreiches Magazin*, but the Vienna *Neue Sammlung* in which her son's own music appeared just months later.[78]

The manuscript score of "Daphne, deine Rosenwangen" is in Leopold's hand, suggesting that he was responsible for the piano reduction and adaptation from Singspiel aria to freestanding children's Lied.[79] Perhaps Leopold saw this as a way to profit from Wolfgang's music, whether or not *Bastien und Bastienne* ended up on stage. The Lied is listed only as "Lied nebst Musik" in the table of contents, suggesting that no association with the Singspiel was intended. Several notable changes to the text (which may have been by Schachtner, Leopold, or even the publisher) also suggest that Leopold had taken the periodical's juvenile audience into account. The addition of the name "Daphne" turns the text into a pastoral lyric, in keeping with others in the *Neue Sammlung*, such as the "Schäferlied" in issue 2 or the poetic dialogue for Chloe and Damon in issue 4.[80] Third person gives way to second person, as the singer addresses his beloved directly, an immediacy more appropriate to a freestanding song. Finally, the third stanza is changed dramatically: the "profiteers" who would exploit Bastienne, "loving her innocence," have given way to "princes" who would envy the narrator if they knew of his happiness with Daphne. This takes the most explicit verse in the poem out of the realm of sexual exploitation and into the virtuous pastoral.

Despite the idealism of Mozart's aria in both of its iterations, the pastoral characters portrayed by child performers in the eighteenth century masked what was often a grim reality, about which the Mozarts (at least Leopold and Nannerl) had close personal knowledge. The acting profession was already one with few protections for actors, and young performers were even more vulnerable to physical and sexual abuse, exploitation, and abduction than their adult counterparts.[81] More than one historian has described the impresario of a French children's troupe as having treated it as his "private harem," while the physical abuse visited on the members of the Piccoli Hollandesi by their troupe leader Nicolini was described in detail—conspicuous for an age in which corporal punishment was treated with nonchalance.[82] Berner was no different than his fellows in these respects. The 1783 volume of the *Theater-Journal für Deutschland* praised Berner's economical management of the troupe, at least for the riches it yielded him, but added that

> the older and the little ones tremble before him, are not allowed to venture one step out of the house without his permission, and put up with every restriction on their small wages (many have none at all), almost bordering on slavery. One must reproach how he keeps the little boys and girls in filthy clothes, and from my list of his performed works you can easily see how much he taxes them with singing, dancing, and performing.[83]

When such conditions are added to the hazards of travel and high mortality rates for youth in general, Garnier's reported mortality rate of

FIGURE 3.3. Silhouette of "Ml[le] Berner," in Garnier, *Nachricht von der Berneri-schen jungen Schauspieler-Gesellschaft* (Vienna, 1786). Courtesy of Wienbibliothek im Rathaus, shelfmark A-12861.

just 12 percent (seven out of fifty-eight members of the troupe named in the 1786 edition of the *Nachricht*) seems suspiciously low.[84] One of the deaths, however, was Berner's own daughter Jeanette. Berner's wife had taken Jeanette and her younger sister Elise away from the troupe after Elise was born, returning in 1776 when the girls were roughly ten and eight.[85] Jeanette died just over a year later—Garnier did not give a cause of death in the *Nachricht*, though he did for other troupe members. Elise and her mother stayed on another four years, leaving Berner and the troupe for good in 1780, when Elise was fourteen.[86] It's unclear which of the Berner daughters are memorialized in the silhouettes labeled

"Ml. Berner" that appeared in the original 1782 edition and the third edition of 1786 of Garnier's *Nachricht* (fig. 3.3). Either way, Berner was paying homage to a daughter who was either dead or estranged.

In 1782, Elise Berner married the singer and actor Johann Nepomuk Peyerl, a marriage that would bring her into the circle of acquaintance of the Mozart family. The couple lived for several years in Salzburg with Madame Berner, before moving to Vienna and later Munich. In 1785, Leopold was writing letters every few days to Nannerl in St. Gilgen, exchanging the most recent gossip and updating her on her son Leopoldl's health. In a September letter, he told her that Peyerl and Elise were living nearby; "consequently I always have music rehearsals either behind me, or in front of me."[87] Three months later, he mentioned an exchange between Elise—now nineteen years old—and her mother, Madame Berner, reported to him by a mutual acquaintance, the composer Joseph Graetz:

> No sooner does the "cher Mama" open her mouth, but the daughter screams, "Shut up, you old liar! You old beast! Or I'll have something to say, you scoundrel!" etc. etc. etc. And what do you think, what beauties come next? "You made me a whore for money, locked me up with cavaliers, etc. etc. etc." Had enough yet? No! there's still more: "My father keeps a whorehouse of young girls, impregnates one after the other, etc. etc." Now that's quite enough! Anyone who comes to Madame Peyerl's is about ready to die.[88]

Leopold concluded this letter with a plea for Nannerl's discretion. "I ask that no one else reads this," he begged his daughter. "I'm only telling you."[89] But this story was already secondhand, suggesting that it was widespread knowledge among Salzburg society: not only that Elise's parents had prostituted her (and possibly also her sister), but that her father was continuing to do so as his troupe toured central Europe. Before the year 1785 was up, Johann and Elise had moved on to Vienna, where they befriended Wolfgang; Johann inspired two off-color canons Mozart composed sometime in 1786: *Difficile lectu mihi Mars* (K. 559) and *O du eselhafter Peierl* (K 560a).[90]

Leopold's secondhand report of Elise Berner's accusations is striking for how it contradicts the narrative around the Berner troupe that was crafted in large part by Garnier. In the 1786 edition of the *Nachricht*, Garnier included the troupe's fourteen rules and regulations, which give an impression of professionalism and even a modicum of actors' rights (the right to contest a casting decision, for instance). Clause 12 states that a company member's contract will be forfeited in the case of "proven immoral conduct [*unsittliche Aufführung*]."[91] Elsewhere, Garnier and others wrote glowingly of Berner, especially for his generous provision for troupe members in his will. The character rehabilitation continued in the twentieth century. In their 1925 survey of Viennese theater, Emil Karl Blümml and Gustav Gugitz asserted that Berner behaved "in a morally impeccable manner," while a 1936 article in the *Salzburger Volksblatt* on "Children's Theater in Salzburg" went out of its way to argue that Berner "was no exploiter of children, but a respectable man who left legacies for 47 of his former child actors in his will."[92] Even in 1973, Robert Münster would only say demurely, "What Father Mozart reported on December 2, 1785 of the family affairs of the Peyerls can be read in the complete edition of the Mozart letters."[93] Yet Münster added that "Elise's mother, Susanne Berner, had 'maliciously' deserted her husband in 1771."[94] It was evidently unthinkable to quote Elise outright, though that did not prevent Münster from casting doubt on Madame Berner's credibility.

This episode does not reveal much about Mozart, except perhaps to cast into relief the additional dangers he and his sister must have faced on their travels as young performers. In a letter a week before the one in 1785 where Leopold shared Elise Berner's accusations with Nannerl, he related another piece of gossip, this time about the Waizhofer troupe, then in a residency at the public theater Archbishop Colloredo had opened ten years earlier. The gossip was that the daughter of a court chamberlain had apparently been impregnated by an actor in Waizhofer's troupe. Leopold gave himself permission to relate some of the more sordid details because, as he puts it, "in my advanced age, nothing in this world troubles [*bekümmere*] me anymore."[95] After the account, he mused on the failures of the girl's parents to protect her from what was evidently an all-too-common fate:

> How many parents make a deal with the devil, for whom children are to be made only for the sake of well-being, but who care little for education, since one should have at least 100 eyes and ears at this time, in order to lead the girl all the way, and to shield her from debauchery [*Verführung*].[96]

Nannerl would surely have caught the autobiographical undertone to Leopold's rueful observation. During all those performances, court visits, and tavern open hours during the 1763–1766 European tour, it is likely that one or both children would have been in danger at some point. From Leopold's letters home to Salzburg, it certainly seems as though he was with the children at all times, and was assiduously protective of their safety. But to expose them to the public as young performers was, inevitably, to place them in harm's way, and it was only a combination of prudence and luck that allowed them to survive that exposure.

The alarmism around children's troupes only rose in the decades after the Berner troupe's heyday. In the 1790s, Kindertruppen were banned in Salzburg, and another troupe led by Xaver Krebs (whose repertoire included, of all things, Mozart's *Die Entführung aus dem Serail*) ran into difficulties with censors and was disbanded.[97] The final straw came in 1821, when it was revealed that the son of a Habsburg foreign minister had been molesting hundreds of young girls in Friedrich Horschelt's popular Viennese *Kinderballett* troupe.[98] Emperor Franz II banned all such troupes in Vienna in response, extending the ban to all the provinces in 1824.[99] Whether this signaled a new attentiveness to the rights of the young, a wish to sequester them from public life, an urgent need to contain an embarrassing scandal, or some combination of all three is an irresolvable question.

The Theatralpflanzschule and Zaide

An alternative to these two theatrical traditions emerged alongside them, one that sought to combine the moral unimpeachability of the Schuldramen with the enduring popularity of the Kindertruppen. In 1772, the actor and playwright Johann Heinrich Friedrich Müller (whom we have already met as one of the librettists of *Bastien und Bastienne*) led a group of children in a Vienna performance of his play *Die Insul der Liebe, oder Amor ein Erforscher der Herzen* (The Island of Love, or Cupid, an Explorer of Hearts), with incidental music by Ignaz Umlauf. *Die Insul der Liebe* was performed alongside two ballets by Noverre as part of an experimental *Kinderballett*, and it appears that Müller may originally have intended the play as just a lark for the young dancers.[100] But *Die Insul der Liebe* was a great success with its audience (which included members of the nobility), and it received a long, positive write-up in the *Wiener Zeitung*.[101]

Müller was already in Joseph II's inner circle, and in 1776 the emperor sent Müller to Wolfenbüttel to meet with Lessing and bring back ideas for improving the Viennese theater, laying the foundation for what would soon become the National Theater and National Singspiel. In his memoir, Müller claimed that it was Lessing who first gave him the idea for a theatrical training institute for the young.[102] "Every art must have its school," Lessing reportedly told Müller. "Only through that, through assiduous study and laborious perspiration, will the actor trained therein earn the right to the esteem and honor of his contemporaries."[103] In Müller's own gloss on this idea, he sums up the pedagogical project and its import for the training of professional actors. His language echoes the appeals of his contemporaries in equating the moral vulnerability of children with theater audiences and the nation as a whole:

> For millennia, experience has proven that the first foundation of the education of the character determines the future character of the people. These impressions are indelible, and their influence works throughout one's whole life. All sensations, passions, inclinations, and abilities must be guided in their first sproutings, where the soft unprejudiced heart obeys every little bend. Just as this is undoubtedly true in regard to moral education, so it is also in consideration of the formation of each artist; and since both can be achieved through a suitably equipped theatrical nursery, the invaluable benefits of such an institute are self-evident and established.[104]

Coming as it did just two years after Maria Theresa's *Allgemeine Schulordnung* (discussed in chapter 2), Müller was employing the language of moral education as a justification for an acting school—another instance of the discourses of childhood and the performing arts industry in dynamic mutual exchange and influence.

In 1777, just as Joseph's National Theater project was taking shape, Müller approached the emperor with a proposal for this Theatralpflanzschule. In his proposal, which he reproduced in full in his memoir, Müller advocated for actors to receive both professional and ethical training, and he proposed to educate students in geography, religion, and history alongside acting, singing, and dancing lessons.[105] Müller saw his Theatralpflanzschule as another vocational opportunity for talented poor children and orphans who might otherwise "waste away."[106] And, as mentioned in chapter 2, it was Joseph's encounter with several talented children at the Vienna Waisenhaus that encouraged him to approve Müller's proposal.

The support was only nominal, however: Joseph II did not initially fund the Theatralpflanzschule, even after appointing Müller the first director of the National Singspiel in December 1777. But Müller did not give up. Six months after the inauguration of the National Singspiel with Ignaz Umlauf's *Die Bergknappen*, Müller programmed a "neues Kinder-Lustspiel" by August Rode at the Burgtheater alongside a revival of *Die Bergknappen*. The "Kinder-Lustspiel" was *Der Ausgang, oder die Genesung* (The Way Home, or The Convalescence), a sentimental play that had already been published in 1776 as one of a set of three dedicated to the Philanthropinum (about which more in chapter 4). Müller's production featured Stephanie himself, Mozart's later collaborator, as the father, and Müller's five children as the sons and daughters, many of whom would go on to careers in the Hoftheater.[107]

Staging this sentimental domestic play in a professional setting must have gone some way toward convincing Joseph that the Theatralpflanzschule was a worthy enterprise. The following year—around the same time that Mozart was collaborating with Schachtner, his *Bastien und Bastienne* collaborator, on the unfinished Singspiel *Zaide*—Joseph II reduced Müller's responsibilities at the National Singspiel, according to him so that Müller could finally establish his Theatralpflanzschule.[108] Müller undertook the endeavor at his own personal cost, taking out a four-page advertisement in a June issue of the *Wienerisches Diarium* to announce the founding of the institution and beg for subscribers.[109] The official premiere took place at the Kärntnertortheater in July 1779, with the Singspiel *Zermes und Mirabella, oder Die vollkommenen Verliebten* (Zermes and Mirabella, or the Perfect Lovers).[110]

Müller's short-lived Theatralpflanzschule staged Shakespeare's *Tempest* and *Hamlet*—the latter a favorite of the Berner troupe—along with many other plays and Singspiels, and ballets by Noverre. But the project never received much promotion; after the debut, *Der Ausgang*, no playbills appear to exist for any subsequent performances. In October 1780, Müller had a two-hour audience with Empress Maria Theresa, in which they discussed the Theatralpflanzschule, with Müller claiming Maria Theresa had offered her earnest support.[111] But with her death just over a month later, and the temporary closing of the theater, interest in the fledgling project proved difficult to resurrect. Müller appealed for subscriptions in an article in the 1781 *Theater-Journal für Deutschland*, and despite advocacy from some critics, Joseph merged the Institute with the National Theater, allowing Müller to retain only the oldest students and compelling him to give up the ballet.[112] In February 1782, the Institute closed with a performance of *Hamlet*, not long before the National Theater project as a whole came to an end.

There is no evidence from the letters that the Mozarts ever discussed Müller's project. The references in the Mozart family correspondence to efforts to court the National Singspiel are vague in their details. But the Theatralpflanzschule was active when Wolfgang arrived in Vienna in March 1781 (though he does not mention having attended any of the performances in any letters home). And one of Mozart's first commissions after arriving in Vienna was *Die Entführung aus dem Serail*, for the National Singspiel (for which Stephanie had by then taken over the directorship from Müller). In the letter in which he reported this, Wolfgang remarked on the failure of an earlier floated project: the *Das Serail/Zaide* Singspiel. Mozart told his father, "As for Schachtner's operetta, there is nothing to be done—for the same reason which I have often mentioned." It's unclear what that reason is, although later Wolfgang does make a reference to the Viennese preferring lighter comedies.[113] Meanwhile, Stephanie offered Mozart the libretto to *Die Entführung*—and because it was this Singspiel that eventually made it to the stage, historians assume that Mozart intended *Zaide* for the National Singspiel as well.[114] It may be, however, that *Zaide* was originally intended not for the National Singspiel, but for Müller's Theatralpflanzschule, the one to which Maria Theresa had reportedly just given her support.

There is some compelling circumstantial evidence to support this hypothesis. First, Mozart was working on *Zaide* in 1780, right around the heyday of the Theatralfplanzschule. In fact, when Leopold told Wolfgang to hold off on the "Schachtner drama" because all the theaters were closed due to the recent death of Maria Theresa, he added, "who knows but that this opera may later give you an opportunity of getting to Vienna?"[115] Second, *Zaide* was based on an original Singspiel in the Berner troupe's repertoire called *Das Serail*—though the means by which Mozart and Schachtner came by *Das Serail*, and the exact nature of their relationship to Berner, are unknown.[116] They certainly had access to a copy of the (anonymous) 1779 Bozen libretto, though we cannot be sure whether they were familiar with the score by Joseph Friebert.[117]

Third is the tantalizing question of *Zaide*'s lone female character. *Das Serail* includes two female characters, Zaide and a "Sclavinn" who sings a meta-theatrical song as part of her audition for the sultan.[118] But this Sclavinn does not make it into Mozart's Singspiel, at least not in the extant portion of the manuscript, which appears to conclude with the finale of act 1. Tyler believes Mozart omitted the Sclavinn due to the difficulty of her dialect aria; but it would still be virtually unthinkable for Mozart to have composed a Singspiel for a permanent theater without it including a second woman.[119] One circumstance where such casting rules could be loosened would have been in Müller's Theatralpflanzschule.

For now, any speculation about a direct connection between *Zaide* and the Theatralpflanzschule must remain speculation. The Mozart family correspondence does not mention Müller's side project, though Mozart and Müller remained friends. We can observe, however, the parallels between the popular sergalio-opera plot of *Zaide* and the circumstances of the Kindertruppen performers: like the inhabitants of the fantastical harem of the eighteenth-century imagination, these child actors all came from "somewhere else" and had little real power.[120] The Sclavinn's audition song in *Zaide*'s source Singspiel *Das Serail* conveys the multiple levels on which she is expected to perform:

> I see, with foolishness one achieves more
> Than with mischievous whimsies,
> I'll act as though I were foolish,
> I'll play along with the fashion.
> They chatter to me about gold and money,
> They want to give half a world to me,
> Yet I wouldn't care about all these things,
> If I could only be back at home again soon.[121]

The comic-relief character, a peasant girl from the "Ländl" now miles away from home, sings this aria directly to the audience after she has been chosen by the Sultan. Speaking "to the parterre," she indicts the economy of the seraglio for revering her as a talented performer and simultaneously debasing her as a "dog" and an "ape." In doing so, the Sclavinn also indicts the Kindertruppen enterprise—its objectification and exploitation of its beloved performers—from within. The language of harems and enslavement that we have seen critics use to describe these troupes came from, and fed back into, the repertoire itself.

From an early age, then, Mozart and his family encountered and worked with a variety of types of child performer, from Benedictine students, to choristers, troupe actors, and the prodigies and young musicians they met on their travels. They knew from experience about the vulnerability of the performing child. And to some, the family was seen as not much different from a wandering troupe themselves. In Beda Hübner's diary from the day of the Mozarts' return from their European tour in November 1766, he wrote that Leopold "appeared in England exactly as in other countries, appearing with his children on public stages and in theaters just like foreign play-actors."[122] Empress Maria Theresa dismissed the family as "useless people" in 1771, warning her son Ferdinand not to take Mozart into his service because they had "go[ne] about the world like beggars [*gueux*]."[123] There was more to these remarks than just class snobbery: the theater's associations with prostitution haunted the Mozarts. This was the price they paid for exhibiting their children on stage.

CHAPTER 4

Kinderlieder and the Work of Play

Anxieties about childhood and virtue did not begin and end in the public arenas of church, orphanage, school, or stage. If anything, the domestic sphere was more contested, with pedagogues debating and prescribing how children should spend their time at home. Long after Empress Maria Theresa's 1774 *Allgemeine Schulordnung*, most of her subjects of all classes still educated their children either at home or not at all.[1] If the Habsburg state could not yet persuade children to attend schools, moralizing and utilitarian education could (indeed, must) be brought to them in their parlors and playrooms.

The juvenile literary market was founded on a venerable advertising stratagem: stoking consumer anxiety to generate and sustain a perceived need for a new product. In this case, the anxiety was about children reading the novels on their parents' shelves. Consider one of the reasons Rousseau gives in *Emile* for initially limiting Emile's literary diet to only the novel *Robinson Crusoe*: "Your greatest care ought to be to keep away from your pupil's mind all notions of social relations which are not within his reach."[2] Similar to the debates reviewed in chapter 3 regarding the representation of moral faults in the *Schuldramen*, pedagogues feared that exposing children to nearly any kind of fiction would preemptively deny them a social innocence that was increasingly being essentialized.

Fears of prematurely exposing child readers to morally questionable content had long predated the pedagogical reforms and publishing trends of the late eighteenth century. But it was only after *Emile* that authors in the German-speaking lands rushed to offer a host of solutions to this "problem," in the form of juvenile literature. Among the most influential series in the young genre was the children's periodical *Der Kinderfreund* (The Child's Friend, Leipzig, 1775–1782), source of the diatribe against children's acting troupes in chapter 3. Its author-editor, Christian Felix Weisse, was a major German poet, playwright, librettist, translator, and pedagogue who based *Der Kinderfreund* on the *moralische Wochen-schriften* (moral weeklies) already popular with adult readers. Like the moral weeklies (and the *Angenehme und lehrreiche Beschäftigung für Kinder in ihre Freistunden*, discussed in chapter 2), *Der Kinderfreund* was an all-in-one digest offering edifying amusements of every stripe: poems, plays, dialogues, riddles, songs, stories, illustrations, and nonfiction content. The material was all presented within a moralizing frame narrative led by a kindly *paterfamilias*, named Herr Mentor (in a clear reference to Telemachus's tutor in Homer's *Odyssey* and Fénelon's *Adventures of Telemachus*). Mentor lives with his four children (ranging in age from five to eleven), his wife (who is very much in the background), and a circle of friends who supply the content that helps convey the intended lessons to the children—and, by extension, *Der Kinderfreund*'s readers.

Der *Kinderfreund* had a print run of 10,000 and may have been read by as many as 100,000 children in Germany alone, according to one estimate (several monasteries and royal households had subscriptions).[3] And it was only the most popular of the nearly fifty German-language children's periodicals published in the last third of the eighteenth century.[4] A second "bestseller" in this genre was the *Kleine Kinderbibliothek* (Little Children's Library, Hamburg, 1779–1784), Joachim Heinrich Campe's semi-annual reader, which went through ten editions in twenty-five years.[5] Campe, a tutor, pedagogue, and writer, wrote in the preface to the first volume of the *Kleine Kinderbibliothek* that his goal was to provide reading material "which would be as understandable as [it was] entertaining and instructive"; for the second edition in 1782, he had added "and by *any consideration, would be completely harmless* to them."[6] Campe even went so far as to divide each volume of his digest into three sections according to the intended age group of the reader (five to seven, eight to ten, and eleven to twelve).[7] A heightened awareness of the phases of child development (a theme explored in chapter 1), combined with anxieties about children's productivity and virtue (chapters 2 and 3), was thus instrumentalized in the formation of this new juvenile literary market.

We have already encountered some of Mozart's contributions to children's periodicals in chapter 2. But the Mozarts were also consumers of this literature themselves. Leopold preferred older pedagogical works: he spoke admiringly of Erasmus, author of two treatises on education (1529 and 1530), and of Fénelon's *Treatise on the Education of Girls* (1687) and *Telemachus* (1699), the latter of which he assigned to Wolfgang to read while father and son were on their first Italian tour.[8] While Wolfgang did not discuss contemporary pedagogues like Weisse, Campe, or Rousseau in his correspondence, he had copies of Weisse's *Lieder für Kinder* (1767)

and Campe's *Kleine Kinderbibliothek* in his library. Four of his Kinderlieder texts, in fact, appear in the *Kinderbibliothek*, and given that the family
had the second edition of 1783, and the songs date from 1787 and 1791, it
appears that the volumes were a part of the family library for their own
sake, not merely as text sources.[9] In addition to the Weisse and Campe,
Wolfgang's library included children's textbooks on geography, natural
history, mathematics, logic, and more, which he and Constanze probably
used in the education of their two surviving children, Carl Thomas and
Franz Xaver.[10]

Also present in Wolfgang's library was a trio of moralizing pedagogi-
cal books by the Munich Jesuit priest Matthias von Schönberg: *Lehrreiche
Gedanken mit kleinen Begebenheiten zur Bildung eines edlen Herzens in der
Jugend* (Educational Thoughts and Small Stories for the Formation of a
Noble Heart in Youth, 1771), *Das Geschäft des Menschen* (The Business of
Humanity, 1772), and *Die Zierde der Jugend* (The Virtue of Youth, 1771).
Schönberg was a severe conservative whom Friedrich Nicolai called an
"extreme bigot" in his 1781 *Beschreibung einer Reise*.[11] Of *Die Zierde der
Jugend*—Mozart's 1777 edition of which was dedicated to Salzburg's Archbishop Colloredo—Jörg-Dieter Kogel writes, "According to Schönberg,
youthful chastity is the source of honor and the mother of all virtues.
Those who do not accustom themselves to a chaste life in youth and recognize its value are lost for the rest of their lives."[12] Ulrich Konrad suspects
these books were given to Wolfgang by Leopold, and that it is unlikely
they were taken seriously by Wolfgang (particularly in light of his bawdy
correspondence with his cousin Maria Anna Thekla Mozart, aka "the
Bäsle," during roughly the same period).[13] Nevertheless, they show how
Mozart was exposed to the most morally conservative pedagogical literature, enshrining the separate education of the sexes and chastity in youth.

In this chapter, I contextualize several of Mozart's Kinderlieder within
other Lieder by Mozart and Kinderlieder by other composers, in order to
uncover the ways that reading, play, work, gender, sexuality, and morality
converge in domestic children's song. Mozart's first and last Lieder ("An
die Freude," K. 53, 1768, and "Das Kinderspiel," K. 598, 1791) were composed for children, and they bookend this chapter. Like the previously
discussed "Die kleine Spinnerin," these songs and others self-consciously
mediate between public and private. And while they embrace rather than
renounce play, they imagine it as a kind of work—both as practice for
adult labor, and as habituation to the increasingly separate spheres of
boyhood and girlhood. In J. W. Smeed's survey of Kinderlieder, he finds
that they portray the child "not as a being whose otherness from adulthood is to be respected, but as a conforming adult in the making, whose

behaviour must be steered as quickly as possible towards the moral and social norms that govern adult society."[14] A Foucauldian reading of this repertoire is almost inevitable: as David Gramit writes of school-based singing pedagogy in this period, "discipline and embodiment are precisely the methods of that pedagogy, which provides a remarkably consistent example of a disciplinary practice in Foucault's sense."[15]

If "Die kleine Spinnerin" reveals anything, however, it is that Kinderlieder are reducible neither to exercises in disciplining, nor to precious expressions of youthful vivacity, "brim[ming] with the sweetest and freshest of melodies," nor to signs of "Mozart's rejuvenation in the last years of his life."[16] Rather, the ways they call upon children, girls, and boys to perform their childhood, girlhood, and boyhood are richly complex, even self-contradictory—as complex and self-contradictory as play itself. Play was a highly contested activity for children in the late Enlightenment, whether impossibly idealized, troublingly sexualized, coopted as training, stubbornly subversive, or utterly indifferent to the adult world.[17] The often conflicting ways various Kinderlieder treat the theme of play serve as a corrective to the tendency to reduce this genre to its dominant strains of didacticism and nostalgia. They also suggest that the notion of childhood as a wholly distinct, protected stage of life was by no means a *fait accompli* in the eighteenth century.

Play as Practice

In chapters 1 and 2, we encountered the Enlightenment pedagogical reformers' belief in play as the cornerstone of education. This meant not just that education could (and should) be playful, but that play could (and should) be educational (the origins of the commonly used phrase "angenehm und lehrreich" and its variants).[18] There is nothing particularly new about this: as J. Allan Mitchell asked rhetorically of medieval toys and playtime, "When is children's recreation *not* education, an introduction to the dominant social habitus or interpellation into the state apparatus?"[19] What was new in the Enlightenment was the audience, and the rationale. The audience was broader, encompassing a middle and upper class beyond the ruling class, while the rationale was twofold: advancing enlightened despotism in noncoercive or "stealth" instruction, while at the same time stoking fears around unstructured, unsupervised play. In *Some Thoughts concerning Education* (a translation of which Campe included in the 1787 volume of his *Allgemeine Revision des gesammten Schul- und Erziehungswesens*), Locke wrote, "All the plays and diversions of children should be directed towards good and useful habits, or else they will introduce ill ones."[20] Rousseau appeared to take a more relaxed approach to play than Locke, asserting in *Emile* (also annotated by Campe for his *Allgemeine Revision*) that "all of childhood is or ought to be only games and frolicsome play," and that play is "nothing but relaxation from" work.[21] But in practice, Rousseau's casual attitude is belied by *Emile*'s conception of a child's surroundings as a vast, intricately designed and totally constrained laboratory of ceaseless moral instruction.

The chief figure in German pedagogical reform—the counterpart to Locke and Rousseau—was the Hamburg-born Johann Bernhard Basedow, who in 1768 founded Philanthropinism, an influential educational philosophy that was promulgated in an experimental school he founded in Dessau in 1774. Influenced by Locke and Rousseau, Basedow advocated an even more playful approach to learning than his predecessors, disguising lessons as games like Simon Says and Twenty Questions in what would come to be known as *Spielpädagogik*.[22] As in *Emile*, this play was by no means free, but rather highly structured and monitored by parents and educators. Basedow's magnum opus was *Das Elementarwerk* (1774), a five-volume picture-based holistic curriculum for children that was addressed not to educators but directly to families.[23] Early in the first volume, Basedow wrote:

> One must not restrict children's freedom to play harmlessly after their liking; but you can make it so that they almost never choose games other than those that you want to tell them about, and which may therefore be useful in promoting certain skills of the body, certain concepts of the mind, and the facilitation of future virtues.[24]

Not even infants were exempt from the pedagogical imperative:

> One likes to play with infants. But one can make this fun more useful than it is. . . . Every game, every joke with infants or with children who are not much older, must be set up with the aim of fostering knowledge of objects and their names, and as preliminary practice in the elements of language and other parts of the body.[25]

The instrumentalizing of play is clear in *Das Elementarwerk*'s *Kupfersammlung*, an accompanying volume of engravings by the illustrator Daniel Chodowiecki.[26] Each of the ninety-six plates were keyed to portions of the main text, which were scripted to be read aloud by "Kinder und Kinderfreunde"—the adult's role was to explain the meaning of each image to the child.[27] Plate 5, the first in a series of three depicting games

FIGURE 4.1. Daniel Chodowiecki, plate 5: "Vergnügungen der Kinder," in *Kupfer-sammlung zu J. B. Basedows Elementarwerke* (Berlin and Dessau, 1774). Courtesy of Österreichische Nationalbibliothek, shelfmark *31.B.7.

and entertainments, represented the youngest children addressed in the book, and was therefore to be read aloud not by a child, but by a mother to a group of children (fig. 4.1). In the scripted exchanges, the children address the reader as "Mama," in keeping with the Rousseauvian promotion of mothers as the primary educators of the very young.[28]

Unsurprisingly, the most athletic of the outdoor games are played by the young boys, while the only indoor space appears to be exclusively female. The group of dancers represents a rare occasion of physical contact between the sexes; it is no surprise, then, that this is the scene shown as requiring adult surveillance and critique. Basedow describes the figure in the window as a grandfather, watching in secret, and wonders "what he will say" about "the ignorant girl raising her foot too high[, which] is not appropriate for girls."[29] In describing the lower-right image of the girls playing with their dolls, "Mama" tells her daughters to treat their dolls according to the manner in which they observe their nannies caring for the small children in their midst. That way, "Mama" urges, the girls will one day be able to help their mothers and aunts with the care of the real children in their own families.[30] Through the scripted close readings

FIGURE 4.2. Daniel Chodowiecki, plate 6: "Andere Vergnügungen der Kinder," in *Kupfersammlung zu J. B. Basedows Elementarwerke* (Berlin and Dessau, 1774). Courtesy of Österreichische Nationalbibliothek, shelfmark *31.B.7.

modeled in the pages of *Das Elementarwerk*, then, children were conditioned to expect a similar level of scrutiny in their own lives, and to seek out a similar level of engagement with their parents.

Plate 6 shows a slightly older group of children, and was scripted to be read aloud by two eight-year-olds (fig. 4.2). A girl is instructed to narrate the top two images, a boy the bottom two. The game shown at upper left is "Besuch" (Visit), a girl's practice for receiving visitors as an adult.[31] The contrast between this image and the one below it, between the girls' rigid comportment, wardrobes, and hairstyles, and the boisterous variety of active poses and free-flowing hair in the boys' outdoor play scene, shows that when playing exclusively with members of their own sex, prepubescent girls were meant to be practicing poise and cordiality, while boys were meant to practice action and exploration. Furthermore, the girls are shown playing together, whereas for the boys, as the narrator explains, "each has his own game and entertainment."[32] None of this is particularly surprising, but it shows how gendered the concepts of cooperation and independence were—themes that we will see at work in several of the Kinderlieder.

Music as Moral Play: The Rise of Kinderlieder

Where play had once been a relatively unstructured respite from other social obligations, Basedow hastened its reconstitution as a kind of training exercise. But what kind of play, and training, was singing? Basedow never granted song the central place in his educational philosophy that he might have — in the Philanthropinum curriculum, it was treated not as an academic subject but only as a form of physical exercise alongside dancing and riding.[33] Locke's and Rousseau's approaches to utilitarian play had left little room for music, as we have already seen in chapter 1. Instrumental music was believed to be particularly dangerous, lacking the moral clarification of an edifying text to counteract its inherent decadence — an exception being Georg Philipp Telemann's short-lived *Der getreue Musicmeister* (The Faithful Music Master, 1728–1729), which, as Steven Zohn reminds us, presented contrapuntal exercises as part of the "moral-instructional landscape" of the periodical.[34] As for children's singing, Rousseau dismissed it, observing that it "never has soul," nor should it, for that would require a level of artifice (and lived experience) undesirable in children.[35] "Imitative and theatrical music is not for his [Emile's] age," Rousseau warned, referring at this point in the book to the years roughly between ages three and thirteen. "I would not even want him to sing words. If he wanted to, I would try to write songs especially for him, interesting for his age and as simple as his ideas."[36] Thus did Rousseau issue a halfhearted, perhaps inadvertent, call for an independent repertoire of children's song.

That call was elaborated and answered by German pedagogues, who were on the whole more optimistic than either the English or the French about song's capacity to serve an edifying purpose for children — or more exercised about its obligation to do so. Over a decade before *Das Elementarwerk* was published, in an issue of the moral weekly *Der Nordische Aufseher* (The Nordic Guardian) that appeared the same year as *Emile* (1762), the Copenhagen-based pedagogue Gottfried Benedict Funk lamented the dearth of contemporary thinkers and writers who were familiar with music.[37] He cited the example of the Greeks, for whom musical knowledge was as essential as general literacy, in support of his assertion regarding the ethical role of fine arts instruction for children. Holding that music was the best of the arts for the young due to its proximity to the rhythms of their natural play, he argued:

> Certain useful exercises can be just as light and fun as their own usual
> games. They learn light and pretty verses as quickly as a vulgar cradle-song

from their wet-nurse. They enjoy listening to a charming fable in verse or in prose, or a marvelous and moving story, as much as they do a gruesome fairy tale from their governess. They are as happy to let themselves be taught to sing or play musical instruments as to build houses of cards; and their taste forms itself as easily and unnoticeably for the beautiful and the regular as it can be corrupted by the bad.[38]

Funk here rationalized the need for a musical repertoire through a subtle vilification of unregulated play and singing. The classist, gendered binary pairs Funk employed, pitting the "vulgar cradle-songs" of female caregivers against the loftier literary and musical offerings of pedagogues like him, cleared a space for ongoing paternalist intervention.[39]

"I have wished," Funk continued,

> that . . . a collection could be made available that one could give to children without concern. The pieces therein would have been selected with care, both as to the intentions of the poetry, and to the music. One would have to seek out light and pretty poems that contained nothing that could present the slightest danger to the innocence of the morals; and the music would have to be likewise light, singable, natural, expressive, and appropriate to the contents of the verse.[40]

Ten years after its appearance in *Der Nordische Aufseher*, Funk's article was reprinted in the 1772 issue of the Bavarian pedagogue Christian Gottfried Böckh's *Wochenschrift zum besten der Erziehung der Jugend* (Weekly for the Improvement of the Upbringing of Youth).[41] In his annotations, Böckh observed approvingly that Funk's wish was "now fulfilled through the excellent composition of the songs of Weisse, Gellert, Hagedorn, and Lavater."[42] Those four poets, along with many other poets and composers, had in the intervening decade been responsible for a proliferation of Lieder oriented specifically toward a young readership, as can be seen in the list reproduced in table 4.1.

These collections were by no means obscure curios. With reviews in the *Allgemeine deutsche Bibliothek*, multiple printings and volumes, and the publishing of individual songs in many of the more prominent children's periodicals of the age, we can assume a sizable readership for Kinderlieder. Mozart had at least one collection of Kinderlieder in his library at the time of his death, in addition to the ones to which he contributed: Johann Adam Hiller's *Vierstimmige Motetten und Arien . . . zum Gebrauch der Schulen und anderer Gesangsliebhaber* (1776). In the preface, Hiller suggested that most schools in large and medium-sized German

TABLE 4.1. Major freestanding Kinderlieder collections, 1760–1799

Year	Title	Text by	Music by	Published in
1766, 1768	*Kleine Lieder für Kinder zur Beförderung der Tugend. Mit Melodien zum Singen beym Klavier, 2 vols.*	Christian Felix Weisse	Johann Adolph Scheibe	Flensburg
1769 [rev. ed. 1775, 1784]	*Lieder für Kinder, vermehrte Auflage. Mit neuen Melodien von Johann Adam Hiller*	Weisse	Johann Adam Hiller	Leipzig
1772	*Lieder für Kinder mit neuen Melodien von Gottlob Gott-wald Hunger*	Weisse	Gottlob Gottwald Hunger	Leipzig
1773	*Kleine Lieder für Kleine Maedchen*	Gottlob Wil-helm Burmann	Burmann	Berlin and Königsberg
1774	*G. W. Burmanns Kleine Lieder für kleine Mädchen und Knaben . . . nebst einem Anhang etlicher Lieder aus der Wochenschrift: Der Greis. Zu Zweyen Stimmen ausgesetzt*	Burmann	"J. G. H."	Zurich
1774	*Fünfzig geistliche Lieder für Kinder, mit Claviermäßig eingerichteten Melodien, zum Besten der neuen Armenschule zu Friedrichstadt*	Christoph Christian Sturm	Hiller	Leipzig
1774	*Lieder eines Mägdchens, beym singen und claviere*	[F. A. C. Werthes]	?	Münster
1774	*Neue Melodien zu G. W. Bur-manns Kleinen Liedern für kleine Mägdchen*	Burmann	Christian Friedrich Schale	Berlin
1775	*Christliche Lieder der vater-ländischen Jugend, besonders auf der Landschaft, gewied-met. Mit Choral-Melodien zu vier Stimmen*	Johann Caspar Lavater	J. G. H.	Zurich
1775	*Wiegenliederchen für deutsche Ammen, mit Melodien*	Friedrich Justin Bertuch	Ernst Wil-helm Wolf	Riga

TABLE 4.1. (*continued*)

Year	Title	Text by	Music by	Published in
1776–1791	*Vierstimmige Motetten und Arien in Partitur, von verschiedenen Componisten, zum Gebrauch der Schulen und anderer Gesangsliebhaber, 6 vols.*	[various]	Hiller	Leipzig
1777	*Kleine Lieder für kleine Jünglinge*	Burmann	Burmann	Berlin and Königsberg
1777	*Kleine Lieder für Kinder. Mit Melodien, zum Singen beym Klavier* [manuscript]	?	?	Leipzig
1780	*Lieder für Kinder mit neuen sehr leichten Melodieen*	?	Georg Carl Claudius	Frankfurt
1781–1790	*Lieder für Kinder aus Campes Kinderbibliothek mit Melodieen, bey dem Klavier zu singen, 4 vols.*	[various]	Johann Friedrich Reichardt	Hamburg, Wolfenbuttel, and Braunschweig
1782	*Sammlung der Lieder aus dem Kinderfreunde, die noch nicht componirt waren, mit neuen Melodien von Johann Adam Hiller*	Weisse	Hiller	Leipzig
1786	*Morgen, Abend und Festgesänge für Kinder beim Clavier*	?	Christian Friedrich Heinicke	Leipzig
1787	*Faßliche Melodien zu Rudolf Christoph Loßius Lieder und Gedichte ein Etui für Kinder. Mit und ohne Clavierbegleitung gesellschaftlich zu singen*	Rudolf Christoph Loßius	Georg Peter Weimar	Erfurt
1789	*Sammlung einiger Lieder für die Jugend bei Industrialarbeiten mit den hiezu gehörigen Melodien*	Franz Štiasny	[various]	Prague

(*continued*)

TABLE 4.1. (*continued*)

Year	Title	Text by	Music by	Published in
1789	*Versuch einiger Lieder mit Melodien für junge Klavier-Spieler. 3 Theile*	?	Carl Gottlieb Hering	Leipzig
1789	*Zwölf Kinderlieder fürs Gesang und Clavier. Ein Geschenk für die Musiclie-bende Jugend*	?	Johann Heinrich Egli	Zurich
1790	*Einfache Clavierlieder*	[various]	[Johann Gottlieb] Karl Spazier	Berlin
1790–1801	*Gesänge zur Beförderung Vaterländischer Tugend. Neujahrsgeschenk ab dem Musiksaal an die Zürcherische Jugend. 12 Stücke*	[various]	[various]	Zurich
1791	*Liedersammlung für Kinder und Kinderfreunde am Clavier: "Frühlingslieder"*	[various]	[various]	Vienna
1791	*Liedersammlung für Kinder und Kinderfreunde am Clavier: "Winterlieder"*	[various]	[various]	Vienna
1792	*25 Lieder für Kinder von Spielmann*	Spielmann	Vincenz Maschek and Franz Duschek	Prague
1794	*Melodien zu Hartungs Lieder-sammlung, zum Gebrauche für Schulen und zur einsamen und gesellschaftlichen Unter-haltung am Klavier*	[various]	[Johann Gottlieb] Karl Spazier	Berlin
1795	*Lieder mit Melodien für Kinder*	?	Georg Friedrich Wolf	Leipzig
1798	*Kinderlieder und Melodien*	Horstig [and various]	Karl Gottlieb Horstig	Leipzig

TABLE 4.1. (*continued*)

Year	Title	Text by	Music by	Published in
1798	*Lieder für Kinder zur Bildung des Herzens, am Klavier*	?	Georg Laurenz Schneider	Coburg
1798	*Wiegenlieder für gute deutsche Mütter*	[various]	Reichardt	Leipzig
1799	*Lieder für die Jugend*, 2 vols.	[various]	Reichardt [and various]	Leipzig
1799	*Lieder für Kinder zur Bildung der Sitten, und das Geschmacks im Singen. 1. Abtheilung*	[various]	Seidel	Prague

Based on Buch, introduction and "Chronological List of Printed Kinderlieder, 1766–1792," in *Liedersammlung für Kinder und Kinderfreunde*, ix–xix and 163; Head, *Sovereign Feminine*, 57; Head, "'If the Pretty Little Hand Won't Stretch,'" 207; Schilling-Sandvoß, "Kinderlieder," 181–83; Brüggemann and Ewers, eds., *Handbuch zur Kinder- und Jugendliteratur*; Schusky, "Illustrationen in deutschen Liederbüchern für Frauen und Kinder," 332–34; and Friedlaender, *Das deutsche Lied im 18. Jahrhundert*.

cities had a choir of which "one could justifiably demand" that they perform his songs; and a later article recommended the collection to Protestant and Catholic readers alike.[43]

With ties to both devotional and folk song, Kinderlieder shared in the didactic aims of the former and the cultural aspirations of the latter. Their subject matter ranged from allegories of nature, to hymns to one's playthings, to the mundane irritants of everyday life, to the sudden death of a playmate, offering young readers a means of coping with and giving expression to a panoply of childhood experiences and emotions, while upholding the moral values that were of such concern. The Lied- and Singspiel-reform debates of the early and mid-eighteenth century had already established German vocal music as an agent of moral instruction and social cohesion, reframing its folklike simplicity as an ethical asset rather than an aesthetic shortcoming—a signifier of the "edle Einfalt" (noble simplicity) so prized in German art.[44] But the lingering associations of song with pleasure (i.e., Mediterranean decadence) caused anxiety on the part of German Enlightenment men of letters. In *Das Elementarwerk*, for instance, Basedow cautioned that music is, "like the fine arts, subject to *misuse*," because of its ability to arouse almost any sentiment or passion.[45]

Protecting children from the perilous "misuse" of music required both internal and external interventions: internal, in the content of the songs, and external, in the composing-in of implied or literal adult supervision. The two often overlapped, as we have already seen in "Die kleine Spinnerin," whose narrator addresses an older, male audience ("Ihr Herr'n") while describing the way she hopes to be praised by others for her diligent labor at the spinning wheel. The implied audience and the staged intergenerational dialogue were common features of children's literature more generally, just as the implied audience for Kinderlieder included parents, tutors, and caregivers.[46] Songs were frequently composed to be sung by parents to their children, or in a duet in which they alternated stanzas with their children in a kind of musical catechism. Several scholars argue that the difficulty of some Kinderlieder suggests that they may have even been primarily aimed at adult performers, with children as the intended audience.[47]

Weisse's own *Lieder für Kinder*, the first collection in the genre, established this tradition of parental participation. His poems were set by at least three different composers—Johann Adolph Scheibe, Hiller, and Gottlob Gottwald Hunger—within the space of just six years.[48] The frontispiece to both Weisse's book of poems, and Hiller's 1769 collection of settings, shows a mother singing to her baby in the cradle, even though there are no lullabies in the collection. Nor do mothers figure prominently in the songs themselves. Instead, as in Weisse's *Der Kinderfreund*, it is the father who speaks and sings to his children. The text-only edition of *Lieder für Kinder* (1767) is bookended by two songs from the perspective of a father: "Zuschrift an ein paar Kinder" (Letter to a Pair of Children) and "Ermahnung an zwei Kinder" (Exhortation to Two Children). The latter is a doting, nostalgic evocation of filial play:

> Sweet girl, lovely boy,
> Play only, play in my lap!
> When I have you in my arms,
> I am as grand as a king.
>
> . . .
>
> Gladly I join in your games
> With a benign indulgence,
> O the happiness that I then feel,
> To be a child once again![49]

FIGURE 4.3. Title page engraving, Scheibe, *Kleine Lieder für Kinder* (Flensburg, 1766). Courtesy of Österreichische Nationalbibliothek, shelfmark SA.82.E.30.

Here, play takes on a romanticizing function: rather than a separate arena of children's lives or a potentially dangerous activity in need of careful monitoring, it is the means by which, through shared games, world-weary fathers might recapture the simple joys of their own remembered boyhoods.

In contrast, the only song that features a mother is one sung to her, the Lied "Ein paar Kinder an ihre Mutter, bey derselben Geburtstage" (A Pair of Children to Their Mother, on Her Birthday), which first appeared in the second edition from 1769, the one with settings by Hiller. The song begins with the two children praising their mother as "best friend," while one verse describes the moment captured in the frontispiece illustration: "Your concerned, alert gaze / Always hangs over our cradles."[50] In Weisse's world, it seems, fathers do the talking, while mothers are there to listen and monitor.

In most other Kinderlieder iconography, the mother is invariably shown as the accompanist. Take for instance the title vignette for Scheibe's *Kleine Lieder für Kinder* (1766), another collection of settings of Weisse's *Lieder für Kinder* that predated Hiller's (fig. 4.3). The engraving shows a family unit at home: a woman at a harpsichord accompanies a man singing from a book, while a young girl follows along at left, the family dog distracting her from her music. Renate Schusky notes the courtly dress of the figures, hypothesizing that the singing man is a private tutor to a well-to-do family.[51] Whether this represents a mother, father, and daughter, two sisters and their tutor, or some other group, the image

FIGURE 4.4. Johann Adolf Rosmaesler, title page engraving, Salzmann, *Unterhaltungen für Kinder und Kinderfreunde, Drittes Bändchen* (Leipzig, 1780). Courtesy of Bayerische Staatsbibliothek München, shelfmark Paed.pr. 2984-3/4.

highlights the function of the collection as an exemplar for younger children. The accompanist's back is to us; dwarfed by the outsized score that sits atop the keyboard, her placement below and to the side of the male singer echoes the position of the dog in relation to the young girl, and even their outstretched arms parallel one another. Both female accompanist and loyal pet thus model attention and subservience.

In another engraving, this time from a children's reader, the woman's role as Kinderlied monitor is made even more explicit. The collection, *Unterhaltungen für Kinder und Kinderfreunde* (Entertainments for Children and the Friends of Children, 1778–1787), was by Christian Gotthilf Salzmann, a fellow teacher of Basedow's at the Philanthropinum. The engraving illustrates a "Lustspiel" from volume 3 of the *Unterhaltungen* entitled "Denk, daß zu deinem Glück dir niemand fehlt, als du!" (Keep in mind, that you do not need anyone but yourself to be happy!) (fig. 4.4).

LIEDERSAMMLUNG
FÜR
KINDER UND KINDERFREUNDE
AM CLAVIER·
FRÜHLINGSLIEDER.

WIEN,
GEDRUCKT BEY IGNAZ ALBERTI, K. K. PRIV. BUCHDRUCKER. MDCCXCI.

M.S.27064

FIGURE 4.5. Christian Sambach, title page engraving, *Liedersammlung für Kinder und Kinderfreunde: Frühlingslieder*, ed. Placidus Partsch (Vienna, 1791). Courtesy of Österreichische Nationalbibliothek, shelfmark MS27064-qu.4°/2,24.

In this play, a grouchy daughter named Mariane keeps alienating herself from her family. In the scene depicted in the engraving, the mother has suggested that her two sons Heinrich and Ferdinand join her to sing the hymn "Lobt den Herrn, die Morgensonne" (Praise the Lord, the Morning Sun). "Maybe you will play the evil spirit out of your sister," she says pointedly, commanding Mariane to "pay attention."[52] But Mariane interrupts her brothers, bickering with them. The mother scolds Mariane, joining her sons to sing the next verse of the hymn. As shown in the engraving, Heinrich stands to play at the clavichord, while Ferdinand sits on his mother's lap as they sing, with Mariane facing the wall. When the mother catches Heinrich teasing Mariane, she chides him, "If you want to encourage others to Praise the Lord, you must not offend them."[53] That this moment of shared music-making is the title page vignette to the entire volume upholds the performative nature of family singing — Mariane's obligation to join in with equanimity, or be cast out of the maternal circle, affirms the participatory mandate for all of Salzmann's readers.

The prominence of the mother in scenes of wholesome domestic music-making is also carried through in the title page vignette (fig. 4.5) of the children's collection to which Mozart contributed his last three Lieder,

the 1791 *Liedersammlung für Kinder und Kinderfreunde.*[54] This collection
(to which I will return later in the chapter) appears to be Vienna's first and
only Kinderlieder publication—evidently the genre was more popular in
Leipzig, Berlin, and Zurich.

Among the gaggle of putti-like child musicians in the vignette, the two
most prominent figures besides the mother are the two boys who stand
on either side of her, presumably her sons. One holds a flute, the other a
violin, and their mouths are slightly open as though they are singing. The
mother makes a conducting gesture toward the older boy with the flute,
while her left hand plucks out the harmony on the clavichord. In the right
background, the eldest daughter performs a supporting role, strumming
a harp in apparent silence. From the very title page, then, this collection
imagines boys as singers and soloists, girls and women as accompanists,
and the collective expression of the family as the ultimate goal.[55] These
songs, in other words, were meant as chamber music, constructing the
sociability of the family.

The Dangers of Play, and the Virtue of Joy

In Kinderlieder, play was not just entrainment, but also an antidote to
indecency. Such was the motivation behind one of the first sets of Kinderlieder to appear in any print medium, the same year as Weisse and Scheibe's *Lieder für Kinder*: a set of nine included in a 1766 issue of the Magdeburg moral weekly *Der Greis* (The Old Man, 1763–1769), edited by the
clergyman, poet, and librettist Johann Samuel Patzke.[56] In the guise of his
alter ego, Patzke's "old man" prefaced the songs with the observation that
children seeking out music to sing were confronted either with large and
inaccessibly difficult works or with collections of short songs that "have
no other contents besides wine and love."[57] The old man's niece, Clelie,
has recently visited some of her girlfriends, one of whom

> would often go to the Flügel and sing and play such Lieder as were the
> expression of an impure heart, and that made me wish, that what might
> in other contexts be a virtue, would not be made into the spoiling of a
> soul.[58]

Such songs, Patzke wrote, might appear harmless to adults, who had
already established a firm moral code. But the weak and impressionable
hearts of the young, he insisted, must be exposed to edifying, age-

appropriate songs that would "instill the most important moral truths in children while they learn music at the same time."[59]

The nine Kinderlieder that follow Patzke's introduction offer just such an alternative for Clelies and their uncles everywhere. The first is a hymn of praise to God, and subsequent songs seek moral lessons in the natural world.[60] One, "Der Rosenstock" (The Rose Bush), is a thinly veiled allegory of the destructive dangers of "the hours of pleasure."[61] It is followed immediately by "Die Freude" ("Joy"), which celebrates the blessings of idyllic, desexualized collective play:

Joy, you companion
Of all my days,
You flow through heart and mind
I know nothing of grief.

The abundance of your blessing
Pervades every part of me,
And the dance lifts my foot
And you teach me songs.

Hopping, I hasten into the ranks
Of laughing playmates,
Where we all are only happy
We all feel just right.[62]

The setting reinforces the aggressively cheerful message of the text, even within a narrow stylistic compass. With an eight-bar strophe easily played by small hands, "Die Freude" proceeds in a robust, martial F major, illustrating the child's "hopping" with murky bass octaves in the left hand and a rising arpeggio that is particularly appropriate under the line "the dance lifts my foot" in the second stanza. One can almost picture the girl in Basedow's *Kupfersammlung* (fig. 4.1) with her lifted foot.

"Die Freude" describes Joy as the teacher of wholesome songs. With this self-referential gesture, Patzke establishes his own songs as both a spur to, and a manifestation of, a wholesome childlike spirit. The message of "Die Freude" is clear: group play of an innocently physical nature is to be welcomed, while the one-on-one "play" of the romantic encounter is to be shunned. The threat of sexual corruption is raised in the subsequent song, "Der Verlust der Freude" (The Loss of Joy), which bookends "Der Rosenstock" with another rumination on deflowering. The narrator bemoans his opaque "wicked deed," advising the reader: "Learn, heart, where joys are. / Joy is the child of innocence. / If you would preserve it / Follow the pleasures of your age."[63]

These moral and even sexual connotations to the word "Freude" may well have been at work in one of the first Kinderlieder Mozart ever composed, "An die Freude" (K. 53), for the 1768 Vienna children's periodical *Neue Sammlung zum Vergnügen und Unterricht*.[64] But whereas the Joy in Patzke's "Die Freude" is a "Begleiterinn" (female companion), "An die Freude" posits Joy as a goddess, the "Königinn der Weisen" (queen of wise men), taking her place alongside such classical figures as Cytheren (Aphrodite), the Graces, Lyäen (Dionysus), and Cynthien (Diana). The more elevated register of this Lied suggests it may have been aimed at an older or more elite readership. This is also a more interior text, with the speaker communing directly with Joy rather than through a shared activity, as shown in the first of its seven stanzas:

> Joy, queen of wise men,
> Who, flower-crowned,
> Praise you on golden lyres,
> Gently, while Folly snorts and snuffles:
> Hear me from your throne,
> Child of Wisdom, whose own hand
> Has always in your crown
> Entwined the fairest roses.[65]

Subsequent verses paint a picture of this mother-queen of wisdom braving threats from Fortune and Death, leading the poet safely through life.

This poem was by the Ansbach poet Johann Peter Uz, and was originally published not in a children's publication, but in Uz's 1768 *Complete Poetic Works*.[66] That same year, Mozart's setting appeared in the *Neue Sammlung zum Vergnügen und Unterricht*, alongside "Daphne, deine Rosenwangen" from Mozart's *Bastien und Bastienne* (as discussed in chapter 3). Mozart's setting of "An die Freude" offers a more sedate, hymnlike melody than "Die Freude" in *Der Greis*, evoking the "geistliche Lieder" of composers like C. P. E. Bach.[67] It is also far more complex than the songs in *Der Greis*, or even in Hiller or Scheibe's *Lieder für Kinder*: a forty-bar strophe with no repeating phrases, it modulates to the dominant and supertonic before returning to the tonic.

The ostensible threats to the virtue of play persisted as the Kinderlieder repertoire blossomed, including in descriptions of collective singing. In 1776, Basedow's fellow Philanthropinist Friedrich Eberhard von

Rochow edited a one-off children's reader for rural schools, also called *Der Kinderfreund*. The section "Von Spielen und Vergnügen" (On Games and Entertainments) begins with an idyll of autonomous play in which collective singing is presented as thoroughly chaste:

> When Wilhelm, Fritz, Martin, Karl, Sophie, Louise, Marie, and Elisabeth were children, they would play after school for several hours, when the weather permitted it. Either one sang Kinderlieder, and the others danced, or they all sang under the shadow of a green tree.[68]

The pastoral innocence of the scene is maintained even after the boys remove their clothes so as not to dirty them while playing a ball game. But when Rochow goes on to interpret his own anecdote for his young readers, he ends with a note of warning:

> And so they remained entertained and healthy, and all people were pleased, when they witnessed the innocent gaiety of these good children.
> Innocent joy is permitted to everyone; only unworthy and impertinent merriness is forbidden.[69]

Rochow here characterizes play as a potentially dangerous pastime, one with threatening undertones. This is in keeping with much contemporaneous children's literature, which warned boys and girls about the dangers of sexual desire. Returning to the 1780 Viennese alphabet of morals mentioned in chapter 2, its entry for the letter V, "Verlangen und Liebe" (Desire and Love), went into fearsome detail about the ruin that would inevitably follow should youths (i.e., boys) succumb to temptation and allow themselves to be "seduced by the harlot, to revel in her lusts."[70] This recalls the vulnerability of innocent joy in Patzke's Kinderlieder, particularly the "hour's pleasure" lamented by the narrator of "Der Rosenstock."

Reading itself was feared to provoke similar dissipation—Matt Erlin has laid out the anxieties expressed by Campe and others about "reading as a potentially dangerous" (because unproductive, unregulated) "form of consumption."[71] The common trope of the paternal interlocutor and fictional family dialogue in juvenile literature served as both a model for real-world parents, and "a direct response to the destabilization of meaning made possible by the circulation of fictional texts in the period."[72] Because reading was also an increasingly solitary act, it was therefore associated with other unruly solitary acts. In the 1780s, a flood of pamphlets and tracts were published around the pathologization of masturbation, led by many of the most prominent Philanthropist authors, including Campe, Schönberg, and Salzmann. This *Broschurenflut* was initiated in part by the Swiss doctor Samuel-Auguste Tissot, whom we first encountered in chapter 1 writing about the nervous systems of child geniuses including Mozart.

The anti-masturbation campaign was arguably the preeminent discursive site for the construction of child sexuality in late eighteenth-century Germany—what Isabel Hull has labeled a "thought experiment" in the regulation of sexuality.[73] The rhetoric of the campaign was almost identical with warnings about children's consumption of illicit song—no surprise, given that many writers contributed to both genres.[74] The danger, in both cases, was premature sexualization, and the parallel illicit activities were even linked in a cause-and-effect relationship. Salzmann, author of the story about grouchy Mariane illustrated in figure 4.4, wrote a 1785 tract, *Ueber die heimlichen Sünden der Jugend* (On the Secret Sins of Youth). In it, Salzmann warned that "love songs, plays, poems, [and] novels" risked "prematurely sensitiz[ing]" children to "temptations . . . whose enjoyment was intended for them many years hence."[75] "The young soul, that had until now no other purpose than to play and learn, to obey and oblige, will begin to fall in love, and dream of pretty girls, at an age when children usually only dream of dolls and hobby horses."[76] This was clearly aimed at boys and their nervous parents. For girls, the threat of sexual awakening was either ignored completely (as in Salzmann), or described as utterly catastrophic. Hull cites Christoph Martin Wieland's comment in 1775 that "ardent girls don't exist, because for those that are, there is nothing further that can be ruined."[77]

The threat to boys was connected to another theme of pedagogical anxiety associated with labor: "Müßiggang" (idleness). Unstructured free time, as we have already seen in chapter 2, was an obsession not just of the middle-class pedagogues but of the heads of orphanages and proponents of industrial education. We already saw how Mozart's Kinderlied "Die kleine Spinnerin" valorizes industriousness. Another Kinderlieder collection, Gottlob Wilhelm Burmann's 1777 *Kleine Lieder für kleine Jünglinge* (Little Songs for Little Youths), includes a Lied called "Müssiggang," in which, to a jolly march in G major, the boy narrator professes never to want to be idle, either as a boy or as a grown man. "Idleness is the path to vice / Work is my desire and inclination!"[78]

Hull ties this moral panic about idleness back to German cameralism, and the same panic shows up when tracts on political economy consider children's role in the welfare of the state. Take for instance

Johann Heinrich Gottlob Justi's 1760–1761 treatise *Grundfeste der Macht und der Glückseligkeit der Staaten* (Foundations of the Power and Happiness of States): "There are a hundred tasks of which children are [already] capable at the age of five or six; and to make work their nature, they must never become acquainted with idleness."[79] Joseph von Sonnenfels also described "idleness as the vice of youth" in his 1770 treatise *Grundsätze der Polizei, Handlung und Finanzwissenschaft* (Principles of Police, Trade, and Finance).[80] And in the Prague educator Karl Heinrich Seibt's 1771 *Von dem Einflusse der Erziehung auf die Glückseligkeit des Staats* (On the Influence of Education on the Happiness of the State), he warned, "What is more advantageous—I would almost say, more essential—to a nation than the industriousness and activity of its citizens? and what more pernicious than sloth and idleness?"[81] Kinderlieder like Mozart's "An die Freude" enshrined these values for both boys and girls, making joy itself into a rehearsal of the ideal subject, and a bulwark (recalling the text of "An die Freude") against cold terror and death.

What Women Must Know: Theaters of Girlhood

Given the moral panic around private reading, it may seem counterintuitive for so many Philanthropinist authors to have lent their imaginations to the production of new Lieder; after all, aside from dancing, there were few public endeavors more intimate than singing a song at the keyboard. Many songs even thematized these qualities, as in the song "Der Liebesgott (Neulich, Schwestern, Darf ich Sagen?)" (The Love God [Recently, Sisters, May I Tell It?]), originally set by Christian Ernst Rosenbaum in 1762, and included in a separate setting in the rather earthy, possibly parodic anonymous 1777 collection *Kleine Lieder für Kinder*.[82] Rosenbaum claimed the poet was "a young fifteen-year-old beauty who will soon be one of the most pleasing of our muses."[83] The poem, a parody of Gotthold Ephraim Lessing's 1747 poem "Der Tod (Gestern, Brüder, könnt ihrs glauben?)" (Death [Yesterday, Brothers, Can You Believe It?]), employs the trope of domestic keyboard performance as a prelude to an act of seduction.[84] As in Lessing's original, the parody presents the narrow escape from a deflowering—for young women a kind of death—in the form of a narrative: a young nun tells it to her fellow "Schwestern."[85] Only the first two verses are included in the *Kleine Lieder für Kinder*, and the identity of the Love-God—whether Cupid or a male suitor—is left ambiguous:

Lately, sisters, may I say it?
Hear what took place:
Recently, at the keyboard [*Clavier*]
The Love-God came to me.

Flirtatiously [*Schäkernd*] he brandished his quiver
Flirtatiously spoke the evil avenger
Feel now what you never felt before
Child, you have played enough.[86]

Rosenbaum's original poem contained seven additional stanzas, in which the girl, revealed to be a novice, successfully kept her suitor at arm's length with her music, finally bargaining with him in order to preserve her chastity.[87] But as it is printed here, with just the first two stanzas, the narrative remains provocatively unfinished. The "sisters" could be siblings or female companions, and the "child's play" of the girl at her clavier suggests similar fears to those obsessively detailed in the anti-masturbation literature. The accompanying illustration shows a rare instance of young women playing and singing together, unsupervised—a moment of ambiguous moral import.

That a collection like *Kleine Lieder für Kinder* could, in 1777, include a song as provocative as "Neulich, Schwestern" suggests that ten years after Patzke's complaint in *Der Greis*, music publishers still were not consistently censoring the songs they marketed to the young. And Weisse himself complained of this inconsistency. In the same article in a 1778 issue of *Der Kinderfreund* in which Weisse had lamented the professional children's troupe, with its "poor innocents being offered for sale" (discussed in chapter 3), he cautioned his young readers not to lend their skills to "shameless wooing songs."[88] Even in private company, Mentor reported,

I have heard children, who have had very talented voices, singing at their parents' request Italian, French, and German *Buhlerlieder* [wooing songs] with true theatrical gestures, and these have been greeted with loud applause by the audience, and heard with the most complacent laughter by their adoring parents. Forgive me, when I sometimes did not applaud myself, and when you might have seen me shake my head disapprovingly! I know well that people may call me simple-minded, or too strict; but it offends me, when I see a young ten-year-old girl singing an "Amabile Idol mio." O what a loud Bravo would you hear from my lips, if the subject were a virtuous sentiment from social and country life, or an encouragement to an obligation appropriate to your age!—And we have, thank

God! songs and Lieder of various kinds, that when played and sung from your sweet innocent mouths, will please Virtue itself.[89]

Weisse's gender slippage from "children" to the "ten-year-old girl" recalls Patzke's "Der Greis" and his anxieties about his niece Clelie.

The high degree of consciousness of audience among girls—the "duty of appearances," in Rousseau's formulation—is part of what has always given girlhood its discomfiting charge.[90] Seth Lerer has identified this as "one of the controlling themes of female fiction, almost from its origin: that girls are always on the stage, that being female is a show," describing it as literature's "theaters of girlhood" (a distant cousin to Judith Butler's performative "girling").[91] Mozart was a deft scribe of Kinderlieder's theaters of girlhood: when the heroine of "Die kleine Spinnerin" eschews the games to which Fritz has invited her on behalf of his companions in favor of remaining indoors and laboring on behalf of her mother, sisters, and "the people," she simply trades one theater for another—even the extended length of her response is itself a theatricality. Such self-conscious staging of virtue is inherently paradoxical: as Tili Boon Cuillé writes of musical tableaus in eighteenth-century fiction, "[a] certain tension between virtue and eroticism is . . . implicit" in the form itself, which invites voyeurism.[92]

Mozart's contributions to the "theaters of girlhood" extend beyond "Die kleine Spinnerin" and Kinderlieder. To take just one example from opera buffa, Despina's aria from *Così fan tutte* (K. 588, 1790), "Una donna a quindici anni" (A Fifteen-Year-Old Woman), begins with a paradox: the "lady" of fifteen, armed for the battle of courtship.

> A lady of fifteen years
> Must know each great fashion,
> Where the devil keeps his tail,
> What is good and what is bad.
> She must know the malicious ways
> That enamour lovers,
> To feign laughter, to feign tears,
> And to invent good reasons.[93]

Despina here outlines for Dorabella and Fiordiligi the sexual knowledge a young woman must have from the age of fifteen—an age which, in 1790 Vienna, would have still been quite young for a woman to be sexually active.[94]

In another of Mozart's Lieder, the threat of premature sexualization in a young woman is thwarted by her mother. The Lied, "Der Zauberer" (The Sorcerer, K. 472), was composed in 1785. Although not a Kinderlied, the poem is by Weisse, from his *Scherzhafte Lieder* (Humorous Songs), the source of three other poems set by Mozart.[95] "Der Zauberer" draws on many of the same tropes as "Neulich, Schwestern." The female narrator is clearly a young unmarried woman, addressing her fellows with a warning: "You girls, keep away from Damoetas!" What follows is a pastoral description of the narrator's sexual awakening on encountering the handsome shepherd: "I felt something I had never felt before." The girl (unnamed, but probably Chloe, since the pair are named in Mozart's other Weisse setting, "Die Verschweigung") allows herself to be drawn by Damoetas into a clump of bushes, stopping only when her mother appears in the nick of time. The girl's concluding expression of relief— "What, o Gods, after so much sorcery / Would have happened to me in the end!"—allows the listener to indulge in the provocatively unspoken, while preserving the same veneer of chastity granted the narrator.[96]

Just as the poem constantly oscillates between familiar erotic opposites—"now red, now white," "yes and no," "flee and follow," "sweet pain"—so too does Mozart's setting, which toggles from the tonic G minor, to a fully harmonized B-flat major, and back to G minor, with abrupt changes in texture and dynamics conveying the psychological conflict described by the speaker.[97] In its suggestive "tension between virtue and eroticism," then, "Der Zauberer" resists the moralizing called for by the Kinderlieder advocates, offering a different image of femininity from the industrious, ascetic spinner-girl of K. 531.

One can find other examples of the "theaters of girlhood" in Mozart's Lieder. Take for instance "Die Alte" (The Old Woman, K. 517, 1787). The poem, by Friedrich von Hagedorn, was one in a series that form a kind of portrait gallery of the ages of man, the others being "Das Kind," "Der Jüngling," and "Der Alte."[98] In "Die Alte" (the only one set by Mozart), an old woman reminisces about how "in my day . . . children grew up / Virtuous girls became brides," and "the husband was governed" by his wife. Now, "o bad times . . . maternal instincts" take over before the young are ready, and husbands "contradict us and herd us around." The austere, contrapuntal bass line and minor mode are undercut by Mozart's highly theatrical expression marking, "Ein bißchen durch die Nase," or "a little nasal." This confirms that the character's age is to be exaggerated to the point of satire, an effect that would be even more pronounced if the singer was a young woman. Mozart's three songs "Die kleine Spinnerin," "Der Zauberer," and "Die Alte" could thus serve as a biography of a single archetypal woman moving through the life cycle, trying on female identities like a series of costumes.

What Men Must Do: Nostalgia and the Singing Boy

Matthew Head has shown how in eighteenth-century domestic music for
"the fair sex," "the categories of the musical amateur and the feminine
intersected in ideals of naturalness, songfulness, instinct, the untutored,
and the gently moving rather than the learned."[99] All of those categories
could also be aligned with the childlike, and Head does include several
collections of songs for girls in his study.[100] But what of the singing boy?
And what sort of juvenile image did Mozart contribute to in some of his
boy-oriented Kinderlieder? As we saw in figures 4.1 and 4.2, boyhood was
just as much a spectacle as girlhood, but what boys performed was bustling, independent activity and exploration. If Kinderlieder presented
girlhood as a process of becoming fluent in social conventions (the musical equivalent of Basedow's game of "Besuch"), then boyhood often took
place out-of-doors, away from society. Girls perform culture, while boys
perform nature.

 An illustration of this can be found in one of Mozart's three Kinderlieder for the 1791 *Liedersammlung für Kinder und Kinderfreunde* — all three
will be discussed in this section, as all three feature boy protagonists.
"Sehnsucht nach dem Frühlinge" (K. 596) sets a poem by Christian Adolf
Overbeck originally entitled "Fritzchen an den Mai" (Little Fritz to May),
and conveys little Fritz's impatience as he waits for the snow to melt so he
and his playmates can venture outside.[101] The verses focus on the active
indoor and outdoor games — cards, blindman's buff, sleigh rides — with
which Fritz passes the time awaiting the spring. In the fourth stanza,
Fritz pities his sister Lottie, as "the poor girl just waits / for the flowers to
bloom."[102] Lottie's passivity — "she sits on her little chair / like a little hen
on an egg" — contrasts with the narrator's energy as he "trot[s] through
the snow."[103] Lottie's performance of responsible girlhood is a sedentary
exercise in forbearance, while Fritz's boyhood is scampering and carefree.

 The earliest freestanding collections of Kinderlieder often distinguished at least some of their songs by gender. And, just as some collections were exclusively aimed at girls, a smaller subset of Kinderlieder
collections were aimed at boys. One example is Burmann's 1777 *Kleine
Lieder für kleine Jünglinge*, whose "Müßiggang" (Idleness) has already
been mentioned.[104] In his preface, Burmann assured the listener that he
had composed his songs with "children's voices" in mind, and he even

indicated with an asterisk those songs in the boys' collection that were probably better off being sung by girls—again, the implication is that none of these collections were meant to be consumed in isolation but rather to be shared among family members.[105] The vast majority of the songs reflect a masculine ideal of virtue and obedience, as in "Der Wunsch: ein braver Mann zu werden" (The Wish: To Become a Good Man), in which the singer professes his integrity and praises "prince and fatherland."[106]

A more contemplative, sentimental strain of boys' subjectivity unfolds in sources like Campe's *Kleine Kinderbibliothek*. The first seven volumes of this reader were in Mozart's library, and the first two volumes contain the texts for the spring songs he contributed to the 1791 *Liedersammlung für Kinder und Kinderfreunde*. His "Der Frühling" (The Spring, K. 597) comes from the section of the *Kleine Kinderbibliothek* aimed at older readers age eleven to twelve.[107] A story elsewhere in this section, "The Reasonable Youth," tells the tale of a young man who eschews the drinking and gambling of his fellow students in favor of communing outdoors with a religious text. Overcome with gratitude for the bounteous nature that surrounds him, he falls to his knees and pledges himself to God's "fatherly guidance."[108] Solitary reading is channeled in the service of a devout sentimentalism. A similar reverence toward both nature and the divine can be found in "Der Frühling." To a regal Adagio in E-flat major—which begins with a piano flourish that prefigures the overture to *Die Zauberflöte*—the narrator reveres the "flower-covered field" as his Creator's altar, praising God "who creates joys" (in a callback to 1768's "An die Freude").

A similarly gentle, divine boyhood is evoked in K. 529, "Des kleinen Friedrichs Geburtstag" (Little Friedrich's Birthday), which Mozart composed in Prague in November 1787 (during the period he was conducting the premiere of *Don Giovanni* in that city). This Lied was not published in Mozart's lifetime, but it may have been originally intended for one of the two publications to which Mozart contributed Kinderlieder in the 1787–1788 period: the Vienna-based *Beschäftigung*, which published his "Die kleine Spinnerin" (K. 531) and "Lied beim Auszug in das Feld" (K. 552); or perhaps even for a publication by the Prague Normalschule, which had published his two *geistliche Lieder* "O Gottes Lamm" and "Als aus Ägypten" in the revised edition of the *Lieder zur öffentlichen und häuslichen Andacht* (see chapter 2 for more on both publications).

We can guess that K. 529 was intended as a Kinderlied because of its publication history prior to Mozart's setting. The poem "Des kleinen Friedrichs Geburtstag" first appeared in print anonymously in the 1778

Philanthropinist publication *Pädagogische Unterhandlungen* (Pedagogical Negotiations), edited by Basedow and Campe, under the title "Liebe um Liebe" (Love for Love).[109] It was in fact by Johann Friedrich Schall, a teacher at the Philanthropinum, and as the original postscript makes clear, it was meant to celebrate not just the ninth birthday of Dessau's crown prince Friedrich, but also the fourth anniversary of the founding of the Philanthropinum.[110] The verses describe Friedrich as "young and tender," "gentle like a little sheep, / and mild like a little dove."[111] "He went diligently / To school and to church"; and when his friends gathered together to celebrate his birthday, "What was seen and heard / Was song and dance and playing." The poem originally ended with a rousing "Es leb' Prinz Friederich!" (Long live Prince Friedrich!), but when Campe included it in a 1779 issue of his *Kleine Kinderbibliothek*, he added a stanza that elevated God as Friedrich's ultimate protector:

> And God in heaven above
> Granted their prayer;
> His blessing follows the boy
> Wherever he goes.[112]

Mozart set Campe's additional stanza as a coda, adding a level of unpredictability rare in Kinderlieder.

It was an oddly dated poem for Mozart to set in 1787: the crown prince was now eighteen, and had joined the Prussian Army the previous year. Neither he nor the Philanthropinum were celebrating any apparent anniversary, nor does Mozart appear to have had any close connections with the Philanthropinum personnel. But the poem seems to have taken on a life independent of its original purpose: the composer Johann Friedrich Reichardt had already set it in his first volume of *Lieder für Kinder aus Campes Kinderbibliothek*, from 1781.[113] It seems, then, that little Friedrich had been fixed at age five, to have come to represent an idealized boyhood, one that might even be emulated across political boundaries. Mozart may even have felt some common ground with this revered boy, frozen in time.

These contradictory attitudes toward boyhood—nostalgic, boisterous, reverent—converge on the last of Mozart's Kinderlieder to appear in the 1791 *Liedersammlung für Kinder und Kinderfreunde: Frühlingslieder*: "Das Kinderspiel" (K. 598). The *Frühlingslieder* had been dedicated to the Archduke Franz and Archduchess Marie Therese, who had married the previous September. The dedication figured the seasons as allegories of the royal succession and the ages of man, suggesting multiple levels on which parents and children were expected to understand the poems, their settings, and the political context of "spring":

> the summer of Austria rejoices in Leopold,
> and its springtime will someday rejoice in Francis. . . .
> So that someday the youth, for whom spring now dawns,
> in their summer will revere you, oh Prince,
> thus let these melting little spring songs here glide into their hearts—
> let them be dedicated to you.[114]

We might consider "Das Kinderspiel" as a counterpart to "Die kleine Spinnerin": it features a boy at play, who tears around outside with his "Brüder" in complete isolation from adults or their cares. Other songs in the *Liedersammlung* catalogue the emblems of spring from a degree of cool remove, in carefully constructed sentences that progress in orderly fashion from one idea to the next. "Das Kinderspiel," in contrast, is an unmediated expression of a boy's interior world: it proceeds in fits and spurts, conveying all the quicksilver energy and distractibility of a child at play. Moreover, it breaks with the pastoral clichés of nature imagery— nightingales, larks, violets, roses, babbling brooks. Instead, verbs take precedence over nouns, as the boys dash around in pursuit of that which strikes their momentary fancy. It is as though we have followed the Fritz of "Die kleine Spinnerin" out the front door of the spinner-girl's house and into the field.

It is worth considering this poem in full, as it paints a striking picture of boyhood as both active and gentle, unburdened yet self-aware. And joy is back, presented here as an indulgence, while keeping eroticism at arm's length.

> 1. We children enjoy [*schmecken*; literally, savor or taste]
> Many pleasures indeed!
> We tease, and play jokes
> (But, of course, only in sport)!
> We shout and we sing,
> And run around,
> And hop and spring
> About on the grass![115]

Stanzas 2 and 3 show a prescience about the cares to come with adulthood; the rejection of those cares in favor of the present moment approaches a radical act. Even the disavowal of description seems a critique of the portraiture found in other seasonal poems.

2. And why not? There's time
Enough yet for grousing!
Any grumbler among us
Would indeed be a fool.
How jolly to see
The corn and the grass!
To describe in words
Is beyond anyone's powers.

3. Hey, my brothers, run
And tumble in the grass!
We're still allowed to do it,
It's not unseemly yet.
If we were older,
It would not be proper;
We would walk around
Stiff-necked and cold.

Stanzas 4–8 narrate encounters with a butterfly and a bird, in which these evanescent, fragile creatures spark wonder and an impulse to shelter rather than to capture or exploit. In a section that recalls the Lied "Der Knabe beim Vogelfang" discussed in chapter 2, nature serves as an allegory for the boys' hesitant entry into the sexual economy, complete with hints of violence and regret.

4. Look, brothers,
There's a butterfly!
Who will catch it?
But please don't hurt it!
There's another,
Probably its friend;
But don't strike it
Or the other will cry!

5. Do I hear singing?
How wonderful it sounds!
Excellent, boys,

It's the nightingale!
There it sits, perched
High in the apple tree;
If we praise it
It will continue its song.

6. Come down to us, darling,
And let us see you!
Who taught you your songs?
You sing them so beautifully!
But don't let us disturb you,
Dear little bird!
All of us
Love to listen to you.

7. Where has it gone?
It's nowhere to be seen!
It's fluttering over there!
Come back, come here!
In vain, our joy
Is gone for the moment!
Someone must have hurt it
One way or another.

The final two stanzas establish family and the security of home, to which
the boy and his playmates will return at close of day. It becomes clear that
this security is the condition for the boys' peaceful, carefree explorations,
and the day is revealed as an allegory of the life cycle itself, with sunset a
harbinger of death.

8. Let us bind wreaths,
There are so many flowers!
Whoever finds violets
Will receive in return
A present from mother:
A sweetmeat or two.
Hurray, I've got one,
I've got one, hurrah!

9. Alas, is the sun
Going down so soon?

We're still lively and merry;
O sun, stay a while!
So, brothers, till tomorrow!
Sleep well! Good night!
Yes, tomorrow again
We'll laugh and we'll play![116]

The poem emerges as a critique of adult artificiality, an ode to the innocent play of the carefree child as an ideal Everyman. It recalls Johann Gottfried Herder's association, in the fourth of his *Kritische Wälder* and elsewhere, of both music and childhood with spontaneous, unmediated emotional expression.[117] This is exactly what Overbeck was after when he published the poem "Das Kinderspiel" in 1781, in a collection he called *Frizchens Lieder* (this collection also included "Fritzchen an den Mai," the poem Mozart set as "Sehnsucht nach dem Frühlinge," K. 596).[118] In his preface to the volume, Overbeck claimed that unlike other poems that might offer the expressions of children but "with the ideas of an adult," in *Frizchens Lieder* "a child really speaks."[119] For all of Fritz's "sauciness" and misbehavior, he possessed a sincerity Overbeck believed to be lacking in the angelic child figures of Weisse and his immediate successors. It was this quality that caused Hans-Heino Ewers to identify *Frizchens Lieder* as the watershed work in the "anti-authoritarian" strain of children's literature, the first work to employ the naïve subject-voice of the child.[120]

Ironically, however, Overbeck's attention to the "genuine" cadences of a child's voice ended up being further removed from the interests of children, and more oriented toward an adult readership, than Weisse's work had ever been. As Overbeck asserted in the preface to *Frizchens Lieder*, "It should remain a pleasure for us adults, to see the little fellow wander here and there."[121] Overbeck even went so far as to mark out fifteen of the forty-nine poems as inappropriate for child readers, betraying an awareness of age categories first established by Campe.[122] A similar adult orientation pervades Mozart's setting of "Das Kinderspiel," owing chiefly to its ambiguous representation of the persona of the singer. To understand what is unusual about this setting, it will be helpful to compare it with two earlier settings of the poem: Georg Carl Claudius's setting of 1780 and Johann Friedrich Reichardt's of 1781. Both of these settings render the amphibrach metrical foot of "Das Kinderspiel" ("Wir *Kin*-der, wir *schmeck*-en die *Freu*-den recht *viel*") in fairly straightforward fashion: Claudius as even eighths in an almost *pesante* 3/8, with an eighth-note anacrusis; and Reichardt as a dactylic rhythm in 2/4 meter, again with an eighth-note anacrusis.

FIGURE 4.6. (a) Georg Carl Claudius, "Das Kinderspiel," in *Lieder für Kinder* (Frankfurt, 1780), 14. Courtesy of SUB Göttingen, shelfmark DD2001.A.395. (b) Johann Friedrich Reichardt, "Das Kinderspiel," in *Lieder für Kinder* (Hamburg, 1781), vol. 1, 3. Courtesy of SLUB Dresden; http://digital.slub-dresden.de/id 415087503; Mus.3922.K.2.

For his setting, Mozart chooses a 3/8 meter akin to Claudius's. However, Mozart shortens the anacrusis from an eighth note to a sixteenth note, resulting in a breathless effect that, on fivefold repetition, paradoxically emphasizes the unstressed syllables ("*Wir* Kinder, *wir* schmecken . . . *Wir* schäkern, *und* näckern, *ver*steht sich im Spiel").

Mozart's rhythmic setting vividly illustrates Fritz's short attention span and almost overwhelmingly propulsive energy, particularly appropriate for the first stanza. After all, what could be more authentically boylike than a tumble of verbs related with such excitement that the pronouns and conjunctions begin to take over in an almost breathless stream

FIGURE 4.7. Mozart, "Das Kinderspiel" (K. 598), in *Liedersammlung für Kinder und Kinderfreunde: Frühlingslieder*, ed. Partsch (Vienna, 1791), XXIV. Courtesy of Österreichische Nationalbibliothek, shelfmark MS27064-qu.4°/2,24.

of consciousness? The hiccupping sixteenth-note anacruses that convey that excitement, however, require a higher degree of skill on the part of the singer than did Claudius's or Reichardt's simpler rhythms. In addition, the keyboard's two-voiced accompaniment, with its sixteenth-note broken-chord pattern in the left hand, demands a fine level of coordination between singer and accompanist. In short, Mozart's "Das Kinderspiel," while childlike in effect, is mature in its technical demands. To put it another way: the more faithfully Overbeck, and after him, Mozart, sought to represent the interior life of a child, the less accessible the Kinderlied became to a child reader.[123]

This paradox will be familiar from writing on a related aesthetic category, *Volkstümlichkeit*: in appropriating folklore for a middle- and upper-class readership, poets cast it in a more elite register. In the preface to the second edition of his *Lieder im Volkston* (1785), Johann Abraham Peter Schulz qualified the *Volkston* thus: "In this appearance of the familiar lies the entire secret of the *Volkston*; but one must not confuse it with the familiar itself; the latter awakens boredom in all artists."[124] A similar fear of the pedestrian marks the discourse surrounding children's poetry: following the publication of *Frizchens Lieder*, a fellow member of the Göttinger Hain warned Overbeck against sinking into the "kindisch."[125]

There was a thin line, it seems, between childlike and childish, just as between the folklike and the folkish.

Connections between the two pairs of terms were made even more explicitly by Herder. Nine years before the first edition of Johann Abraham Peter Schulz's *Lieder im Volkston*, and five years before Herder's own *Volkslieder* (1778–1779), he coined the term *Kinderton*, in his 1773 *Von deutscher Art und Kunst* (On German Character and Art). In the context of a discussion of Ossian, Herder quoted from Goethe's "Heidenröslein," a poem that is still held up as the exemplar of *Volkstümlichkeit*:

> . . . In our time there is so much talk of songs for children. Do you want to hear an older German [one]? It contains no transcendental wisdom and morality, with which children will soon enough be bombarded—it is nothing but a childish fable-songlet.[126]

Herder did not interpret Goethe's poem as a *Volkslied*. Nor did he seek to apologize for or explain away the childish in "Heidenröslein." Rather, after quoting the poem, including its "childish refrain," Herder concluded, "Ist das nicht Kinderton?"[127] This poem, in other words, was a Kinderlied before it was a Volkslied. And the category of the *kindertümlich* made a path for the *volkstümlich*.[128]

In the Kinderlieder of Mozart and his contemporaries, then, we find song marshalled as an aspect of the Philanthropinist *Spielpädagogik*, and a tool of moral education. Kinderlieder represent in this way a coopting of playtime, an invasion of domestic space. At the same time, the self-reflexive stance of Kinderlieder like "Die kleine Spinnerin" and "Das Kinderspiel" also captures a threshold moment, between music for children and music invoking childhood as a form of spiritual antidote or inoculation—between Lieder "für Kinder" and "für Kinderfreunde." This is the reason for the premature nostalgia expressed in "Das Kinderspiel," as when Fritz observes, "There's time enough yet for grousing! . . . If we were older . . . we would walk around stiff-necked and cold." That sense—expressed before the fact, by the child himself—that time is running out on the idyll of youth, is part of the Romantic idealization of childhood that was by 1791 already well underway.

Kinderlieder constitute, for perhaps the first and only time in European music, an amateur repertoire meant to be shared between young and old. To imagine these songs in performance is to imagine a space where parents, children, and siblings might listen to one another as they traded verses in a song, taking turns and developing together a vocabulary of shared sentiment (one that, as we will see in the next chapter, extended to instrumental music). At the same time, Kinderlieder established and inculcated gender roles in the family, training boys and girls in the proper ways to view and practice playing and reading, always under the watchful eye of an equally trained parent. An attention to Mozart's Lieder that thematize play and childhood, and to the repertoires and traditions from which they accumulate their meanings, reveals the complex blend of obedience and rebellion that Mozart embodied and helped reify as "childlike."

CHAPTER 5

Cadences of the Childlike

Just as Kinderlieder represented children's play as both metaphor and training ground for adult labor, so too could chamber music serve as both metaphor and training ground for familial affection. In this chapter, I interpret Mozart's instrumental music for siblings, parents, and children as a form of musical family portrait, and also as an opportunity to rehearse the new ideal of the affectionate family. This is not to say that adults did not feel affection for children until the Enlightenment (or a decrease in infant mortality) gave them permission to do so. The many responses to Philippe Ariès's foundational historicizing study of childhood, *Centuries of Childhood* (*L'Enfant et la vie familiale sous l'ancien régime*, 1960), have confirmed that truism.[1] What was new, however, was the notion that this love was worthy of sustained reflection, cultivation, and display. We have already encountered the ideal of an all-consuming love for children in the Philanthropinist movement and in literature for "Kinderfreunde." In the first issue of Christian Felix Weisse's *Der Kinderfreund*, for instance, the fictional *paterfamilias* Mentor professes to love his children "more than all the treasures of the earth, more than the whole world, yes, I almost want to say, more than my life."[2] Chamber music ritualized this all-consuming familial devotion, allowing middle-class families to join their aristocratic counterparts in ritualizing the closely bonded family.

Three instrumental works by Mozart exemplify the musical family ritual: the Concerto for Three Keyboards, K. 242 (composed in Salzburg in 1776), the Concerto for Flute and Harp, K. 299 (composed in Paris in 1778), and the Sonata for Four Hands, K. 521 (composed in Vienna in 1787). All three pieces were composed or published with specific parents, children, and siblings in mind. K. 242 was composed for the Countess Antonia Lodron and her two daughters, Aloisia and Josepha, who were at the time aged fourteen and eleven. K. 299 was composed for the

Duc de Guînes to perform with his daughter, Marie-Louise-Philippine. As for K. 521, Mozart originally shared it with one of his students, Franziska von Jacquin, but when it was published, the sonata was dedicated to two unmarried sisters, Nanette and Babette Natorp.

In all three pieces, the historical personas of the original performers and dedicatees suggest instrumental personas based on family bonds. Like all portraitists, Mozart knew he was expected first and foremost to flatter his patrons.[3] But these works are portraits of archetypes as well as of individuals. The four-hand sonata layers a close sisterly bond over the teacher-student relationship. The triple concerto stages compromise and turn-taking between a mother and her two daughters. The concerto for flute and harp enshrines cooperation and autonomy between a father and daughter. In explicitly associating this music with particular family members, Mozart thematized those relationships, inviting identification on the part of performers and listeners, just as the sentimental novels and plays of the period did for their readers and audiences.

As Edward Klorman and Simon Keefe have shown, the act of imputing allegorical personas to instrumental voices in chamber and orchestral music goes back at least as far as Heinrich Christoph Koch's *Musical Lexicon* (1802), and arguably to Johann Georg Sulzer's *General Theory of the Fine Arts* (1774).[4] Meanwhile, Wye J. Allanbrook argues that the instrumental music of Mozart is suffused with "comic-opera values," as topics are arranged in an interplay of sharply drawn characters.[5] But whereas music historians like Allanbrook, Keefe, Klorman, and others interpret the instrumental music of this period through metaphors of conversation or drama, we might just as easily consider these pieces as a kind of dance: a wordless, circumscribed, yet also fundamentally dynamic and unpredictable form of social engagement and display.[6]

There is nothing particularly new about associating eighteenth-century music with dance—it is, after all, the foundation of topic theory. But while topic theory describes music's materials and vocabulary as rooted in dance, what I intend by the association between this music and dance is something broader: the phenomenological, corporeal experience of making music with family members, and—crucially—the silence that accompanies these acts. The lack of words attached to both dance and instrumental music was a frequent source of concern for critics and philosophers intent on the moral function of the arts. It could also be a respite: in a society teeming with conversation, it afforded, in the words of one of Jane Austen's characters, the "luxury of silence."[7] John Dussinger writes that the most revealing moments in Austen are moments of encounter, which he defines as "a radically focused interaction, to reveal

nuances of behavior."[8] Like balls and card games in Austen, these three
works by Mozart offer equally revealing pretexts for encounter—in this
case, an encounter between family members. And the nuances of behavior they reveal, as well as the social implications attending such encounters, were still very much in flux.

Mozart knew well what it meant to be part of a music-making family:
it was not just his lived experience, but also a key aspect of his brand from
the beginning of his public career, as the 1763 Delafosse engraving discussed in chapter 1 (which his family continued to peddle in the 1770s)
makes clear.[9] Mozart's close bonds with his father and sister were played
out on the stages of Europe when he was still a preadolescent—and these
bonds were entwined with the genre of the keyboard duet itself. The kind
of close-knit family exemplified both by the Mozarts themselves, and by
Mozart's music for families, was mediated through performances and
prints that traversed public and private spaces. This informed the ways
audiences might have heard (and the way we now might hear) sibling and
parent-child exchanges in his later music—just as Mozart's own childhood, like the Delafosse engraving, followed him into his adult years.

Interpreting this music benefits from an attention to "multiple agency,"
an approach to chamber music articulated by Klorman that foregrounds
"the role musicians play in enacting the social interplay for which the
score is but a script."[10] This narratological method, driven by texture,
bears resemblances to Jessica Waldoff's "reading for the plot" in Mozart's
operas. Like operas, four-hand sonatas and multiple concertos involve
"characters in action on the stage who have motivations and goals and
who become embroiled in conflicts that depend for their resolution on
the course of events."[11] We might imagine "performing and/or listening
personae," as Tom Beghin does when interpreting the music Haydn composed for his students.[12] Or, with Roger Moseley, we might hear such
music embodying a ludic impulse that reaches back to the *lazzi* of the
commedia dell'arte, and prefigures the cooperative multiplayer games of
the digital age.[13] To return to the dance metaphor, I see such scores as
functioning less like scripts or librettos, and more like scenarios for pantomimes, or step notations for ballets or ballroom dances. Characters or
personae are still involved, but their movements possess both spatial and
temporal meanings, both fixed and flexible aspects, unfolding wordless
plots that rely heavily on convention and improvisation for their legi-
bility.

The music's emotional registers may be equally protean—after all,
until one of Austen's characters speaks, they might be feeling or thinking
anything during a ballroom dance, and their physical movements might

often be in witty or poignant opposition to their thoughts or conversation. Klorman writes that the string quartet can suggest "gamesmanship and competition" just as easily as cooperation and compromise.[14] The same is true of any music for more than one player. Family dynamics are complex, and allegories of family dynamics across all kinds of media addressed far more than just affection or obedience. Naomi Miller has described sibling relations in Shakespeare's *Tempest*, for instance, as "portals into constructions of domination and desire, longing and loss, across a range of social and familial relations."[15] Mozart's three pieces under consideration here offer similar representations of family bonds, in all their irreducibility.

Intimacies at the Keyboard: Music for Four Hands

Although the 1763 Carmontelle portrait did not depict Wolfgang and Nannerl sitting together at the keyboard, keyboard duos were a staple of their performances throughout their European tour.[16] The varying press accounts suggest that the siblings performed a combination of concerto reductions, sonatas, pieces with improvised obbligatos (sometimes at a separate keyboard), and even parlor tricks involving handkerchiefs covering the keys.[17] They also performed on newly invented instruments, such as the large two-manual harpsichord by Burkat Shudi in 1765.[18] The novelty of the pair of siblings was often matched, therefore, by the novelty of the instruments at which they sat.

Music for keyboard four-hands was equally novel in the 1760s. For a long time, it was believed that the Sonata for Four Hands, K. 19d (pub. 1788), no longer attributed to Mozart, was the first publication in the genre. As Cliff Eisen has shown, there are references to manuscript four-hand sonatas in the 1760s, now lost, but the first surviving four-hand print dates to 1772: Louis-Joseph Saint-Amans's punningly titled *Quartetto per il cembalo, qui doit s'éxécuter par deux personnes sur le meme Instrument*.[19] A "quartet for keyboard" must have sounded like science fiction in 1772, given that string quartets themselves were still relatively new (Haydn's Opus 1 was first published in 1764). Mozart's first definitively attributable sonatas for four hands, K. 381 (123a) and K. 358 (186c), also date from the period 1772–1774, though they were not published until 1783. The five sonatas and one set of variations he composed for four hands were all published during his lifetime—which, as Marianne Stoelzel points out, is rare for Mozart's music.[20] This suggests an immediate connection between this genre and the marketplace, which, as we shall see, led to a response to the genre from within printed children's literature.

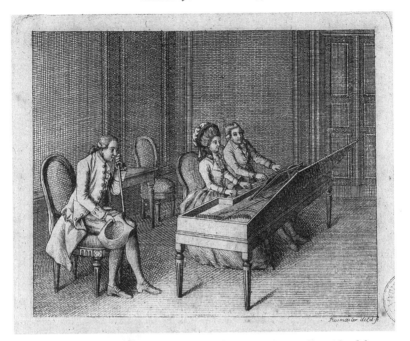

FIGURE 5.1. Johann August Rosmaesler, title page engraving, Franz Seydelmann, *Sechs Sonaten für Zwo Personen auf einem Clavier* (Leipzig, 1781). Courtesy of SLUB Dresden, shelfmark Mus.3550-T-2.

What might this new genre have meant to its first consumers? The intimacy of two bodies in close proximity at a single keyboard was surely noteworthy in an age that, as we have already seen, choreographed with anxious precision even the most benign and fleeting forms of public physical contact between adult men and women. The risks of unsupervised contact were already evidently of concern in 1781, when Franz Seydelmann published his *Six Sonatas for Two Persons at One Clavier* (fig. 5.1).[21] The title page engraving shows an adult man and woman at a clavichord, the woman taking the primo, the man the secondo. A decorous distance is maintained between their bodies, while a male onlooker assures the reader that the couple are not alone. The onlooker, however, leans forward as though captivated—whether by the music or by the closeness of the players, it's difficult to say.

The onlooker recalls Basedow and Chodowiecki's grandfather supervising the children's outdoor dance in *Das Elementarwerk* (discussed in chapter 4), a bulwark against arousal. After all, the theorist Meinrad Spiess's 1745 treatise on composition—a copy of which was in Leopold Mozart's library—had described chamber music as, among other things,

Die Musik.

FIGURE 5.2. Chodowiecki, "Music," from "Occupations des Dames," *Almanac de Berlin* (Berlin, 1781). Courtesy of Herzog August Bibliothek, shelfmark Uh 4° 47 (161).

"zur Lieb reitzend" (love-provoking).[22] And the close proximity at a single instrument partook in a long painterly tradition, from Vermeer to Jean-Honoré Fragonard to Pietro Longhi, of the music lesson and domestic music-making as a prelude to courtship.[23] Another engraving showing two bodies at one keyboard is "Music," from the 1781 series *Occupations des Dames*, again by Chodowiecki (fig. 5.2). Although not strictly speaking a four-hands duo, the young man pokes suggestively at one of the keys. And in contrast to the Seydelmann engraving, the closeness

FIGURE 5.3. Attr. Johann Nepomuk della Croce, *The Mozart Family* (1780/1781). © Internationale Stiftung Mozarteum.

between the two bodies leaves little doubt that music is here a pretext for physical intimacy.[24]

The keyboard could, however, be a site of platonic rather than romantic encounters, whether between teachers and students or family members. The famous portrait of the Mozart family by Johann Nepomuk della Croce, also from 1780–1781, sets the intimacy of four-hand music within a domestic space that also referenced the Mozarts' public personas (fig. 5.3). In one sense, it can be viewed as a kind of sequel or response to the 1763 Carmontelle portrait.

Leopold has replaced Nannerl as the odd one out, no longer shown playing his violin as in the Carmontelle portrait or the frontispiece to his *Violinschule*, but waiting expectantly while holding the symbol of his most noteworthy contribution to music history. Meanwhile, his two children, grown but as yet unmarried, take equal charge of the harpsichord. Samuel Breene has written of the foregrounding of "digital dexterity" in the portrait, describing the entwining of Wolfgang's right hand and Nannerl's left hand as "a stylized display of sibling warmth and affection. . . . His transgression of her melodic space appears as a gesture of tenderness rather than aggression."[25] To my knowledge, none of Mozart's keyboard duos feature this explicit of a hand-crossing, but of course, as Leppert argues of the conversation piece portrait, such paintings are revealing not so much of actual musical practices but of the family bonds and social conventions that gave them meaning.[26]

The portrait of the Mozarts, especially when read in dialogue with the earlier Carmontelle portrait, has something of an air of nostalgia. Wolfgang and Nannerl were now in their twenties, but there were multiple accounts of the siblings continuing to play four-hands throughout this period, particularly when guests were visiting.[27] Beyond tenderness, then, Wolfgang's right arm overlapping Nannerl's left also conveys a certain comedy in their grown bodies struggling to make space together at the keyboard—something that would have been much easier when they were children. In 1789, Daniel Gottlob Türk's *Klavierschule* (School of Clavier Playing)—which was written with the clavichord in mind—recommended four-hand sonatas by Mozart and others for cultivating accuracy in counting and entrances.[28] Türk went on to warn, however, against playing too many keyboard duets, "because they can have a detrimental effect on finger placement and especially on the position of hands and arms; because for the most part both people must sit fairly pressed together, their hands twisted, and so on."[29] Although Türk had a clavichord in mind in the *Klavierschule*, and this is a harpsichord, the challenge of maintaining physical composure and decorum while pressed together has always been part of the spectacle of four-hands repertoire.

Keyboard music for four hands was particularly suited to families, where the bodies of women and children might more easily (and irreproachably) accommodate the close proximity called for by the instrument. In 1777, Charles Burney composed a set of *Four Sonatas or Duets for Two Performers on One Piano Forte*, to which he appended a preface noting that they are particularly well suited when there are "two students upon the same keyed-instrument in one house." With Burney's music, rather than being in each other's way, "they become reciprocally useful, and necessary companions in their musical exercises."[30] Burney seemed here to acknowledge a common struggle within larger families for keyboard time, turning it into a pedagogical asset. Music could thus be marshalled as a means of smoothing over domestic conflict.

Four-hands music was also touted as a pedagogical tool, something Mozart took part in as a teacher. We know that he played his early four-hand sonatas, K. 381 and 358, from manuscript with several of his students.[31] He also performed duets with Johann Nepomuk Hummel, his live-in student from 1786 to 1788, and he composed K. 448 (the Sonata in D Major for Two Keyboards) to perform with his Vienna student, Josepha Auernhammer.[32] This was a common enough practice to be satirized in Joseph Haydn's four-hand theme and variations, *Il Maestro e [lo] scolare*, composed ca. 1768–1770 and published by Hummel in 1781. The piece is an extended essay in call-and-response between the *secondo* "maestro" and his *primo* "scolare."[33] Tom Beghin has offered three equally compelling interpretations of the excessively difficult cut-key fingerings in the *secondo* part, whose counterparts in the *primo* are easy to sight-read. If the *secondo* was not intended to be playable, it could have been Haydn's way of mocking mediocre teachers. Alternatively, if the "Maestro" is able to pull off the fingerings, it could either be a skit (autobiographical?) about the overqualified teacher combating boredom, or an effort to flatter a lesser student by making them sound more virtuosic than they were.[34] Whatever the implication—and of course none are mutually exclusive—a platonic exchange of hands, voices, personalities, and personas is at the heart of this little comedy.[35] The popularity of these and other keyboard duos likely prompted Mozart to decide to publish the first of his duos in 1783 with Artaria, as his Opus 3 with the publisher.

Sibling Harmony in the Sonata in C Major for Keyboard Four Hands, K. 521

The attribution of personas to Haydn's *Il Maestro e scolare* requires no great effort of imagination, given the piece's programmatic title. But what if the four-hands piece is simply a numbered sonata, as with K. 521? We might look first to the dedication on the 1787 print: "aux Demoiselles Nanette, et Babette de Nattorp." Maria Anna (Nanette) and Maria Barbara (Babette) Natorp were twenty-two and eighteen years old, and both were still living at home, the unmarried daughters of a Vienna merchant, Franz Wilhelm Natorp, who was a friend of the Mozarts and the Jacquins. One or both of the daughters may have been students of Mozart's, or of his other student Auernhammer.[36]

Several details suggest that we pay close attention to this dedication. The first is that this is the only work of Mozart's for keyboard four-hands that was published with a dedication. Moreover, as already mentioned, Mozart originally sent the manuscript sonata to his student Franziska von Jacquin, offering it to her through her husband, Mozart's friend Gottfried von Jacquin.[37] But when Hoffmeister first published the sonata, it was dedicated not to Franziska, but to the Natorps. Furthermore, the sisters' Christian names were not used, but rather their childhood nicknames, Nanette and Babette. Mozart was not the first to dedicate music to a pair of sisters: Haydn had published a set of six solo keyboard sonatas in 1780 as Opus 30 (his first Artaria publication), which were dedicated to the virtuoso keyboardists Marianna and Katarina Auenbrugger.[38] But Mozart's sonata was for keyboard duo, and that, along with the nicknames, would have encouraged those who purchased the print to imagine the sisters playing the piece together.

Another clue as to the dramatic implications of K. 521 appears in a story for children published a year after the sonata. The story first appeared in the 1788 *Moralische Kinderklapper für Kinder und Nichtkinder* (Moral Children's Rattle for Children and Nonchildren), a story collection by Johann Karl August Musäus printed in Gotha.[39] The collection was freely adapted from a 1784 French volume, *Les hochets moraux*, but this story, "Harmonie" (Harmony), was new to the German version. "Harmonie" is a story of two pairs of sisters, one bad and one good. The bad sisters, Hannchen and Fiekchen, are spoiled by their father (a magistrate) and mother, respectively. There is always quarreling in the house, with each daughter pitting their favored parent against the other. In an effort to remedy the situation, their aunt offers to take the sisters with her for a visit to her city residence. They willingly come along for the urban adventure, and are soon introduced to the good pair of sisters in the city, Lottchen and Gustgen. Unlike the bickering country sisters, Lottchen and Gustgen are "adorned with every charm of youth, gentle as the first morning light in the spring sky, twinned more through sympathy more than through birth, one heart and one soul."[40]

No sooner have Hannchen and Fiekchen arrived for their visit than they begin once again to argue. In order to cover up the discord ("Mißlaut"), Lottchen sits down "full of grace" at the keyboard, Gustgen follows her, and "the two conjured forth, in Mozart's mellifluous chords, the most entrancing sonata for four hands." It is remarkable to see a composer singled out and named in this way—the collection includes no other such callouts, and children's fiction from this period rarely references living artists in passing.

The story continues:

> In sweet harmony, soul and heart were combined with every swan-white hand that, here with quick suspensions [*Wechselgängen*], there with melodious union, fluently translated the artist's musical notation from the page into something familiar [i.e., music].[41]

As in Breene's discussion of the Della Croce portrait, the focus again is on hands.[42] In "Harmonie," the "swan-white hand[s]" of the sisters become disembodied, serving as the conduits between the souls and hearts of the

FIGURE 5.4. Illustration to "Harmonie," in Johann Karl August Musäus, *Moralische Kinderklapper* (Gotha, 1794), 77. Courtesy of Bayerische Staatsbibliothek München, shelfmark Augsburg, Staats- und Stadtbibliothek LD 4966.

two exemplary sisters, just as Mozart himself is the conduit between Harmony itself and the sisters. Even the use of the term "Wechselgängen" allegorizes the resolution of musical tension in terms of sisterly "consonance."[43] When the *Moralische Kinderklapper* was reprinted in 1794, an engraving was included above the title of the story, depicting this moment, which was clearly seen by the engraver and editor as the crux of the story (fig. 5.4).

Once the music has ended, the aunt tells the two bickering sisters:

> "See there an example of like-minded souls, and feel the effect of sisterly harmony. . . . Concord [*Eintracht*] was the creatress of the silver tones that delighted you and me; she alone animated Lottchen's hand, ruled Gustgen's finger. But where Discord [*Zwietracht*] moves the tangents [*Tangenten*], there is wailing: because she breeds only vain dissonance, and to such a harsh melody, one can hardly sing or dance."[44]

The country sisters, chastened, turn to each other, and the story concludes with their pledge to improve their behavior and cultivate that sisterly harmony so expertly modeled to them at the keyboard.

The identity of the sonata played by Lottchen and Gustgen remains a mystery, but it is unlikely to have been K. 521.[45] Musäus died in Weimar on October 28, 1787, and the posthumous preface by the publisher Friedrich Justin Bertuch is dated November 14. Musäus might have had in mind one of Mozart's two earlier four-hand sonatas published in 1783 (K. 381 and 358), which were still in print in 1787. Given that the sonata was completed on May 29, 1787, but not published by Hoffmeister until 1788, after the *Moralische Kinderklapper* was published, there is a tantalizing (though slim) possibility that Mozart, or Hoffmeister, might have chosen to dedicate K. 521 to the Natorp sisters in order to chime with the story in the *Moralische Kinderklapper*, rather than the other way around. Regardless, one can imagine a family reading Musäus's story aloud, perhaps even acting it out and playing one of Mozart's keyboard duos as they came to that point in the action, as they would have done with countless other skits, plays, and operas included in the children's periodicals and collections of the day. Musäus, in a sense, was creating the music cue for his own play; and the didactic functions of both would have been familiar to Mozart and his consumers. As the physician and amateur musician Amand Wilhelm Smith had written in his *Philosophical Fragments on Practical Music*, published in Vienna the same year as K. 521 (and in Mozart's library at the time of his death), "in education, music is as appropriate as any other method that is used to make humans compliant and civilized."[46]

Tracking "sisterly harmony" in K. 521 involves a focus on changes in texture, for it is in textural expanse and variety that the extra pair of hands at the keyboard is most marked. The serene second movement is an Andante in ternary form with a stormy B section.[47] The opening period of the A section is relatively blocky, with repetitive rests at the end of each two-bar phrase (ex. 5.1). This might have come across as stilted were it not for the shifting configurations of voices between the four hands. In the first two-measure phrase, the four hands form a kind of trio, with the *primo*'s right hand establishing the *cantabile* theme. The *secondo*'s leap to the F above middle C in m. 1 puts it a mere third away from the *primo*'s left hand, bringing the two players' hands and bodies into extraordinarily close proximity right at the outset. In the second phrase (mm. 3–4), the texture expands to five lines, and the voices proceed in a chorale-like homophonic texture. The third phrase (mm. 5–6) changes the texture again, with the low F in the *secondo* ushering in a passage of parallel tenths

EXAMPLE 5.1. Mozart, Sonata in C for Keyboard Four Hands, K. 521, movement 2 (Andante), mm. 1–8

that gives way to counterpoint, the two right hands diverging away from each other, then twining back at the end in a curlicue, duet at its most tender. The five-voice chorale returns in the final phrase (mm. 7–8) to create a textural (and topical) "rhyme" between the second and fourth phrases.

The give-and-take in this passage is unlike anything Mozart had written for four hands up to now. The slow movements of K. 381, 358, and 497 all maintained a relatively static texture that we might call "superkeyboard," where the two outer hands take the melody and bass, sometimes trading roles, while the inner hands offer arpeggiated accompaniment patterns.[48] In the second movement of K. 521, though, the variety of textural combinations in just these first eight bars evokes the multilayered conversations of a string quartet—appropriate, since Mozart's acclaimed and highly self-conscious "Haydn" quartets had been published two years earlier, in 1785.

The third and final movement of K. 521 is a rondo that proceeds at an unhurried Allegretto tempo. The unassuming, singsong, *volkstümlich* quality of the *dolce* rondo theme (ex. 5.2, mm. 20–27) recalls Mozart's variations on "Ah, vous dirais-je maman," K. 265, also in C major, which had been published in Vienna in 1785. The tonic drone in the *secondo*'s left hand evokes those pastoral notes Allanbrook traced in *The Marriage of Figaro*, composed the previous year: glimpses of a "green world" where, as she put it, "human nature can discover—or is it rediscover?—the dim traces of its most natural bonds."[49] It is fitting that in a sonata dedicated to two sisters, the final movement should begin with such a childlike pastoral tune.

Like all green worlds, the *Eintracht* or "concord" of this movement must be threatened if there is to be any drama, and the contrasting episode kicks off at mm. 28–29 with military fanfares in four octaves—an energetic contrast to the *dolce* rondo theme. (These fanfares also recall the opening gestures of movement 1.) It is the way these fanfares are eventually absorbed back into the rondo theme that is so striking about this movement. In the first episode, the fanfare winds down for a smooth transition to the theme. The second, minor-mode episode barrels through, even including a crescendo, until it is replaced by the return of the *dolce* rondo theme, like the reveal at the end of a magic trick (ex. 5.3, mm. 142–43). This moment is echoed in Musäus's story, when the bickering sisters are drowned out by Lottchen and Gustgen's "silver tones," *Eintracht* overcoming aggression. As Allanbrook writes, the "shelter" of the pastoral "is substantial precisely because it can coexist with the harsher realities of the daylight world."[50] Here, the singsong pastoral rondo theme casually displaces the fanfare and brilliant topics that had briefly threatened its serenity.

In the final bars of the movement, the two voices cooperate to reinterpret the X-section music from the rondo theme as material for the cadential close. This device recalls the conclusion to the letter duet from act 3 of *Figaro*, with "Che soave zeffiretto" another hymn to sisterly companionship and cooperation. Susanna and the Countess's vocal lines begin to loop around one another at the end of the duet, as the harmonic motion both speeds up and becomes simpler. The steady reassertion of the cadence in each piece reminds us of Allanbrook's other observation about the pastoral: it is that "special place in which [women] move, beyond the ordinary limits [of] men, strenuously occupied by their particular callings."[51] Like the letter duet, K. 521 exalts the female bond.

We cannot know what inspired Musäus (if it was even him) to write

EXAMPLE 5.2. K. 521, movement 3 (Allegretto), mm. 20–29

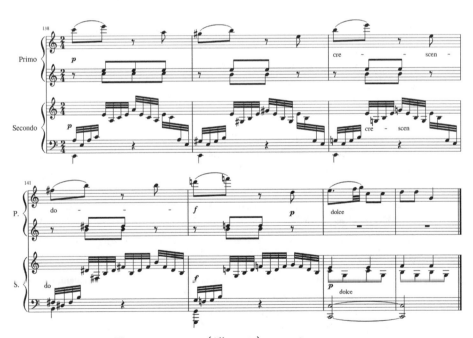

EXAMPLE 5.3. K. 521, movement 3 (Allegretto), mm. 138–44

"Harmonie," or to associate Mozart with the ennobling of sisterly affection. But the subsequent editions of the *Moralische Kinderklapper* all retained the "Harmonie" tale, the engraving, and the reference to Mozart, up to the revised edition of 1823, nearly forty years later. The affinity between Mozart's four-hands music and sibling bonds evidently had a long reach. Rebecca Cypess has interpreted music for two keyboards in the context of Enlightenment sympathy and Moses Mendelssohn's ideal of "unity in variety." As Cypess describes it, "united in both bodily motions and musical sentiments, players of keyboard duos could rehearse the formation of sympathetic bonds even as they articulated their individual identities."[52] If anything, those bonds were even closer when the two players were seated together at one instrument.

Music as a marker of, and catalyst for, sibling affection also appears in Kinderlieder like "Brüderliche Eintracht" (Brotherly Concord), from the second edition of Weisse's *Lieder für Kinder* (1769) set by Johann Adam Hiller. This Lied unfolds over four verses that are traded between a brother and sister, followed by a closing verse for both siblings. The first refrain reads: "These must truly be siblings, / Because their love is tremendous!"[53] For the final stanza, not only do the brother and sister sing together—they sing in ("brotherly") harmony. The right hand of the keyboard splits into two staves, with the sister presumably taking the top line and the brother harmonizing a third below. At the final appearance of the refrain, Hiller adds a point of imitation, allowing the upper voice to ascend higher than in the previous verses, enhancing the poignancy of the duet. The text now reads: "Where hearts stand in alliance, / Only there is the first blood-relationship beautiful!"[54] Like "Brüderliche Eintracht," K. 521 captures an everyday intimacy between siblings (both the Natorp sisters and the Mozart siblings), while also inculcating values of harmony and collaboration. Literary historians Naomi Miller and Naomi Yavneh have noted that sibling relations are often eclipsed by "the family ties most obviously associated with issues of power and authority— parenthood and marriage."[55] If that was where the Natorp sisters, and the Mozart siblings, were eventually headed, Mozart's four-hand keyboard works nevertheless make room for this unique sibling bond in order to demonstrate its redemptive power.

Making Room and Taking Turns in the Concerto in F Major for Three Keyboards, K. 242

Mozart's multiple concertos for parents and children do not appear to have been memorialized in fiction as Mozart's keyboard duos were in the *Moralische Kinderklapper*. But they still staged domesticity within the (semi-)public space of the concert. Between 1774 and 1780, Mozart composed six double or multiple concertos, some identified as *concertone* or *symphonie concertante*. There are several possible explanations for the uptick in this period. To begin with, these were fashionable genres in the two cities, Mannheim and Paris, in which Mozart was living and working in the late 1770s.[56] The genre may have also appealed to Mozart as a compositional challenge, a chance to tackle complexities of texture and orchestration, not to mention the special delight of a shared cadenza.

Of these multiple concertos, K. 242 and K. 299 appear to have been the only two composed to order for specific family members, both in spring 1778. Might we then, as with K. 521, listen for family dynamics in these concertos? Given what we know, and what Mozart knew, about the people for whom he was composing, it stands to reason that such a theatrically minded composer might approach the concerto as he would an opera role. After all, just two years later Mozart would include in a letter to his father the oft-quoted remark about liking "an aria to fit a singer as perfectly as a well-made suit of clothes."[57]

Yet a multiple concerto is not just theatrical. In his book on dramatic dialogue in Mozart's piano concertos, Simon Keefe has argued that while the more public genre of the concerto represents "the dialogue principle" in its theatrical register, chamber music invokes a more domestic register of dialogue.[58] K. 242 and 299, then, are compelling candidates for an exploration of the overlap between these two registers. In placing a duo or trio on stage in front of an orchestra, they nest the conversational within the theatrical.[59] Perhaps we might stretch Keefe's dialogical interpretation of the piano concertos to encompass networks of dialogue among the soloists as well as between the soloist group and the orchestra. And, as with J. S. Bach's concertos for three and four harpsichords (BWV 1063–1065, ca. 1730), or C. P. E. Bach's concerto for keyboard and piano (Wq. 47, 1788), another key aspect of the multiple keyboard concerto is the sheer spectacle of multiplying large, expensive, often novel instruments onstage.[60] To perform one in one's residence, for instance, one had to possess or have access to multiple keyboards, inevitably a sign of great wealth.

As its dedication makes clear, K. 242 was composed for the Countess Lodron to perform with her two daughters, fourteen-year-old Aloisia and eleven-year-old Josepha.[61] When scholars do refer to the concerto, it is usually to dismiss the third keyboard part as little more than bench-warming for Josepha, assuming the parts were distributed in descending order of age. This dismissal is especially tempting since Wolfgang later adapted the work for two pianos for performance with his sister Nannerl—an arrangement, Marius Flothius writes witheringly, "in which [Mozart] needed to sacrifice very little of the substance."[62] But perhaps we should not be so quick to dismiss Josepha Lodron. We know that the sisters studied keyboard with Leopold, and that they played in Salzburg's preeminent amateur orchestra. Of course, as one of Salzburg's most prominent aristocratic families, the Lodrons hosted the orchestra's weekly concerts. But Leopold reported with pride to Wolfgang that by June 11, 1778, they had "each played three times already" (perhaps including the premiere of K. 242) and "did themselves and myself great credit," including a June 7 performance at which Aloisia played a concerto by Andrea Lucchesi "very well indeed."[63] Leopold was never one to mince words about other musicians' skills, especially with his own son, so he was clearly satisfied with their playing.

Two subsequent performances of the concerto show what a crowd-pleaser it was. The first took place in Augsburg the following October, at a publicity event promoting the piano builder Johann Andreas Stein, who took one of the parts alongside Mozart. The performance earned a rave review in the local paper that confirmed the novelty of three soloists sharing the spotlight: "One hardly knew what to give attention to first, and all the listeners were enraptured."[64] The following March, three young women in Mozart's Mannheim circle—Rosa Cannabich, Aloysia Weber, and Therese Pierron—performed the concerto for him as part of a farewell event before he and his mother left for Paris. At the time, these three performers would have been fourteen, nineteen, and fifteen years old, respectively. Cannabich was an accomplished student of Mozart's, and he praised her in several letters to his father, including one in which he refers to her as being "very intelligent and steady for her age."[65] Weber was arguably Mozart's first love, while Pierron was the Webers' housekeeper. So clearly this concerto, in its original three-keyboard scoring, had a rich performance history among Mozart's acquaintance within the first few years after its composition.

The Lodron family were not just neighbors to the Mozarts; they were also important advocates for them at court, with connections to the Arcos and the Firmians.[66] But Wolfgang was not the daughters' teacher at the time of the concerto's composition, nor would he ever be. Rather, they studied first with the court organist Anton Adlgasser, and after his death in December 1777 with Leopold and (later) Nannerl.[67] The concerto, then, was part of a network of flattery, influence, and patronage that would involve several prominent Salzburg families. Given all these circumstances, the so-called "superfluous" third keyboard part for eleven-year-old Josepha might actually have been a generous balancing act

EXAMPLE 5.4. K. 242, movement 1 (Allegro), mm. 111–16, solo parts only

between accessibility and participation, one that choreographs the give-and-take between parents and children with patience and humor.

The staging of familial collaboration and reciprocity is at its most salient in the concerto's outer movements. The first example is a fleeting but significant moment from the opening Allegro, one that only pays off in performance, suggesting a drama of blocking that operates independently of the notes on the page. The moment occurs at the close of the exposition, where the cadential phrase consists of a call-and-response between keyboards I and II (mm. 111–13) (ex. 5.4). The call-and-response is then repeated, this time by keyboards II and III (mm. 114–16).

On the surface, mm. 114–15 are no more than an exact repetition of mm. 111–12—the pitches, registers, and rhythms are identical. But in performance, one hears and sees it as a 1–2, 2–3 pattern: keyboard I passes the phrases to keyboard II, and II then passes the same phrase to III. Assuming the parts were distributed in descending order of age, the result is a call-and-response between mother and elder daughter that is immediately repeated between elder and younger daughter.[68] It is a moment, then, that gains significance primarily through its visual blocking—or, to put it another way, it only registers for those who are present at its performance, to witness the handoff.

The middle movement, an Adagio, behaves much more like a duo for keyboards I and II, with III far in the background providing only accompaniment figures. But in the final movement, a sonata-rondo in minuet tempo, III has a prominent role to play, one that is apparent at the cadential extension in each appearance of the rondo theme, and in each of the three Eingänge that close the intervening episodes. "Josepha," in other words, is a catalyst of closure.

I and II introduce the rondo theme together at the outset of the movement, but III initiates the cadential extension with which the theme closes (ex. 5.5). I and II begin the cadence in sixteenth notes (mm. 16–19), while III replies in easygoing triplets (mm. 20–21), reestablishing the triplet rhythm of the theme's opening statement, in a pace that is then adopted by I (m. 21). This pattern will be repeated every time the rondo theme returns, suggesting that III's job is to "pump the brakes" as it were on the cadence's rhythm. At the close of the recapitulation, before the final Eingang, III once again interrupts I and II's pattern of sixteenth notes to reestablish the triplet rhythm (ex. 5.6). This time, however, III takes a leading role in a cadential extension with a harmonic progression we have not yet heard in this movement: I^6-vi-IV-V. The prevailing texture has been turned on its head: while III has been in the background on the main melodic material, now III takes the lead with the most active part, and I and II are in the supporting role, providing the punctuating chords that reinforce the harmony. For a moment, then, III is in charge. In mm. 186–89, III continues the triplets even as I and II reassert the sixteenth notes, and the orchestra plays duple eighths—resulting in a layering of subdivisions during which III holds its own. As though responding to III's blossoming leadership role, in the last measures of the final orchestral ritornello, the strings adopt III's triplet cadential extension in triplets of their own for the first time. At the movement's end, III's influence has extended beyond the "domestic space" of the three soloists to the "public audience" of the orchestra.

EXAMPLE 5.5. K. 242, movement 3 (Rondeau, tempo di minuetto), mm. 16–22, solo parts only

Imagining a performance of this concerto by Countess Lodron and her daughters, we might ask what sort of mother-daughter and sororal bonds it allowed them to explore. Patience, the ceding of place, the internalization of maternalism, and the replication of the pedagogical imperative all appear in the work. As Mary Hunter reminds us, opera buffa could trade on the humor of "see[ing] characters locked in disagreement or

EXAMPLE 5.6. K. 242, movement 3, mm. 180–90, solo parts only

EXAMPLE 5.7. K. 242, movement 3, mm. 207–12, string parts only

misunderstanding but still, in a spirit of obvious cooperation, singing the same music."[69] In the wordless "opera buffa" that is a triple concerto, the performers and the audience could interpolate any scenario they wished: the sisters could still be bickering even as they made *Silbertöne* together (gritting one's teeth through the family portrait, as it were). What mattered was not what each family member might have been feeling in their heart of hearts—those petty rivalries, grudges, or more serious conflicts that anyone with a sibling will recognize as part and parcel of everyday family life. What mattered instead was what Hunter calls the "cadential unanimity," bringing all the voices into the fold, for this fleeting moment of familial intimacy before the mother's daughters went on to form their own "chamber ensembles" with husbands and children.[70]

A more ennobled variation on this theme pervades a story that appeared in Weisse's *Der Kinderfreund* in 1778, the same year in which K. 242 was composed. Although it does not thematize music as did "Harmonie," the story, "Die Geschwisterliebe" (Sibling Love), shows how children could be called upon even to deceive their parents in service of what Emily Bruce calls the "elevation of sensibility and horizontal relationships."[71] In the cautionary tale, little brother Carl accidentally wounds his older sister Julchen with a gun belonging to their father, an army major. Upon recovering, Julchen lies to protect Carl from their father's wrath. All is confessed and forgiven in the play's final scene.

Bruce describes the frame story, in which the Mentor family discusses the applicability of this melodramatic model in their own everyday lives, and it emerges that the play was inspired by a more mundane act of altruism by seven-year-old Fritz on behalf of his younger sister Luischen, five.[72] Mentor sums up the moral: "When siblings are so attuned to one another that the painful sensation of one does the other more pain than their own pain, I can be content with that, and will praise and admire such children."[73] A family friend even quotes from Plutarch's "De fraterno amore" (On Brotherly Love), in the *Moralia*:

> The friendships of those bound in close intimacy are in reality only shadows and imitations of that first love that Nature instilled in siblings towards one another. And as for the man who does not revere and practice this love, how can one expect him to be loving and benevolent to other people?[74]

The sibling altruism glorified here—in one of the most popular, influential children's periodicals of the time—transcends filial duty, even honesty, at least temporarily.

Ute Dettmar has explored how the performing of domestic theatricals reinforced the new image of the insular, emotionally bonded family. Musical family rituals like the triple keyboard concerto achieved a similar goal, as the three women on stage—and all the families in attendance— would have spent time contemplating the turn-taking, cooperation, and ceding of place choreographed by Mozart's music.

> The family is constituted and experienced in the private space as a cohesive ensemble; it instantiates itself in its rituals and at the same time cel-

ebrates itself in its staging. [Fictional] setting and performance venue blend together, and the family-theater does not seek to build a "fourth wall"; the amateur actors perform as family members and as such are addressed as spectators.[75]

This cooperative learning process suggests that sympathetic bonds between members of a close-knit family could be practiced with the help of periodicals like *Der Kinderfreund* and concertos like K. 242 alike.

Leading, Following, and Letting Go in the Concerto in C Major for Flute and Harp, K. 299

In the summer of 1777, just a few months after he completed the concerto for the Lodrons, Mozart professed his values regarding filial responsibility in a letter to Archbishop Colloredo. Mozart was petitioning his employer to grant his father permission to travel, and in the letter, Mozart summarized all the obligations his upbringing had encouraged him to value, advocating for his father in a way his father had advocated for him time and again. It was an emulation of Leopold, one that subtly asserted Mozart's position as the dominant, most powerful musical figure in the family.

> Most Gracious Prince and Lord! Parents endeavor to place their children in a position to earn their own bread; and in this they follow alike their own interest and that of the State. . . . My conscience tells me that I owe it to God to be grateful to my father, who has spent his time unwearyingly upon my education, so that I may lighten his burden, look after myself and later on be able to support my sister.[76]

Mozart might as well have taken this statement word for word from a book like Basedow's *Elementarwerk* or Weisse's *Kinderfreund*; he had mastered the Josephinian language of filial duty and the utilitarian aims of education.

Less than a year later, Mozart staged the ideal of parenthood to which he professed subscribing in the letter—the cultivation of the child's self-sufficiency—in his Concerto in C Major for Flute and Harp, K. 299. The concerto was commissioned by Adrien-Louis de Bonnières, the Count (later the Duc) de Guînes, a short time after Mozart's arrival in Paris, and was intended for performance by the count himself on flute, and his daughter, Marie-Louise-Philippine, on harp. At the time of its composition, Marie-Louise was eighteen or nineteen years old, and in just a few months she would be married. The concerto was likely intended for private or semiprivate performance by a chamber orchestra, perhaps even as part of the betrothal or wedding festivities.[77] We have no evidence of a performance at the count's residence—apparently, he never paid Mozart for the concerto and underpaid him for the lessons, which greatly annoyed Mozart.[78]

Joseph Frank, a doctor who knew Mozart, claimed in 1852 that Mozart had told him he "hated" the flute and harp.[79] Whether or not this is true, Mozart admired the de Guines's talent, describing the father as "incomparable" and the daughter as "*magnifique*."[80] In fact, Marie-Louise was the dedicatee of a number of other works for harp, including a harp duo by Francesco Petrini and a set of twelve preludes and airs for harp by Johann Baptist Krumpholtz.[81] And, in addition to being Mozart's dedicatee, Marie-Louise was also one of his composition students, to whom he gave daily lessons that he detailed in letters home.

As was the case with musical portraits, the concerto depicted not just the Duc and Mademoiselle de Guines, but a father and daughter. In the concertos closest to it—K. 242 and K. 365—the textural give-and-take is fluid, with antecedent-consequent pairs of phrases being traded equally between the voices, frequently in sequences and call-and-response patterns. K. 299, however, unfolds a distinctive textural plot over its three movements: from true duet in movement 1, to minimally separated phrasing (mostly echo effects) in movement 2, and finally to extended solos for each instrument in movement 3. The effect is one of increasing autonomy between the voices, which, given the circumstances—a daughter on the brink of leaving her father's home for her husband's—would have taken on special poignancy in performance.

The concerto begins in bonded intimacy, with the first movement enshrining the inseparability of flute and harp. The two instruments enter together in octaves, sharing the fanfare gesture with which the orchestra had opened the movement. Thereafter, flute and harp sound together for the vast majority of the movement. In both the primary and secondary themes, and the new material in the dominant, it is as if the two are one hybrid instrument, a "flute-harp." The only exception is in the transition section, when the two engage in a single, brief call-and-response passage.

In the ensuing development section, the two instruments depart from one another for the first time, completing a modulating progression over call-and-response phrases initiated by the flute. The recapitulation reinstates their simultaneous sounding, as though once again they are a single hybrid instrument. If the development, then, represents a splitting of the composite "flute-harp," the recapitulation shows the two knitted back

EXAMPLE 5.8. K. 299, movement 2 (Andantino), mm. 88–100, flute and harp parts only

together. Mozart includes a fermata before the cadenza, but leaves it unrealized, suggesting that he trusted these talented musicians to compose out—or perhaps even improvise in tandem—their own joint cadenza.

In contrast to the "flute-harp" texture that prevails in the first movement, the second, an Andantino, is dominated by echo effects, representing the first sustained distancing between flute and harp. This process is further extended when the closing material returns in the recapitulation (ex. 5.8), with the unit of repetition extending from one (mm. 88–92), to three measures (mm. 92–97), followed by a cadential arpeggio in imitation at the hyper-abbreviated unit of the eighth note (m. 98). In other words, where the flute and harp nearly always sounded together in movement 1, movement 2 has them establish a limited but unmistakable independence from one another.

The third movement continues this narrative of increasing independence, using a sonata-rondo form with a bewildering variety of themes.[82] In contrast to the previous movements, the number of measures during which one of the two solo instruments plays alone is now much longer, with stretches of eight, twelve, fourteen, and fifteen measures for just one or the other instrument. The fusion of instruments that prevailed in the first movement has given way to an alternation that also stages acts of listening: flute falls silent and listens to harp, harp falls silent and listens to flute. Their union is rarer now, and even their alternations are asymmetrical, following no predictable pattern.[83]

Not only do the two instruments appear independently from one another for much of this section, and for the movement as a whole; they are also no longer in conversation with one another or engaging in byplay over the same melodic material as they did in movement 2. Now, each time the flute or harp plays solo, the instrument is introducing new thematic material, tunes that have not even been heard in the opening ritornello. And the only time the two instruments introduce new material together is in the transition sections between the tonic and dominant key areas. The overall impression, therefore, is of two independent voices, perhaps even two independent concertos, which come together only for cadences. To be sure, the two join together for the final solo statement of the movement, and the entire concerto. But this is the winking coda theme, which was originally introduced by the orchestra, and it is one of the only themes that the two play together.

Over its three movements, then, the concerto enacts a plot that might be understood as an allegory of upbringing and filial autonomy. And it appears to be something of an anomaly: I have not come across other eighteenth-century concertos for flute and harp, though there were plenty of collections of accompanied sonatas for the configuration. What, then, might have been the connotations for a father performing alongside his harpist daughter with an orchestra or chamber ensemble? The gender roles of the instruments themselves were certainly predictable: playing the harp was a favorite accomplishment for aristocratic young women (most famously Marie Antoinette), though as such it was frequently depicted in paintings and engravings as a symbol of *galant* erotics. Meanwhile, professional harpists were almost exclusively male, and many had reputations for debauchery.[84]

As for flutists, both professionals and amateurs were almost exclusively men—for example, Johann Joachim Quantz and Frederick the Great—due in large part to the visible labor of breath and facial contortions required to play the instrument, which were considered unbecoming in women.[85] We have already encountered this gendering of flute and harp in chapter 4, in the title page illustration to the *Liedersammlung für Kinder und Kinderfreunde: Frühlingslieder*, where the elder son plays flute in the foreground while the elder daughter doubles the accompaniment of her mother on harp. The father's presence would thus have mitigated any risqué implications of a young unmarried woman performing a concerto on harp. Like the images from chapter 4 of parents supervising and guiding the reading and games of their children, K. 299 enacts a dramaturgy of supervision.

Mozart had performed alongside talented young women throughout his life, from his sister to the violinist Regina Strinasacchi and the keyboardists Maria Theresia von Paradies and Josepha Auernhammer.[86] He even crossed paths with the female harp prodigy, Mademoiselle Schencker, who made her debut at the Concert Spirituel in 1765 at age twelve, earning a glowing report in the *Mercure de France*.[87] Schencker was sponsored by the music patron Louis François de Bourbon, Prince de Conti, who made her a member of his orchestra the following year.[88] On the Mozarts' return to Paris in 1766, they performed at the court of this same Prince de Conti, an event memorialized in a painting by Michel-Barthélémy Ollivier.[89] Like Mozart, Schencker was the child of a musical family who sought to parlay her youthful fame into a permanent court appointment. Both children navigated the overlapping networks of patronage and public concert life. Their common background may have been a distant reference point for Mozart as he composed the concerto.

Mozart may also have been influenced by the tradition of bourgeois tragedy. As Susan Gustafson has shown, in plays such as Lessing's 1772 *Emilia Galotti* and Schiller's 1784 *Kabale und Liebe,* fathers and daughters navigate a fraught sexual-political dynamic that reinscribes the patriarchal order.[90] The comic foil to this trope is, of course, the *commedia dell'arte* plot where the young lovers outsmart the father figure, something Mary Hunter has read as a social allegory of generational change and that can be found again and again in Mozart's *opere buffe*.[91] Mozart's concerto, then, could be said to operate on many levels—biographical, autobiographical, allegorical, archetypal—staging both an occupation of and a retreat from the public stage, a hinge-point between unmarried and married, a tension between father and daughter at the moment of the transfer of guardianship from father to husband. On a more prosaic level, it would also have provided a ready excuse for father and daughter to reunite on future occasions after her marriage. It staged both the paternalism and surveillance, the letting go and the possibility of reunion, all at once.

Reaching Out

Johann Jakob Engel's 1785 *Ideas on Mimicry* is essentially an actor's treatise on theatrical gesture. In this publication, the German Enlightenment philosopher categorized bodily movements and positions according to their motivation and function.[92] Engel included numerous engravings

FIGURE 5.5. Johann Wilhelm Meil, figures 17 and 18, in Johann Jakob Engel, *Ideen zu einer Mimik, Erster Theil* (Berlin, 1785). Courtesy of Bayerische Staatsbibliothek München, shelfmark Res/L.eleg.g. 126-1.

over the two-volume treatise to illustrate his classification system, juxtaposing tableaus from classical dramas with more generic characters that might be found in the bourgeois tragedies of Lessing or Diderot. In one pair of illustrations, a child reaches out to its mother, and the mother reaches out to the child (fig. 5.5). Engel painstakingly describes the parts of each body that bend, stretch, and strain toward the other: the boys' arms raised overhead, "all the muscles tensed," while the mother "lowers her arms invitingly."[93] The figures are depicted separately, with the child on top reaching up, the mother on the bottom reaching down. This can be explained as simply a response to the order of Engel's description of the two figures in the text. But in an illustrative intervention, the engraving has both characters facing away from each other on both the horizontal and vertical axes. The existing orientation encourages a more comparative approach, and the viewer has to work harder to turn this into a composite image of a single scene.

Engel's was, to be sure, a manual for professional actors, not a children's reader or a conduct book for parents. But the pictures ennoble the gesture of parents and children reaching out to one another as "Kinder" and "Kinderfreunde." Friedrich Schiller had already spoken of children in similar terms in his *On Naïve and Sentimental Poetry* (1795–1796). We delight in natural things, and in children, Schiller argued, because "they represent to us our lost childhood," and "the divine or the ideal emerges, only when the differences"—between reason and imagination, between free and necessary, between young and old—"are blended."[94] The sentimental encounter between parents and children, with music as the unit of emotional currency, ritualizes this interdependence of young and old.

So many studies of childhood in the eighteenth century focus on the molding or "fashioning" of children, or on children as reservoirs of adult fantasy. But to take this image of Engel's archetypal mother at face value is to consider the inclining of the adult toward the child in this period. Influenced by Marah Gubar and other writers who are working to recuperate the historical child as an agent, we might reconsider the relationship between parent and child as one of mutual transformation. It was a lopsided power dynamic, to be sure, but one with a degree of reciprocity, and the self-fashioning of the parent was at least as effortful as the fashioning of the child.

We can see this at work in Mozart's own self-fashioning as a composer-parent, in the dedication to the Opus 10 "Haydn" quartets in 1785. Mozart's dedication broke with the conventions of dedicating musical works to a royal patron: instead, he dedicated his music to an admired colleague, mentor, and most significantly, "Friend."

> To my dear friend Haydn,
>   A father who had resolved to send his children out into the great world took it to be his duty to confide them to the protection and guidance of a very celebrated Man, especially when the latter by good fortune was at the same time his best Friend.[95]

In figuring his quartets as his own children, Mozart looked forward to them providing comfort to him later in life:

Here they are then, O great Man and dearest Friend, these six children of mine. They are, it is true, the fruit of a long and laborious endeavor, yet . . . I flatter myself that this offspring will serve to afford me solace one day.[96]

And finally, he gave up these children to the care of this Friend, extending the metaphor so that Haydn became their adoptive parent, their "Mentor":

> May it therefore please you to receive them kindly and to be their Father, Guide and Friend! From this moment I resign to you all my rights in them, begging you however to look indulgently upon the defects which the partiality of a Father's eye may have concealed from me, and in spite of them to continue in your generous Friendship for him who so greatly values it, in expectation of which I am, with all of my Heart, my dearest Friend, your most Sincere Friend.[97]

The language of fatherhood, tutelage, and friendship could have come straight out of the inaugural issue of *Der Kinderfreund*. Furthermore, it bears no small resemblance to Mozart's letter to Archbishop Colloredo of eight years earlier. Then, Mozart wrote of his obligation to lighten his father's burden; now, he speaks as a parent himself, entrusting his children to their appointed guardian.

"We know nothing of childhood," Rousseau famously stated in his 1762 treatise, *Emile, or On Education*.[98] On the one hand, his rhetorical device was just a sales pitch—yet, in this stark sentence, Rousseau also articulated a new preoccupation with childhood's essential alterity. As Chris Jenks puts it, "Children, through this period of Enlightenment, had . . . escaped into difference."[99] I might rephrase that to "Children had been consigned to difference." In seeking a greater intimacy with children, Rousseau (and the pedagogical reformers he inspired across Europe) felt—or believed they needed to feel—the distance between young and old more keenly than ever before. That distance now needed to be intolerable. Like Engel's archetypal mother, parents needed to strain their bodies toward their children, across the gulf. What was once benign indifference, or affection taken for granted, gave way to ostentatious concern, which tumbled over in the next century into full-blown yearning. Mozart's instrumental music for family members preserved the ultimate unresolvability of this impasse. It gave space for children and parents to encounter one another, to contemplate what separated them, and to fill the intervening space with harmonious music, gesture, tenderness, and witty exchange. But it did not seek to resolve the contradictions and tensions inherent in the encounter, or to smooth them away with words. Instead, such music merely called the steps, created the shapes, set the bodies in "felicit[ous] rapid motion."[100] The rest, it seems, we may not overhear.

CHAPTER 6

Toying with Mozart

In 1802, Mozart's Missa Brevis in C ("Sparrow Mass," K. 220, 1775–1777) was performed at the Laxenburg residence of Empress Marie Therese (wife of Franz II), but not as Mozart had originally composed it. Mozart's former lodge brother and family friend, the composer and conductor Paul Wranitzky, arranged the Sparrow Mass for toy instruments manufactured in Berchtesgaden, a town twenty miles south of Salzburg. Berchtesgaden was a major center of woodcraft for centuries, and to this day is famous for its decorated boxes, Christmas ornaments, figurines, and toys. The toy instruments made by Berchtesgaden woodworkers included bird calls, pipes, trumpets, bells, tambourines, rattles, and others (fig. 6.1). John Rice speculates that the chirping motif in Mozart's Sanctus, which gives the Mass its nickname, may have prompted Wranitzky to associate the piece with Berchtesgaden bird calls.[1]

Adding toy instruments to a Mass setting may seem to push the bounds of taste, but Wranitzky had precedent. A whole subgenre of music for toy instruments, "Berchtesgaden Musik," had been in existence since the 1760s.[2] One symphony, *Berchtoldsgaden Musick* (ca. 1760s), by the composer and Benedictine choirmaster Edmund Angerer, was performed throughout Europe, appearing on the program of a Vienna benefit concert in April 1791 (a concert which, it was later claimed, Mozart himself had attended).[3] The symphony appeared in print beginning in 1811, and subsequent German, French, and English prints variously attributed the symphony to Joseph Haydn, Michael Haydn, and Leopold Mozart.[4] Although these attributions are spurious, we know that the Mozart family was familiar with Berchtesgaden toys and the toy symphony genre. In 1764, Leopold wrote a letter home from the tour that reported how the women of Paris did their makeup "like the dolls [*Docken*] of Berchtesgaden"; and in 1770, Wolfgang wrote to Nannerl from Bologna about his

FIGURE 6.1. A selection of toy instruments made in Berchtesgaden. Top, left to right, Ratchet with Whistle (MIR 2118); Whistle-rider (MIR 2145). Bottom, left to right, Music box with Whistle (MIR 2147); Birdcall (MIR 2150). Courtesy of Germanisches Nationalmuseum.

homesickness, saying he wished he could play a little trumpet or fife in a "Pertelzkammersinfonie."[5]

Rice identifies Wranitzky's toy-instrument arrangement of the Mozart Mass as belonging to Marie Therese's collection of "Scherzmusick" (Joke Music)—she was fond of pieces that evoked and parodied the Bavarian countryside and traditional music. "Joke music" can be found at the edges of the Mozart family repertoire as well, beginning with Leopold's *Die musikalische Schlittenfahrt* (The Musical Sleigh-Ride, 1755), with parts for sleigh bells, and *Die Bauernhochzeit* (The Country Wedding, also 1755), with parts for bagpipes and hurdy-gurdy. Wolfgang composed a number of humorous pieces in the 1780s, from the terzett *Liebes Mandel, wo*

FIGURE 6.2. (a) *Oberammergau. Kraxenträger aus dem Stammhaus Lang sel. Erben um 1750* [postcard]. Courtesy bpk-Bildagentur / Museum Europäischer Kulturen der Staatlichen Museen zu Berlin -Preußischer Kulturbesitz / Art Resource, New York. (b) Alberti, Papageno, in Schikaneder, *Die Zauberflöte. Eine große Oper in zwey Aufzügen* [libretto] (Vienna, 1791). Courtesy of Österreichische Nationalbibliothek, shelfmark 580065-A.

is's *Bandel* (K. 441) to the scatological canons to the *Musikalischer Spass* (K. 522), and that spirit animates the panpipe and glockenspiel music in Mozart's final Singspiel, *Die Zauberflöte* (K. 620, 1791).[6] In one way, Papageno provides a direct link to the "Kraxenträger" of Mozart's youth, the peddlers from Berchtesgaden who carried handmade toys, icons, and chip boxes in a wooden frame on their backs and traversed the mountain passes to sell their wares to the cities and villages of Bavaria and Tyrol.[7] Undoubtedly the most famous Kraxenträger during Mozart's lifetime was Anton Adner (ca. 1705–1822), celebrated by King Ludwig, who was reported to have reached the age of 117. He would have come through Salzburg numerous times, and Wolfgang and Nannerl might even have met him in their youth. The resemblance between Kraxenträger like Adner, and the earliest images of Emanuel Schikaneder as Papageno in *Die Zauberflöte*, are unmistakable (fig. 6.2); one can even picture Adner playing a little panpipe or "Berchtesgadener Fleitl" (fife) to announce his arrival in town, perhaps even to a tune similar to "Der Vogelfänger [Kraxenträger] bin ich ja."[8] The glockenspiel and panpipe music played by Papageno in *Die Zauberflöte* were among the most frequently published excerpts from that Singspiel in early prints and collections. Now ubiquitous in wind-up music boxes to this day, they continue to serve as major signifiers for Mozart in popular culture. For many, toy Mozart *is* Mozart.

In this final chapter, I explain how Mozart was first made *gemütlich*— cozy, appealing, accessible to the general public. As "radio-friendly" as he might be today, Mozart did not begin his posthumous career with that kind of mass appeal. Toward the end of his life and for some years afterward, he was characterized by many as a talented but rather eccentric composer, his music challenging to perform and often bewildering for listeners. The phrases "extremely difficult," "too difficult," "too artificial/ contrived," and even culinary metaphors like "over-seasoned" appear again and again in critical assessments of Mozart's music up to the end of the eighteenth century.[9] Even those defending Mozart acknowledged his inscrutability, as when the pastor, theologue, and musician Johann Karl Friedrich Triest (in an 1801 eleven-part article for the *AmZ* tracing the development of eighteenth-century German music) explained some of the "Bizarrerien" in Mozart's instrumental works by drawing a comparison with Shakespeare. Both men, Triest wrote, had a "propensity and talent for the grotesque" and "a certain indifference to the old rules of art. . . . Shakespeare drew criticism for his astonishing situations, Mozart for his astonishing modulations."[10] In the early nineteenth century, this Romantic strain of Mozart reception began to coexist with assessments that emphasized Mozart's "simplicity," "elegance," "lightness," and "purity."[11] John Daverio calls this "the assimilation of Mozart's music to an aesthetic of the beautiful," and it represents a popular foil to the "sublime Mozart" that continues to prove so tenacious among listeners and scholars.[12]

One easily overlooked aspect of this early trend in Mozart reception is his emergence on the juvenile market in the first third of the nineteenth century, which coincided with the continued expansion of children's print. This includes biographies of Mozart for young readers; anthologies for young and beginner musicians that excerpted and simplified Mozart's music; child-oriented music and musical games spuriously attributed to Mozart; and finally, the print debut of Mozart's first compositional sketches from the *Nannerl Notenbuch*. This corpus ranges widely both generically and geographically. Rather than representing a coordinated campaign, it seems more likely that various publishers simply caught on to the idea that there was a profit to be made from peddling the pre-eminent ex-prodigy to a juvenile readership. However opportunistic each individual decision was, together they had a transformative effect on the broader reception of Mozart, influencing biographies for the general reader and printed music for the general public. Child-friendly Mozart prints helped domesticate the composer, smoothing out his eccentricities and laying the foundation for the "safe," infantilized Mozart that is just as misleading as his sacralization.

We might call the child-friendly curios explored here *Mozartetti*: they are short, often fragmentary, seemingly inconsequential, scattered across the print landscape like confetti, and they are notoriously difficult to eradicate—even when, as in the case of the spurious music, the attribution is corrected. They continue to affect Mozart's status in the popular imagination to this day, yet they occupy something of a historiographical blind spot among Mozart scholars—even those, like Ruth Halliwell and Gernot Gruber, who have outlined the establishment of the "Mozart industry" by the composer's survivors and publishers.[13] Once the spurious works are identified as such, they tend to be ignored, and the few juvenile biographies that are mentioned by historians are seen as no more than a footnote to Georg Nikolaus Nissen's problematic "first authoritative" biography of 1828 (completed by Constanze Mozart after Nissen's death in 1826).

Rather than dismissing *Mozartetti* as arcane Mozartiana, I see them as evidence of the important role played by the juvenile market in effecting the fundamental shift in Mozart reception, a shift that was endorsed in Nissen's biography. When Nissen included among Mozart's works a spurious Wiegenlied (lullaby) whose attribution was imputed to its "Mozartisch" qualities, the circular nature of that argument—it must be by Mozart, because it sounds Mozartian—affirmed what the previous thirty years had helped establish: the essentializing of qualities such as naïve, whimsical, and pleasing as Mozartian.[14] This chapter, in other words, offers one account for how the eponymous adjective "Mozartisch" underwent a connotative transformation from difficult to delightful.

Mozart in Children's Biographies

Making Mozart child-friendly was a business decision first and foremost. Mozart's widow Constanze, and to a lesser extent his sister Nannerl, were effectively the executors of his artistic estate, and Constanze in particular was anxious to maximize the profits from that estate. For years she was engaged in complex, tense negotiations with Breitkopf &

Härtel over the rights to Mozart's music, negotiations that intensified in 1798 when Breitkopf announced their forthcoming Complete Works edition in their house journal, the *AmZ*. The *AmZ* was Breitkopf's Mozart "publicity machine," as Halliwell calls it, and biography was one of their chief promotional tools.[15] At the same time as the Complete Works edition began, the *AmZ* ran the Friedrich Rochlitz, Constanze, and Nannerl anecdotes, which helped establish the twin poles of the Mozart-and-childhood mythos: the privileging of Mozart's years as a child prodigy, and the image of the adult Mozart as a perpetual man-child.[16]

From the earliest contribution to Mozart's posthumous biographical tradition—Friedrich Schlichtegroll's obituary in his *Nekrolog auf das Jahr 1791* (first published in 1793)—Mozart's startling maturity as a child performer and composer, and the immaturity that he was believed to have retained throughout his short life, had already begun to be linked in a reciprocally deterministic way.[17] As I mentioned in chapter 1, this pairing of Mozart the "child-man" and Mozart the "man-child" has been interpreted by scholars as a manifestation of Romantic notions of divinely inspired genius. But it also had a more prosaic cause: Schlichtegroll's main informants for the *Nekrolog* were figures from Mozart's childhood—his sister Nannerl and family friend Johann Andreas Schachtner, the court trumpeter in Salzburg who would later collaborate with Mozart on *Bastien und Bastienne* and *Zaide* (see chapter 3). Both Nannerl and Schachtner contributed vivid anecdotal reminiscences of the child Mozart that were reproduced again and again in the biographical literature leading up to Nissen. To trace the repetition and variation of these Wunderkind anecdotes—a process of embroidery that likely began before they were even transmitted to Schlichtegroll—is to observe the mythography of Mozart in its earliest stages.

One such anecdote, which originated with Schachtner and was reproduced in virtually all the early biographies, gained particular visual prominence on the page by including dialogue that was almost always set off from an otherwise unbroken set of descriptive paragraphs. The episode appears to have taken place in Mozart's fourth or fifth year of age, although it is difficult to determine whether it dates before or after Mozart began learning composition. The story goes that Schachtner and Leopold come home from church one day to find Wolfgang scribbling on a sheet of music paper. Leopold asks what Wolfgang is working on, and he replies, "A clavier concerto." He protests that it is not yet finished, but Leopold insists on seeing it. At first, Leopold and Schachtner chuckle at the many ink spots caused by Wolfgang's dipping his quill down to the bottom of the well. But as Leopold reads more closely, tears begin to spring in his eyes, and he says to Schachtner, "Look . . . see how correctly and properly it is all written." He praises Wolfgang but tells him the music is too difficult to play, to which Wolfgang answers without hesitation, "That's why it's a concerto, you must practise it till you can get it right." Wolfgang then begins to play, and even he is unable to execute his own music sufficiently well. But even this failure demonstrates to Schachtner that Wolfgang "had the notion that to play a concerto and work a miracle must be one and the same."[18] Mozart ostensibly grasped the conventions of florid concerto writing even before he knew how to compose, or had the keyboard training to play a concerto.

This anecdote, the last in the biographical narrative before Leopold puts Wolfgang and his sister before the public eye, was reproduced almost wholesale in all the major early nineteenth-century biographical sources.[19] But in the Nissen biography of 1828, a new layer was added, and with it a new spin on the anecdote. Nissen's version prefaced the anecdote with an imagined backstory that goes as follows:

> As a boy, our Mozart had as yet no knowledge of composition; nonetheless, he hit upon the idea of composing a keyboard concerto. Although he could not produce a true artwork, nevertheless he showed a childish attempt at what he would be able to accomplish, if the rules of art came to the aid of his talent. He crossed out, spilled, and dribbled at the concoction for a long time, until he believed it to have been completed.[20]

Thereafter follows the anecdote as Schachter recounted it, with the two elder gentlemen marveling at the concerto's correctness.

Nissen did not come up with these sentences on his own. Rather, he cribbed them word for word from a lesser-known Mozart biography from 1803, entitled *Mozarts Geist* (Mozart's Spirit), a source Nissen acknowledges in the preface and bibliography to his own volume. *Mozarts Geist* is familiar to Mozart scholars, but what is usually only mentioned in passing, if at all, is the fact that it was the first Mozart biography intended chiefly for young readers. It was subtitled *An Educational Book for Young Musicians*, and the author—Ignaz Ferdinand Arnold, a novelist and organist based in Erfurt—wrote in the preface that he hoped to show young artists the way to the "nameless pleasure of new discoveries" in the genius of the composer.[21]

Arnold's gargantuan 452-page biography begins with a hundred-page overview of the composer's life, before turning to detailed studies

of a number of the individual works. His expanded version of the concerto anecdote does not appear where one might expect it to—in the
biographical chapter—but rather in the next chapter, which is entitled
"On Artists' Talent or Genius." This was Arnold's original contribution to
the early posthumous assessment of Mozart, and it was undertaken with
his young readership in mind. Arnold sought to correct parents and educators who call a child a genius merely when he or she shows an aptitude
for learning. Genius, Arnold argued, occurs when someone is able to create something that follows certain rules of which they themselves could
not possibly be aware, or could only be dimly aware. "They change and
reshape the thing until they are satisfied with it and can say to themselves
that now the result is beautiful. These people are artists. And that which
they possess before their peers, who do not know how to do such things,
is called Genius."[22]

The concerto anecdote, Arnold asserted, is "the unmistakable expression of genius in our Mozart"—genius understood here as a combination
of instinct and effort, undertaken autonomously.[23] Arnold hastened to
remind his readers that "While Nature gave [Mozart] much, he earned
far more through his hard work and his untiring perseverance."[24] Between
this comment about hard work, and the embroidery on the concerto
anecdote to emphasize Mozart's tenacious crossing-out and rewriting,
Arnold clearly meant for young musicians to model themselves after
Mozart. Both passages are repeated word for word in Nissen's biography.[25] This is how a child-oriented take on Mozart became a governing
trope of his biographical tradition.

Even before its adoption in the Nissen biography, *Mozarts Geist*
had a more immediate impact on the market. On its publication, it was
reviewed favorably in the *AmZ*, which, while noting the book's debt to
existing sources, praised Arnold for his careful study of Mozart's scores
and affirmed his claim about the book's value to young readers.[26] In
1810, Arnold paired it with a biography of Haydn, and that same year he
included both in a two-volume biographical collection of composers that
would itself be reprinted in 1816.[27] Arnold was evidently not the only one
to recognize that there was money to be made in a juvenile biography of
Mozart. A number of them appeared in the first two decades of the nineteenth century, as listed in table 6.1.

In addition to the better-known biographies already discussed, various biographical sketches and anecdotes of Mozart (skewed, predictably,
toward his childhood years) also appeared in some of the many children's
periodicals and almanacs that had emerged in the late eighteenth century
and flourished in the early nineteenth. One biographical sketch from 1813,

TABLE 6.1. Comparative list of selected early Mozart biographies, 1793–1828

	General audience		Juvenile audience	
Year	Author, short title (city)	Format	Author, short title (city)	Format
1793	Friedrich Schlichtegroll, "Mozart," in *Nekrolog auf das Jahr 1791* (Gotha)	Article in periodical		
1798	Thomas Busby, "Life of Mozart," *Monthly Magazine/Walpoliana* (London)	Article in periodical		
	Franz Xaver Niemetschek, *Leben des Mozart* (Prague)	Monograph		
	Friedrich Rochlitz, "Verbürgte Anekdoten aus Mozarts Leben," *AmZ* (Leipzig)	Article in periodical		
1799	Constanze Mozart, "Einige Anekdoten aus Mozarts Leben," *AmZ* (Leipzig)	Article in periodical		
1800	Nannerl Mozart, "Noch einige Anekdoten aus Mozarts Kinderjahren," *AmZ* (Leipzig)	Article in periodical		
	Christian Siebigke, "Wolfgang Gottlieb Mozart," in *Museum deutscher Gelehrten und Kuenstler* (Breslau)	Article in biographical collection		
1801	Théophile Frédéric Winckler, *Notice biographique sur Mozart* (Paris)	Monograph		
1803			Ignaz Arnold, *Mozarts Geist* (Erfurt)	Monograph

(continued)

TABLE 6.1. (*continued*)

	General audience		Juvenile audience	
Year	Author, short title (city)	Format	Author, short title (city)	Format
1804	Jean-Baptiste-Antoine Suard, *Anecdotes sur Mozart* (Paris)	Article in collection		
1806			Peter Blanchard [and Friedrich Karl Kraft], "Mozart, ein sehr berühmter Tonsetzer," in *Neuer Plutarch* (Vienna)	Article in biographical collection
1807	"Mozart in England," *Zeitung für die elegante Welt* (Leipzig)	Article in periodical	Joseph Freiherr von Hormayr, "Wolfgang Gottlieb Mozart," in *Oesterreichischer Plutarch* (Vienna)	Article in biographical collection
1810			Ignaz Arnold, "Wolfgang Amadeus Mozart und Joseph Haydn. Versuch einer Parallele," in *Gallerie der berühmtesten Tonkünstler* (Erfurt)	Article in biographical collection
1813			Lenke, "Anekdoten und Züge aus dem Leben Mozarts," *Neue Jugend-Zeitung* (Leipzig)	Article in periodical
			Theodor Christian Ellrodt, "Das musikalische Kind Mozart," in *Taschenbuch zur nützlichen Unterhaltung für die Jugend und ihre Freunde* (Leipzig)	Article in periodical
1814	Stendhal, "Vie de Mozart," in *Vies de Haydn, de Mozart et de Métastase* (Paris and London)	Monograph		
1818	"Einiges aus Mozarts Kinderjahren," *Der Aufmerksame* (Graz)	Article in periodical	"Einiges aus Mozarts Kinderjahren," *Morgenblatt für gebildeten Stände* (Tübingen) [same article]	Article in periodical

TABLE 6.1. (*continued*)

Year	General audience Author, short title (city)	Format	Juvenile audience Author, short title (city)	Format
1826			Karl Müchler, "Wolfgang Mozart," in *Erinnerungen aus dem Leben berühmter Männer* (Berlin)	Article in biographical collection
1827			Johann Friedrich Franz, "Wolfgang Amadeus Mozart," in *Interessante Züge aus dem Jugendleben berühmter Künstler . . .* (Aarau)	Article in biographical collection
1828	Johann Aloys Schlosser, *Mozarts Biographie* (Prague)	Monograph		
	Georg Nikolaus von Nissen, *Biographie W. A. Mozarts* (Leipzig)	Monograph		

"Das musikalische Kind Mozart," appeared in a children's reader edited by the botanist Theodor Christian Ellrodt. Ellrodt's sketch concluded with a note of mourning on the composer's passing, only to insist that his spirit had not entirely left us, "because we still hear so often—and long and with pleasure may our grandchildren hear!—the echo of his lovely tones."[28] Mozart also appeared in several biographical collections for young readers. He was usually the lone musician or composer alongside figures like Homer and Julius Caesar, Newton and Napoleon, once again affirming his influence outside music history (as discussed in chapter 1). In the 1806 *Neuer Plutarch*, for instance, he took his place among the venerated British, French, and Russian statesmen of his day (fig. 6.3).[29]

These volumes helped correct the image of Mozart as an *outré* composer. The *Neuer Plutarch*, for instance, referred to Mozart having been underappreciated and even thwarted during his lifetime, his music dismissed as "too difficult to perform."[30] The *Oesterreichischer Plutarch*, published a year later by the same publisher, praised Mozart's "inexhaustible abundance of happy, partly charming, partly sublime, but always original ideas," his "admirable universality in a variety of subjects, from the smallest Lied . . . to the terrifyingly sublime Don Juan . . . from his littlest

FIGURE 6.3. Portrait of physician Johann Peter Frank, Count Mirabeau, Wolfgang Amadeus Mozart, William Pitt, Victor Moreau, and Tsar Alexander I of Russia. In Pierre Blanchard [and Friedrich Karl Kraft], *Neuer Plutarch* (Vienna, 1806), vol. 2, after 254. Courtesy of Österreichische Nationalbibliothek, shelfmark 287621-B.2.

keyboard sonatas, to the great symphony in C major, this canon of musical craft and beauty."[31] In the process of canonizing Mozart, these popular biographies sought to expand the variety of genres included in that canon from the most modest to the most ambitious works. Each end of the spectrum, it seems, mitigated the more off-putting extremes of the other.

Mozart Made Easy, Part 1: Anthologies for Piano Students

A Mozart for the masses, and for the ages, required a technology through which future generations could, in Ellrodt's words, make those "echoes of his lovely tones" audible. That technology was printed music, and Breitkopf & Härtel courted the domestic music market from the first, with their *Oeuvres Complettes* favoring Mozart's Lieder, chamber music, and above all, sonatas and variations for piano.[32] In Mozart's own thematic catalogue, he had described two works from 1788 as "kleine Sonaten für Anfänger" (little sonatas for beginners)—these are the keyboard sonata in C, K. 545, and the violin sonata in F, K. 547.[33] When K. 545 was first printed in 1805, its title was translated to "*sonate facile*"; and arrangements of his music with the words "easy," "little," "light," and "beginner" in the titles began to proliferate.[34]

"Easy" Mozart appeared no more frequently in publishers' catalogues than "light" Reichardt, or "little" Haydn, or "short and light" Wanhal, and these other composers were also anthologized in collections for beginning pianists and singers. But "easy Mozart" soon became paradigmatic. An 1813 *AmZ* review of a *Sonate facile* by Friedrich Kuhlau compared the quality of Kuhlau's work favorably to "the smaller [*kleiner*] Mozart sonatas."[35] This suggests that Mozart's more modest music had by then become a standard for emulation within the student keyboard repertoire.

A comparison of the first and second editions of Türk's *Klavierschule* (already mentioned in chapter 5) provides a revealing case study. In a section in the first edition of 1789 recommending literature for "raw beginners" (*ganz rohe Anfänger*), Türk recommended students seek out four-hand sonatas by Mozart and his contemporaries, alongside Kinderlieder by Reichardt, Hiller, and others, and solo sonatas by Haydn, C. P. E. Bach, and others.[36] When Türk revised this passage for the 1802 edition, he added "similar, very useful, short compositions by Mozart, (*XII petites pieces* etc.) by Haydn, (*Sammlung leichter Klavierstücke* &c.) and by various other composers" to his list.[37] Alongside the recommendations, this second edition now included hundreds of short musical excerpts from Mozart and other composers, as real-world examples for Türk's suggestions on everything from fingering to hand-crossing to expression.

Other piano tutors and student collections also began to excerpt Mozart around the turn of the nineteenth century. In Johann Peter Milchmeyer's 1801 *Kleine Pianoforte-Schule für Kinder*, simplified versions of "Se vuol ballare" (*Le nozze di Figaro*) and "Fin ch'han dal vino" (*Don Giovanni*) appear alongside lullabies, folk songs, and themes by Grétry,

Haydn, and Beethoven's *Abschiedsgesang an Wiens Bürger* (Farewell Song to Vienna's Citizens, WoO 121, 1796), as well as a waltz attributed to Mozart that was actually by Anton Hammer.[38]

By 1819, a pedagogical collection entitled *W. A. Mozarts Clavierschule* was published in Prague.[39] Despite the title, the treatise portion of the text does not mention Mozart at all. The first musical excerpt following the finger exercises is a simplified adaptation of the "Es klinget so herrlich" chorus from *Die Zauberflöte*. Of the seventeen graded excerpts that follow, not even half are by Mozart. The last one by him is No. 11, a transcription of his orchestral Minuet and Trio K. 604/1 (1791). The more difficult excerpts that follow are by composers like Beethoven, Haydn, and Maria Theresia von Paradies; and the final and most complex excerpt is a movement from one of the sonatas C. P. E. Bach included with his *Essay on the True Art of Playing Keyboard Instruments* (1753). It is tempting to interpret the presence of Mozart's name in the title as little more than opportunistic branding, given the dearth of Mozart excerpts and references. But the fact that his contributions fall out of the collection the more advanced the music gets suggests that a deliberate choice was made—not only to use Mozart's simpler music, but to associate Mozart with the simple.

Mozart Made Easy, Part 2: Dice Games and Musical Alphabets

As the *Neuer Plutarch* confirmed, soon after Mozart's death "collections and editions of his compositions followed one after the other with the greatest speed; every trifle from his estate was sought out."[40] Music was sometimes erroneously or misleadingly attributed to Mozart—we have already seen one example in the spurious waltz in the 1801 *Kleine Pianoforte-Schule für Kinder*. In spurious music for children, we find further examples of the growing cultural traction of child-friendly Mozart.

The first example, the musical dice game, was a genre not always or even mostly aimed at the young—but it later came to be associated with them. Today, musical dice games are often interpreted as either an exemplar of Enlightenment rationalist philosophy, an anticipation of Romantic originality and freedom of invention, or even a distant forebear of twentieth-century serial and algorithmic compositional procedures.[41] In the eighteenth century, however, they were commonly promoted as a kind of magical shortcut to the production of simple dance tunes. One Viennese print from the 1780s described dice-game composition as "One of the newest fashionable pastimes in French society."[42]

Mozart was apparently familiar with the fad, and even sketched what appears to be a table of minuet measures (K. 516f) in May 1787. Scholars are not certain, however, whether Mozart intended this as a dice game or just as, in the words of Neal Zaslaw, a "modular minuet machine."[43] Regardless, Mozart's sketch was never published in his lifetime; it was not even catalogued until the third edition of the Köchel catalogue in 1937. But his name came to be associated with one musical dice game in particular that was popular in German cities at the turn of the nineteenth century.

Piracy and misattribution were common in dice-game prints, revealing both the fluidity of authorship in a genre that is only tenuously "composed," and the responsiveness of the market to celebrity. One musical dice game composed (designed?) by Maximilian Stadler—the composer and cleric, then a monk at the Benedictine Abbey of Melk, and later a cataloguer of Mozart's works—was republished numerous times in the 1780s, including once under Joseph Haydn's name. The two dice games attributed to Mozart were originally published anonymously in 1793 by the Berlin publisher Rellstab. We do not know their original composer; it may well have been Stadler again. One game was for generating contredanses, the other for waltzes, and their titles echoed the "you can, too" rhetoric of others in circulation: "Instruction for Composing with Dice as Many [Waltzes or Contredanses] as One Could Want, Without Being Musical or Understanding Composition." Of the two, the waltz game was apparently especially popular, for within a year, Rellstab came out with a set of 24 *Waltzes after the Anleitung, by 24 different, for the most part unmusical* [!], *persons.*[44] This print was described in a capsule review in the *Allgemeine Literatur-Zeitung* as proof to anyone who still doubted that a toss of the dice could result in a successful waltz.[45]

Rellstab's two dice games were soon pirated by the Hummel firm, and this time Hummel added Mozart's name prominently to the title page.[46] Five years later, in 1798, the Simrock firm in Bonn printed both the waltz and the contredanse games, again with Mozart's name.[47] And three years after that, in 1801, two other music publishers sold the games under Mozart's name: Johann Michael Götz, based in Worms, and G. P. Arnold, in Hamburg.[48] That these musical dice games were attributed to Mozart by multiple geographically disparate music publishers attests to the popularity of the composer at the turn of the century. But Mozart's name also appears to have raised the cachet of what was otherwise an indisputably trivial genre of music. When in 1813 the *AmZ* disavowed Mozart's composition of the two *Anleitung* prints, the author of the article looked back ruefully on the errors of his forefathers, who had taken a "little plaything" for something "so deep and wonderful, that it was believed their invention was to be attributed to none other than the God-given genius that was at hand, namely Mozart, who had never in his life thought of such a thing!"[49] The author's embarrassment at the glorification of these musical trifles suggests that someone in Mozart's estate might have intervened; or perhaps by then the fad had simply run its course. The author went on to spend four more pages on an elaborate series of calculations about the possible combinations of bars in an eight-bar melody. The association with Mozart had served its purpose, elevating what was originally a parlor game into a sophisticated mathematical problem.

As both Zaslaw and Hans Pimmer have noted, the frequency with which these dice games were marketed to people "without the least knowledge of music" meant that children were also an intended consumer for this genre.[50] Several dice games—such as N. Bigant's *Domino musical* (1779, Paris) and the *Musical Domino* (1793, London)—made this goal explicit, addressing themselves to children or students.[51] The same was true for the Rellstab dice games, even after the misattribution to Mozart was corrected. Around 1810, the London-based music publisher Charles Wheatstone printed yet another pirated version of the *Anleitung* material, this time entitled *Mozart's, [sic] Musical Game, or the Christmas Musical Gift, to juvenile amateurs, being an ingenious, easy & systematical method, of composing any number of pleasing and entertaining Waltzes, without the slightest knowledge of composition, by the turn of a te totum.* The teetotum, or numbered spinning top, was seen by many as an acceptable tool for the young to use in gaming, since it did not have the same unsavory connotations as dice.[52] In a prefatory address to the reader, Wheatstone claimed that

> This work was chiefly intended by the late celebrated MOZART, to excite curiosity [and] at the same time calculated to amuse and entertain; and tho it does not embrace the principles of the Science; yet it affords an opportunity for the Juvenile practitioner to form a just Idea of the construction of melody; likewise some practice in writing Music.[53]

This was all fabricated ballyhoo, of course, but it made use of that familiar trope of children's music and literature: the "amuse and instruct" binary. The advertisement for G. P. Arnold's 1801 pseudo-Mozart dice game had used this language, addressing "all parents who wish to give their children a very *pleasing and beneficial gift.*"[54] The misattribution has continued to prove tenacious, being reproduced in several modern editions of the score as well as on the 1991 Philips Complete Mozart Edition recording. This cemented the reciprocal strains of early Mozart reception: the

FIGURE 6.4. *W. A. Mozarts Alphabet. Ein musikalischer Scherz* (Berlin, ca. 1820s). Courtesy of Bayerische Staatsbibliothek München, shelfmark Mus.pr. 2009.135.

association of Mozart with youthfulness, and the elevation of his "trivial" genres.

The association of Mozart and "pleasing and beneficial" entertainments for children was further cemented in a musical "Alphabet . . . for Children's Voices" published in Berlin in the 1820s, with Mozart's name under the title (fig. 6.4). The "arranger" may have been Carl Eduard Pax, a Berlin-based music teacher who was responsible for several other sets of waltzes, contredanses, and children's choral works published by Lischke.[55] But this musical alphabet turns out to be neither by Mozart, nor by Pax.[56] It appears, rather, to have been plagiarized from a collection of songs by a composer known only as "Dillenberg," entitled *Ernst und Scherz*, published by Simrock in Bonn in 1813.[57] *Ernst und Scherz* was by no means intended for children: it includes a drinking song and a song repudiating marriage, and the "Alfabet" that is the seventh of its twelve songs is more a joke than a pedagogical exercise. The collection closes with a Quodlibet that includes quotations from *Die Zauberflöte* alongside several bawdy puns. The *AmZ* was scandalized by this collection, calling its texts "vile" and questioning the "social class [Volksklasse]" of its author.[58] But it must have been relatively popular, for it was still in print in 1845, along with a separate print of the Quodlibet. Pax's pseudo-Mozart alphabet was still in print as well.[59] Like the dice game, the "Mozart" alphabet had a tenacious hold on the popular imagination: to this day it is a favorite of amateur children's choirs and recording artists of children's music, particularly in France, where it is still published by Editions Salabert under Mozart's name.[60]

The spurious musical dice games and alphabet suggest that there was an incentive for publishers to invoke Mozart's name in connection with musical games and jokes, and not just because of his celebrity status. These works appealed to those "with no knowledge of composition," reinforcing the "easy, light" persona exemplified in the sonatas aimed at beginners. The lighthearted music also capitalized on the composer's image as a playful, sociable gentleman, a bit of a scamp even. This may also account for the frequency with which "Papa Haydn's" name was attached to similar genres.[61] But Mozart's biographical tradition, far more than Haydn's, emphasized his career as a composing prodigy. He thus continued to be closely associated with children and childhood throughout and after his life, which meant that music printers with a piece of playful and child-friendly music readily attached that music to the Mozart brand.

Mozart Made Easy, Part 3: "Relics" in the Nissen Biography

Perhaps the ultimate *Mozartetti* are the juvenile and child-oriented compositions that appeared in Nissen's 1828 biography. Nissen chose just three pieces for inclusion as score excerpts in the text of the biography, and four others as "Musikblätter" or tipped-in sheets.[62] Given that the biography and its appendix together totaled 921 pages, these scant appearances of notated music take on major significance in the *mise en livre*. Of the seven, six are by Mozart, and three date from before he turned ten. Granted, Nissen's publisher Breitkopf may have wished to avoid any duplication of music already sold separately in their catalogue, and to entice customers with musical arcana one could find nowhere else. Whatever the motivation, the effect of these examples was to create a narrative running in parallel to the text, one that reified Mozart's youthful works as "precious relics," as Nissen himself referred to them.[63]

The first we might consider in this gallery is the *Wiegenlied* (lullaby), which was considered an authentic Mozart work (K. 350) up until the end of the nineteenth century (fig. 6.5). This piece, like the dice games and alphabet, has become nearly inextricable from Mozart: by the time Max Friedlaender proved in 1892 that it was not actually by Mozart, it was the second most well-known Mozart Lied after "Das Veilchen," and it has continued to be recorded throughout the twentieth century.[64] The simple

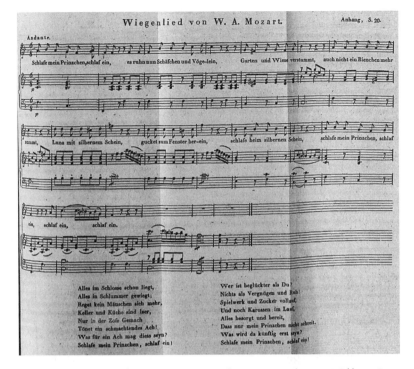

FIGURE 6.5. "Wiegenlied von W. A. Mozart," in Nissen, *Anhang zu Wolfgang Amadeus Mozart's Biographie* (Leipzig, 1828), after p. 20. Courtesy of Universitätsbibliothek Frankfurt, Nachlass Arthur Schopenhauer, urn:nbn:de:hebis:30-1137524.

tune, on a text from Friedrich Wilhelm Gotter's play *Esther*, is in fact by the dilettante composer Bernhard Flies, and was first published in 1795.[65]

Exactly how this *Wiegenlied* first came to be associated with Mozart is uncertain, but an anonymous copy was in Constanze's possession in 1825, and she handed it over to the publisher André with an equivocal authentication. Constanze's comments on the Wiegenlied in the letter to André began: "Totally charming, in many ways recognizably Mozartian [*Mozartisch*], naïve, whimsical."[66] This part of the description was reproduced verbatim in Nissen's biography (perhaps by Constanze herself). The spurious lullaby appears in the *Anhang* (appendix) to Nissen's biography, as part of the "List of musical fragments and drafts found in Mozart's estate, which have for the most part been prepared by Abbé Maximilian Stadler."[67] What the *Anhang* leaves out, however, is the continuation of Constanze's comments on the lullaby in the original letter. After the observations about its "recognizably Mozartian" style, she admitted that Nannerl knew nothing of the song, though Mozart would have had to have composed it in his youth, because he did not compose it in Vienna. Furthermore, Constanze admitted, nothing in the lullaby "betrayed the youth of the composer."[68] In other words, she could not definitively attribute the lullaby to Mozart. Nevertheless, the lullaby was not only included in the *Anhang*, but also given pride of place as one of the tipped-in *Musikblätter*; and it was singled out as "quite lovely" in the first of two reviews of the biography published in *Caecilia*.[69] Could Breitkopf & Härtel perhaps have intended for readers to remove the unassuming little lullaby for occasional performance at bedtime? Could they have foreseen that "Schlafe, mein Prinzchen" would soon be cited as the paradigmatic example of a "Wiegenlied" in the definition of that word in the 1840 *Musikalisches Conversations-Lexikon*?[70] Regardless, this spurious work managed to become part of the Mozart canon for over a century, based solely on the circular argument that it struck Constanze as "recognizably Mozartian."[71]

That eponymous adjective "Mozartisch," first recorded in Constanze's authentication of the lullaby, gained more connotative force when it began to be used to describe other composers. To my knowledge, the earliest time "Mozartisch" was used in a positive sense to describe a composer other than Mozart occurs in the early criticism of Beethoven's first two symphonies (published 1801 and 1804). An 1821 article in the *Berlin Allgemeine musikalische Zeitung* described Beethoven's first symphony as "straightforwardly *Mozartisch*," and his second as "already somewhat beyond Mozart's symphonies."[72] This review ended up in Nissen's biography, in a section on Beethoven.[73] No longer did "Mozartisch" suggest bizarre and excessive; now it meant graceful, delicate, and pleasant. In an unexpected way, Beethoven was living up to his premature identification as "a second Mozart" (as discussed in chapter 1). The emergence of his eccentric, difficult music made possible a more charming, accessible Mozart.[74] Tia DeNora suggests that the Mozartian values of elegance and "pleasingness" did not leave room for the "force" of Beethoven; but to read some of the critical literature that paired the two composers, it may have been that Beethoven's "force" made room for Mozart's "pleasingness."[75] Putting it in terms of the Dillenberg collection: Beethoven's "Ernst" enabled Mozart's "Scherz," and vice versa.

A final pair of artifacts, again reproduced in full in the Nissen biography, confirms the privileging of child Mozart, and takes us back to a period preceding the years, and the music, with which this book began. These are the sketches from the *Nannerl Notenbuch*, in which Leopold copied out pieces for Nannerl to practice, and also notated the first compositional efforts of the five- and six-year-old Wolfgang (K. 1–5).[76]

For a composer who started publishing at age seven, only these unpublished movements and movement fragments can accurately be termed juvenilia. Already in 1817, the Würzburg-based theorist and music pedagogue Joseph Fröhlich had breathlessly reported the acquisition of these first efforts of the "Hero of Composition."[77] While he admitted that they were slight in themselves, Fröhlich claimed they showed "the unique direction of this great spirit."[78] Nissen repeated Fröhlich's words, and lovingly reproduced a number of Mozart's own movements, and some of the movements copied out for him and Nannerl to learn at the keyboard, in twelve pages of *Musikblätter*—by far the longest musical example in the biography. The length of this example even raised some eyebrows among its early readership: in a second, more critical review of the biography in *Caecilia*, the reviewer reported somewhat peevishly that he was "quite unable to perceive any progress" over the course of the *Musikblätter*.[79]

The extraordinary amount of space Nissen gives to the *Nannerl Notenbuch* excerpts in his biography does not mean that he considered K. 1–5 to be of greater significance than, say, *Don Giovanni* or the Jupiter Symphony. But including such obscure Mozartiana would surely appeal to devotees, completists, and antiquarians, while the ease with which the music could be played would have been a strong selling point for homes with a piano. In devoting a lavish amount of space to these little exercises, Nissen monumentalized the most unassuming products of the preprofessional child Mozart.[80]

The *Nannerl Notenbuch* sketches were not even the most juvenile of Mozart's juvenilia to appear in the *Biographie*. Nissen also included a nonsense lullaby that Mozart supposedly devised as a bedtime routine with his father (fig. 6.6). The anecdote was translated nearly in full in the review of the Nissen biography published in the London *Foreign Quarterly Review*, showing just how much traction this little song had in the reception of the book:

> Mozart loved his parents, particularly his father, so tenderly, that every night before going to bed he used to sing a little air that he had composed on purpose, his father having placed him standing in a chair, and singing the second to him. During the singing he often kissed his father *on the top of the nose*, (the epicurism of childish fondness,) and as soon as this solemnity was over, he was laid in bed, perfectly contented and happy.[81]

The account in Nissen claimed that this tradition was maintained until Mozart was ten, years after his first sonatas were published. Nissen went on, "The words were approximately: *oragna figata fa marina gamina fa*."[82]

This Italian-doggerel lullaby, then, is presented as Mozart's "first com-

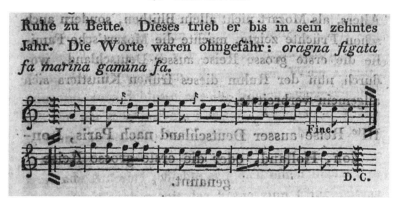

FIGURE 6.6. Mozart[?], "Schlaflied," in Nissen, *Biographie W. A. Mozarts* (Leipzig, 1828), 35. Courtesy of Bayerische Staatsbibliothek München, shelfmark Mus.th. 4904.

position." Whether related by Mozart to Constanze, recalled by Schachtner or Nannerl, or a complete fabrication, it is presented as a transcription, the mediation of a fantasy of immediacy. That Leopold harmonized with Wolfgang encapsulates the inseparability of the playful and the pedantic in the Mozart household (why should they be separated at this time, after all?)—although the harmony is inexplicably omitted from the transcription. That the text is a loving parody of Italian, rather than German or Salzburg dialect, presents Wolfgang as a cosmopolitan even before he was a musician.[83]

Early in book 1 of his 1782 *Confessions*, Rousseau wrote, "I felt before thinking—this is the common fate of humanity."[84] If Nissen's bedtime litany is to be believed, we might say that Wolfgang sang before playing or writing. And now the most extreme endpoint of his oeuvre was a bedtime litany, an intimate ritual of reassurance between father and son, one that he had presumably shared with Constanze frequently enough that she had memorized it. Thanks to her, an engraver set that litany in type, Breitkopf included it on page 35, and that intimate ritual was now enshrined in print for all time, and for all the world to read—just as Rousseau had laid bare his own interiority to a shocked readership. When Nissen made not just Mozart's most rudimentary, juvenile, and private compositional efforts but even his own musical security blanket something to be transcribed and consumed, Mozart's transformation of the relationship between childhood and the marketplace was complete.

Acknowledgments

I am humbled by the many individuals whose generosity helped me see this book through to completion. I would like to begin by thanking the obliging staff at the following libraries and archives: the Augsburg University Library, Bayerische Staatsbibliothek München, British Library, British Museum, ETH (Eidgenössische Technische Hochschule) Bibliothek Zürich, Germanisches Nationalmuseum, Herzog August Bibliothek, Internationale Stiftung Mozarteum, Niedersächsische Staats- und Universitätsbibliothek Göttingen, Österreichisches Nationalbibliothek, Salzburg University Library, Scripta Paedagogica Online at Bibliothek für Bildungsgeschichtliche Forschung des Deutsches Institut für Internationale Pädagogische Forschung, Sächsische Landesbibliothek—Staats- und Universitätsbibliothek Dresden, Smithsonian Libraries, Stadtarchiv Salzburg, Universitätsbibliothek Frankfurt, and Wienbibliothek im Rathaus. I would also like to thank the staff at Mount Holyoke College Library, Information, and Technological Services, particularly Ethan Powers and the Interlibrary Loan department, for their assiduous help in acquiring materials for my research over the years.

Many admired colleagues read and commented on the manuscript at various stages. For their insightful observations on early drafts, I wish to thank Rebekah Ahrendt, Katherine Butler, Melanie Gudesblatt, Jonathan Hicks, Lisa Jakelski, Jonathan Morton, Emily Richmond Pollock, Laura Protano-Biggs, Megan Robb, and Anicia Timberlake. These colleagues and friends from my years as a graduate student at the University of California, Berkeley, and a Junior Research Fellow at New College, University of Oxford, offered thoughtful input that sharpened the focus of each chapter and of the project as a whole. They often made connections that I could not see, and their treasured companionship meant that I will always look back on those years with fondness.

At the University of Chicago Press, I wish to thank Marta Tonegutti for her patient and encouraging shepherding of the book, as well as Tristan Bates and Dylan Montanari, who each demonstrated an admirable blend of friendliness and exactitude in handling the myriad details of the manuscript's preparation and submission. I would also like to thank the anonymous readers for reports that were at once reassuring, challenging, and highly entertaining to read, and I appreciate the precise copyediting and careful editorial supervision of Marianne Tatom and Tamara Ghattas, as well as the index prepared by June Sawyers.

I developed the material for this book over a number of conferences and colloquia that allowed me to receive valuable input from a variety of scholars at various stages in my research. Thanks go to the organizers of colloquia at the University of California, Berkeley; King's College London; the Five College Childhood Studies Seminar; the University of Oxford; the Presidential Scholars in Society and Neuroscience conference, Columbia University (*The Transmission of Songs in Birds, Humans, and Other Animals*); the Don Juan Archiv Symposium; the American and British Societies for Eighteenth-Century Studies; the Mozart Society of America; and the American Musicological Society. Fellow eighteenth-centuryists who shared information and ideas, and whose cordiality continue to make our collaborations and reunions a joy, include Jessica Waldoff, Martin Nedbal, Estelle Joubert, Bruce Alan Brown, Paul Corneilson, and Rupert Ridgewell.

The support and engagement of now-far-flung colleagues sustained me and expanded my thinking about the issues I explore here and the wider historical, political, and ethical concerns from which they cannot pretend to be disentangled. In addition to those listed above, I would like to thank Olga Panteleeva, Tiffany Ng, Bill Quillen, and Sean Curran, among the many bright souls from 107 Morrison, for stimulating exchanges of ideas and for serving as models of how to live an engaged intellectual life. At Oxford, in addition to those already named, I wish to thank Peter Franklin, Jennifer Thorp, Daniel Grimley, Steven Grahl, Rachel Moore, Benedict Taylor, and Michael Burden, for inspiring conversations, collaborations, and even a few harebrained schemes as I fell down Alice's rabbit hole over three idyllic years.

My greatest debts are to my mentors from UC Berkeley. Nicholas Mathew and James Davies continue to serve as models for how to keep the historical quirks, the big questions, and the pleasures of sound in productively colliding orbits. Nick encouraged me to think ever more expansively about my project; this book is the richer for it. Mary Ann Smart has long been my exemplar for writerly precision and imagination. Her discerning guidance while I was first formulating these questions, and the compassion and insight she has shown in our exchanges since then, are gifts I can only repay by following her example with my own students. She also showed me how to make peace with my inner critic—or, at least, how and when to establish temporary détentes. Richard Taruskin taught me how to read quickly and teach nimbly, and how teaching can be a kind of writing; I think of him nearly every time I'm in the classroom. Finally, this book owes an incalculable debt to the late Wye J. Allanbrook. My Austen reference in chapter 5 is, in part, a tribute to a conversation between her and my mother after she delivered the keynote address at a conference I organized on *Die Zauberflöte*. Listening in as those two women I admired talked Austen was a moment I will never forget.

This book was begun at UC Berkeley and Oxford but completed at Mount Holyoke College, where my colleagues in the Department of Music—particularly chairs Gary Steigerwalt, David Sanford, and Olabode Omojola—have welcomed me warmly and supported my pedagogical and scholarly development from day one. Words cannot convey my gratitude to the Friday morning faculty writing group, begun by Cathy Luna, for five years of weekly accountability, mentoring, and quiet fellowship, especially Sarah Bacon, Mara Benjamin, Holly Hanson, Serin Houston, Jacquelyne Luce, Katherine O'Callaghan, Karen Remmler, Mary Renda, Megan Saltzman, and Monika Schmitter. My other writing partners Vivian Leung and Amy Coddington, as well as the Faculty Success Program at the National Center for Faculty Development and Diversity, have also helped me immeasurably in fine-tuning my writing practice. For their careful review of my translations, I would like to thank Anna Karapin-Springorum and Beth Siegling. Finally, I want to thank my students at Mount Holyoke, whose dedication, creativity, candor, and activism challenge me every day to become a more thoughtful and ethical professor. I can think of no place I would rather be at this difficult, transformative moment in American history.

My deepest thanks go to my family and friends, for unwavering moral support, the occasional cold splash of perspective, and a welcome sense of humor. It is because of my mother and father that I am most at home in classrooms and around books and popular culture. My dad, Robert, taught me to appreciate the sublime in comedy, the craft of the journeyman actor, and the endlessly fascinating in nature. My mom, Linda, taught me that there's no business like show business, and nothing quite as heartwarming as a backstage musical. "As you from crimes would pardoned be, / Let your indulgence set me free." We always will—

ideally from the front row, with tears in our eyes, and the first to rise to our feet.

My husband, Ian, has been my greatest champion and companion for more than half my life now. Even in times of trial, his wisdom and easy wit never fail to astonish me, and he always seems to know exactly when we need to stop whatever we're doing, crank up the speakers, and dance. A devoted archivist, cine- and TV-phile, reader, gardener, and father, he brings delight to the everyday. This book is dedicated with love to our daughter Nora, a budding artist with the soul of a scientist (or is it the other way around?). If I have had anything to do with her goodwill and restless curiosity, I will count the strange journey of motherhood—which first prompted this book's line of inquiry—a success.

Notes

Introduction

1. Leopold described this portrait in a letter (Paris) to Lorenz Hagenauer (Salzburg), April 1, 1764, *MBA* 83:155–58; trans. in Anderson, 44.

2. Letter from Leopold (Munich) to Maria Anna (Salzburg), December 30, 1774, *MBA* 308:5–11; trans. in Anderson, 255.

3. Letter from Leopold (Salzburg) to J. G. I. Breitkopf (Leipzig), October 6, 1775, *MBA* 320:26–28; trans. in Anderson, 265.

4. Letter from Leopold (Salzburg) to Maria Anna and Wolfgang (Mannheim), January 26, 1778, *MBA* 410:61–67; extract not trans. in Anderson.

5. Letter from Mozart (Paris) to Leopold (Salzburg), July 31, 1778, *MBA* 471:165–67; trans. in Anderson, 587.

6. "Verzeichnis jetzlebender Componisten in Deutschland," *Musikalischer Almanach für Deutschland auf das Jahr 1784*, ed. Johann Nicolaus Forkel (Leipzig); in *Dokumente*, 195–96; *Documents*, 220.

7. Letter from Leopold (Munich) to Breitkopf & Son (Leipzig), February 12, 1781, *MBA* 582:11–12; trans. in Anderson, 710.

8. Letter from Nannerl (St. Gilgen) to Breitkopf & Härtel (Leipzig), September 24, 1799, *MBA* 1268:70–75; not in Anderson.

9. Siskin and Warner, "This Is Enlightenment: An Invitation in the Form of an Argument," 1.

10. Siskin and Warner, "This Is Enlightenment," 22.

11. See in this regard van Orden, introduction, in *Music and the Cultures of Print*; and Taruskin, *Text and Act*. On music and mediation, see Born, "On Musical Mediation."

12. Cunningham, *Children and Childhood*; Melton, *Absolutism*; Cook, "Children's Consumption in History"; and Cook, "Children as Consumers."

13. Blanning, *The Culture of Power*; Beales, *Enlightenment and Reform*; and Morrison, "Authorship in Transition." On the peculiar nature of the "Austrian Enlightenment," see the writings of Ritchie Robertson, most recently the essays reprinted in part 2 of *Enlightenment and Religion in German and Austrian Literature*.

14. For critical overviews of the historiography of childhood, see Cunningham, "Histories of Childhood"; Jenks, *Childhood*; and Fass, "Is There a Story?"

15. See for instance Marten, "Childhood Studies and History"; Spyrou, *Disclosing Childhoods*; and Cook, ed., *Symbolic Childhood*.

16. Müller, ed., *Fashioning Childhood*; Cunningham, *The Invention of Childhood*; and Langmuir, *Imagining Childhood*.

Chapter One

1. See Archard, "John Locke's Children"; and Yolton and Yolton, "Introduction," in Locke, *Some Thoughts concerning Education*.

2. This philosophy was enshrined in the first sentence of Rousseau's *On the Social Contract*: "Man is born free, and everywhere he is in chains." Rousseau, *Du contrat social*, 2. See also Heywood, *Growing Up in France*, esp. 52–63, on "the innocent child."

3. Rousseau, *Émile*, vol. 1 (1762), 203; trans. in *Emile*, 226.

4. On the child as noble savage, see Jenks, *Childhood*, 4–6; and Cunningham, *Children of the Poor*, 99. For a study of the period between Locke and Rousseau that attempts to account for the transformations in educational philosophy in eighteenth-century France, see Gill, *Educational Philosophy in the French Enlightenment*.

5. Among the classical and early modern antecedents are Quintilian's *Institutio oratoria* (ca. 95 CE), Ersamus's *On Education for Children* (1529), and Michel de Montaigne's *De l'institution des enfants* (ca. 1578–1580). See King, "The School of Infancy."

6. Gubar, *Artful Dodgers*, 6.

7. See *Dokumente*; *Documents*; *NMD*; and Edge/Black.

8. Gubar, *Artful Dodgers*, 6.

9. Krupp, *Reason's Children*, 15.

10. Kivy writes, for instance, that Mozart's "marvelous juvenilia were produced before any knowledge or 'method' *could* have been acquired, even if there were such, thus proving beyond doubt that no such knowledge or method is necessary, even if available, for creative activity at the highest level." Kivy, *The Possessor and the Possessed*, 92. See also Kivy, "Child Mozart as an Aesthetic Symbol"; Solomon, "Mozart: The Myth of the Eternal Child"; Flaherty, "Mozart and the Mythologization of Genius"; Pesic, "Child and the Daemon"; and Hausfater, "Etre Mozart: Wolfgang et ses émules."

11. See Rasch, "The Dutch Republic as a Place of Publication," 95, 100; and Baragwanath, "Mozart's Early Chamber Music with Keyboard," 25–26.

12. Igor Kopytoff writes that, after its initial purchase, a commodity's "status is inevitably ambiguous and open to the push and pull of events and desires, as it is shuffled about in the flux of social life." Kopytoff, "The Cultural Biography of Things," 83. See also van Orden, "Introduction," in *Music and the Cultures of Print*, xiii.

13. Taruskin, *Text and Act*.

14. Letter from Leopold (Paris) to Maria Theresia Hagenauer (Salzburg), February 1, 1764, *MBA* 80:155–157; trans. in Anderson, 38.

15. See for instance Edge and Black, "10 May 1765: Defending the Truth of Mozart's Age," in Edge/Black. Perhaps the most famous example of this, though fictional, is the teenage "Infant Phenomenon" in Charles Dickens's 1839 novel *Nicholas Nickleby*. See Gubar, "The Drama of Precocity," 63, 75–76.

16. For an overview of musical prodigies in the eighteenth century, see McLamore, "Mozart in the Middle"; Cooper, *Child Composers and Their Works*; Bodsch,

ed., *Beethoven und andere Wunderkinder*; Sacquin and Ladurie, eds., *Le printemps des génies*, 52–129; McVeigh, *Concert Life in London*, 85–86; Stevens, *Das Wunderkind in der Musikgeschichte*; and Traudes, *Musizierende "Wunderkinder."*

17. Elisabeth-Claude Jacquet de la Guerre was described in the *Mercure galant* in 1677 as playing her own pieces from age ten, but she did not publish her first piece until age twenty-two. See Jackson, "Musical Women of the Seventeenth and Eighteenth Centuries," 72. Françoise-Charlotte de Ménetou (b. 1680, fl. 1691), a pupil of François Couperin, published her *Airs sérieux à deux* in 1691 at age eleven, but no mention was made of her age in the print. Jean-Baptiste Cardonne (1730–ca. 1792), a page in the Royal Music under Louis XV, had a *chanson* published in the *Mercure de France* in 1746, when he was sixteen, and his youth was remarked at the time. But this was not an independent opus, nor did one appear later in his youth. See *Mercure de France* (February 1746), 146. Finally, in Nuremberg in 1756 and 1757, Anna Bon (1740?–after 1767) published two sets of sonatas, the first for flute and the second for clavier. If the supposed date of her birth is correct, then she would have still been in her teens, but no mention is made of her age in the original prints or, as far as can be determined, in any contemporary reviews. See Schleifer and Glickman, eds., *Women Composers*, vol. 3, 16–24.

18. Dedication to *Sinfonie da chiesa à tre . . .* (Modena: Fortuniano Rosati, 1699), trans. in Sven Hansell, "Fiorè, Andrea Stefano," *OMO* (2001). I can find no evidence of the early reception of this work; Estienne Roger reprinted it in 1700 for Amsterdam and numerous times over the next forty years, but without retaining Fiorè's original dedication. Rasch, *Music Publishing House of Estienne Roger*, 20.

19. Burney, *Present State of Music in France and Italy*, 228; reproduced in Flaherty, "Mozart and the Mythologization of Genius," 296.

20. When a boy "loses his voice," Leopold Mozart wrote, "he is taken care of for a good two or three years more (according to his good behaviour), so that he gains time to perfect himself and put himself in a position to enter the service of the Court, which the majority of them attain because, if they are fit for service, they are given preference over others." Mozart, "Nachricht," 194–95; trans. in Zaslaw, *Mozart's Symphonies*, 555. Translation Zaslaw's. As to when the voice break could take place, one study cites J. S. Bach's report of boy altos in Leipzig to surmise that male voices at mid-century began to break between sixteen and eighteen. Daw, "Age of Boys' Puberty in Leipzig." Scholars continue to disagree about the reliability of such figures; see also Ong et al., "Timing of Voice Breaking in Males."

21. See for instance Loughnan, *Manifest Madness*, 67–94; and Crofts, *Criminal Responsibility*.

22. See for instance G[eorge] L[ong], "Infans, Infantia," in Smith, ed., *Dictionary of Greek and Roman Antiquities*, 636: "*Infans* properly means *Qui fari non potest* [who does not have the power of speech]. The expression *Qui fari potest* expressed not only that degree of intellectual development which is shown by the use of intelligible speech, but also a capacity for legal acts in which speech was required." I am grateful to Nicholas Mathew for this observation.

23. Frisch, *Teutsch-Lateinisches Wörter-Buch*, vol. 1 (1741), 514.

24. Taddei, "*Puerizia, Adolescenza* and *Giovinezza*," 20–21.

25. See again Crofts, *Criminal Responsibility*; and Cipriani, *Children's Rights*.

26. See [Maria Theresa], *Constitutio Criminalis Theresiana*, 21–22.

27. Rousseau, *Émile*, vol. 1 (1762), 191, 202; trans. in *Emile*, 222, 226. Rousseau here departs somewhat from Diderot and d'Alembert's *Encyclopédie*, which claims that at seven or eight years of age, one is capable of rational thought. [Arnulphe d'Aumont], "Enfance," in Diderot and d'Alembert, eds., *Encyclopédie*, vol. 5 (1756), 651–52.

28. Locke, *Some Thoughts concerning Education* (1693), 90, 91–92, and 140; see also Archard, "John Locke's Children," 88.

29. See for instance Neuhouser, *Rousseau's Theodicy of Self-Love*.

30. This was Locke's reason for discouraging corporal punishment in the very young; for below the age of seven, "What Vices can a Child be guilty of, but Lying, or some ill-natur'd Tricks." Locke, *Some Thoughts concerning Education* (1693), 96.

31. Locke, *Some Thoughts concerning Education* (1693), 235; Rousseau, *Émile*, vol. 1 (1762), 403; trans. in *Emile*, 289.

32. Rousseau, *Émile*, vol. 1 (1762), 418; trans. in *Emile*, 293.

33. German-language editions of, and commentaries on, Locke's *Some Thoughts on Education* from 1700 to 1763 included: *Des Herrn John Locke Gedanken von Erziehung junger Edelleute* (Greiffswald: Fickweiler, 1708); *Herrn Johann Locks [sic] Unterricht von Erziehung der Kinder* (Hanover: Förster und Sohn, 1729); *Abhandlung von der Erziehung der Kinder und besonders der Prinzen: worinn die Wichtigkeit der ersten sieben Jahre des Lebens gezeigt wird* (Berlin: Rüdiger, 1758); and *Herrn Johann Lockes Gedanken von Erziehung der Kinder* (Leipzig: Krauß, 1761). Rousseau's *Émile* was translated and published in Germany the year of its original publication: *Aemil, oder Von der Erziehung* [trans. Johann Joachim Schwabe] (Berlin, Frankfurt, and Leipzig: [n.p.], 1762).

34. Hübner, from the "Diarium Patris Bedae Hübner" (April 26, 1766); in *Dokumente*, 53; *Documents*, 55. See also *Lloyd's Evening Post* (February 22, 1765), 183; and letter of Joseph Yorke (The Hague), October 1, 1765; both reproduced in *NMD*, 6 and 9, respectively.

35. Anonymous, "Ein Tonkünstler von 7 Jahren und seine Schwester von 11 Jahren," *Historisch-Moralische Belustigungen des Geistes oder Ermunternde Betrachtungen über die wunderbare Haushaltung Gottes in den neuesten Zeiten* (Hamburg, 1765), 693; in *Dokumente*, 46; *Documents*, 47.

36. Letter to the Printer, *Public Advertiser* (May 10, 1765), in Edge and Black, "10 May 1765: Defending the Truth of Mozart's Age," in Edge/Black.

37. See also Christoph von Zabuesnig's 1769 poem in honor of Mozart, which refers to "the proofs of your art" (die Proben deiner Kunst); in *Dokumente*, 80; *Documents*, 87.

38. Barrington, "Account of a Very Remarkable Young Musician," 54–55n; cited in Chrissochoidis, "London Mozartiana": 84.

39. Loughnan, *Manifest Madness*, 70.

40. Antonín Kammel, letter of April 30, 1765, State Regional Archives Prague, quoted and reproduced in Volek and Bittner, *Mozartiana of Czech and Moravian Archives*, 4 and 14–16. Translation authors'. Volek and Bittner add that Kammel's account "should, henceforward, be referred to if we are confronted—as it happens time and again—with absurd hints at Mozart's alleged infantility."

41. Burney, *Account of an Infant Musician* (1779), 24.

42. See in this context Rose, *The Case of Peter Pan*; Gubar, *Artful Dodgers*; and Nelson, *Precocious Children and Childish Adults*.

43. See Abert, 59–61; and Irving, *Mozart's Piano Sonatas*, 20–23. The genre

appears to have originated with Jean-Joseph Cassanéa de Mondonville in 1734 (*Pièces de clavecin en sonates avec accompagnement de violon*, Opus 3).

44. See Hawkins and Ives, eds., *Women Writers and the Artifacts of Celebrity*. On music arrangements as a form of merchandising, see Wheelock, "Marriage à la Mode"; and Thormählen, "Playing with Art," esp. 343 and 345. Michael Burden has shown how printed sets of "Favourite Songs" from London operas functioned throughout the century to sustain the celebrity of certain singers, a kind of cross-promotional "myth-making" that in turn fueled the industry as a whole. Burden, "Divas and Arias." See also Carter, "Printing the 'New Music.'"

45. *Mercure de France* (February 1765); in *Dokumente*, 42; *Documents*, 42.

46. *Public Advertiser* (March 20, 1765); in *Dokumente*, 45; *Documents*, 45.

47. See for instance Semonin, "Monsters in the Marketplace," 72–75; and Ridley, *Clara's Grand Tour*, 53–63.

48. Many of the practical details of viewings as outlined in the poster for Clara the rhinoceros are similar to those for the Mozarts' appearances (especially in London), as is the overall trajectory of Clara's European and British tour (1741–1758). This is not to suggest that Leopold modeled his tour after Clara's. A pointed reference to a rhinoceros's skin in his letter of December 8, 1763, suggests that Leopold might have been familiar with Clara, but there is no evidence that she passed through Salzburg on her way from Vienna to Regensburg in 1746–1757. Ridley, *Clara's Grand Tour*, xii–xiii, 62–63, and 77.

49. I have found no evidence of such ephemera accompanying the tours of other musical prodigies like Johann Gottfried Wilhelm Palschau (1741–1815) or Gertrud Elisabeth Mara (née Schmeling, 1749–1833). See Rainer Kaiser, "Palschaus Bach-Spiel in London"; and Rasch, *Muziek in de Republiek (Oude Versie): Hoofdstuk Dertien: Concerten*.

50. Alec Hyatt King describes his proportions as "doll-like"; King, *A Mozart Legacy*, 23.

51. Anonymous, "Ein Tonkünstler," 691; in *Dokumente*, 46; *Documents*, 47; and Pater Beda Hübner, "Diarium" (November 29, 1766); in *Dokumente*, 63; *Documents*, 68. For another contemporary comparison of the two siblings, see Grimm, *Correspondance littéraire* (December 1, 1763); in *Dokumente*, 27; *Documents*, 26.

52. On musical family portraits as idealizing and ideological, see Leppert, *Music and Image*.

53. King, *A Mozart Legacy*, 5–24.

54. Dodsley, Preface, *The General Contents of the British Museum*, vi. See also Nannerl's list of items viewed on their visit to the British Museum; Reisenotizen (London), April 23, 1764, to September 4, 1765; *MBA* 100:9–15; not trans. in Anderson.

55. Burney, *Account of an Infant Musician*, 24. Emphasis mine. Barrington, too, described published scores as "printed proof" of a prodigy's compositional abilities, in his account of Samuel Wesley. See Barrington, "Account of Master Samuel Wesley," 306. Both Barrington and Burney include musical excerpts in their accounts of Wesley and Crotch, respectively.

56. Letter from Leopold (London) to Lorenz Hagenauer (Salzburg), December 3, 1764, *MBA* 93:16–18; trans. in Anderson, 53.

57. Davies, "Julia's Gift," 307.

58. Pesic, "Child and the Daemon," 93: "several of the published sets of variations seem to be Mozart's attempts to notate these extempore performances." James

Webster has identified a host of improvisatory gestures in Haydn's keyboard sonatas and trios whose effect is "a kind of slippage between composer, persona, and performer." Webster, "Rhetoric of Improvisation," 208.

59. Mozart, *Versuch*, 255–56; trans. as *Treatise*, 218. Emphasis mine.

60. Bach, *Versuch*, 122; *Essay*, 152. See also Kramer, "Diderot's *Paradoxe* and C. P. E. Bach's *Empfindungen*."

61. Wiebke Thormählen has identified an imaginative function in domestic arrangements of works like Haydn's *Creation* around the turn of the nineteenth century. Thormählen argues that such arrangements transformed spectatorship into something much more participatory: in playing through a celebrated work, the consumer was meant "not only to experience its effects but to reenact its creative processes." Thormählen, "Playing with Art," 341.

62. Stewart, "From the Museum of Touch," 32, 35.

63. Mozart[?], Dedication to Opus 1; in *Dokumente*, 30; *Documents*, 29.

64. Leach, *Sung Birds*, chapter 1, especially 11, 20–21, and 41–43.

65. Augustine, "De musica," in *Writings of St. Augustine*, vol. 4, 179. See also Tommasi, "*De musica*," 341–45. As Leach summarizes it, for Augustine, "Only the deployment of the human capacity for rational understanding (*scientia*) in the production of the sound can guarantee its musicality." Leach, *Sung Birds*, 42.

66. On the generic conventions of the composer dedication, see Bernstein, *Print Culture and Music*, esp. 105; and Green, *Dedicating Music*. Wayne Erickson is among those who have traced the rhetorical strategy of false modesty in literary paratexts; see Erickson, "The Poet's Power."

67. See, among others, Kivy, "Mainwaring's *Handel*."

68. Young, *Conjectures*, 31.

69. Young, *Conjectures*, 31.

70. Lessing, "Über die Regeln der Wissenschaften," 145; translated in Flaherty, "Mozart and the Mythologization of Genius," 291 and 304n.

71. Sulzer, "Originalgeist," in *Allgemeine Theorie*, vol. 3, 625–28; trans. Thomas Christensen, in Baker and Christensen, eds., *Aesthetics and the Art of Musical Composition*, 34; emphasis Sulzer's. See also Abrams, *Mirror and the Lamp*, 187; Bauman, "Becoming Original," 338; and Woodmansee, "The Genius and the Copyright."

72. Mozart[?], Dedication, *Six Sonates pour le clavecin qui peuvent se jouer avec l'accompagnement de violon ou flaute traversiere . . . Oeuvre III* (London, 1765), n.p.; in *Dokumente*, 39; *Documents*, 39. It is Alec King who supposes Leopold to be the author of the dedication; see King, *A Mozart Legacy*, 14.

73. Mozart[?], Dedication, n.p. The word "*Nature*" does not appear in this dedication, as it did in Opus 1 — although that is perhaps moot, since both "nature" and "genius" ultimately derive from the same root. Vallini, "*Genius/ingenium*: derive semantiche." I am grateful to Jonathan Morton for this reference.

74. See for instance Cook, "On Genius and Authorship," 617: "There existed . . . an alternative tradition coeval with the cult of nobly wild genius as popularized by Addison, one in which genius and learning were joined in a sort of discordant harmony."

75. On the roots of these binaries in classical and medieval philosophy, see Lippman, *History of Western Musical Aesthetics*, 14–15; and Leach, *Sung Birds*, 12–16.

76. Quantz, *Versuch*, 12–13; *On Playing the Flute*, 20. Quantz reasserts later that "Only if exceptional natural ability is supported by thorough instruction, by industry,

pains, and inquiry; only in this fashion, I repeat, can a special degree of excellence be achieved." Quantz, *Versuch*, 15; *On Playing the Flute*, 22.

77. See for instance Johann Wolfgang von Goethe, *Eckermann's Conversations with Goethe*, trans. R. O. Moon (London: Morgan, Laird, n.d.), 301, quoted in Kivy, *Possessor and the Possessed*, 91.

78. Grimm, *Correspondance littéraire* 7 (July 15, 1766), 81; in *Dokumente*, 55; *Documents*, 56.

79. Hiller, "Wien," *Wochentliche Nachrichten und Anmerkungen die Musik betreffend* 22 (November 25, 1766): 174; in *Dokumente*, 63; *Documents*, 67.

80. See Rose, *Musician in Literature*, 183–92. Rose argues that Telemann's 1718 autobiography "pioneered an early Enlightenment view of musical talent, portraying himself as a self-taught prodigy for whom nature alone had been the guide" (12).

81. The phenomenon is traced by François Waquet in *"Puer doctus*, les enfants savants de la République des lettres," and by Michèle Sacquin in "Les jeunes savants," both in Sacquin and Ladurie, eds., *Le printemps des génies*.

82. Traudes, *Musizierende "Wunderkinder"*, 76–80 and 428-431; and Bodsch, "'Merckwürdige Nachricht'," 103-111.

83. Hiller, *Wochentliche Nachrichten* (November 25, 1766): 174; in *Dokumente*, 63; *Documents*, 67.

84. All three published their first works at the age of sixteen.

85. Baillet, *Des enfans devenus célèbres*. I have as yet found no evidence that Locke read this volume.

86. Baillet, *Des enfans devenus célèbres*, 8.

87. It may be that this was a confusion of correlation with causation: sickly children were simply more likely to stay in bed, and thus to spend more time reading and writing, than healthy ones. For a discussion of the pathologization of child virtuosity that takes in Kant, Tissot, Baillet, and other figures mentioned in the present chapter, see Traudes, *Musizierende "Wunderkinder,"* 422–48; and Bodsch, "Merckwürdiges Nachricht," 103–8.

88. Baillet, *Des enfans devenus célèbres*, 5–6.

89. Baillet, *Des enfans devenus célèbres*, 6–7.

90. *Des enfans devenus célèbres* was reprinted in Paris in 1722 and Amsterdam in 1725, and remained popular well into mid-century. It was referred to by Louis-René de la Chalotais in his 1763 *Essai d'éducation Nationale* (Essay on National Education), and was even parodied in Laurence Sterne's *The Life and Opinions of Tristram Shandy*, vol. 6 (1762), 24.

91. See, for Heinecken: [Anonymous], Review of *Des Lübeckischen dreyjährigen Knabens, Christ. Henr. Heineckens. . .* , ed. Johann Gottlieb Krause, 70 (Leipzig, August 1725): 688. For Baillet: Formey, *Vie de Baratier*, 42.

92. Valentin, "'Was die Bücher anlaget . . . ,'" 105. Formey's biography, *La Vie de Mr. Jean Philippe Baratier*, went through multiple printings in the Netherlands, England, and Germany between 1741 and 1755.

93. Kant, *Anthropology from a Pragmatic Point of View*, 122–23.

94. See Bastian, "Wunderkinder," 2068.

95. Jürgen Neubacher writes that Telemann had a special fondness for prodigies, having promoted the three Cröner brothers from Munich (violinists) in addition to his advocacy for Heineken. See Neubacher, "Zwischen Auftrag und künstlerischem Anspruch," 73–74.

96. The poem is signed "Puffendorff," perhaps indicating the Aulic Councillor Konrad Friedrich von Pufendorf, but the poet has not yet been definitively identified. In *Dokumente*, 20; *Documents*, 19. Emphasis mine.

97. Barrington, "Account of a Very Remarkable Young Musician," 63.

98. Barrington, "Account of a Very Remarkable Young Musician," 64.

99. Baratier also seems to surpass Handel in the index to Barrington's article, which reads "*Mozart*, J. C. a very surprizing child, famous by his musical performances, p. 55. Short account of his life, ibid. Compared with the famous Baratier, p. 63." Index to *Philosophical Transactions* (1771), 562. There is no similar callout of Handel in the index.

100. [Anonymous], "Article IV: *Voyages de* Rabbi Benjamin [review]," *Bibliotheque Germanique ou Histoire Litteraire de l'Allemagne, de la Suisse, et des Pays du Nord* 30 (Amsterdam: Pierre Humbert, 1734): 115–16. Baratier followed up the *Voyages* with two large monographs, another extensive translation with commentary, a set of successfully defended master's theses, and six periodical articles.

101. Hiller, *Wöchentliche Nachrichten* (November 25, 1766): 174; in *Dokumente*, 63; *Documents*, 67.

102. Tissot, "XVI. Discourse," *Aristide* (October 11, 1766): 66. None of these personages appear in Baillet's *Des enfans devenus célèbres*.

103. Tissot, *De la santé*, 117–18. An earlier version was published as *Avis aux gens*. See also [Anonymous], "Mozart and Dr. Tissot," *Notes* 8, no. 1 (1950): 60 and 62.

104. Tissot, "XVI. Discourse," *Aristide ou Le citoyen* (October 11, 1766), 69; in *Dokumente*, 61; *Documents*, 65.

105. A translation of Tissot's article was sent to the Mozarts in 1771; in *Dokumente*, 125; *Documents*, 139–40. A German translation of Tissot's writings, *Aristides oder der bürgerliche Philosoph* (1771), was in Mozart's library at the time of his death.

106. Draft of a letter by Hennin (September 20, 1766), reproduced in Staehelin, *Reise der Familie Mozart*, 93–94; also in *NMD*, 15. Eisen does not hazard a guess as to the identity of the "young Frenchman."

107. Witmore, *Pretty Creatures*, 38. Emphasis Witmore's. See also Wasyliw, *Martyrdom, Murder, and Magic*, 17.

108. Böldicke, *Methodus Lockio-Baratieriana*, Sectio Secunda, Membrum 1 ("Von einer solchen *Methode* überhaupt"), §4, n.p.

109. Proposal of the Vienna Court Chancery, January 19, 1765; in *Dokumente*, 40; *Documents*, 40. See also Wolf, *Judentaufen in Österreich*, 52–53.

110. Chrissochoidis suggests the same was true in England, where Mozart was referred to by many as "the eight-year-old boy" throughout his fifteen-month stay in 1764–1766. Chrissochoidis, "London Mozartiana," 86.

111. Martha Feldman identifies a similarly paradoxical phenomenon in *opera seria*, which "mimicked the miraculous world of the sovereign's court but thrived amid ever-expanding publics and spaces." See Feldman, *Opera and Sovereignty*, 437.

112. A similar attitude prevailed in colonial America during the Great Awakening (1730s–1740s), where, as Holly Brewer and Courtney Weikle-Mills have shown, questions about child conversion and religious participation hinged on children's perceived capacity both to reason and to feel. Although the age of first communion was still held at fourteen by the most prominent of these revivalist preachers, revivalists encouraged young converts to go against their parents' wishes. See Brewer, *By Birth or Consent*, 45–86, esp. 64–70; and Weikle-Mills, *Imaginary Citizens*, 57–62.

113. Caffiero, *Forced Baptisms,* 57.

114. See Timothy Kelly, "Catholicism," in Fass, ed., *Encyclopedia of Children and Childhood,* vol. 1, 135.

115. Wolf, *Judentaufen in Oesterreich,* 42n. For a fuller discussion of Benedict XIV's ruling and the issue of illicit and forced baptisms in eighteenth-century Europe, see Caffiero, *Forced Baptisms,* 44–60.

116. Empress Maria Theresa, "Baptismus Infantum Judaeorum," in *Corpus Juris Ecclesiastici Bohemici, et Austriaci* . . . (Vienna: Kurzböck, 1770), 117; quoted in Wolf, *Judentaufen in Österreich,* 54.

117. Solomon has made a related argument stemming from the Tissot, but our interpretations of similar material differ slightly. "Mozart was considered, then, to represent a superlative example of the child's unlimited potentiality for creative and moral development, which could be unlocked by enlightened upbringing . . . one whose small body exemplified the infinite perfectibility of the child and, by inference, of mankind." Solomon, "Mozart: The Myth of the Eternal Child," 9. I interpret the early reception of Mozart's precocity primarily in terms of something that *exceeds* enlightened upbringing, and yet not necessarily as perfect, miraculous, or unique.

118. Others besides the 1765 Court Chancery conflated Mozart's talent and his perceived moral maturity. In 1766, Tissot wrote: "A well-ordered mind appears to be made for a virtuous soul and sweet ways; experience has verified this in several great artists, & little Mozart supplies a new proof of it." Tissot, "XVI. Discourse," *Aristide* (October 11, 1766), 191; in *Dokumente,* 61; *Documents,* 65. This conflation might explain Rousseau's caution, in the entry on "Musicien" for the *Encyclopédie,* that the word "virtuoso" does not mean that the musician is virtuous, but rather reflects the Italian word for talent or skill, "virtù." [Rousseau], "Musicien," in Diderot and d'Alembert, eds., *Encyclopédie,* vol. 10 (1765), 898.

119. [Mainwaring], *Memoirs of the Life of Handel,* 6.

120. Coleman, *Neither Angel nor Beast,* 28–29.

121. Rose, *Musician in Literature,* 180–81 and 202–11.

122. Macartney, ed., *Habsburg and Hohenzollern Dynasties,* 148. See also Derek Beales, *Joseph II, Volume 2,* chap. 5 ("Toleration of Protestants, Greek Orthodox and Jews").

123. Edict of Toleration, issued January 2, 1782, §25. English translation from Macartney, ed., *Habsburg and Hohenzollern Dynasties,* 168.

124. In a related move toward Protestants, on May 22, 1781, Joseph instructed the Hungarian Chancery that Protestant orphans must not be approached about conversion until reaching the age of sixteen. Letter of April 29, 1781, reproduced in Mályusz, ed., *Iratok a türelmi rendelet történetéhez,* 160. See also Beales, *Joseph II, Volume 2,* 182.

125. Court Chancery, Votum of March 11, 1782, quoted in Wolf, *Judentaufen in Österreich,* 88.

126. Wolf, *Judentaufen in Österreich,* 87.

127. Wolf, *Judentaufen in Österreich,* 87.

128. Joseph II, Resolutions of March 28 and 31, 1782, in Joseph II, *Codex Juris Ecclesiastici Josephini,* vol. 1, 159–61. Joseph based his decision chiefly on three factors: parity with the law for Protestant child baptism; an increased recognition of parental rights (until eighteen, Joseph decreed, religious choice required the consent of the

parents); and finally, an implicit sense of children's religious freedom. See Karniel, *Die Toleranzpolitik*, 465.

129. Joseph II, resolution of March 28, 1782, in *Codex Juris Ecclesiastici*, 160. See also Wolf, *Judentaufen in Österreich*, 90–97.

130. See "Mündig, Volljährig, Voigtbar, Majorenn," in Zedler, *Universal-Lexikon*, vol. 22 (1739), 401.

131. Joseph's cooler, more skeptical attitude toward both Mozart and the baptism debate was motivated by broader concerns: he was determined to purge Catholic practice of its more superstitious aspects, to reduce papal juristic power, and to promote Jewish assimilation (largely on economic grounds). See Wolf, *Judentaufen in Österreich*, 90.

132. Historians of the position of Jews in the Austrian Enlightenment seem to be more sensitive to this than Mozartians. See Wolf, *Judentaufen in Oesterreich*, 53n, cited in Hanslick, *Geschichte des Concertwesens in Wien*, vol. 1, 121; and Karniel, *Die Toleranzpolitik Kaiser Josephs II*, 298–99 and 460.

133. Douthwaite, *The Wild Girl*, 135.

134. Melton, *Absolutism*, 212–14.

135. Hofkanzleidirekt, February 18, 1787, quoted in Krause, *Kinderarbeit und Gesetzlicher Kinderschutz*, 23. See also Seebauer, *Kein Jahrhundert des Kindes*, 32.

136. "Patent vom 13ten January 1787, für alle Länder," in *Joseph des Zweyten Römischen Kaisers Gesetze*, 9.

137. The current minimum age of criminal responsibility in Austria and Slovenia is fourteen; in the Czech Republic, fifteen; in Hungary, twelve. See [Child Rights International Network], "Minimum Ages of Criminal Responsibility."

138. "Stand," in Zedler, *Grosses vollständiges Universal-Lexicon*, vol. 39 (1744), 1101. "Kind," Adelung, *Versuch*, vol. 2 (1775), col. 1577.

139. *Three Lessons for the Harpsichord or Piano Forte . . . by Elizabeth Weichsell, a Child Eight Years of Age* (London: Welcker, [1775]).

140. Burney, *Account of an Infant Musician*, 21.

141. Burney, *Account of an Infant Musician*, 21.

142. The claims reach Shandyesque levels: "two years and three quarters," "two years eleven months," "twelve months," and so on. Barrington, "Account of Mr. Charles Wesley," and "Account of his son Samuel from the Rev. Mr. Charles Wesley," in *Miscellanies*, 289 and 291n, respectively.

143. Barrington, "Account of his son Samuel," in *Miscellanies*, 293 and 306–7. See also Forsaith, "Pictorial Precocity."

144. This Percy is the nephew of the editor of *Reliques of Ancient Poetry*. Barrington seems to have been fond of promoting such prodigy encounters: he brought Samuel Wesley with him to visit (and test) William Crotch. See Barrington, "Some Account of Little Crotch," in *Miscellanies*, 313–16.

145. Barrington, "Some Account of Little Crotch," in *Miscellanies*, 316. Original emphasis.

146. For a fuller examination of Crotch's career, see Traudes, *Musizierende "Wunderkinder,"* 94–187.

147. Georg Christoph Lichtenberg, "William Crotch, das musikalische Wunderkind," in *Taschenbuch zum Nutzen und Vergnügen fürs Jahr 1780* (Göttingen: Johann Christian Dieterich, 1780), 8–19.

148. Grimm, "April 1772," in *Correspondance littéraire*, vol. 9, 482, 481. See also

David Fuller and Bruce Gustafson, "Darcis, François-Joseph," *OMO* (2001); and *NMD*, 126–127.

149. Tissot, "24. Discours," *Aristide* (December 6, 1766), 287, reproduced in Staehelin, *Die Reise der Familie Mozart*, 102; and translated in *NMD*, 18. For more on public musical prodigies in the wake of Mozart, see Hausfater, "Être Mozart: Wolfgang et ses émules"; and Adelson and Letzter, "*Mozart fille*."

150. Zelizer, *Pricing the Priceless Child*, 15.

151. Rose, *The Case of Peter Pan*, xii; and Kincaid, *Child-Loving*.

152. See Heywood, *Growing Up in France*, 62–63.

153. Beethoven[?], Dedication, *Drei Sonaten fürs Klavier* [WoO 43] (Speier: Bossler, 1783), n.p.

154. Neefe, "Nachricht von der churfürstlich-cöllnischen Hofcapelle zu Bonn und andern Tonkünstlern daselbst," in Cramer, *Magazin der Musik* (March 30, 1783), 395, quoted in Thayer et al., *Thayer's Life of Beethoven*, vol. 1, 66. See also Sisman, "The Spirit of Mozart from Haydn's Hands."

155. Anonymous, "Auszüge aus Briefen, in- und ausländische musikalische Nachrichten enthaltend," *Musikalischer Alamanch für Deutschland auf das Jahr 1784*, ed. Johann Nicolaus Forkel (Leipzig: Schwickert, 1784), 195; quoted in Derry, "Ludwig van Beethoven," 585.

156. Anonymous, "Auszüge aus Briefen," 195–96. The phrase "boys of twelve years" apparently refers to the prodigy Bonifazio Asioli, mentioned later in the review.

157. Rousseau, *Émile*, vol. 1 (1762), 199; trans. in *Emile*, 290. On the "English girl," see Rasch, *Muziek in de Republiek*, 13–14. To my knowledge, she has never been identified, though she performed in the Netherlands in 1743–1745 as "Beroemde Engelse juffrouw." She is also mentioned in Imhof, *Des Neu-Eröffneten Historischen Bilder-Saals*, 1359. However, I have not yet discovered any mention of her in French-language texts. Charles Burney's daughter Esther was a prodigy harpsichordist who performed on a London prodigy concert in 1760, but her tour of France took place in 1764–1767. See "Burney, Mrs Charles Rousseau, Esther, née Burney," in Highfill, Burnim, and Langhans, *Biographical Dictionary of Actors*, vol. 2, 429.

158. Rousseau, *Émile*, vol. 1 (1780), 337. The 1780 edition appears to be the first to include the footnote. On the 1780 complete works edition, see Alston, *Order and Connexion*, 103.

159. Opus 2 was reprinted in Paris in 1785, but after that none of the Opus 1–4 works reappeared in print until the *Oeuvres complettes* by Breitkopf & Härtel included Opus 4 (K. 26–31) in its volume 15 (1804) and K. 6–8 in its volume 17 (1806).

Chapter Two

1. Letter from Leopold (Vienna) to Lorenz Hagenauer (Salzburg), August 6, 1768, *MBA* 136:27–38; excerpt not in Anderson.

2. See Halliwell, 90–92.

3. See Ulbricht, "Debate about Foundling Hospitals," esp. 236.

4. See Wheatcroft, *Habsburgs*, 208–9, 226.

5. "Wien den 1. Weinm. 1768," *Wienerisches Diarium* (October 1, 1768), n.p.

6. Ulbricht, "Debate about Foundling Hospitals," 235.

7. Letter from Leopold (London) to Lorenz Hagenauer (Salzburg), June 28, 1764, *MBA* 90:142–45; trans. in Anderson 1:49.

8. This was part of a broader program of centralized poor relief that began under Maria Theresa and Joseph; see Scheutz, "Demand and Charitable Supply."

9. For an introduction to Enlightenment philanthropy in Europe, see Cunningham, "Introduction," 2–4; and Garrioch, "Making a Better World."

10. For more on Basedow and the Philanthropinum, especially its reception in the Habsburg lands, see chapter 4.

11. [Anonymous], *Nachricht an das Publikum*, n.p. The publication date of 1771 is noted in Melton, *Absolutism*, 203n.

12. See also Seebauer, *Kein Jahrhundert des Kindes*, 19.

13. "Denkschrift des Kaisers Joseph über den Zustand der österreichischen Monarchie" (1765), in *Maria Theresia und Joseph II. Ihre Correspondenz*, vol. 3, 344; quoted in Blanning, *Joseph II*, 79. Translation Blanning's.

14. Hörnigk, *Oesterreich über Alles*, 44–45. See Macartney, *Habsburg and Hohenzollern Dynasties*, 70–78; Seibt, *Von dem Einflusse der Erziehung*; and Blanning, *Joseph II and Enlightened Despotism*, 21.

15. Melton, *Absolutism*, especially chapters 5 and 6.

16. Ulbricht, "Debate about Foundling Hospitals," 229: "child labor was generally accepted and even approved of by the most prominent pedagogues of the time and practiced in orphanages." On the rise in manufacturing: as Ernst Bruckmüller notes, the number of Lower Austrians employed in manufacturing and industry rose from around 50,000 in 1782, to 120,000 in 1785, and 180,000 in 1790. Bruckmüller, *Sozialgeschichte Österreichs*, 179.

17. Historians have used the term repeatedly in reference to Habsburg public communications going back to Maximilian I; see for instance Spielman, *City & The Crown*, 103; Silver, *Marketing Maximilian*, ix; and Wangermann, *From Joseph II to the Jacobin Trials*. Habsburg historians like Michael Yonan, Tim Blanning, and Andrew Wheatcroft adumbrate a public-relations culture, even if they do not call it by that name. See Yonan, *Empress Maria Theresa*; Blanning, *Culture of Power*; and Wheatcroft, *Habsburgs*.

18. Cunningham, "Introduction," 10.

19. See, among others, Safley, "Introduction," 10–12.

20. Miller, *Orphans of Byzantium*, 212–20.

21. This pattern was established in the previous generation of Habsburg rulers; see Janet Page, *Convent Music and Politics*, 4: "Piety, music, and the political need for constant visibility combined in a yearly cycle of state visits to churches, monasteries, and convents, which court calendars and the newspapers of the day reported to the larger world."

22. See for instance Chimani, *Vaterländischer Jugendfreund*, Th. 3, 52; Pezzl, *Johann Pezzl's Chronik von Wien*, 223–24; "Das Vaterland. Schulen, Unterrichts-, Erziehungs- und Bildungsanstalten in Wien. Das Waisenhaus," in J. B. Weis, *Der österreichischer Volksfreund, für das Jahr 1831*, vol. 1 (Vienna: Franz Wimmer, 1831), 58; and Rieder, *Ignaz Parhamer's*, 95.

23. See Hull, *Sexuality, State, and Civil Society*, 111–15, here, 111: "infanticide was the crime that officials, legal reformers, and social critics used to discuss the pros and cons of sexual law reform generally. And sexual law reform, thought necessary to eliminate the causes of infanticide, was a major impetus for general reform of all criminal laws during the Enlightenment."

24. Massie, *Farther Observations*. See Ristelhueber, *Wegweiser zur Literatur*, 6–7.

25. See for instance "Gedanken über die Frage, ob Waysenhäuser nützlich sind," *Hannoverisches Magazin* (February 3, 1766), 145–60; and Jacobs, *Der Waisenhausstreit*.

26. [Anonymous], *Jährlicher Bericht* (1772), quoted in Jacobs, *Der Waisenhausstreit*, 72–73.

27. Nicolai, *Beschreibung einer Reise*, vol. 3, 229, 230; quoted in Scheutz, "Pater Kindergeneral und Janitscharenmusik," esp. 42. See also Polenghi, "'Militia est vita hominis.'"

28. Scheutz, "Pater Kindergeneral und Janitscharenmusik," 41. When Joseph finally closed the orphanage in 1784, he ordered it to be converted into a military training school.

29. See Black, "Mozart and Musical Discipline."

30. Weiß, *Geschichte der öffentlichen Anstalten*, 180; quoted in Rieder, *Ignaz Parhamer's*, 20.

31. Scheutz, "Pater Kindergeneral und Janitscharenmusik," 68; and [Anonymous], *Vollkommener Bericht von der Beschaffenheit* (1774), 72.

32. [Anonymous], *Vollkommener Bericht von der Beschaffenheit* (1774), 57–62 ("Musickordnung"). See also Weiß, *Geschichte der öffentlichen Anstalten*, 181.

33. [Anonymous], *Vollkommener Bericht von dem Music-Chor* (1764), 2. Mentioned in Black, "Mozart and Musical Discipline," 24–26.

34. Letter from Leopold (Vienna) to Lorenz Hagenauer (Salzburg), September 13, 1768, *MBA* 137:37–40. See Black, "Mozart and Musical Discipline," 19.

35. Black, "Mozart and Musical Discipline," 19.

36. Letter from Leopold (Vienna) to Lorenz Hagenauer (Salzburg), December 14, 1768, *MBA* 143:16–21; trans. in Anderson, 94.

37. "Wien den 10. Christm. 1768," *Wienerisches Diarium* (December 10, 1768), n.p.; in *Dokumente*, 78; *Documents*, 84.

38. Weschel, *Die Leopoldstadt bey Wien*, 383; not in *Dokumente*, *Documents*, *NMD*, or Edge/Black.

39. Black, "Mozart and Musical Discipline," 20.

40. See Abert, 108n and 223n.

41. As Black notes, "That the orphans, aged between six and sixteen, could rise to the occasion and perform works of considerable technical difficulty is a testament to the rigorous education instituted by their director." Black, "Mozart and Musical Discipline," 31.

42. Black hypothesizes that the concerto may have been intended for Ignatz Schmatz, soon to enter the service of Graf Theodor von Batthyani. Black, "Mozart and Musical Discipline," 22–23.

43. Abert, 224.

44. Mozart was often recorded as improvising arias to his own keyboard accompaniment, and we already know that he "joined the choirboys in the singing of the motets," so there's an outside chance—though it would have been highly unorthodox—that the commensurate showman and prominent "event headliner" might have entrusted this difficult, one-off passage only to himself.

45. The Ospedali and Vivaldi were still renowned in German circles in the late eighteenth century. See for instance Volkmann's section on Venice in *Historisch-kritische Nachrichten von Italien*, vol. 3, 616–17; and Jean-Baptiste Ladvocat's entry on Vivaldi in *Historisches Hand-Wörterbuch*, vol. 4, 906. Vivaldi is also listed in an

exhaustive review of John Hawkins's *General History of the Science and Practice of Music* in Johann Nicolaus Forkel's *Musikalisch-kritische Bibliothek*, vol. 2 (Gotha: Ettinger, 1778), 211.

46. For reports of each of these events, see *Wienerisches Diarium*, May 14, 1768; June 1, 1768; and May 9, 1770, respectively.

47. "Wien den 9. Maym. 1770," *Wienerisches Diarium* (May 9, 1770), n.p. See also Black, "Mozart and Musical Discipline," 21.

48. "Wien, den 9. May 1772," *Wienerisches Diarium* (May 9, 1772), n.p.

49. Rieder, *Ignaz Parhamer's*, 78.

50. Müller, *Johann Heinrich Friedrich Müller's Abschied*, 243.

51. Müller, *Johann Heinrich Friedrich Müller's Abschied*, 237. See also Tar, *Deutschsprachiges Kindertheater*, 27. In the end, the Theatralpflanzschule was as short-lived as the Nationaltheater, lasting only from 1779 to 1782. See chapter 3.

52. Kuebach, *Trauerrede auf den tödtlichen Hintritt Josephs*, 8.

53. Aristotle, *De Sensu et Sensibili*, chapter 1, 437a.

54. Such false remedies were catalogued in [Anonymous], *Ueber Taubstumme*, 5.

55. Diderot, *Lettre sur les aveugles* and *Lettre sur les sourds et muets*.

56. See Davis, *Enforcing Normalcy*, 53–54; and Renate Fischer, "Abbé de l'Epée."

57. Davis, *Enforcing Normalcy*, 51, 60, and 61. More recent studies on the role of print in nineteenth-century histories of deaf people include Werner, "*Why Give Him a Sign*," and Murray, "Transnational Interconnections."

58. Schott, *Das k. k. Taubstummen-Institut*, 57–59.

59. Stork, *Anleitung zum Unterrichte der Taubstummen*, 145.

60. [Anonymous], *Nachricht an das Publikum*, n.p.

61. Revealing in this regard is the litany with which May's reader for Taubstummeninstitut students begins: "I am a person [Mensch]. / You are a person. / My father is a person. / My mother is a person. . . . / We are all people." [May], *Erste Kenntnisse für Taubstumme*, 3–4.

62. [Anonymous], *Festschrift zum 175-Jährigen Bestande*, 81.

63. [Anonymous], "Innländische Begebenheiten. Wien," *Wiener Zeitung* (October 1, 1783), [1].

64. Nicolai, *Beschreibung einer Reise*, vol. 4, 795 and 798, respectively. This turned out to be the prelude to an even more reform-minded critique of rote learning for all children, deaf and hearing alike. Nicolai ended up railing against "dogmatic" and "thoughtless" memorization, and accusing L'Épée of being a "well-intentioned old man but a weak head." Nicolai, *Beschreibung einer Reise*, 809.

65. Pezzl, *Skizze von Wien*, vol. 2, 125–26.

66. [Anonymous], "Ankündigung der öffentlichen privil. Buchdruckerey des k. k. Taubstummeninstituts," *Wiener Zeitung* (May 13, 1786), 1125.

67. Pezzl looked forward to the day when the Taubstummeninstitut would offer the girls a similar means of "mechanical employment." Pezzl, *Skizze von Wien*, vol. 2, 126.

68. The image can be seen at Pictura Paedagogica Online: http://opac.bbf.dipf.de /cgi-opac/bil.pl?t_direct=x&fullsize=yes&f_IDN=h0087783berl.

69. Schott, *Das k. k. Taubstummen-Institut in Wien*, 83; Mozart's salary, Abert, 706.

70. [Anonymous], "Ankündigung der öffentlichen privil. Buchdruckerey des k. k. Taubstummeninstituts," *Wiener Zeitung* (May 13, 1786), Anhang, 1125.

71. [Anonymous], "Ankündigung eines Wochenblattes für Kinder zur angenehmen und lehrreichen Beschäftigung in ihren Freystunden," *Wiener Zeitung* (February 24, 1787), 432–33.

72. ["Den Herausgebern"], "Liebe Kinder, Theure junge Freunde!," *Angenehme und lehrreiche Beschäftigung,* vol. 1, [3].

73. ["Den Herausgebern"], [3–4].

74. ["Den Herausgebern"], [4]; and Kant, "Beantwortung der Frage," 481–94.

75. *Angenehme und lehrreiche Beschäftigung . . . Herbstquartal 1787, Erstes Bändchen,* n.p.

76. *Beschäftigung,* vol. 1, [4].

77. *Beschäftigung . . . Herbstquartal 1787, Erstes Bändchen,* n.p.

78. *Beschäftigung,* vol. 1, 63.

79. *Beschäftigung,* vol. 1, tipped-in sheet after p. 63. "Der Knabe beim Vogelfang" is credited to a "Franz Wolf," who also composed a "Morgenlied als ein Gebeth im Türkenkriege," which appeared in vol. 4 (1788), tipped in after p. 91. I have been unable to locate any further information about Wolf.

80. Davis, *Enforcing Normalcy,* 59.

81. [May], *Erste Kenntnisse für Taubstumme,* 87. The terms "mute" and "deafmute" are outdated and offensive.

82. The title vignette to each volume of the *Beschäftigung* uses a remarkably similar Masonic visual vocabulary to that on Alberti's frontispiece to *Die Zauberflöte.* No libraries appear to own a copy of volume 2 of the four-volume *Beschäftigung,* so the attribution of any illustrations in that volume cannot be confirmed. On Alberti's relationship to Mozart, see Senigl, "Ignaz Alberti"; and Buch, "Placidus Partsch, the *Liedersammlung für Kinder und Kinderfreunde.*"

83. [Anonymous], "Ankündigung der öffentlichen privil. Buchdruckerey des k. k. Taubstummeninstituts," *Wiener Zeitung* 38, Anhang (May 13, 1786), 1125. It is well known that Mozart and Torricella did not have the best working relationship: like other Viennese publishers, Torricella often reprinted Mozart's older music without securing his permission.

84. *NMD,* 53. See also *Dokumente,* 498, *Documents,* 588.

85. Beales, "Court, Government and Society in Vienna," 15–17. On the consequences of this war, which ended up claiming approximately 192,000 lives and putting many of Joseph's reform projects on hold, leading to inflation and bread riots in Vienna and elsewhere, see Edge, "Mozart's Reception in Vienna, 1787–1791," 67–68, esp. n5. The casualty statistics come from Roche, *Exploring the Sociology of Europe,* 108.

86. Head, *Orientalism, Masquerade, and Mozart's Turkish Music,* 38–39.

87. "An alle wahren Edeln der Staaten Josephs und Katharinens der Zweiten," *Angenehme und Lehrreiche Beschäftigung,* vol. 4, 90.

88. "An alle wahren Edeln," 92.

89. "An alle wahren Edeln," 91.

90. "Die Denkmäler der Helden vom Bunde Josephs und Katharinens der Zweiten," *Beschäftigung,* vol. 4, 95–96.

91. Beales, "Court, Government and Society in Vienna," 16–17.

92. "Die Denkmäler der Helden," *Beschäftigung,* vol. 4, 97, 98.

93. "M. v. S.," "An die Herrn Herausgeber des Wochenblatts für Kinder," *Beschäftigung,* vol. 1, 154.

94. "Antwort. Liebster junger Freund," *Beschäftigung*, vol. 1, 156.

95. "Von der Bauart des Bibers," *Beschäftigung*, vol. 1, 165.

96. "Von der Bauart des Bibers," 177.

97. Translation in Dixon et al., "English Translations of the Lieder Texts," 74-75.

98. [Anonymous], *Schmuckkästchen für die Jugend*, 21–26 and 44–45.

99. Rousseau, *Émile*, vol. 2, 3 and 9; trans. as *Emile*, 532 and 536.

100. Ernst-August Ballin, *Das Wort-Ton-Verhältnis in den Klavierbegleiteten Liedern Mozarts* (Kassel: Bärenreiter, 1984), 47. Gottfried August Bürger's 1776 poem *Die Spinnerin* ("Hurre, hurre, hurre") was set numerous times before Haydn's *Die Jahreszeiten* of 1800, and many of these settings represent the movement of the spinning wheel in the piano accompaniment. See also Max Friedlaender, *Das deutsche Lied im 18. Jahrhundert: Quellen und Studien*, vol. 2 (Stuttgart: Gotta, 1902), 223.

101. Ballin, *Das Wort-Ton-Verhältnis*, 46–47. Ballin identifies six stylistic categories of Lieder (based more on music than text); he assigns "Die kleine Spinnerin" to the third category, "Dem Wiener Singspiellied nahestehende Lieder." "Männer suchen stets zu naschen" and "Die kleine Spinnerin" are the only Lieder in Mozart's output to exhibit this combination of Singspiellied characteristics. "Das Veilchen" (K. 476) of 1785 comes close, but its through-composed form, slower tempo, more variable rhythm, and more adventurous harmonic motion mitigate the singsong quality. Two other Lieder with something of the Singspiellied tone, "An Chloe" (K. 524) and the Kinderlied "Des kleinen Friedrichs Geburtstag" (K. 529), both of 1787, utilize an Alberti bass accompaniment that softens the rhythmic profile.

102. See Maria Theresa, *Spinnschulen-Aufrichtungs-Patent* (1765), discussed in Bruckmüller, *Sozialgeschichte Österreichs*, 180.

103. *Anleitung* (1786), 140.

104. Gramit, *Cultivating Music*, chapter 4 ("Education and the Social Roles of Music").

105. Quoted in Schott, *Das k. k. Taubstummen-Institut in Wien*, 83; the phrase appears to be attributed to Strommer, but Schott does not cite the source. It is not in the 1786 *Wiener Zeitung* announcement of the press, or in the prefaces to the *Anleitung zum Unterrichte der Taubstummen* or the *Angenehme und lehrreichte Beschäftigung für Kinder*.

106. *Beschäftigung*, vol. 1 (1787), [5].

107. Melton discusses the "invention" of free time in Halle under Pietist pedagogues: "By establishing a period of time free from the normal demands of work, Francke's schools also created a period that was to be devoted to nothing but work. Francke's bifurcation of time merely accentuated the Pietist labor imperative, reinforcing rather than attenuating the obligation to work." Melton, *Absolutism*, 41.

108. *Rapport von Wien* (November 29, 1788), 276; in *Dokumente*, 289; *Documents*, 330; see also Buch, *Liedersammlung für Kinder und Kinderfreunde*, xix n54. The two other composers who contributed settings to the *Beschäftigung* were: Franz Wolf ("Der Knabe beim Vogelsang," vol. 1, and "Morgenlied als ein Gebeth im Türkenkriege," vol. 3) and Josef Hugelmann ("Das Kind am neuen Jahre," vol. 2).

109. *Beschäftigung*, vol. 2 (1788), n.p. The engraver was an "Engelman f.V.," possibly Wenceslaus Engelman (1713–1762), who appears to be responsible for some engravings in other late 1780s publications in Vienna. This was not, apparently, the only such error. In that same year, another short-lived publication edited by May

and Franz Anton Gaheis, *Neue Kinderbibliothek* (1788), included in the preface to its second volume an apology for the printing errors in the first volume by the young apprentices. See Lang, Lang, and Büchinger, eds., *Bibliographie der Österreichischen Zeitschriften, 1704–1850,* vol. 2, 101–2.

110. Furthermore, Mozart allowed his name to be added to the list of subscribers to volume 2. He no longer appears on the list in volumes 3 and 4, despite the presence of his "Lied beim Auszug in das Feld" in volume 4.

111. Maria Theresa, *Allgemeine Schulordnung,* n.p.

112. Blanning, *Joseph II,* 68–69.

113. One example of the criticism this policy elicited comes from Joseph Richter, who wrote, "A people with our kind of constitution not only needs elementary knowledge; it needs the higher sciences and the fine arts." Richter, *Warum wird Kaiser Joseph von seinem Volke nicht geliebt?* (Vienna, 1787), 32, translated in Wangermann, *The Austrian Achievement,* 142.

114. Like Joseph, Frederick opposed universal secondary education, writing in 1779, "one must teach the peasants what they need to know, but in such a manner that they will not flee the countryside, but remain there contentedly." Frederick, "Kabinets-Schreiben an den Etats-Minister von Zedlitz" (1779), quoted in Melton, *Absolutism,* 183.

115. Melton, *Absolutism,* 176–83.

116. Melton, *Absolutism,* 191.

117. Melton, *Absolutism,* 202.

118. Melton, *Absolutism,* xxii.

119. Felbiger, "Vorrede," *Die Christlich-katholische Lehre in Liedern,* vii.

120. Felbiger, "Circulare, darin der Gebrauch der im Druck gegebenen Lieder beym Gottesdienste und bey Begräbnissen empfohlen . . ." (October 14, 1768), in *Kleine Schulschriften,* 100. Felbiger also wrote at length about how schoolteachers should teach their students to sing, as in his *Eigenschaften, Wissenschaften, und Bezeigen.*

121. *Katholisches Gesangbuch* and *Verbesserte katechetische Gesänge.* See Melton, *Absolutism,* 219.

122. "Wien, den 5. Augustm.," *Wiener Zeitung* (August 5, 1780), n.p.

123. Melton, *Absolutism,* 221. Many of these schools folded quickly, however, due to families keeping their children at home for farming and housework; see Seebauer, *Kein Jahrhundert des Kindes,* 34.

124. On the school reforms in Bohemia, see Weiss, *Geschichte der theresianischen Schulreform in Böhmen,* 63; and Grečenková, "Enlightened Absolutism and the Birth of a Modern State," esp. 277–78. On the history of the Normalschule press in Prague, see Hall, "Schulverlagsanstalt für Böhmen und Mähren in Prag."

125. Pařízek, *Ausführliche Beschreibung,* 61. See also Weiss, *Geschichte der theresianischen Schulreform in Böhmen,* 17.

126. Steinsky, *Uiber die Pflicht,* 7.

127. Burney, *Present State of Music in Germany,* vol. 2, 4–5; and Christoph Willibald von Gluck, paraphrased in Johann Christian von Mannlich, "Gluck à Paris en 1774," *La Revue Musicale* (1934), quoted in Heartz, "Coming of Age in Bohemia," 521. See Murray, *Career of an Eighteenth-Century Kapellmeister,* 14–17.

128. Melton, *Absolutism,* 9.

129. Kindermann, *Nachricht von der Landschule zu Kaplitz*, 2nd ed. (Prague: Schönfeld, 1774), 8–9, quoted in Helfert, *Die Gründung der österreichischen Volksschule*, vol. 1, 54.

130. See, for instance, *Sammlung gottesdienstlicher Lieder für die öffentliche und häusliche Andacht* (St. Petersburg: Johann Karl Schnoor, 1773); *Neueste Kirchen-Lieder aus den besten Dichtern zum Gebrauch der öffentlichen sowol als häuslichen Andacht* (Lemgo, 1773); *Verbessertes Gothaisches Gesangbuch zum Gebrauch beym öffentlichen Gottesdienst und bey häuslicher Andacht* (Gotha: J. C. Reyhers Wittwe und Erben, 1778); and *Allgemeines Gesangbuch, auf Königlichen Allergnädigsten Befehl zum öffentlichen und häuslichen Gebrauche der Deutschen in Kopenhagen herausgegeben* (Copenhagen: Christ. Gottl. Prost, 1782).

131. Weiss, *Geschichte*, 65.

132. "Anmerkung," [Anonymous], *Lieder zur öffentlichen und häuslichen Andacht*, n.p.

133. "Vorrede," [Anonymous], *Lieder zur öffentlichen und häuslichen Andacht*, xii. On Štěpán's contributions to the Andachtslieder, see Picton, *The Life and Works of Joseph Anton Steffan*, 209–10.

134. "Steinsky (Franz Anton)," in Hamberger and Meusel, *Das Gelehrte Teutschland*, vol. 7, 644.

135. "Vorrede," [Anonymous], *Lieder zur öffentlichen und häuslichen Andacht*, ix–x.

136. "Vorrede," xi and x, respectively.

137. Despite the pedigree of many of the contributing composers, the *Andachtslieder* was not received favorably by all critics, particularly north Germans, who it seems looked down on Catholic Lieder. See "Qf" [= Friedrich Germanus Lüdke], "Wiener Schriften [review]," *Allgemeine deutsche Bibliothek*, vol. 57, no. 2 (1784), 545; and Nicolai, *Beschreibung einer Reise*, vol. 4, 551n. As David Black notes, Nicolai disdained most Catholic songs as "simple and singable," but "empty of harmony" and "without expression." Quoted in Black, "Mozart and Musical Discipline," 27–28.

138. [Anonymous], *Künftige Gottesdienstes- und Andachtsordnung für Prag*. See also David Black, after Ernst August Ballin, "1787—Mozart Sacred Songs for St. Nicholas Church in Prague," in Edge/Black.

139. Weiss, *Geschichte*, 200. The Czech edition was entitled *Pjsně k weřegné y domácý pobožnosti s melodyemi, též y modlitby* (Prague: Normalschulbuchdruckerey, 1789).

140. Wangermann, *Aufklärung und staatsbürgerliche Erziehung*, 67.

141. See for instance Black, *Mozart and the Practice of Sacred Music*, 158–61; and Buch, "Introduction," in Buch, ed., *Liedersammlung*, xix, 56n.

142. The songs may even have been included in a celebratory Mass that took place at St. Nicholas in 1787, for which Mozart was described as providing the music (now lost). Black argues that Mozart's relationship with Strobach probably led to the commission. See Black, *Mozart and the Practice of Sacred Music*, 157; and Black, after Ballin, "1787—Mozart Sacred Songs for St. Nicholas Church in Prague," in Edge/Black. The relationship between Strobach and Mozart has been identified as far back as Jahn's biography, vol. 4, 618; quoted in Ernst August Ballin, *Kritischer Bericht, Lieder*, NMA III/8 (1964), 116. As Black notes, we still do not know the nature of the connection between Mozart, Strobach, Steinsky, and Kindermann, or how it led to Mozart's two Lieder appearing in the *Andachtslieder*.

143. Melton cites the following attendance rates in *Absolutism*, 8 and 220–21: Vienna in 1770, about one-third of school-age children; Passau in 1772, 10–20%; Lower Austria, 16% in 1771 and 34% in 1779; Graz, 17% in 1772 and 30% in 1780; Salzkammergut, 24% in 1773 and 66% in 1778; Bohemia in 1790, about two-thirds.

144. Melton, *Absolutism*, 135–36.

145. Melton, *Absolutism*, 222; see also 137–39.

146. The emphasis on textile arts reflects the rapid expansion in the textile industry in the Habsburg lands, especially in Bohemia, and efforts to alleviate a persistent shortage of rural spinners. Melton, *Absolutism*, 121 and 126–27.

147. See Nettl, "Prager Lieder aus der Mozart-Zeit," 120. Nettl notes the presence of the Lied "Fritz prahlte sehr mit Menschenliebe" in both the *Prager Kinderzeitung* and the *Liedersammlung für Kinder und Kinderfreunde: Winterlieder* (Vienna: Alberti, 1791), but does not mention that "Die kleine Spinnerin" appears in both the *Lieder für die Jugend bei Industrialarbeiten* and the *Angenehme und lehrreiche Beschäftigung für Kinder*. Nettl also shows how another song in the *Arbeitslieder* collection, by Johann Henneberg (the first conductor for *Die Zauberflöte*), also appeared in the 1791 *Liedersammlung für Kinder und Kinderfreunde* to which Mozart contributed the three last songs, K. 596–98. I will return to this collection and these songs in chapter 4, but Nettl rightly observes that they are at least in part the result of a conversation between Prague Kinderlieder and Viennese Kinderlieder. See also Buch, "Placidus Partsch," 71n.

148. See Allanbrook, *Rhythmic Gesture in Mozart*, 79–82.

149. Stiasny, *Sammlung einiger Lieder*, 4.

150. Arnold, *Beobachtungen in und über Prag*, vol. 2, 14.

151. Arnold, *Beobachtungen in und über Prag*, vol. 2, 15.

Chapter Three

1. Sibylle Dahms prefers the term "Benedictine drama" to "Schuldrama," though that is because she includes adult monastic dramas in her study; see Dahms, "Barockes Theatrum Mundi," 175.

2. In 1769, Schrattenbach made Wolfgang Konzertmeister of the Salzburg court, though the position was unpaid until Schrattenbach was succeeded by Colloredo in 1772.

3. Bruckmüller, *Sozialgeschichte Österreichs*, 181.

4. Hull, *Sexuality, State, and Civil Society*, 1.

5. See for instance Töpelmann, "Salzburg"; Lederer, "Clemency of Rufinus Widl"; Boberski, *Das Theater der Benediktiner*; and Kutscher, *Das Salzburger Barocktheater*.

6. Kutscher, *Das Salzburger Barocktheater*, 43. See also Graubner, "'Sind Schuldramata möglich?,'" 93.

7. See Rainer, "Die Salzburger Szenare," esp. 189.

8. Lederer, "Clemency of Rufinus Widl," 223.

9. Kutscher, *Das Salzburger Barocktheater*, 58–61. For a list of fourteen dialect interludes to university plays between 1678 and 1772, see Huber, *Die Literatur der Salzburger Mundart*, 6–8.

10. Boberski, *Das Theater der Benediktiner*, 30, 38; and Fischer, "Das Salzburger Theater," 153–54. On sex-segregated performances in the Jesuit university theater, see Münster, "Neues zu Leopold Mozarts," 58.

11. While the scenarios for these pantomimes do not appear in the *Perioche*, and

the composer is not identified, it was most likely Eberlin himself. He had composed at least one other Singspiel featuring Steffl and his wife Gredel: *Die geadelte Bauren, oder Die ihr selbst unbekannte Alcinde* (1750). See Angermüller, "Personae Musicae," 6. Roland Tenschert suspects that the pantomime characters were more appealing to audiences than Sigismund or Tobias. Tenschert, *Mozart: Ein Leben für die Oper*, 31.

12. Dahms, Schneider, and Hintermaier, "Die Musikpflege an der Salzburger Universität," 199.

13. Rommel, *Die alt-wiener Volkskomödie*, cited in Sieveke, *Johann Baptist Adolph*, 12. See also Paumgartner, "Introduction," in Haydn, *Die Hochzeit auf der Alm*, [n.p.].

14. Carlson, *Vocal Music of Leopold Mozart*, 6; Layer, "Zasianellulus," 71; and Münster, "Neues zu Leopold Mozarts," 57–60.

15. See letter from Leopold (Vienna) to Lorenz Hagenauer (Salzburg), January 30–February 3, 1768, MBA 125:103–37; translated in Anderson, 82.

16. Lederer, "Clemency of Rufinus Widl"; and Prince, "Ovid Metamorphosed."

17. Apollo's act of clemency, motivated by virtue, is thus an echo or allegory of Croesus's clemency in the spoken tragedy.

18. Based on Alfred Orel, foreword to *Apollo et Hyacinthus*, ed. Orel, NMA II/5/1 (1959), xvi–xvii; Boberski, "Spielplan des Universitätstheaters (1617–1778)," in *Das Theater der Benediktiner*, 219–310; Catanzaro and Rainer, *Anton Cajetan Adlgasser*; and various Periochen.

19. Alfred Orel expresses surprise that a seventeen-year-old could still perform an alto part. Orel, foreword to *Apollo et Hyacinthus*, ed. Orel, NMA II/5/1 (1959), xvii. In the next two year-end *Schuldramen* after *Clementia Croesi/Apollo et Hyacinthus*, Vonderthon does not have singing roles, but is rather the leading mime, Dromus (in 1767's *Hannibal Capuanae/Sibylla/Dromus und Bromia*, 1767), and a dancer (in 1768's *Clementia Theodosii/Lycus et Arethusa*).

20. See also Schmid, *Mozart und die Salzburger Tradition*, 94–96.

21. Orel, foreword to *Apollo et Hyacinthus*, ed. Orel, NMA II/5/1 (1959), xvii.

22. Lindner, *Beitrag zu Schulhandlungen*.

23. Lindner, "Vorrede: Anmerkungen über das Schuldrama," in *Beitrag zu Schulhandlungen*, n.p. See also Graubner, "'Sind Schuldramata möglich?,'" 105.

24. Lindner, quoted in Graubner, "'Sind Schuldramata möglich?,'" 106.

25. Herder, "Ueber Thomas Abbts Schriften," 314.

26. Herder, "Ueber Thomas Abbts Schriften," 314.

27. Herder, "Ueber Thomas Abbts Schriften," 316.

28. For an introduction to these debates, see Outram, *Four Fools in the Age of Reason*, chapter 5 ("Two Deaths: the Hanswurst and the Fool"), 106–24; and Nedbal, *Morality and Viennese Opera*.

29. Weiskern, "Vorrede," in *Die deutsche Schaubühne zu Wienn, nach Alten und Neuen Mustern, Fünfter Theil* (1755), quoted in Nedbal, *Morality and Viennese Opera*, 28.

30. Kutscher, *Vom Salzburger Barocktheater*, 116n. See also Fuhrich, *Theatergeschichte Oberösterreichs*, 312.

31. Kutscher, *Vom Salzburger Barocktheater*, 63–64.

32. See Weidenholzer, "Bürgerliche Geselligkeit und Formen," 56–57; and Kramml, Veits-Falk, and Weidenholzer, *Stadt Salzburg*, 54.

33. See Boberski, *Das Theater der Benediktiner*, 127–28; and Kutscher, *Das Salzburger Barocktheater*, 95.

34. Letter from Wolfgang (Vienna) to Leopold (Salzburg), June 16, 1781, *MBA* 606:80–81; translated in Anderson, 746 (as "Merry Andrew").

35. Komorzynski, "Ist Papageno ein 'Hanswurst'?"

36. Dopsch and Hoffmann, *Geschichte der Stadt Salzburg*, 347.

37. Rainer, "Die Salzburger Szenare," 193.

38. Kutscher, *Das Salzburger Barocktheater*, 90.

39. See for instance Lamb, *Performing Childhood in the Early Modern Theatre*; Austern, *Music in English Children's Drama*; and Shapiro, *Children of the Revels*. On the boy companies and the "little eyases" passage in *Hamlet*, see Knutson, "Falconer to the Little Eyases."

40. Tar, *Deutschsprachiges Kindertheater*; Tar, *Gyermek a 18. és 19. századi*; and Dieke, *Die Blütezeit des Kindertheaters*, 54–118. See also Mueller, "Youth, Captivity and Virtue."

41. Rousseau, *Émile*, vol. 1, 406; *Emile*, 290. Diderot, "Conversations on *The Natural Son* [1757]," in Diderot, *Selected Writings*, 71.

42. [Mattheson], "Vorbericht," *Abhandlung von den Pantomimen*, n.p.

43. Lessing wrote about the Piccoli Hollandesi on no fewer than four occasions: "Zwölfter Brief. An den Herrn A** [1747]"; "Hamburg [review of Carl Samuel Geißler, Abhandlung von den Pantomimen," *Berlinische privilegirte Zeitung* 32 (March 15, 1749); *Abhandlung von den Pantomimen der Alten* [1750]; and "Versuch einer Beurtheilung der pantomimischen Opern des Hrn. Nicolini, entworfen von Johann Gottlieb Benzin [review]," *Critische Nachrichten* (1751). All in Gotthold Ephraim Lessing, *Werke und Briefe*, vol. 1 ("Werke 1743–1750") and vol. 2 ("Werke 1751–1753").

44. Betzwieser, "Zwischen Kinder- und Nationaltheater." On the Piccoli Hollandesi's role in the circulation of the intermezzo, see Charles E. Troy and Piero Weiss, "Intermezzo (ii)," *OMO* (2001).

45. Garnier, *Nachricht* (1782).

46. Ages based on Garnier, *Nachricht* (1782), 18–23.

47. As Peter Schmitt has shown, the average age of debut for actors in late eighteenth- and early nineteenth-century German companies was sixteen to eighteen. Schmitt, *Schauspieler und Theaterbetrieb*, 45–46. Schmitt surveyed records for 2,000 actors who debuted between 1775 and 1850. See also Dieke, *Die Blütezeit des Kindertheaters*, chapter 2 ("Kinderaufführungen in den Erwachsenentruppen"), 140–54.

48. See for instance, Anonymous, "Auszüge aus Briefen: Dünkelsbühl, den 20. Sept. 1778," *Theater-Journal für Deutschland* 10 (1779), 86–87: "It is true that the eyes and ears lose much of the natural, for those spectators who are used to adults. There are a couple of adults, like the Ballet Master, the Music Director Gspan, Mlle Rentin, [and] Madame Gspan, who plays the first lover, and who shows appropriate sensations to the children."

49. This is akin to the phenomenon of female singers in operatic trouser roles, who "exist onstage in an almost angelic condition of being not-men, not-women." Corinne E. Blackmer and Patricia Juliana Smith, "Introduction," in Blackmer and Smith, eds., *En Travesti*, 5.

50. "K. [Christian Gottlob Klemm?]," "Theatralnachrichten. Acht und dreyßigs-

ter Brief," *K[aiserlich] K[önigliche] allergnädigst privilegierte Realzeitung* 6 (February 4, 1777), 90; quoted in Dieke, *Die Blütezeit des Kindertheaters*, 118. For more on the *Realzeitung* as the chief periodical of the Viennese Enlightenment, see Morrison, *Pursuing Enlightenment in Vienna*, 144-72.

51. Weisse, "Ueber Tanz und Gesang," *Der Kinderfreund* 12, no. 161 (August 1, 1778), 75-76. It is difficult to know to which troupe Weisse is referring; Dieke uncovered no evidence of a Leipzig sojourn by Berner's or Nicolini's troupes in the early 1770s, and I can find no evidence of Sebastiani's troupe having passed through the city at this time.

52. These domestic Kinderschauspiele are discussed briefly in Bauman, *North German Opera in the Age of Goethe*, 209-11, and at greater length in German studies such as: Dettmar, *Das Drama der Familienkindheit*; Betzwieser, "Zwischen Kinder- und Nationaltheater; and Cardi, *Das Kinderschauspiel der Aufklärungszeit*.

53. "Der großen Kaiserin weil. Maria Theresia in unterthänigster Ehrfurcht geweiht, von der kleinen Thalia, unter der Bernerischen Schauspieler-Gesellschaft zu Schönbrunn in einer neuerrichteten Hütte den 11. Oct. 1775," in Garnier, *Nachricht* (1782), 38-39.

54. For more on this trend in the repertoire, see Mueller, "Youth, Captivity and Virtue," 84.

55. "Das Milchmädchen an das Parterre, nach der Opperette [*sic*], gesprochen von Mlle. Liskin der ältern, in Würzburg," in Garnier, *Nachricht* (1782), 35. The reference is to the faun's lament in Salomon Gessner's idyll "Der zerbrochene Krug" ("The Broken Jug," from *Idyllen von dem Verfasser des Daphnis* [Zurich, Gessner, 1758]). *Die Milchmädchen und die beiden Jäger* is based on the 1763 opéra comique *Les deux chasseurs et la laitière*, by Louis Anseaume and Egidio Duni.

56. "Das Milchmädchen an das Parterre," 36.

57. Garnier, *Nachricht* (1782), 15. The number of editions of Garnier's *Nachricht*, and the sheer number of engravings that accompany each edition, also indicates that the Berner troupe had a strong following and made a healthy profit. There are eighteen engravings in the 1782 edition, twenty-four in 1784, and thirty-one in 1786, with many actors commissioning new silhouette portraits for subsequent editions, and the 1782 edition also includes six elaborate engravings depicting scenes from Berner troupe operas and pantomimes.

58. Kutscher, *Das salzburger Barocktheater*, 96-97.

59. Pirckmayer, *Ueber Musik und Theater*, 24.

60. Garnier, *Nachricht* (1782), 6.

61. See Tyler, "*Bastien und Bastienne*," 529n; Loewenberg, "*Bastien und Bastienne* Once More," 178; and Rudolf Angermüller, foreword to *Bastien und Bastienne*, ed. Angermüller, NMA II/5/3 (1974), ix-x and xiv.

62. As Tyler summarizes, Mozart was given the Weiskern-Müller version, which he began setting to music, and only after he completed his composition did Schachtner make some changes to the text, which Mozart then incorporated into the final version. Tyler, "*Bastien und Bastienne*," 530.

63. Tyler, "*Bastien und Bastienne*," 530-31.

64. Nissen, *Biographie W. A. Mozart's*, 127; Tyler, "*Bastien und Bastienne*," 531n; and Abert, 96n.

65. Tyler, "*Bastien und Bastienne*," 534.

66. Schäffer, *Das fürstbischöfliche und königliche Theater zu Passau*, 43; and Garnier, *Nachricht* (1782), 10.

67. Tar, *Deutschsprachiges Kindertheater*, 151. The reviewer seems to think that the company was composed exclusively of "girls in men's clothing." Anonymous, "Von. den Schauspielgesellschaften, welche hier in Salzburg gespielt haben," *Theaterwochenblatt zu Salzburg* 1–3 (November 18, 22, 25, 1775), 17.

68. Dialogue following Aria (Colas), "Befraget mich ein zartes Kind," no. 4. This and subsequent English translations by Ian Page, from liner notes to *Mozart: Grabmusik, Bastien und Bastienne*, The Mozartists, cond. Ian Page (Classical Opera/Signum Records SIGCD547, compact disc, 2018).

69. Aria (Bastienne), "Wenn mein Bastien im Scherze," no. 5.

70. Aria (Bastienne), "Würd ich auch, wie manche Buhlerinnen," no. 6.

71. Dialogue following Duet (Colas and Bastienne), no. 7.

72. Aria (Bastien), "Meiner Liebsten schöne Wangen," no. 11.

73. Tyler, "*Bastien und Bastienne*," 541.

74. The *Gesammelte Schriften* was edited by Christian Gottlob Stephanie "der ältere," whose younger brother, Johann Gottlieb "der jüngere," would collaborate with Mozart on *Die Entführung aus dem Serail*, K. 384, 1782, and *Der Schauspieldirektor*, K. 486, 1786.

75. See the advertisement for the *Neue Sammlung*, "Nachricht," *Gelehrte Beytraege zu dem Wienerischen Diarium* (March 9, 1768), n.p.; and a brief notice of issues 1–4 in *Nachtrag zu dem wienerischen Diarium* 62 (August 3, 1768), n.p. The only other children's periodical listed in the *Handbuch zur Kinder- und Jugendliteratur* as published in Vienna before 1774 was the *Kurzer Auszug der Sittenlehre über die Pflichten des Menschen zum Gebrauche der adelichen Jugend der frommen Schulen* (Vienna: Kaliwoda, 1768). I could find no announcements about this periodical in the Viennese press. "Kurzer Auszug der Sittenlehre," in Brüggemann and Ewers, eds., *Handbuch zur Kinder- und Jugendliteratur*, 1410.

76. Letter from Leopold (Vienna) to Lorenz Hagenauer (Salzburg), March 30, 1768, *MBA* 127:43–44.

77. See for instance *MBA Kommentar* to 127:43–44; and Töpelmann, *Mozart Family and Empfindsamkeit*, 154. On the *Magasin des enfans*, see Miglio, *Le Magasin des enfants*. The *Magasin* was wildly popular, and in Germany it found its most fervent and sustained audience, going through five printings of a full translation of the four-volume set. For a complete account of all the Austrian editions of this work, see Lang, Lang, and Büchinger, eds., *Bibliographie der Österreichischen Zeitschriften*, vol. 2, 30–32; and Dagmar Grenz, "1758: Jeanne-Marie LePrince de Beaumont (1711–1780): Lehrreiches Magazin für Kinder," in Brüggeman and Ewers, eds., *Handbuch zur Kinder- und Jugendliteratur*, 494–506.

78. The *Neue Sammlung* is mentioned much later in the Mozart family correspondence: in November 1785, Leopold wrote to Nannerl that he was sending her "the *Neue Sammlungen zum Vergnügen*," presumably on her request. At the time, her five stepchildren ranged in age from three to fourteen, meaning that several of them would have been an ideal age for the periodical. Letter from Leopold (Salzburg) to Nannerl (St. Gilgen), November 28, 1785, *MBA* 905:66.

79. See Angermüller, foreword to *Bastien und Bastienne*, ed. Angermüller, *NMA* II:5:3 (1974), xiv; and Ballin, "Zu Mozarts Liedschaffen," 21–22.

80. "Komm, Doris! Mit vergnügten Schritten," in *Neue Sammlung zum Vergnügen und Unterricht, Zweytes Stück* (Vienna: Friedrich Bernhardi, 1768), 117-19; "Das Gewitter," in *Neue Sammlung zum Vergnügen und Unterricht, Viertes Stück* (Vienna: Friedrich Bernhardi, 1768), 139-41.

81. On this subject see Straub, *Sexual Suspects*; and Nussbaum, *Rival Queens*.

82. On the French impresario, Nicolas-Médard Audinot, see Root-Bernstein, *Boulevard Theater and Revolution*, 151-52; and Isherwood, *Farce and Fantasy*, 181 and 286n. On physical abuse by Nicolini, see Klingemann, *Kunst und Natur*, vol. 2 (1821), 478-79, quoted in Dieke, *Die Blütezeit des Kindertheaters*, 22.

83. "A.," "Ueber einige Vorstellungen der Bernerschen Schauspielergesellschaft zu Kaufbeuren," *Theater-Journal für Deutschland* 21 (1783): 57.

84. Three troupe deaths occurred on the same day, June 26, 1772, in Cremsir in Moravia, where the troupe had performed for the Count of Ollmütz. I have so far been unable to find any report of the cause of the three deaths; it could have been an accident, a crime, or a virulent infection.

85. We know that Jeanette was nine in 1775 because of a poem by Christian Daniel Friedrich Schubart, "Epilog von der neunjährigen Nanette Berner gesprochen—1775," which concludes with the exhortation "Take everything, you wise connoisseurs, / That a child can give you in innocence; / Take my thanks, illustrious men, / And these tears." Schubart, *Gedichte aus der Gefangenschaft*, 449-50.

86. Garnier, *Nachricht* (1782), 21.

87. Letter from Leopold (Salzburg) to Nannerl (St. Gilgen), September 9, 1785, *MBA* 876:59-60; not in Anderson.

88. Letter from Leopold (Salzburg) to Nannerl (St. Gilgen), December 2, 1785, *MBA* 906:49-52 and 81-89; not excerpted in Anderson.

89. Letter from Leopold to Nannerl, *MBA* 906:102-3; not excerpted in Anderson. See also Halliwell, 497.

90. Albert Dunning, foreword to *Canons*, ed. Dunning, NMA III/10 (1974), xv. See also Münster, "Aus Mozarts Freundeskreis," 32; and Münster, *"Ich bin hier sehr beliebt,"* 150. The Peyerls eventually settled in Munich in 1787, where Elise became court singer in 1796. After Joseph died in 1800, Elise remarried (to a horn player also known to Mozart), and continued to perform as a singer in Munich until 1819 as Elise Lang, dying in 1824. Münster, "Aus Mozarts Freundeskreis," 35.

91. "Reglement für die Bernerische Schauspielergesellschaft," in Garnier, *Nachricht* (1786), 48.

92. Garnier, *Pilgerfahrt*, quoted in Blümml and Gugitz, *Alt-Wiener Thespiskarren*, 189; and Schönwald, "Kindertheater in Salzburg," 5.

93. Münster, "Aus Mozarts Freundeskreis," 31.

94. Münster, "Aus Mozarts Freundeskreis," 31.

95. Letter from Leopold (Salzburg) to Nannerl (St. Gilgen), November 28, 1785, *MBA* 905:55-56; not in Anderson.

96. Letter from Leopold to Nannerl, *MBA* 905:61-65; not in Anderson.

97. Kutscher, *Das Salzburger Barocktheater*, 100; Schönwald, "Kindertheater in Salzburg," 5; and Dieke, *Die Blütezeit des Kindertheaters*, 129-30.

98. The prince in question, Count Aloys, son of Wenzel Anton, Prince of Kaunitz-Rietberg, was given the equivalent of probation. See Gerstner, *Das Kinderballett von Friedrich Horschelt*; and Feigl and Lunzer, *Das Mädchen-ballett des Fürsten Kaunitz*, 193-247.

99. Tar, *Deutschsprachiges Kindertheater*, 89.

100. Müller, preface, *Genaue Nachrichten*, vol. 2, n.p.

101. "Wien, den 26. Augustmon.," *Wienerisches Diarium* 69 (August 26, 1772), [6].

102. Hadamowsky, *Wien Theater Geschichte*, 463.

103. Müller, *Abschied*, 133.

104. Müller, *Abschied*, 133.

105. Müller, *Abschied*, 239–45.

106. Müller, *Abschied*, 242; quoted in Blümml and Gugitz, *Alt-Wiener Thespiskarren*, 170.

107. Theaterzettel, *Der Ausgang, oder Die Genesung* (October 14, 1778, performance). Österreichisches Theatermuseum, Signatur BIBT 773042 DTh 17781004.

108. See Müller, "Kinderschauspiel des Herrn Müller zu Wien," *Theater-Journal für Deutschland* 17 (Gotha, 1781), 71–74; Müller, *Theatererinnerungen*, 34–35; and Dieke, *Die Blütezeit des Kindertheaters*, 156–63.

109. Müller's advertisement in the *Wienerisches Diarium* (June 16, 1779), quoted in Teuber, *Die Theater Wiens*, vol. 2, 65n3. See also Dieke, *Die Blütezeit des Kindertheaters*, 157.

110. The Singspiel was based on a French comedy by German-François Poullain de Saint-Foix. The music to *Zermes und Mirabella*, now apparently lost, was by Anton Teyber, a member of a family of Viennese court musicians and singers with whom the Mozarts were quite friendly. Anton was the brother of Therese Teyber, who would eventually originate the role of Blonde in Mozart's *Die Entführung aus dem Serail*.

111. Müller, *Abschied*, 268.

112. Announced in "Vereinigung der Theatralpflanschule mit dem Nazionalteater," *Allgemeiner Theater Allmanach von Jahr 1782* (Vienna: Joseph Gerold, 1782), 145–50.

113. Letter from Wolfang (Vienna) to Leopold (Salzburg), April 18, 1781, *MBA* 590:27–29; translated in Anderson, 725.

114. See for instance Tyler, "'Zaide,'" 216: "Thus, it seems, the unfinished opera was permanently shelved after Stephanie—one of the five directors of the National Theatre and a prominent playwright, librettist, and translator there—rejected it."

115. Letter from Leopold (Salzburg) to Wolfgang (Munich), December 11, 1780, *MBA* 558:46–47, 50–51; trans. in Anderson, 685; see also Tyler, "'Zaide,'" 215–16.

116. *Das Serail, / eine / Teutsche Operette. / Auth: Gius. Friebert. / MDCo in Passavia / 1779.* The lone extant copy of this score, at the Don Juan Archiv in Vienna, is now being prepared for publication in a forthcoming critical edition by Hollitzer Wissenschaftsverlag. The libretto, [Anonymous], *Ein musikalisches Singspiel, genannt: Das Serail*, is reproduced in Friedrich-Heinrich Neumann, *Kritischer Bericht, Zaide*, ed. Neumann, *NMA* II/5/10 (1963), 74–91. On the circumstances surrounding the conception and eventual abandonment of Zaide, see Hüttler, "Hof- und Domkapellmeister Johann Joseph Friebert"; Betzwieser, "Mozarts *Zaide* und *Das Serail*"; Tyler, "'Zaide,'" esp. 218–20; Neumann, "Zur Vorgeschichte der *Zaide*"; Senn, "Mozarts 'Zaide'"; and Einstein, "Die Text-Vorlage zu Mozart's 'Zaide.'" I will follow convention in referring to this singspiel as *Zaide*, even though its intended title is not known.

117. While there is no evidence that either of them witnessed a performance of *Das Serail*, the Berner troupe had passed through Salzburg and Vienna several times before, as outlined earlier in this chapter (1766–1767 and 1774). At the time, Bozen/Bolzano was a principality in the Tyrol; the Berner troupe's only documented sojourns here occurred in 1767, and again in 1784. The libretto thus might have been

pirated, or passed into the repertoire of another *Wandertruppe*, before being printed there. For a comparison of the numbers in *Das Serail* and *Zaide*, see Tyler, "'Zaide,'" 219–20. The only known connection between Mozart and Friebert is the fact that Mozart had a copy of the *Sammlung Deutscher Lieder für das Klavier* (Vienna, 1780) in his estate, and no. 14 in that collection, "Das Veilchen," was in a setting by Karl Frieberth, Joseph's younger brother. See Konrad and Staehelin, *"allzeit ein buch,"* 109–10.

118. See Mueller, "Youth, Captivity and Virtue," 81.

119. Tyler, "'Zaide,'" 218.

120. Grosrichard, *The Sultan's Court*, 132 and 128; quoted in Mueller, "Youth, Captivity and Virtue," 68.

121. [Anonymous], *Ein musikalisches Singspiel, genannt: Das Serail*, n.p. [act 2, scene 4].

122. Hübner, *Diarium* (November 29, 1766); in *Dokumente*, 64; *Documents*, 68.

123. Letter from Maria Theresa (Vienna) to Archduke Ferdinand (Milan), December 12, 1771; in *Dokumente*, 124; *Documents*, 138; quoted in Halliwell, 137.

Chapter Four

1. See Bruckmüller, *Sozialgeschichte Österreichs*, 240–42; and Melton, *Absolutism*, 220.

2. Rousseau, *Émile*, vol. 2, 82; trans. in *Emile*, 333.

3. Hurrelmann, *Jugendliteratur und Bürgerlichkeit*, 169. Hurrelmann arrives at her figure as follows: the first three printings of *Der Kinderfreund* were 3,000, 3,000, and 4,000 copies, respectively. Hurrelmann estimates ten to twenty readers per copy (given the average size of households and schools holding subscriptions, and taking into account formal and informal lending libraries). This does not count the 15,000 copies claimed by Weisse to have been printed in Austria, nor foreign translations. See "Christian Felix Weiße," *Saxonia: Museum für sächsische Vaterlandskunde* 16 (December 1835), 78.

4. In all, some forty-three German-language children's periodicals were published in the last third of the eighteenth century, which together totaled an estimated readership of nearly 500,000, or around 1.6 percent of the 30 million inhabitants of the German lands. Uphaus-Wehmeier indicates forty-three in her *Zum Nutzen und Vergnügen*, cited in Ewers and Völpel, "Kinder- und Jugendzeitschriften," 141. Sophie Köberle, writing twelve years earlier, had a more conservative number (nineteen). See Köberle, *Jugendliteratur zur Zeit der Aufklärung*, 77. See also Heckle, "'Ein lehrreiches und nützliches Vergnügen,'" 328.

5. Ewers, "1778–1784. Joachim Heinrich Campe (1746–1818): *Kleine Kinderbibliothek*," in Brüggemann and Ewers, eds., *Handbuch zur Kinder- und Jugendliteratur*, 192–206.

6. Campe, "Vorbericht," *Kleine Kinderbibliothek*, vol. 1 (Hamburg: Heroldschen Buchhandlung, 1779), 4–5; and Campe, "Vorbericht," *Kleine Kinderbibliothek*, vol. 1 (Hamburg: Heroldschen Buchhandlung, 1782), no page numbers; Campe's emphasis.

7. In subsequent editions, Campe excised more and more material as indecorous, and, in 1785, he renounced the excerpting of literature for young children altogether, as inappropriate and contrary to the natural development of the child. See Hains-

Heino Ewers, "1778–1784. Joachim Heinrich Campe (1746–1818): *Kleine Kinderbibliothek*," in Brüggemann and Ewers, eds., *Handbuch zur Kinder- und Jugendliteratur*, 205.

8. The two Erasmus works are *Declamatio de pueris statim ac liberaliter instituendis* (1529) and *De Civilitate Morum Puerilium* (1530). Thomas Ford has identified strains of both Erasmus's and Fénelon's thought in Leopold's approach to the education of his son and daughter. See Ford, "Between *Aufklärung* and *Sturm und Drang*," 18–23. See also Mueller, "Learning and Teaching," 10–12.

9. They may have been purchased by or given to the family after the birth of Mozart's first son, Raimund, in 1783. On Mozart's library, see Konrad and Staehelin, *"allzeit ein buch"*; and Stiftung Mozarteum Salzburg, "W. A. Mozart's library," *Bibliotheca Mozartiana (ISM)*, https://digibib.mozarteum.at/BibliothekWAMozart/nav /classification/843031, accessed January 10, 2019.

10. These books included Joseph Spengler, *Öffentlichen Lehrers der Mathematik auf der hohen Schule zu Dillingen, Anfangsgründe der Rechenkunst und Algebra* (Augsburg: Matthias Riegers sel. Söhnen, 1779); Friedrich Osterwald, *Anfangs-Gründe der Erdbeschreibung, zum Nutzen junger Kinder vorzüglich eingerichtet* (Straßburg: Bauer und Treuttel, 1777); Johann Jakob Ebert, *Naturlehre für die Jugend* (Leipzig, 1776–1778); Heinrich Braun, *Einleitung in die Götterlehre der alten Griechen und Römer. Zum Gebrauch der Schulen* (Augsburg: Elias Tobias Lotter, 1776); and *Atlas des enfans, ou Méthode Nouvelle, courte, facile et démonstrative, pour apprendre la Geographie* (Amsterdam: J. Schneider, 1760). See Konrad and Staehelin, *"allzeit ein buch"*; and Töpelmann, *The Mozart Family and Empfindsamkeit*, 127–31.

11. Nicolai, *Beschreibung einer Reise*, vol. 6, 542 and 619–20.

12. Kogel, "1771. Matthias von Schönberg (1734–1792): *Die Zierde der Jugend*," in Brüggemann and Ewers, eds., *Handbuch zur Kinder- und Jugendliteratur*, 545.

13. Konrad, "Schönbergs Geschäfte des Menschen, Zierde der Jugend, und lehrreiche Gedanken in Begebenheiten. 3 Thl.," in *"allzeit ein Buch*," 85–86.

14. Smeed, "Children's Songs in Germany," 235. Other surveys of Kinderlieder from this period include Buch, "Introduction," in Buch, ed., *Liedersammlung*; Boock, *Kinderliederbücher*, 55–59; Freitag, *Kinderlied*; and Schilling-Sandvoss, "Kinderlieder."

15. Gramit, *Cultivating Music*, 94.

16. Brown, "Mozart's Songs for Voice and Piano"; and Cliff Eisen, "Songs," in Eisen and Keefe, eds., *The Cambridge Mozart Encyclopedia*, 21 and 476, respectively.

17. See also in this respect Pesic, "Child and the Daemon," and Moseley, *Keys to Play*, "Key 1: Ludomusicality" and "Key 3-2: Pantomimes and *Partimenti*."

18. See for instance Steven Zohn on making "instruction agreeable and . . . Diversion useful" (in Addison's *Spectator* 1, no. 10 [March 12, 1711]: 1); Zohn, "Morality and the 'Fair-Sexing,'" 70.

19. Mitchell, *Becoming Human*, 66–69.

20. Locke, *Some Thoughts* [1989], 101. For Campe's edition, trans. Ludwig Rudolphi, see Campe, *Allgemeine Revision, Neunter Theil* (Vienna and Wolfenbüttel: Rudolph Gräffer, 1787). See also Brehony, "Theories of Play," in Fass, ed., *Encyclopedia of Children and Childhood*, vol. 3, 827–28; and Yolton, "Locke: Education for Virtue," 184.

21. Rousseau, *Émile*, vol. 1, 427, and vol. 2, 50–51, respectively; trans. in *Émile*, 296 and 323, respectively. For Campe's edition, trans. C. F. Cramer, see Campe, *All-*

gemeine Revision, Zwölfter Theil—Fünfzehnter Theil (Vienna and Wolfenbüttel: Rudolph Gräffer, 1789–1791).

22. [Schummel], *Fritzens Reise nach Dessau*, 54 and 56. See Ulbricht, "Spielpädagogik des Philanthropismus."

23. *Das Elementarwerk* was an expansion of a 1770 publication by Basedow, *Des Elementarbuchs für die Jugend und für ihre Lehrer und Freunde in gesitteten Ständen*. See Jörg-Dieter Kogel, "1774. Johann Bernhard Basedow (1724–1790): *Des Elementarwerkes*," in Brüggemann and Ewers, eds., *Handbuch zur Kinder- und Jugendliteratur*, 969–84.

24. Basedow, *Das Elementarwerk*, vol. 1, 35–36.

25. Basedow, *Das Elementarwerk*, vol. 1, 33 and 35.

26. See Theodor Brüggeman, "1770–74. *Kupfersammlung zu J. B. Basedows Elementarwerke*," in Brüggemann and Ewers, eds., *Handbuch zur Kinder- und Jugendliteratur*, 984–91.

27. Basedow, *Das Elementarwerk*, vol. 1, 5.

28. Basedow, *Das Elementarwerk*, vol. 1, 133.

29. Basedow, *Das Elementarwerk*, vol. 1, 132–33.

30. Basedow, *Das Elementarwerk*, vol. 1, 133.

31. "Inhalt der Tafeln," Basedow, *Kupfersammlung*, 5.

32. Basedow, *Das Elementarwerk*, vol. 1, 136.

33. "Drey Stunden zum regelmässigen Vergnügen in Bewegung, als Tanzen, Reiten (Fechten), Musik, u. s. w." Basedow, *Das in Dessau errichtete Philanthropinum*, 17. In *Fritzens Reise nach Dessau*, the eponymous narrator describes a music concert at the Philanthropinum at length. [Schummel], *Fritzens Reise nach Dessau*, 76–79. See also Hans-Heino Ewers, "1776. Johann Gottlieb Schummel (1748–1813): *Fritzens Reise Nach Dessau*," in Brüggemann and Ewers, eds., *Handbuch zur Kinder- und Jugendliteratur*, 161–66.

34. Zohn, "Morality and the 'Fair-Sexing,'" 77. Zohn emphasizes Telemann's "pedagogical light touch" and use of humor throughout the *Getreue Music-meister*; see esp. 70, 73–74.

35. Rousseau, *Émile*, vol. 1, 412; trans. in *Emile*, 291.

36. Rousseau, *Émile*, vol. 1, 413; trans. in *Emile*, 291–92.

37. Funk, "Die Musik, als ein Theil einer guten Erziehung," *Der Nordische Aufseher* 80 (1762): 239–57. See Luehrs, *Der Nordische Aufseher*, 103. Funk would later become rector of the Domschule in Magdeburg, site of the *Mittwochgesellschaft* that brought together Johann Heinrich Rolle and Johann Samuel Patzke, about whom more later in this chapter. See Pyatt, *Music and Society in Eighteenth-Century Germany*, 65.

38. Funk, "Die Musik," 247–48.

39. See James Parsons, "Lied, III: Lieder c1740–c1800," *OMO* (2001, updated 2011).

40. Funk, "Die Musik," 254–55.

41. Böckh, "Von dem Einfluß der Musik in eine gute Erziehung," *Wochenschrift zum besten der Erziehung der Jugend* 4, no. 27 (Stuttgart and Tübingen, 1772), 409–24. See Susanne Hahn, "1771–1772. *Wochenschrift zum Besten der Erziehung der Jugend*," in Brüggemann and Ewers, eds., *Handbuch zur Kinder- und Jugendliteratur*, 108–13.

42. Böckh, "Von dem Einfluß der Musik," 420.

43. Hiller, "Vorbericht," *Vierstimmige Motetten und Arien*, n.p. See also "Nachrichten," *Litteratur- und Theater-Zeitung* 36 (Berlin, September 4, 1784), 152.

44. On this subject see, for instance, Joubert, "Songs to Shape a German Nation"; Parsons, "The Eighteenth-Century Lied"; and "Einfalt," in Sulzer, *Allgemeine Theorie der schönen Künste*, vol. 1, 295.

45. Basedow, *Das Elementarwerk*, vol. 2, 485. Emphasis Basedow's.

46. See Heckle, "'Ein lehrreiches und nützliches Vergnügen,'" 328.

47. See for instance Buch, introduction, *Liedersammlung*, xi; and Smeed, "Children's Songs in Germany," 245 and 234.

48. Scheibe, *Kleine Lieder für Kinder* (1766 and 1768); Hiller, *Lieder für Kinder* (1769); and Hunger, *Lieder für Kinder* (1772).

49. Hiller, *Lieder für Kinder*, 32–33.

50. Hiller, *Lieder für Kinder*, 136.

51. Schusky, "Illustrationen in deutschen Liederbüchern," 327.

52. Salzmann, *Unterhaltungen für Kinder und Kinderfreunde* 3 (1780): 11–12.

53. Salzmann, *Unterhaltungen für Kinder und Kinderfreunde* 3 (1780): 14.

54. See Buch, ed., *Liedersammlung*. The *Liedersammlung* was intended to be a four-part publication, one volume for each of the four seasons. In the event, only the *Frühlingslieder* and *Winterlieder* volumes were published. Alberti was a member of the Masonic Lodge "Crowned Hope," along with Mozart.

55. See Corneilson, "*Liedersammlung.*"

56. Patzke was a pastor in Magdeburg, Saxony-Anhalt. *Der Greis* was an adult *moralische Wochenschrift*. For a brief English-language introduction to the narrative conceit, contents, and aesthetic orientation of *Der Greis*, see Pyatt, *Music and Society in Eighteenth-Century Germany*, 86–91.

57. Patzke, *Der Greis* 158–59 (February 12, 1766), 101.

58. Patzke, *Der Greis*, 100.

59. Patzke, *Der Greis*, 102.

60. Patzke did not identify the composer, saying only that he was "einem unsrer besten Tonkünstler in Musik"; Patzke, *Der Greis*, 103. It was probably one of two men: Johann Heinrich Rolle or Gottlob Wilhelm Burmann. Rolle had been the music director for Magdeburg's six parish churches since 1751; he was Patzke's friend and frequent collaborator, and the two belonged to the intellectual club called the *Mittwochgesellschaft* (Wednesday Society). See Thomas Bauman, revised by Janet B. Pyatt, "Rolle, Johann Heinrich," in *OMO* (2001). The second candidate, Burmann, would go on to publish several collections of Kinderlieder in the 1770s in which he included these nine songs. When the songs were reprinted for two voices in G. W. *Burmanns Kleine Lieder für kleine Mädchen und Knaben . . . nebst einem Anhang etlicher Lieder aus der Wochenschrift: Der Greis. Zu Zweyen Stimmen ausgesetzt* (Zurich: David Bürgkli, 1774), the composer was credited as "J. G. H." I have not yet been able to identify this composer.

61. Patzke, *Der Greis* 158–59 (February 12, 1766), 113.

62. Patzke, *Der Greis*, 114–15.

63. Patzke, *Der Greis*, 116–17.

64. Mozart, "An die Freude," in *Neue Sammlung zum Vergnügen und Unterricht, Siebentes Stück* (Vienna: Rudolph Gräffer, 1768), 80–82.

65. Translation in Dixon et al., "English Translations of the Lieder Texts," 69.

66. Uz, *Sämtliche Poetische Werke*, 283–86.

67. Bach, *Herrn Professor Gellerts Geistliche Oden und Lieder*. On "geistliche Lieder," see Bach, *Gellert Songs*; and Hinton, *Poetry and Song in the German Baroque*.

68. Rochow, *Der Kinderfreund*, 19; excerpted in Ewers, ed., *Kinder- und Jugendliteratur der Aufklärung*, 68.

69. Rochow, *Der Kinderfreund*, 20; in Ewers, *Kinder- und Jugendliteratur der Aufklärung*, 68–69. For more on Rochow, see Mayer, "Friedrich Eberhard von Rochow's Education," esp. 25–26, on *Der Kinderfreund*.

70. "Verlangen und Liebe," in [Anonymous], *Schmuckkästchen für die Jugend*, 62.

71. Erlin, "Book Fetish," 356.

72. Erlin, "Book Fetish," 365–66, and see 372, on Campe's Robinsonade *Robinson der jüngere*: "The sometimes lively conversations among audience members may give the impression that interpretations of events in the novel are being generated intersubjectively, rather than being imposed from above, but it is important to remember that the father is always the ultimate authority and that the correct interpretation is never in question."

73. Hull, *Sexuality, State, and Civil Society*, 257.

74. Hull, *Sexuality, State, and Civil Society*, 260.

75. Salzmann, *Ueber die heimlichen Sünden*, 125 and 124; trans. in Hull, *Sexuality, State, and Civil Society*, 266. On eighteenth-century anxieties about child masturbation, see also Heywood, "Innocence and Experience," esp. 49–50 and 55–56; and Richter, "Wet-Nursing, Onanism, and the Breast," 1–22.

76. Salzmann, *Ueber die heimlichen Sünden*, 125.

77. Wieland, "Unterredung zwischen W** und dem Pfarrer zu ***," *Teutsche Merkur* 1 (1775), 90; trans. in Hull, *Sexuality, State, and Civil Society*, 252–53.

78. Burmann, *Kleine Lieder für kleine Jünglinge*, 51.

79. Justi, *Grundfeste der Macht*, vol. 2, 117; quoted in Bruckmüller, *Sozialgeschichte Österreichs*, 180.

80. Sonnenfels, *Grundsätzen der Polizey*, 100; quoted in Bruckmüller, *Sozialgeschichte Österreichs*, 180.

81. Seibt, *Von dem Einflusse der Erziehung*, 18.

82. Rosenbaum, *Lieder mit Melodien*, 28–29; and [Anonymous], *Kleine Lieder für Kinder*, reprinted in Friedlaender, ed., *Neujahrsgrüsse empfindsamer Seelen*, 23. This may have been meant as a parody of Scheibe's 1766–1768 *Kleine Lieder für Kinder*.

83. Rosenbaum, "Vorbericht," *Lieder mit Melodien*, n.p.

84. On this subject see chapter 5, and Cuillé, *Narrative Interludes*, 70; Leppert, *Music and Image*, 61–65; and Huff, "Lotte's Klavier."

85. Friedlaender, *Das deutsche Lied*, vol. 2 ("Dichtung"), 86–87. Lessing's "Der Tod" was first published in Christlob Mylius, *Ermunterungen zum Vergnügen des Gemüths*, part 5 (Hamburg: Johann Adolph Martini, 1747), then in Lessing, *Kleinigkeiten* (Frankfurt and Leipzig: [s.n.], 1751).

86. [Anonymous], *Kleine Lieder für Kinder*, no. 2, n.p.

87. It is a somewhat Faustian bargain: she offers him the Abbess instead, who he then causes to fall in love with the Father; in exchange, the protagonist is now able to sing "mit neuer Krafft." Rosenbaum, *Lieder mit Melodien*, 29.

88. Weisse, "Ueber Tanz und Gesang," *Der Kinderfreund* 12, no. 161 (August 1, 1778): 51.

89. Weisse, "Ueber Tanz und Gesang," 51–52. I have found no evidence of an aria or art song entitled "Amabile Idol mio"—I assume Weisse is here constructing a generic title to convey the erotic nature of the repertory he disdains.

90. "These are the reasons which put even appearances among the duties of women, and make honor and reputation no less indispensable to them than chastity." Rousseau, *Émile*, vol. 2, 9; trans. as *Emile*, 536; also quoted above, in chapter 2.

91. Lerer, *Children's Literature*, 228–29. On "girling," see Judith Butler, "Critically Queer," 22–23.

92. Cuillé, *Narrative Interludes*, 18–19.

93. *Così fan tutte*, ed. Faye Ferguson and Wolfgang Rehm, NMA II/5/18 (1991). Translation adapted from Schoep and Harris, *Word-by-Word Translations*, 223.

94. See for instance Schmidt, *Lebensregeln für Jungfern*, 72–73, which asserted that while doctors generally deem women "mature" around fourteen, eighteen is a better age for marriage, "because a maiden of eighteen years is generally complete [*vollkommen*] in body, and there is also nothing lacking in the emotional faculties."

95. The three other Lieder are "Die Zufriedenheit" (Contentment, K. 473, 1785), "Die betrogene Welt" (The Deceived World, K. 474, 1785), and "Die Verschweigung" (Discretion, K. 518, 1787). None of the four Weisse settings were published in Mozart's lifetime, and this was during a period when no letters survive from Mozart, so we do not know for whom they were originally intended. Mozart's copy of the *Scherzhafte Lieder* was bound with Weisse's *Lieder für Kinder* and his *Amazonenlieder*, as the three-volume *Kleine lyrische Gedichte*.

96. A similar theme is found in Weisse's poem "Die zu späte Ankunft der Mutter" (The mother's too-late arrival), set by Joseph Haydn in his *XII Lieder für das Clavier* (1781), no. 12.

97. Such abrupt modal shifts seem to be a feature of the Viennese Lied; see Brown, "Joseph Haydn and Leopold Hofmann's 'Street Songs,'" 369.

98. The set appears to have been first published in Görner, *Sammlung neuer Oden und Lieder, Teil 2* (1744), then in Hagedorn, *Oden und Lieder in fünf Büchern*, vol. 3, 92–93.

99. Head, *Sovereign Feminine*, 50–51. See also Clark, "Reading and Listening"; and Zohn, "Morality and the 'Fair-Sexing.'"

100. Head, *Sovereign Feminine*, 56–59.

101. "Fritzchen an den Mai," in *Musenalmanach für das Jahr 1776 von den Verfassern des bish. Götting. Musenalmanach*, ed. Johann Heinrich Voß (Lauenberg: Johann Georg Berenberg, [1776]), 49–51.

102. Trans. in Buch, ed., *Liedersammlung*, xxi.

103. Buch, *Liedersammlung*, xxi.

104. Burmann also published a collection for girls, *Kleine Lieder für kleine Mädchen*, and a joint collection, mentioned earlier in connection with Patzke's *Kinderlieder*: G. W. Burmanns Kleine Lieder für kleine Mädchen und Knaben. See Theresa Rixen and Susanne Hahn, "1777. Gottlob Wilhelm Burmann (1737–1805): *Kleine Lieder für kleine Mädchen, und Jünglinge*," in Brüggemann and Ewers, eds., *Handbuch zur Kinder- und Jugendliteratur*, 187–93.

105. Burmann, "Vorerinnerung," *Kleine Lieder für kleine Jünglinge*, n.p.

106. Burmann, "Vorerinnerung," 6–7.

107. Campe, ed., *Kleine Kinderbibliothek, Zweite Auflage, Vierter Theil, welcher das siebente und achte Bändchen der ersten Auflage enthält* (Hamburg: Heroldschen Buchhandlung, 1783), 208–10. See also Ernst August Ballin, *Kritischer Bericht, Lieder*, ed. Ballin, NMA III/8 (1963), 162.

108. "Der verständige Jüngling," in Campe, *Kleine Kinderbibliothek* 1 (1779), 116.

109. "Liebe um Liebe," *Pädagogische Unterhandlungen*, vol. 5, 481–82.

110. Postscript to "Liebe um Liebe,"482.

111. Schall's original lines had referenced Friedrich's parents rather than animals. "Liebe um Liebe," 481.

112. "Der Kleinen Friedrichs Geburtstag," in Campe, *Kleine Kinderbibliothek, Erstes Bändchen* (Hamburg: Heroldschen Buchhandlung, 1779), 28.

113. Reichardt, *Lieder für Kinder aus Campes Kinderbibliothek*, 2.

114. Dedication, *Liedersammlung: Frühlingslieder*; trans. in Buch, *Liedersammlung*, 2.

115. Translation in Dixon et al., "English Translations of the Lieder Texts," 76.

116. Mozart, "Das Kinderspiel," in *Lieder*, ed. Ernst August Ballin, *NMA* III/8 (1963), 60–61.

117. Herder, "Viertes Wäldchen," 161. See also Herder, "On Recent German Literature," 105.

118. Overbeck, *Frizchens Lieder*. See also Freitag, *Kinderlied*, 91–92; and Susanne Hahn, "1781. Christian Adolf Overbeck (1755–1821): *Frizchens Lieder*," in Brüggemann and Ewers, eds., *Handbuch zur Kinder- und Jugendliteratur*, 269–77. Overbeck's poem first appered in print in 1777, and was anthologized in Campe's *Kleine Kinderbibliothek* in 1779 (vol. 1, 34–37).

119. Overbeck, "Vorrede des Herausgebers," in *Frizchens Lieder*, n.p.; quoted in Hahn, "1781. Christian Adolf Overbeck," 269. ("A boy" would have been more accurate than "a child.")

120. Ewers, "Pippi Langstrumpf als komische Figur [1992]," quoted in Hofmann, *Der kindliche Ich-Erzähler*, 39.

121. Overbeck, "Vorrede des Herausgebers," in *Frizchens Lieder*, 4.

122. This caused the young Ulm-based pastor and writer Samuel Baur to wonder in 1790 how one could hope to keep certain poems off-limits to a child reader—and, in a notable departure from the Campe-Weisse line, Baur went on to question why one would wish to do so in the first place. Baur, *Charakteristik der Erziehungsschriftsteller Deutschlands*, 340.

123. Lawrence Kramer makes a similar observation about Schubert's 1815 setting of *Heidenröslein* in "Beyond Words and Music: An Essay on Songfulness [2002]," quoted in Hirsch, *Romantic Lieder*, 209: "Thanks to the high note, the folk tone becomes self-conscious."

124. Schulz, Preface, *Lieder im Volkston* (1785), quoted in Gramit, *Cultivating Music*, 67. See also Gelbart, *Invention of Folk Music and Art Music*, 266–70.

125. Johann Martin Miller, letter of 1785; quoted in Grantzow, *Geschichte des Göttinger*, 126. See also Schiller, *Über naïve und sentimentalische Dichtung* (1795–1796), trans. in Schiller, *Essays*, 187: "It is, moreover, not at all easy, always correctly to distinguish childish from childlike innocence."

126. Herder, "Auszug aus einem Briefwechsel," 56–57.

127. Herder, "Auszug aus einem Briefwechsel," 57.

128. "Kindertümlich" would not emerge as a term for juvenile writing until the late nineteenth century. See Kümmerling-Melbauer, *Kinderliteratur, Kanonbildung und literarische Wertung*, 67–69.

Chapter Five

1. Ariès, *Centuries of Childhood*. See for instance Retford, "Philippe Ariès's 'Discovery of Childhood'"; King, "Concepts of Childhood"; Cunningham, *Children and Childhood in Western Society*; Heywood, *"Centuries of Childhood"*; and Linda Pollock, *Forgotten Children*.

2. Weisse, *Der Kinderfreund. Ein Wochenblatt* 1–5 (October 2–16, 1775), 4.

3. "Every artist understood that he worked for patrons. To the extent that the demands of the patrons evolved, so did the 'look' of the artworks." Leppert, *Music and Image*, 177.

4. Klorman, *Mozart's Music of Friends*, 29, 33–35; and Keefe, *Mozart's Piano Concertos*, 10 and 18–20.

5. Allanbrook, *Secular Commedia*, 129.

6. See in particular Klorman, *Mozart's Music of Friends*, chapter 2 ("Chamber Music and the Metaphor of Conversation"), esp. 26–30; and Le Guin, "A Visit to the Salon de Parnasse."

7. Austen, *Mansfield Park*, 229. On silence and dancing in Austen, see Bander, "Jane Austen and the Uses of Silence," esp. 47–48.

8. Dussinger, *In the Pride of the Moment*, 2.

9. In 1774, Leopold wrote to his wife to ask that Nannerl pack five or six copies of the engraving with her when she came to join them in Munich. Letter from Leopold (Munich) to Maria Anna (Salzburg), December 30, 1774, *MBA* 308:6–11; trans. in Anderson, 255.

10. Klorman, *Mozart's Music of Friends*, xxiii.

11. Waldoff, *Recognition in Mozart's Operas*, 80. The phrase "reading for the plot" is adapted from Brooks, *Reading for the Plot*.

12. Beghin, *The Virtual Haydn*, xxviii. Emphasis Beghin's.

13. See Moseley, *Keys to Play*, "Key 3: The Emergence of Musical Play."

14. Klorman, *Mozart's Music of Friends*, 40.

15. Miller and Yavneh, "Introduction: Thicker Than Water," 10.

16. Maunder, "Mozart's Keyboard Instruments," 210.

17. See for instance advertisements in the *Ordentliche Wochentliche Franckfurter Frag- und Anzeigungs-Nachrichten* (August 16, 1763, and August 20, 1763); and *Public Advertiser* (May 13, 1765, and July 9, 1765); in *Dokumente*, 25–26 and 44–45; *Documents*, 24–25 and 45–46. Cited in Eisen, "Mozart and the Four-Hand Sonata K. 19d," 98.

18. "London, 5. July 1765," *Europäische Zeitung* (August 6, 1765); in *Dokumente*, 47; *Documents*, 48. Discussed in Maunder, "Mozart's Keyboard Instruments," esp. 210. It was believed that Mozart composed the Sonata in C, K. 19d, for this occasion and instrument, but the authenticity of that sonata has been called into question since the *NMA* edition of 1955. See Eisen, "Mozart and the Four-Hand Sonata K. 19d."

19. Eisen, "Mozart and the Four-Hand Sonata K. 19d," 97–98. This work is also mentioned in Stoelzel, "Mozarts letzte vierhändige Sonate," 716.

20. Stoelzel, "Mozarts letzte vierhändige Sonate," 716.

21. Seydelmann, *Sechs Sonaten für Zwo Personen*. Klorman mentions, and reproduces, this engraving in *Mozart's Music of Friends*, 271–72.

22. Spiess, *Tractatus Musicus Compositorio-Practicus*, 162; cited in Breene, "The

Instrumental Body," 244. See also Rowen, "Some 18th-Century Classifications," 95. On Leopold's library, see Irvine, "Der belesene Kapellmeister," 14–15.

23. See for instance Wallace, "Lessons in Music, Lessons in Love"; and Leppert, *Music and Image*, 61–66.

24. "Occupations des Dames," *Almanac de Berlin* (Berlin, 1781). Although not discussed in Klorman, *Mozart's Music of Friends*, Chodowiecki's illustration appears on the companion website's gallery of "Other Illustrations: Musical Scenes and Portraits," http://mozartsmusicoffriends.com/chodowiecki-daniel-music-from-occupation-des-dames-engraving-from-almanac-de-berlin/, accessed July 17, 2019.

25. Breene, "The Instrumental Body," 241.

26. Leppert, *Music and Image*, 4.

27. See for instance the accounts in Burney, *The Present State of Music in Germany*, vol. 2, 325; and Joachim Ferdinand von Schiedenhofen (August 15, 1777); in *Dokumente*, 145; *Documents*, 161. Both are mentioned in Maunder, "Mozart's Keyboard Instruments," 210.

28. Türk, *Klavierschule* (1789), 16–17; trans. as *School of Clavier Playing*, 352; cited in *NMD*, 117. On Türk's understanding of "Klavier" as clavichord, and the predominance of that translation of the word in late eighteenth-century German texts, see Haggh, "Translator's Introduction," in Türk, *School of Clavier Playing*, xiv–xix.

29. Türk, *Klavierschule* (1789), 17n.

30. Burney, "Preface," *Four Sonatas or Duets*, n.p.

31. Letter from Leopold (Salzburg) to Wolfgang (Mannheim), December 8, 1777, *MBA* 387:100–102; trans. in Anderson, 412; quoted in Eisen, "Mozart and the Four-Hand Sonata K. 19d," 96.

32. On Hummel, see Kroll, *Johann Nepomuk Hummel*, 13. On Auernhammer, see Lorenz, "New and Old Documents."

33. The gendering of teacher and student as male is noteworthy here, given the popularity of the instrument as a female accomplishment, as well as the prevalence of women among Haydn's students.

34. ". . . amus[ing] himself in an attempt to fight the boredom of yet another tedious lesson, or, with subtle calculation, to create a situation in which he can, with greater effect and credibility, turn to his noble pupil as she copies him with her more easily executed fingering and exclaim, 'Bravo!'" Beghin, *The Virtual Haydn*, 123–24. Beghin's rhetorical device of using the female pronoun for Haydn's students here means that he ignores the masculine "scolare"—though Haydn could just as easily have intended the title diplomatically, reassuring his female students that none were parodied in the piece.

35. In the 1780s, other composers wrote "maestro e scolare" variations, including Jean Michel Pfeiffer, who included an "Il maestro e la scolara" in the second edition of his 1784 keyboard method, *La bambina al cembalo* (Venice). The "bambina"/"scolara" was Pfeiffer's female student, Elizabeth Wynne, the five-year-old dedicatee of the original method.

36. Lorenz, "New and Old Documents," 321; and Senn, "Zwei Schülerinnen Mozarts," 346–47.

37. In the accompanying letter, Mozart warned Gottfried that Franziska would have to practice it, "for it is rather difficult." Letter from Mozart (Vienna) to Gottfried von Jacquin (Vienna), end of May 1787, *MBA* 1053:5–7; trans. in Anderson [as May 29], 908. Senn maintains that the sonata was originally composed with

Nanette and Babette, not Franziska von Jacquin, in mind; see Senn, "Zwei Schülerinnen Mozarts," 347.

38. Haydn, *Sei Sonate per il clavicembalo*. On these sonatas, see Sisman, "Haydn's Career and the Rise of the Multiple Audience," 12–14.

39. Musäus, *Moralische Kinderklapper für Kinder und Nichtkinder*. The term "Nichtkinder" in the title is an unusual one, and may even be a neologism—it would have been far more likely for Musäus to have used "Kinderfreunde." The only other book title I found from this period with the word "Nichtkinder" is Friedrich Caspar Oesterlin, *Der kleine Zauberer, oder Anweisung zu leichten und belustigenden Kunststücken aus der natürlichen Magie: Für Kinder und Nichtkinder* (Stuttgart: Löfflund, 1799). Musäus also published the collection *Volksmärchen der Deutschen* (Gotha: C. W. Ettinger, 1782–1787).

40. "Harmonie," in Musäus, *Moralische Kinderklapper*, 69.

41. "Harmonie," 69–70.

42. This recalls the keyboard music for "pretty little hand[s]" about which Matthew Head has written (see discussion in chapter 4). Head, "If the Pretty Little Hand," and *Sovereign Feminine*, esp. 62. See also Zohn, "Morality and the 'Fair-Sexing.'"

43. See Marpurg, *Handbuch bey dem Generalbasse*, 83–84. I am grateful to Anna Karapin-Springorum for directing me to this reference.

44. "Harmonie," 70.

45. See Eisen, "Mozart and the Sonata K. 19d"; Temperley, ed., *A Selection of Four-Hand Duets*; and Stoelzel, *Die Anfänge vierhändiger Klaviermusik*. I am grateful to Rupert Ridgewell for clarifying some of the publisher timelines in this section. See his "Mozart's Publishing Plans with Artaria in 1787"; and "Artaria Plate Numbers and the Publication Process, 1778–87."

46. Smith, *Philosophische Fragmente*, 39; quoted in Breene, "The Instrumental Body," 235.

47. On the sarabande topic in K. 521/ii, see Irving, "Performing Topics in Mozart's Chamber Music," 546–47.

48. The ensuing dense texture is a distant forerunner of music for player piano, suggesting an instrument that seeks to transcend the limitations, but still reference the sound, of a single player. See Drott, "Conlon Nancarrow and the Technological Sublime."

49. Allanbrook, "Human Nature in the Unnatural Garden," 92.

50. Allanbrook, "Human Nature in the Unnatural Garden," 92.

51. Allanbrook, *Rhythmic Gesture in Mozart*, 172.

52. Cypess, "Keyboard-Duo Arrangements," 185. See also Cypess, "Duets in the Collection of Sara Levy."

53. Hiller, *Lieder für Kinder*, 131.

54. Hiller, *Lieder für Kinder*, 133.

55. Miller and Yavneh, "Introduction: Thicker Than Water," 2.

56. See Barry S. Brook, revised by Jean Gribenski, "Symphonie concertante," *OMO* (2001); and Christoph-Hellmut Mahling, foreword to *Concertone, Sinfonia concertante*, ed. Mahling, NMA V/14/2 (1975), xi–xii.

57. Letter from Mozart (Mannheim) to Leopold (Salzburg), February 28, 1778, *MBA* 431:26–27; trans. in Anderson, 497. Adena Portowitz has also discussed how K. 242 and K. 246 (composed for Countess Antonia Lützow) appear to honor their

first performers, with K. 242 reflecting "the Countess's maternal exemplarity." Porto-witz, "Mozart and Aristocratic Women Performers in Salzburg."

58. Keefe, *Mozart's Piano Concertos*, 2–3 and 52. Keefe draws on writings by Koch and others to show how central theatrical and musical theories of dialogue were to eighteenth-century understandings of instrumental music.

59. Keefe does not discuss K. 242 in his book because, as he puts it, the inter-soloist exchanges of the multiple concerto "would require an approach to dialogue and piano/orchestra relations grounded in inter-soloist as well as solo/orchestra interaction." Keefe, *Mozart's Piano Concertos*, 6.

60. See Cypess, "Keyboard-Duo Arrangements," 209–10; and Cypess, "Duets in the Collection of Sara Levy," 187–90.

61. "Concerto for 3 Harpsichords . . . Dedicated to the Incomparable Merit of Her Excellency Signora Countess Lodron née Countess d'Arco, and to her Daughters Contessa Aloisia and Giuseppa, From their Most Devoted Servant Amadeo Wolf-gango Mozart." Title page to manuscript copy by Leopold Mozart.

62. Marius Flothius, foreword to *Klavierkonzerte Band 1*, ed. Flothius, *NMA* V/15/1 (1972), viii. See also Irving, *Mozart's Piano Concertos*, 178–79. According to Nannerl's diary, the performance of the two-keyboard version took place in Salzburg on September 3, 1780, at which she and Wolfgang also revisited the four-hand sonata, K. 381. See Nannerl Mozart's diary, September 3, 1780, *MBA* 533:108–9. This event may even have prompted Della Croce's portrait to depict the siblings together at the keyboard.

63. Letter from Leopold (Salzburg) to Maria Anna and Wolfgang (Paris), June 11, 1778, *MBA* 452:25 and 38–40; trans. in Anderson, 545. There is no record of the date of the concerto's premiere. Mozart also composed the "Lodron Serenades" (K. 247 and K. 287) for Countess Lodron in 1776–1777.

64. "Augsburg vom 24 Oct.," *Augsburgische Staats- und Gelehrten Zeitung* (Octo-ber 28, 1777); in *Dokumente*, 150; *Documents*, 168. Deutsch posits that the author of the October 21 notice and the October 28 review was Johann Christoph von Zabuesnig. The third soloist on this occasion was Johann Michael Demler, the organ-ist of Augsburg Cathedral.

65. Letter from Wolfgang (Mannheim) to Leopold (Salzburg), December 6, 1777, *MBA* 386:28–29; trans. in Anderson, 408. See also *Dokumente*, 156; *Documents*, 174.

66. Halliwell, 203–6; and see family tree, fig. 3, pp. 204–5.

67. Halliwell, 282.

68. In Mozart's adaptation for two keyboards, the order of call-and-response is resolved into a I-II, II-I, a neat symmetry that tells an altogether different story than the original I-II, II-III.

69. Hunter, *Culture of Opera Buffa*, 179.

70. Hunter, *Culture of Opera Buffa*, 225.

71. Bruce, *Reading Agency*, 64.

72. Bruce, *Reading Agency*, 65.

73. "Die Geschwisterliebe, ein Schauspiel für Kinder (Fortsetzung)," *Der Kinder-freund, Ein Wochenblatt*, 41 (April 15, 1776), 31–32.

74. "Die Geschwisterliebe," 33. See Plutarch, "De fraterno amore," 21.

75. Dettmar, *Das Drama der Familienkindheit*, 20.

76. Letter from Mozart (Salzburg) to Archbishop Colloredo (Salzburg), August 1,

1777; *MBA* 328:25–28, 33–36; trans. in Anderson, 267. See also Mueller, "Learning and Teaching," 12.

77. On the possible performance configurations of this concerto, see Zaslaw, "Wolfgang Amadeus Mozart. *Konzert*," 388. See subsequent letter to the editor from Ralph Leavis, "Communications," and Zaslaw's reply, "Communications."

78. See letter from Wolfgang (Paris) to Leopold (Salzburg), July 31, 1778, *MBA* 471:163–64; trans. in Anderson, 587.

79. Frank, "Aus den ungedruckten Denkwürdigkeiten der Aerzte Peter und Joseph Frank," *Deutsches Museum* (Leipzig: January 1852); in *Dokumente*, 476; *Documents*, 561. See also letter from Mozart (Mannheim) to Leopold (Salzburg), February 14, 1778, *MBA* 423:56–57; trans. in Anderson, 481: "you know that I become quite powerless whenever I am obliged to write for an instrument which I cannot bear." This statement is generally thought to refer to the flute; see *MBA Kommentar* to 423:56–57; and Bowers, "Mozart and the Flute," 33.

80. Letter from Mozart (Paris) to Leopold (Salzburg), May 14, 1778, *MBA* 449:57–61; trans. in Anderson, 538. See also Zaslaw, "Wolfgang Amadeus Mozart, *Konzert*," 387.

81. Petrini, *Duo pour deux harpes, dédié à Mlle de Guines, Op. VII* (Paris, 1773/1774); and Johann Baptist Krumpholtz, *Recueil de douze préludes et petits airs pour la harpe ... Opera 2* (Paris, 1776).

82. This may have been another of Mozart's efforts to demonstrate to Marie-Louise how "easy" it was to compose a tune; she struggled with confidence in generating original melodies, and at one point he gave her the first four bars of a minuet, claiming to be unable to finish it, in order to overcome her resistance and self-doubt. See letter from Mozart (Paris) to Leopold (Salzburg), May 14, 1778, *MBA* 449:86–91; trans. in Anderson, 538–39.

83. Compare this to the third movement of the Concerto in E-flat for Two Keyboards K. 365 (1779), where the soloists trade phrases with much greater regularity.

84. See Rensch, *Harps and Harpists*; and Hoffmann, *Instrument und Körper*, 131–37.

85. Hoffmann, *Instrument und Körper*, 208–9.

86. He apparently supported Auernhammer's secret plan to remain unmarried and make a living as a professional. See letter from Wolfgang (Vienna) to Leopold (Salzburg), June 27, 1781, *MBA* 608:29–35; trans. in Anderson, 748.

87. "Concerts Spirituels, Du Jeudi, 16 Mai, fête de l'Ascencion," *Mercure de France* (Paris: June 1765), 191. See Gétreau, "Une harpiste au Concert spirituel"; and Pierre, *Histoire du Concert Spirituel*, 288.

88. Turrentine, "The Prince de Conti."

89. Michel-Barthélémy Ollivier, *Le Thé à l'anglaise servi dans le salon des Quatre-Glaces au palais du Temple, mai 1766*, oil on canvas, Chateau Versailles, MV 3824.

90. Gustafson, *Absent Mothers and Orphaned Fathers*, esp. 14–15.

91. Hunter, *Opera Buffa in Mozart's Vienna*, 74. Hunter cites Northrop Frye on comedy as "the mythos of spring."

92. Engel, *Ideen zu einer Mimik, Erster Theil*, 170–71. See Kendon, *Gesture*, 86–87.

93. Engel, *Ideen zu einer Mimik, Erster Theil*, 170.

94. Schiller, "On Naïve and Sentimental Poetry," 180–81. I am grateful to Nicholas Mathew for this reference.

95. Mozart, *SEI QUARTETTI*, n.p.; in *Dokumente*, 220; *Documents*, 250.

96. Mozart, *SEI QUARTETTI*, n.p.

97. Mozart, *SEI QUARTETTI*, n.p.

98. Rousseau, *Émile*, vol. 1, iii; *Emile*, 157 (Kelly translates this sentence as "Childhood is unknown").

99. Jenks, *Childhood*, 58.

100. "It may be possible to do without dancing entirely. Instances have been known of young people passing many, many months successively, without being at any ball of any description, and no material injury accrue either to body or mind;—but when a beginning is made—when the felicities of rapid motion have once been, though slightly, felt—it must be a very heavy set that does not ask for more." Austen, *Emma*, 205.

Chapter Six

1. Rice, "Adding Birds to Mozart's 'Sparrow Mass.'" The manuscript parts are held at A-Wn Mus. Hs. 10235. See also Rice, *Empress Marie Therese and Music at the Viennese Court*, 143–51.

2. See Croll, ed., *Musik mit Kinderinstrumenten*.

3. See Black, "1793—Mozart comments on 'Haydn's' *Toy Symphony*," in Edge/Black. On the symphony and Angerer's authorship, see Angerer, *Berchtoldsgaden Musick: Kindersinfonie*; Herrmann-Schneider, "Edmund Angerer OSB (1740-1794)"; and Illing, *Berchtoldsgaden Musick*, 2–3.

4. Black, "1793—Mozart comments on 'Haydn's' *Toy Symphony*." See also Illing, *Berchtoldsgaden Musick*; and Gerlach, "Textkritische Untersuchungen," 153.

5. Letter from Leopold (Paris) to Maria Theresia Hagenauer (Salzburg), February 1, 1764, *MBA* 80:5–6; trans. in Anderson, 33–34. Wolfgang, postscript to letter from Leopold (Bologna) to Maria Anna (Salzburg), October 6, 1770, *MBA* 213:37–39; trans. in Anderson, 165.

6. See Buch, "Mozart's Bawdy Canons."

7. Bachmann, *Berchtesgadener Volkskunst*, 43–45. On the childlike elsewhere in *Die Zauberflöte*, see Mueller, "Who Were the Drei Knaben?"

8. See Bruckner, "Die Pfeifenmacherei in Berchtesgaden."

9. For example: "extremely difficult": "Prag, den 1. November [review of *Don Giovanni*]," *Prager Oberpostamtszeitung* (November 3, 1787); in *Dokumente*, 267; *Documents*, 303; "difficult . . . rather unsettling": Adolf von Knigge, "Den dritten October: Belmonte und Konstanza, oder: die Entführung aus dem Serail," *Dramaturgische Blätter* 2 (Hannover, October 11, 1788); in *Dokumente*, 288–89; *Documents*, 327–28. "too artificial/contrived [*gekünstelt*]": "Wien vom 3ten Mai. (aus Privatnachrichten)," *Münchner Zeitung* (May 9, 1786), in Dexter Edge, "3 May 1786: A report on the premiere of *Le nozze di Figaro*," in Edge/Black; and "over-seasoned": Carl Friedrich Cramer, "Wien, den 29sten Januar [review of "Haydn" Quartets]," *Magazin der Musik* (April 23, 1787); in *Dokumente*, 255–56; *Documents*, 290.

10. Triest, "Bemerkungen über die Ausbildung der Tonkunst in Deutschland im achtzehnten Jahrhundert," *AmZ* 23 (March 4, 1801): 393 and 391n.

11. See for instance Nissen, *Biographie W. A. Mozart's*, 640–41.

12. Daverio, "Mozart in the Nineteenth Century," 177; Allanbrook, "Is the Sublime

a Musical Topos?" See also DeNora, *Beethoven and the Construction of Genius*, 11–15, on the aesthetics of "pleasingness."

13. Halliwell, 567–642 (Part 6: "The Biographical Legacy"); Gruber, *Mozart and Posterity*, 12–15, 24–29, and 52–57.

14. Nissen, *Anhang zu Wolfgang Amadeus Mozart's Biographie*, 20.

15. Halliwell, 591 and 603. On Breitkopf & Härtel's *Oeuvres complettes* (1798–1806), see Eisen, "The Old and New Mozart Editions."

16. Friedrich Rochlitz, "Biographieen. Verbürgte Anekdoten aus Wolfgang Gottlieb Mozarts Leben, ein Beytrag zur richtigern Kenntnis dieses Mannes, als Mensch und Künstler," *AmZ* (October 10, 1798—December 5, 1798), collected and transcribed in http://mozartsocietyofamerica.org/embp/RochlitzAnekdoten.pdf, accessed July 10, 2019; Constanze Mozart, "Biographie. Einige Anekdoten aus Mozarts Leben, von seiner hinterlassenen Gattin uns mitgetheilt," *AmZ* 1 (September 11, 1799): 854–56; Nannerl Mozart, "Noch einige Anekdoten aus Mozarts Kinderjahren, Mitgetheilt von dessen Schwestern, der Reichsfreyin, Frau von Berthold zu Sonnenburg," *AmZ* 2 (January 22, 1800): 300–301.

17. Schlichtegroll, "Mozart," 109. Traudes also surveys this biographical tradition in *Musizierende "Wunderkinder*," 27–51.

18. Schlichtegroll, "Mozart," 89–90, based on letter from Schachtner (Salzburg) to Nannerl (St. Gilgen), April 24, 1792; in *Dokumente*, 396; *Documents*, 452. On this anecdote and its variations from Schachtner to Schlichtegroll, see Clarke, *The Annotated Schlichtegroll*, 21–23.

19. Niemetschek, *Leben des K. K. Kapellmeisters Wolfgang Gottlieb Mozart*, 4–5; Busby, "Life of Mozart," 445; Siebigke, "Wolfgang Gottlieb Mozart," 9–11; Winckler, *Notice biographique sur Jean-Chrysostome-Wolfgang-Théophile Mozart*, 9–10.

20. Nissen, *Biographie*, 18.

21. [Arnold], *Mozarts Geist*, ix–x.

22. [Arnold], *Mozarts Geist*, 108–9.

23. [Arnold], *Mozarts Geist*, 110.

24. [Arnold], *Mozarts Geist*, 105–6.

25. Nissen, *Biographie*, 653–54 and 696.

26. *Mozarts Geist* was also advertised in the *Intelligenzblatt der Zeitung für die elegante Welt*, listed as an anonymous "Bildungsbuch für Damen" (though as far as I can tell there were no such editions with that subtitle) and advertised alongside other books suitable as "Christmas gifts for the fair sex." "Empfehlungswerthe Schriften als Weihnachtsgeschenke für das schöne Geschlecht," *Intelligenzblatt der Zeitung für die elegante Welt* 5, no. 62 (December 14, 1805): n.p.

27. [Arnold,] *Wolfgang Amadeus Mozart und Joseph Haydn*, and *Gallerie der berühmtesten Tonkünstler*. This latter collection also includes biographies of Zumsteeg, Dittersdorf, Cherubini, Paisiello, Cimarosa, Winter, and Himmel, all of which appear also to have been issued separately.

28. Elliodt, "Das musikalische Kind Mozart," 109. This sketch is paired with one on "Das gelehrte Kind, Baratier," the two together constituting an entry entitled "Kleine Bildergallerie merkwürdige und berühmter Kinder." For more on Baratier, see chapter 1.

29. Blanchard [and Kraft], *Neuer Plutarch*. The work was a translation of, and expansion on, Blanchard's *Le Plutarque de la jeunesse* (1803). Mozart does not appear

in *Le Plutarque;* Kraft and the Austrian editors added new entries on Mozart and other Austro-German figures.

30. Blanchard and Kraft, *Neuer Plutarch,* 275.

31. Hormayr, *Oesterreichischer Plutarch,* vol. 7 (1807), 139. On this title, see Davies, *The Wallenstein Figure,* 115–16.

32. Gruber, *Mozart and Posterity,* 24–26. For an overview of genre preferences (and genre fluidity) in the early nineteenth-century print music market, see Carew, "The Consumption of Music."

33. Mozart listed K. 545 (composed June 26, 1788) as "Eine kleine klavier Sonate für anfänger," and K. 547 (composed July 10, 1788) as "Eine kleine klavier Sonata für Anfänger mit einer Violin." See Mozart, *Thematisches Verzeichniss,* 38. For more on K. 545, see Irving, *Mozart's Piano Sonatas,* 85–86.

34. Mozart, *Sonate facile pour le Pianoforte* (Vienna: Bureau d'Arts et d'Industrie, 1805); Mozart, *Sonate facile pour Piano-Forté* (Offenbach am Main: Johann André, 1805); and Mozart, *Sonate facile pour le Clavecin où Pianoforte* (Vienna: Johann Cappi, 1809). Examples of the "easy," "little," "light," and "beginner" prints include: "easy": Mozart, *Duettini facili p. 2 Viol.* (Vienna: Artaria, n.d.); Mozart, *3 Duos faciles p. 2 Viol. Ou Fl. et Viol* (Hamburg, Boehme, n.d.), advertised in Carl Friedrich Whistling, *Handbuch der musikalischen Literatur . . .* (Leipzig: Hoffmeister, 1815), 101; "little": Mozart, *XII petites pièces pour le piano forte* (Vienna: Hoffmeister, [1795?]); "light": Mozart, *Zwölf leichte Klavierstücke* (Leipzig: Peters, 1814); and "beginner": Justin Heinrich Knecht, *Kleine und leichte Uebungsstücke im Klavierspielen für die ersten Anfänger mit angemerktem Fingersatze, von Haydn, Mozart, Clementi, Pleyl, Vogler, Knecht &c.* (Freyburg and Konstanz: Herder, 1815), 3 vols.

35. "Sonate facile p. le Pianof. av. accomp. de Violon ad libitum, par Fred. Kuhlau [review]," *AmZ* 15, no. 27 (July 7, 1813): 449–50.

36. Türk, *Klavierschule* (1789), 15–17; *School of Clavier Playing,* 23–24. See Riggs, "Authenticity and Subjectivity in Mozart Performance."

37. Türk, *Klavierschule* (1802), 25.

38. Milchmeyer, *Kleine Pianoforte-Schule für Kinder,* vol. 2, pp. 6, 28, and 30, respectively. On the Hammer waltz, see RISM ID no. 450063518.

39. Cramer, *W. A. Mozart's Clavierschule.*

40. Blanchard [and Kraft], *Neuer Plutarch,* 276.

41. See for instance Nierhaus, *Algorithmic Composition,* esp. 36–38; Schmidt, "Den Zufall denken"; Pimmer, *Würfelkomposition;* Hedges, "Dice Music in the Eighteenth Century"; and Ratner, "Ars Combinatoria."

42. "Einleitung," [Stadler], *Neues Musikalisches Würfel-Spiel,* n.p.

43. Zaslaw, "Mozart's Modular Minuet Machine."

44. Anonymous, *24 Walzer nach der Anleitung.* I have not yet been able to locate any extant copies of this print, which may have been the first piece of printed music by a group of supposed "non-composers."

45. "III. Neue Musikalien," *Intelligenzblatt der Allgemeine Literatur-Zeitung* 100 (September 21, 1793), 800.

46. "Mozart," *Anleitung: so viel Engl. Contre Tänce* and *Anleitung: so viel Walzer.*

47. "Mozart," *Anleitung englische Contretänze* and *Anleitung Walzer oder Schleifer.*

48. Götz prints: advertised in [Anonymous], *Catalogue des livres,* 28. I have not yet been able to locate any extant copies of these prints. Arnold prints: "Mozart,"

Anleitung für zwey Violinen, advertised in *Intelligenzblatt der Allgemeine Literatur-Zeitung* 226 (December 8, 1802), 1823.

49. "Auflösung einer mathematisch-musikalischen Aufgabe," *AmZ* 15, no. 22 (June 2, 1813): 357–58. Mozart had, of course, "thought of such a thing," namely K. 516f, the unpublished "musical minuet machine" mentioned on pp. 188–89.

50. Zaslaw, "Mozart's Modular Minuet Machine," 225; and Pimmer, *Würfelkomposition*, 103–4.

51. Bigant, *Domino musical*, in Zaslaw, "Mozart's Modular Minuet Machine," 223; and [Anonymous], *Musical Domino*; Hayn, *Anleitung, Angloisen mit Würfeln zu komponieren*, preface; quoted in Pimmer, *Würfelkomposition*, 123. I have not yet been able to locate any extant copies of this last print.

52. See for instance Strutt, *Sports and Pastimes*, 288, which mentions the teetotum in the chapter on children's games: "the usage of the *te-totum* may be considered as a kind of petty gambling."

53. Wheatstone, "Address," *Mozart's*, [sic] *Musical Game*, 2.

54. Arnoldt [sic], "Musikalisches Würfelspiel," *Intelligenzblatt der Allgemeine Literatur-Zeitung*, 1823. Emphasis mine.

55. The *Alphabet* is listed in Whistling, *Handbuch der musikalischen Literatur* (1828), 1018.

56. Mozart's closest melody to that of the *Alphabet* is the puzzle canon no. 11 from the *14 Canonic Studies* (K. 73x, 1772). As is obvious, the *Alphabet* tune bears no resemblance to the "Ah! vous dirai-je maman" melody with which Mozart would come to be associated with the more familiar alphabet song through his variations K. 265 (1781–1782) (which I have traced only as early as 1834, M. Cochin, *Manuel des fondateurs et des directeurs des premières écoles de l'enfance*, 2nd ed. (Paris: Hachette, 1834), 5.

57. I can find no biographical information on this "Dillenberg"—it might be a pseudonym.

58. "Kurze Anzeigen: *Ernst und Scherz. Sammlung verschiedener Lieder und Romanzen mit Begleitung des Fortepiano oder der Guitarre, zusammengetragen von Dillenberg*," in *AmZ* 15, no. 20 (May 19, 1813): 338–39.

59. *Mozarts Alphabet* continued to be listed in Whistling, *Handbuch der musikalischen Literatur*, vol. 3 (1845), 72; by this time the version by Dillenberg had been reprinted by Simrock (Bonn); see Whistling, *Handbuch*, 58.

60. "Mozart," *Alphabet pour choeur à 3 voix* (Paris: Editions Salabert, 1987).

61. I am grateful to Rebekah Ahrendt for pointing out this important comparison. On "Papa Haydn," see James Webster, "§6. Character and Personality," in Georg Feder and Webster, "Haydn, (Franz) Joseph," *OMO* (2001).

62. The score excerpts in the body of the text are: the "Schlaflied" (to be discussed in this section), the first six bars of K. 9/1, and a Rondeau by the thirteen-year-old Louise d'Orléans dedicated to Mozart in 1766; Nissen, *Biographie*, 35, 65, and 114–16, respectively. The *Musikblätter* are twelve pages of excerpts from early compositions from the *Nannerl Notenbuch* through K. 8, Mozart's audition piece for the Accademia Filarmonica (K. 86, 1770), the spurious *Wiegenlied* (K. 350, to be discussed in this section), and the first thirty-five bars of the concert aria "In te spero o sposo amato" (K. 440, 1782); Nissen, *Biographie*, after 14 and 226, and Nissen, *Anhang*, after 20 and 28.

63. Nissen, *Biographie*, 15n.

64. Friedlaender, "Mozart's Wiegenlied" (1892) and "Mozarts Wiegenlied" (1897).

65. Flies, *Wiegenlied, von Gotter*. A similar but not identical setting, by Friedrich Fleischmann, was published the following year in Offenbach by André as *Wiegenlied aus Gotters Esther*, with a dedication to Gotter's own daughter.

66. Letter from Constanze (Salzburg) to Johann Anton André (Offenbach), October 28, 1825, *MBA* 1403:93–94; not in Anderson; reproduced in Köchel 6, 847.

67. Nissen, *Anhang*, 10.

68. *MBA* 1403:98–99; see also Friedlaender citations in note 64 above.

69. "Ds." [Friedrich Deycks], "Recensionen. Biographie *W. A. Mozart's*," *Caecilia* 10, no. 40 (Mainz, 1829), 237. Strangely, no specific mention is made of the music examples and tipped-in sheets in the review of Nissen's *Biographie* in the *AmZ*. "Recensionen, *Biographie W. A. Mozart's. . .*," *AmZ* 22 (June 3, 1829): 356–60.

70. Gathy, *Musikalisches Conversations-Lexikon*, 511.

71. No individual print of the lullaby appears to have been published under Mozart's name, but this was likely only due to the fact that Constanze's misgivings about the authenticity of the lullaby had grown by 1828. See entry in Köchel 6, 847.

72. [Anonymous?], "Etwas über die Symphonie und Beethovens Leistungen in diesem Fache." *Berlin Allgemeine musikalische Zeitung* 1, no. 20 (May 19, 1824), 173.

73. Nissen, *Anhang*, 161.

74. [Anonymous], "den 30sten März 1783. Nachricht von der churfürstlich-cöllnischen Hofcapelle zu Bonn und andern Tonkünstlern daselbst," *Magazin der Musik* 1 (Hamburg, 1783), 395. On Beethoven as a "second Mozart," see Lockwood, "Beethoven before 1800: The Mozart Legacy"; and DeNora, *Beethoven and the Construction of Genius*, chapter 5 ("'From Haydn's Hands': Narrative Constructions of Beethoven's Talent and Future Success"), esp. 85.

75. DeNora, *Beethoven and the Construction of Genius*, 15–16.

76. For more on the *Nannerl Notenbuch*, see Tyson, "A Reconstruction of Nannerl Mozart's Music Book (Notenbuch)"; and Wolfgang Plath, foreword to *Klavierstücke Band 1: Die Notenbücher*, ed. Plath, NMA IX/27/1 (1982): xii–xxi.

77. [Joseph Fröhlich], "Recension. Grande Sinfonie . . . par Vogler. à Offenbach, chez J. André," *AmZ* 6 (February 5, 1817): 96.

78. [Fröhlich], "Recension," 96.

79. G[eorg] C[hristoph] Grosheim, "Biographie W. A. Mozart's von Georg Nicolaus von Nissen . . . Zweite Recension," *Caecilia* 11, no. 44 (1831): 282.

80. The sketches were printed on their own sometime after 1831, as *Die Wunder der Tonkunst, Oder 12 Musikstücke welche der unsterbliche W. A. Mozart in seinem 6ten Lebensjahre komponiert hat* (Augsburg). The title "Wunder der Tonkunst" might allude to Fröhlich's 1817 description of Mozart as "dieser Heros der Tonkunst."

81. [Anonymous], "Biographie W. A. Mozarts. Von G. N. von Nissen [Review]," in *Foreign Quarterly Review* 4 (April & August) (London: Treuttel and Würtz, 1829), 407.

82. Nissen, *Biographie W. A. Mozart's*, 35.

83. In this way, it is of a piece with his demonstration arias for Daines Barrington, with their "jargon recitatives" preceding the Love Song on "*affetto*" and Song of Rage on "*perfido*." Barrington, "Account of a Very Remarkable Young Musician," 60–61.

84. Rousseau, *The Confessions* [1782], 7.

Bibliography

Printed Music (Including Modern Editions)

Angerer, Edmund. *Berchtoldsgaden Musick: Kindersinfonie*. Ed. Hildegard Herrmann-Schneider. Beiträge zur Musikforschung in Tirol 3. Innsbruck: Eigenverlag des Instituts für Tiroler Musikforschung, 1997. Available online at http://www.musikland-tirol.at/html/html/musikedition/komponisten/angerer/kindersinfonie/kindersinfonieframe.html, accessed July 9, 2019.

[Anonymous]. *24 Walzer nach der Anleitung, Walzer mit Würfeln zu componiren, von 24 verschiedenen, grösstentheils unmusikalischen Personen.* [Vienna?]: n.p., 1793[?].

———. *Katholisches Gesangbuch auf allerhöchsten Befehl ihrer k. k. apost. Majestät Marien Theresiens*. Vienna: Verlag der katechetischen Bibliothek, 1774.

———. *Kleine Lieder für Kinder mit Melodien, zum singen beym Klavier*. Leipzig: [s.n.], 1777.

———. *Lieder zur öffentlichen und häuslichen Andacht, mit vielen Melodien von den besten vaterländischen Meistern. Herausgegeben auf Veranlassung der k. k. Normalschuldirektion*. Prague: K. k. Normalschulbuchdruckerey, 1783.

———. *Musical Domino: A New Game. This Game was invented for the Improvement of young Scholars in Music*. London: John Wallis, 1793.

———. *Verbesserte katechetische Gesänge, welche nun nach der Ordnung und dem Inhalte des für die k. k. Staaten vorgeschriebenen Katechismus sind abgeändert worden*. Vienna: Verlagsgewölbe der deutschen Schulanstalt bei St. Anna in der Johannesgasse, 1779.

Bach, Carl Philipp Emanuel. *Gellert Songs*. Ed. Darrell M. Berg. In *The Complete Works, Series VI, Songs and Vocal Chamber Music*, vol. 1. Los Altos, CA: Packard Humanities Institute, 2009.

———. *Herrn Professor Gellerts Geistliche Oden und Lieder mit Melodien*. Berlin: George Ludewig Winter, 1758.

Bigant, N. *Domino musical, ou L'art du musicien, mis en jeu, jeu utile, instructif, intéressant et amusant, à la portée de tout le monde et les enfans*. Paris: Bigant, 1779.

Buch, David, ed. *Liedersammlung für Kinder und Kinderfreunde am Clavier* (1791): *Frühlingslieder and Winterlieder*. Recent Researches in the Music of the Classical Era, 95. Middleton, WI: A-R Editions, 2014.

Burmann, Gottlob Wilhelm. *G. W. Burmanns Kleine Lieder für kleine Mädchen und Knaben, In Musik gesetzt von J. G. H. Nebst einem Anhang etlicher Lieder aus der Wochenschrift: Der Greis*. Zürich: David Bürgkli, 1774.

———. *Kleine Lieder für kleine Jünglinge.* Berlin and Königsberg: G. I. Decker and G. L. Hartung, 1777.

———. *Kleine Lieder für kleine Mädchen.* Berlin and Königsberg: G. I. Decker and G. L. Hartung, 1773.

Burney, Charles. *Four Sonatas or Duets for Two Performers on One Piano Forte or Harpsichord.* London: Bremner, 1777.

Claudius, Georg Carl. *Lieder für Kinder mit neuen sehr leichten Melodieen.* Frankfurt am Mayn: Brönner, 1780.

Cramer, A. M. W. *A. Mozart's Clavierschule, nebst dem bei dem Conservatorium der Musik zu Paris angenommenen Grundsätzen der richtigen Fingersetzung auf dem Piano-Forte; durch praktische Beispiele und fortschreitende Uibungsstücke von den besten Meistern erläutert.* Prague: Carl Wilhelm Enders, 1819.

Fleischmann, Friedrich. *Wiegenlied aus Gotters Esther, mit Begleitung einer Guitarre oder des Klaviers, gesetzt und den Gotterschen Tochter gewidmet.* Offenbach: André, 1796.

Flies, Bernhard. *Wiegenlied, von Gotter.* Berlin: G. F. Starcke, [1795].

Friedlaender, Max, ed. *Neujahrsgrüsse empfindsamer Seelen: Eine Sammlung von Liedern mit Melodien und Bilderschmuck aus den Jahren 1770–1800.* Veröffentlichungen der Musik-Bibliothek Paul Hirsch 3. Berlin: M. Breslauer, 1922.

Görner, Johann Valentin. *Sammlung neuer Oden und Lieder, Teil 2.* Hamburg: J. C. Bohn, 1744.

Haydn, Joseph. *XII Lieder für das Clavier.* Vienna: Artaria, 1781.

———. *Il maestro e scolare, o Sonata con variazioni a quadri mani per un clavi-cembalo.* Berlin: J. J. Hummel, 1781. Ed. Sonja Gerlach. Munich: Henle, 2007.

———. *Sei Sonate per il clavicembalo, o forte piano . . . opera XXX, dedicate alle ornatissime signore Caterine e Marianna d'Auenbrugger.* Vienna: Artaria, [1780].

Haydn, Michael. *Die Hochzeit auf der Alm: Ein dramatisches Schäfergedicht.* Ed. Bernhard Paumgartner. Salzburg/Stuttgart: Das Bergland-Buch, 1959.

Hayn, Friedrich Gottlob. *Anleitung, Angloisen mit Würfeln zu komponieren.* Dresden: C. A. Kirmse, 1798.

Hiller, Johann Adam. *Lieder für Kinder, vermehrte Auflage. Mit neuen Melodien von Johann Adam Hiller.* Leipzig: Weidmanns Erben und Reich, 1769.

———. *Vierstimmige Motetten und Arien in Partitur, von verschiednen Componisten, zum Gebrauch der Schulen und anderer Gesangsliebhaber.* Leipzig: Dykische Buchhandlung, 1776.

Hunger, Gottlob Gottwald. *Lieder für Kinder mit neuen Melodien.* Leipzig: Weidmanns Erben und Reich, 1772.

"Mozart, Wolfgang Amadé" [i.e., spurious]. *Alphabet pour choeur à 3 voix.* Paris: Editions Salabert, 1987.

———. *Anleitung englische Contretänze mit zwei Würfeln zu componiren, so viele man will, ohne etwas von der Musik oder der Composition zu verstehen. Par W. A. Mozart.* Bonn: Simrock, 1798.

———. *Anleitung für zwey Violinen, Flöte und Baß, so viele Contra-Tänze mit zwey Würfeln zu componiren als man will; ohne musikalisch zu seyn, noch etwas von der Composition zu verstehen.* Hamburg: G. P. Arnold and Christian Gottfried Kratsch, 1801.

———. *Anleitung für zwey Violinen, Flöte und Baß, so viele Contra-Tänze mit zwey Würfeln zu componiren als man will; ohne musikalisch zu seyn, noch etwas von der*

Composition zu verstehen. Par Mr. W. A. Mozart. Hamburg: G. P. Arnold and Christian Gottfried Kratsch, 1801.

———. *Anleitung: so viel Engl. Contre Tänce mit zwei wurfeln zu componieren als man will, ohne musikalisch zu seyn, noch etwas von der Composition zu verstehen.* Berlin: Hummel, 1793.

———. *Anleitung: so viel Walzer oder Schleifer mit zwei Würfeln zu componiren so viel man wil, ohne musikalisch zu seijn noch etwas von der Composition zu verstehen.* Berlin: Hummel, 1793.

———. *Anleitung Walzer oder Schleifer mit zwei Würfeln zu componiren, so viele man will, ohne etwas von der Musik oder Composition zu verstehen. Par W. A. Mozart.* Bonn: Simrock, 1798.

———. *Mozart's, [sic] Musical Game, or the Christmas Musical Gift, to juvenile amateurs, being an ingenious, easy & systematical method, of composing . . . waltzes, without the slightest knowledge of composition, by the turn of a te totum . . . To which is prefaced three German waltzes.* London: C. Wheatstone, [ca. 1810].

———. *W. A. Mozarts Alphabet. Ein musikalischer Scherz. Für drei Kinder-Stimmen arrangirt von C. F. Pax.* Berlin: Lischke, [ca. 1820s].

Mozart, Wolfgang Amadé [i.e., authentic]. *Sämtliche Lieder für mittlere Stimme* [transposition]. Ed. Ernst August Ballin. Kassel: Bärenreiter, 1999.

———. *SEI QUARTETTI per due Violini, Viola, e Violoncello, Composti e Dedicati al Signor GIUSEPPE HAYDN, Maestro di Cappella di S. A. il Principe d'Esterhazy &c &c Dal Suo Amico W. A. MOZART, Opera X.* Vienna: Artaria, 1785.

———. *Wunder der Tonkunst! Oder 12 Musikstücke welche der unsterbliche W. A. Mozart in seinem 6ten Lebensjahre theils für das Klavier, theils für die Orgel komponirt hat* Augsburg: Verlag von Anton Böhm, [n.d., after 1831].

Partsch, Placidus, ed. *Liedersammlung für Kinder und Kinderfreunde am Clavier. Frühlingslieder.* Vienna: Ignaz Alberti, 1791.

Reichardt, Johann Friedrich. *Lieder für Kinder aus Campes Kinderbibliothek.* Hamburg: Heroldschen Buchhandlung, 1781.

Rosenbaum, Christian Ernst. *Lieder mit Melodien.* Altona und Lübeck: David Iversen, 1762.

Scheibe, Johann Adolph. *Kleine Lieder für Kinder zur Beförderung der Tugend.* Flensburg: Johann Christoph Korte, 1766–1768. 2 vols.

Schoep, Arthur, and Daniel Harris. *Word-by-Word Translations of Songs and Arias, Part II: Italian.* New York: Scarecrow Press, 1972.

Schulz, Johann Abraham Peter. *Lieder im Volkston.* Berlin: Decker, 1782 (1st ed.), 1785 (2nd ed.), 1790 (3rd ed.).

Seydelmann, Franz. *Sechs Sonaten für Zwo Personen auf einem Clavier.* Leipzig: Breitkopf, 1781.

Stadler, Maximilian. *Neues Musikalisches Würfel-Spiel, oder: die Kunst, mit Hilfe zweyer Würfel, Menuetts und Trios bis ins Unendliche zu komponiren.* Vienna: Musikalisch-Typographischen Gesellschaft, n.d.

Stiasny, Franz. *Sammlung einiger Lieder für die Jugend bei Industrialarbeiten mit den hiezu gehörigen Melodien.* Prague: Normalschul-Buchdruckerey, 1789.

Stoelzel, Marianne. *Die Anfänge vierhändiger Klaviermusik: Studien zur Satztypik Muzio Clementis.* Europäische Hochschulschriften 36/7. Frankfurt: Peter Lang, 1984.

Temperley, Nicholas, ed. *A Selection of Four-Hand Duets Published between 1777 and*

1857; *Works for Two Pianos Published between 1778 and 1860. The London Piano-forte School 1766–1860*, xix–xx. New York: Garland, 1986.

Selected Periodicals

Allgemeine deutsche Bibliothek
Allgemeine Literatur-Zeitung
Allgemeine musikalische Zeitung (AmZ)
Allgemeiner Theater Allmanach von Jahr . . .
Almanach de Berlin
Angenehme und lehrreiche Beschäftigung für Kinder in ihre Freistunden
Aristide, ou le citoyen
Berlin Allgemeine musikalische Zeitung
Bibliotheque Germanique ou Histoire Litteraire de l'Allemagne, de la Suisse, et des Pays du Nord
Briefwechsel der Familie des Kinderfreundes
Caecilia
Europäische Zeitung
Foreign Quarterly Review
Der Greis
Hannoverisches Magazin
K[aiserlich] K[önigliche] allergnädigst privilegierte Realzeitung
Der Kinderfreund
Kleine Kinderbibliothek
Litteratur- und Theater-Zeitung
Lloyd's Evening Post
Magazin der Musik
Mercure de France
Mercure galant
Musenalmanach für das Jahr . . .
Musikalischer Almanach für Deutschland
Musikalisch-kritische Bibliothek
Neue Kinderbibliothek
Neue Sammlung zum Vergnügen und Unterricht
Der Nordische Aufseher
Der österreichischer Volksfreund
Pädagogische Unterhandlungen
Public Advertiser
Salzburger Volksblatt
Saxonia: Museum für sächsische Vaterlandskunde
Taschenbuch zum Nutzen und Vergnügen fürs Jahr . . .
Theater-Journal für Deutschland
Theaterwochenblatt zu Salzburg
Unterhaltungen für Kinder und Kinderfreunde
Wienerisches Diarium
Wiener Zeitung
Wochenschrift zum Besten der Erziehung der Jugend

Wochentliche Nachrichten und Anmerkungen die Musik betreffend
Zeitung für die elegante Welt

Other Primary and Pre-1850 Sources
(including Modern Editions and Translations)

Adelung, Johann Christoph. *Versuch eines vollständigen grammatisch-kritischen Wörterbuches der Hochdeutschen Mundart.* Leipzig: Breitkopf & Co., 1775–1780. 5 vols.

Anderson, Emily, trans. and ed. *The Letters of Mozart and His Family.* 2nd ed., prepared by A. Hyatt King and Monica Carolan. London: Macmillan, 1966 [1938]. 2 vols.

[Anonymous]. *Catalogue des livres de musique qui se vendent chez Jean Michel Götz.* Mannheim, Joseph Ableshauser, 1802.

———. *Ein musikalisches Singspiel, genannt: Das Serail. Oder: Die unvermuthete Zusammenkunft in der Sclaverey zwischen Vater, Tochter, und Sohn.* Botzen: Karl Joseph Weiß, 1779.

———. *Jährlicher Bericht des Wiener Waisenhause unser lieben Frau am Rennwege . . .* [Vienna]: Joseph Gerold, 1772, 1777.

———. *Künftige Gottesdienstes- und Andachtsordnung für Prag, mit Anfange des 1. des Monats May 1784.* Prague: Schönfeld, 1784.

———. *Nachricht an das Publikum. Von der Absicht und dem Nutzen des auf allerhöchsten Befehl verbesserten Schulwesens in Oesterreich unter der Enns.* [Vienna]: n.p., [1771].

———. *Schmuckkästchen für die Jugend, oder auserlesene Moral für das Herz. In alphabethischer Ordnung.* Vienna: Gerold, 1780.

———. *Ueber Taubstumme, Eine Einladungsschrift zur öffentlichen Prüfung der Taubstummen, welche den 22. August 1795 im k. k. Taubstummen-Institute zu Wien auf dem Dominikaner-Platze Vormittag von 9 bis 12 Uhr gehalten wird.* Vienna: Seizer, 1795.

———. *Vollkommener Bericht von dem Music-Chor deren Knaben in dem Waysenhaus Unser Lieben Frau auf dem Rennweeg* [sic] *. . . , Im Jahr, 1764, den 22. Novemb.* Vienna: Johann Jacob Jahn, [1764].

———. *Vollkommener Bericht von der Beschaffenheit des Waisenhauses Unser lieben Frau auf dem Rennwege zu Wien in Oesterreich . . . im Jahre 1774.* Vienna: Kaliwoda, 1774.

Aristotle. *De Sensu et Sensibili.* In *The Parvu Naturalia.* Trans. J. I. Beare. *The Works of Aristotle Translated into English.* Oxford: Clarendon Press, 1908.

Arnold, Friedrich. *Beobachtungen in und über Prag, von einem reisenden Ausländer.* Prague: Woflgang Gerle, 1787. 2 vols.

[Arnold, Ignaz]. *Gallerie der berühmtesten Tonkünstler des 18. und 19. Jahrhunderts.* Erfurt: Müller, 1810, rev. 1816. 2 vols.

———. *Mozarts Geist. Seine kurze Biografie und ästhetische Darstellung seiner Werke. Ein Bildungsbuch für junge Tonkünstler.* Erfurt: Hennings, 1803.

———. *Wolfgang Amadeus Mozart und Joseph Haydn: Nachträge zu ihren Biografieen und ästhetischer Darstellung ihrer Werke. Versuch einer Parallele. Bildungsbuch für junge Tonkünstler.* Erfurt: J. K. Müller, 1810.

Augustine. *Writings of St. Augustine.* Ed. Robert C. Taliaferro. Fathers of the Church. Washington, DC: Catholic University of America Press, 1947.

Austen, Jane. *Emma.* London: John Murray, 1816 [orig. pub. 1815].

———. *Mansfield Park: A Novel.* London: J. Murray, 1816 [orig. pub. 1814].

Bach, Carl Philipp Emanuel. *Essay on the True Art of Playing Keyboard Instruments.* Trans. and ed. William J. Mitchell. New York: W. W. Norton, 1949.

———. *Versuch über die wahre Art, das Clavier zu spielen.* Berlin: C. F. Henning, 1753.

Baillet, Andre. *Des enfans devenus célèbres par leurs etudes ou par leurs ecrits: Traité historique.* Paris: Antoine Dezallier, 1688.

Barrington, Daines. "Account of a Very Remarkable Young Musician. In a Letter from the Honourable Daines Barrington, F. R. S. to Mathew Maty, M. D. Sec. R. S." In *Philosophical Transactions, Giving Some Account of the Present Undertakings, Studies, and Labours, of the Ingenious, in Many Considerable Parts of the World.* London: Royal Society, 1771, vol. 60 ("For the Year 1770").

———. "Account of Master Samuel Wesley." In *Miscellanies by the Honourable Daines Barrington.* London: J. Nichols, 1781, 291–310.

———. "Some Account of Little Crotch." In *Miscellanies by the Honourable Daines Barrington.* London: J. Nichols, 1781, 311–17.

Basedow, Johann Bernhard. *Das in Dessau errichtete Philanthropinum, Eine Schule der Menschenfreundschaft und guter Kenntnisse für Lernende und junge Lehrer, arme und reiche.* Leipzig; Siegfried Lebrecht Crusius, 1774.

———. *Das Elementarwerk: Ein geordneter Vorrath aller nöthigen Erkenntniß; Zum Unterrichte der Jugend, von Anfang, bis ins academische Alter, Zur Belehrung der Eltern, Schullehrer und Hofmeister, Zum Nutzen eines jeden Lesers, die Erkenntniß zu vervollkommnen; In Verbindung mit einer Sammlung von Kupferstichen, und mit französischer und lateinischer Uebersetzung dieses Werkes.* Dessau, 1770. 4 vols.

———. *Kupfersammlung zu J. B. Basedows Elementarwerke für die Jugend und ihre Freunde.* Berlin and Dessau: n.p., 1774.

Basedow, Johann Bernhard, and Joachim Heinrich Campe, eds. *Pädagogische Unterhandlungen.* Dessau and Leipzig: Steinacker and Crusius, 1777–1778. 12 Stücke.

Bauer, W. A., Otto Erich Deutsch, and Joseph Heinz Eibl, eds. *Mozart: Briefe und Aufzeichnungen, Gesamtausgabe.* Rev. ed. Kassel: Bärenreiter, 2005 [1962–1975]. 7 vols.

Baur, Samuel. *Charakteristik der Erziehungsschriftsteller Deutschlands: Ein Handbuch für Erzieher.* Leipzig: Johann Benjamin Georg Fleischer, 1790.

Blanchard, Peter [Pierre], [and Friedrich Karl Kraft]. *Le Plutarque de la jeunesse, ou Abrégé des vies des plus grands hommes de toutes les nations, depuis les temps les plus reculés jusqu'a nos jours.* Paris: Le Prieur, 1803.

———. *Neuer Plutarch, oder kurze Lebensbeschreibungen der berühmtesten Männer aller Nationen von den ältesten bis auf unsere Zeiten. Aus dem Französischen frey übersetzt, und mit neuen Biographien vermehrt.* Vienna: Anton Doll, 1806. 2 vols.

Böldicke, Joachim. *Methodus Lockio-Baratieriana, Das ist, Ein Vorschlag Durch Hülffe des Spielens, der Music, Poësie, und anderer Ergötzlichkeiten, Wodurch man die wichtigsten Wahrheiten vortragen kan, Zum Ruhm des Schöpfers, Binnen 12. Jahren Zehn vornehme Kinder dergestalt zu erziehen . . .* Berlin: Christian Albrecht Gäbert, 1735, repr. 1750.

Burney, Charles. *Account of an Infant Musician, Read at the Royal Society, Feb. 18, 1779.* London: Nichols, 1779.

————. *The Present State of Music in France and Italy, or, The Journal of a Tour through Those Countries, Undertaken to collect Materials for A General History of Music.* London: T. Becket and Co., 1771.

————. *The Present State of Music in Germany, The Netherlands, and the United Provinces . . .* London: Becket, Robson, and Robinson, 1773. 2 vols.

Busby, Thomas. "Life of Mozart, The Celebrated German Musician." *Monthly Magazine* 6, no. 39 / *Walpoliana* 9 (December 1798): 445–50.

Campe, Joachim Heinrich. *Allgemeine Revision des gesammten Schul- und Erziehungswesens von einer Gesellschaft praktischer Erzieher.* Hamburg, Vienna, Wolfenbüttel, and Braunschweig, 1785–1792. 16 vols.

————. *Kleine Kinderbibliothek.* Hamburg: Heroldschen Buchhandlung, 1779–1784. 12 vols.

Chimani, Leopold. *Vaterländischer Jugendfreund. Ein belehrendes und unterhaltendes Lesebuch ur Veredlung des Herzens, Beförderung der Vaterlandsliebe und gemeinnütziger Kenntnisse für die Jugend des österreichischen Kaiserstaates.* Vienna: Anton Doll, 1814. 6 Theile.

Deutsch, Otto Erich. *Mozart: A Documentary Biography.* Trans. Eric Blom, Peter Branscombe, and Jeremy Noble. Stanford, CA: Stanford University Press, 1965.

————. *Mozart: Die Dokumente seines Lebens.* Kassel: Bärenreiter, 1961.

Diderot, Denis. *Lettre sur les aveugles à l'usage de ceux qui voient.* London: n.p., 1749.

————. *Lettre sur les sourds et muets à l'usage de ceux qui entendent et qui parlent.* [Paris]: n.p., 1751.

————. *Selected Writings on Art and Literature.* Trans. and ed. Geoffrey Bremner. London: Penguin Books, 1994.

Diderot, Denis, and Jean le Rond d'Alembert, eds. *Encyclopédie, ou Dictionnaire raisonné des sciences, des arts et des métiers, etc.* Paris: Briasson, David, Le Breton, and Durand, 1751–1772. 28 vols. ARTFL Encyclopédie Project, http://encyclopedie.uchicago.edu/.

Dixon, Graham, et al., "English Translations of the Lieder Texts." In *W. A. Mozart, Sämtliche Lieder für hohe Stimme.* Ed. Ernst August Ballin. Kassel: Bärenreiter, 1991, 69–76.

Dodsley, Robert. *The General Contents of the British Museum: With Remarks. Serving as a Directory in Viewing that Noble Cabinet.* London: R. and J. Dodsley, 1761.

Edge, Dexter, and David Black, eds. *Mozart: New Documents.* First published June 12, 2014. https://sites.google.com/site/mozartdocuments/.

Eisen, Cliff. *New Mozart Documents: A Supplement to O. E. Deutsch's Documentary Biography.* London: Macmillan, 1991.

Ellrodt, Theodor Christian. "Das musikalische Kind Mozart." In *Taschenbuch zur nützlichen Unterhaltung für die Jugend und ihre Freunde.* Ed. Ellrodt. Leipzig: n.p., 1813.

Engel, Johann Jakob. *Ideen zu einer Mimik, Erster Theil.* Berlin: August Mylins, 1785.

Felbiger, Johann Ignaz von. *Die Christlich-katholische Lehre in Liedern; das ist: Catechetische Gesänge zum Gebrauche der Saganischen Schulen: mit einer Vorrede von der Absicht und dem Gebrauche dieser Lieder.* Sagan: Verlag der katholischen Trivialschule, 1766.

————. *Eigenschaften, Wissenschaften, und Bezeigen rechtschaffener Schulleute, um nach dem in Schlesien für die Römischkatholischen bekannt gemachten Königl. General-Landschulreglement in den Trivialschulen der Städte, und auf dem Lande der Jugend nützlichen Unterricht zu geben.* Bamberg and Würzburg: Göbhardt, 1772.

————. *Kleine Schulschriften, nebst einer ausführlichen Nachricht von den Umständen und dem Erfolge der Verbesserung der katholischen Land- und Stadt-Trivialschulen in Schlesien und Glatz.* Bamberg and Würzburg: Göbhardt, 1772.

Formey, Johann Heinrich Samuel. *La Vie de Mr. Jean Philippe Baratier, Maître [d]ès Arts, & Membre de la Société Royale des Sciences de Berlin.* Utrecht: Etienne Neaulme, 1741.

Frisch, Johann Leonhard. *Teutsch-Lateinisches Wörter-Buch.* Berlin: Christoph Gottlieb Nicolai, 1741. 2 vols.

Garnier, Franz Xaver. *Meine Pilgerfahrt aus Mutters Schoos in das Welgetümmel.* Breslau: n.p., 1802.

————. *Nachricht von der Bernerischen jungen Schauspieler-Gesellschaft, von der Aufnahme und dem Zuwachse derselben, mit einigen Anhängen, und 24. am Ende beygefügten Silhouettes mit Verwilligung und Beytrag des Herrn Berners zusammengetragen von M. I. R. Einem Zögling derselben, im Jahre 1782.* Erlangen: n.p., 1782.

————. *Nachricht von der im Jahre 1758 von Herrn Felix Berner errichteten jungen Schauspieler-Gesellschaft, von den bis jezt gethanenen Reisen, von der Aufnahme und dem Zuwachse derselben, einigen Anhängen, und vielen am Ende beigefügten* Silhouettes *von Schauspielern und Schauspielerinnen dieser Gesellschaft. Mit Bewilligug und Beitrag des Herrn Berner.* Vienna: Johann Joseph Jahn, 1786.

Gathy, August. *Musikalisches Conversations-Lexikon, Encyklopädie der gesammten Musik-Wissenschaft . . .* Hamburg: G. W. Niemeyer, 1840.

Grimm, Friedrich Melchior von. *Correspondance littéraire, philosophique et critique, depuis 1753 jusqu'en 1790.* Ed. Maurice Tourneux. Paris: Garnier Frères, 1877–1882. 16 vols.

Hagedorn, Friedrich. *Oden und Lieder in fünf Büchern.* Hamburg: Johann Carl Bohn, 1747.

Hamberger, Georg Christoph, and Johann Georg Meusel. *Das Gelehrte Teutschland oder Lexikon der jetzt lebenden teutschen Schriftsteller,* 5th ed. Lemgo: Meyerschen Buchhandlung, 1798. 7 vols.

Herder, Johann Gottfried von. "Auszug aus einem Briefwechsel über Ossian und die Lieder der alten Völker." In *Von Deutscher Art und Kunst: Einige fliegende Blätter.* Hamburg: Bode, 1773, 3–70.

————. "On Recent German Literature: First Collection of Fragments [1767]." In *Selected Early Works, 1764–1767: Addresses, Essays, and Drafts; Fragments on Recent German Literature.* Ed. Ernest A. Menze and Karl Menges. Trans. Menze with Michael Palma. University Park: Pennsylvania State University Press, 1992, 85–165.

————. "Ueber Thomas Abbts Schriften. Zweites Stück. Aus der Handschrift. (1768)." In *Herders Sämmtliche Werke.* Ed. Bernhard Suphan, vol. 2: 295–363. Berlin: Weidmannsche Buchhandlung, 1877.

————. "Viertes Wäldchen" [1769, unpublished]. In *Sämmtliche Werke.* Ed. Bernhard Suphan. Berlin: Weidmann, 1878, vol. 4: 3–198.

Hormayr, Joseph Freiherr von. *Oesterreichischer Plutarch, oder Leben und Bildnisse aller Regenten und der berühmtesten Feldherren, Staatsmänner, Gelehrten und Künstler des österreichischen Kaiserstaates.* Vienna: Doll, 1807–1814. 20 vols.

Hörnigk, Wilhelm von. *Oesterreich über Alles wann es nur will, Das ist: wohlmeinender Fürschlag Wie mittelst einer wolbestellten Lands-Oeconomie, die Kayserliche Erb-Land in kurzem über alle andere Staat von Europa zu erheben* . . . [Nuremberg]: n.p., 1684.

Imhof, Andreas Lazarus von. *Des Neu-Eröffneten Historischen Bilder-Saals, Zehender Theil. Das ist Kurtze, deutliche und unpartheyische Beschreibung der Historiae Universalis* . . . *von dem Jahr 1734. bis auf das Jahr 1743.* Nurnberg: Buggel and Seitz, 1744.

Joseph II. *Codex Juris Ecclesiastici Josephini, oder vollständige Sammlung aller während der Regierung Joseph des Zweyten ergangenen Verordnungen im geistlichen Fache.* Frankfurt and Leipzig, 1788–1789. 2 vols.

———. *Joseph des Zweyten Römischen Kaisers Gesetze und Verfassung im Justiz-Fache* . . . *In dem siebenten Jahre seiner Regierung. Jahrgang von 1786 bis 1787.* Vienna: K. K. Hof- und Staats-Aerarial-Druckerey, 1817.

Justi, Johann Heinrich Gottlob. *Grundfeste der Macht und der Glückseligkeit der Staaten, oder ausführliche Vorstellung der gesamten Policey-Wissenschaft.* Königsberg and Leipzig: Gebhard Ludewig Wolkersdorfs Wittwe, 1760–1761. 2 vols.

Kant, Immanuel. *Anthropology from a Pragmatic Point of View* [1798]. Trans. Robert B. Louden. Cambridge: Cambridge University Press, 2006.

———. "Beantwortung der Frage: Was ist Aufklärung?" *Berlinische Monattschrift* 12 (December 1784): 481–94.

Klingemann, August. *Kunst und Natur: Blätter aus meinem Reisetagebuche.* Braunschweig: G. C. E. Meyer, 1819–1828. 3 vols.

Kuebach, P. Stansislaus. *Trauerrede auf den tödtlichen Hintritt Josephs des II.* . . . *die hohe Trauercerimonie feyerte den 18. März 1790.* Augsburg, Matthäus Riegers sel. Söhnen, 1790.

Ladvocat, Jean-Baptiste. *Historisches Hand-Wörterbuch, worinnen von den Patriarchen, Kaysern, Königen, Fürsten* . . . *und andere Helden des Alterthums.* Ulm: Gaum, 1763. 4 vols.

Lessing, Gotthold Ephraim. *Gotthold Ephraim Lessing: Werke und Briefe in zwölf Bänden.* Ed. Jürgen Stenzel. Frankfurt: Deutscher Klassiker, 1989. 12 vols.

———. "Über die Regeln der Wissenschaften zum Vergnügen; besonders der Poesie und Tonkunst." In *Der Critische Musicus an der Spree*, ed. Friedrich Wilhelm Marpurg, vol. 18 (July 1, 1749): 141–46.

Lindner, Johann Gotthelf. *Beitrag zu Schulhandlungen.* Königsberg: Gebh. Ludwig Woltersdroffs Wittwe, 1762.

Locke, John. *Some Thoughts concerning Education* [1693]. London: A. and J. Churchill, 1693.

———. *Some Thoughts concerning Education* [1989]. Ed. and intr. John W. and Jean S. Yolton. Oxford: Clarendon Press, 1989.

[Mainwaring, John]. *Memoirs of the Life of the Late George Frederic Handel.* London: R. and J. Dodsley, 1760.

Maria Theresa. *Allgemeine Schulordnung, für die deutschen Normal- Haupt- und Trivialschulen in sämmtlichen Kaiserl. Königl. Erbländern d. d. Wien den 6ten December 1774.* Vienna: Trattner, 1774.

———. *Constitutio Criminalis Theresiana oder der Römisch-Kaiserl. zu Hungarn und Böheim &c. &c. Königl. Apost. Majestät Maria Theresia Erzherzogin zu Oesterreich, &c. &c. peinliche Gerichtsordnung.* Vienna: Edlen von Trattner, 1769.

————. *Maria Theresia und Joseph II. Ihre Correspondenz.* Ed. Alfred Ritter von Arneth. Vienna: Carl Gerold's Sohn, 1867–1868. 3 vols.

————. *Supplementum Codicis Austriaci, oder Chronologische Sammlung, aller vom 1ten Jäner 1759 bis letzten Dezember 1770 . . . Generalien, Patenten, Satz-Ordnungen, Rescripten, Resolutionen, dann Landesobrigkeitlichen Edikten, Mandaten und Dekreten . . .* Vienna: Trattner, 1777. 6 vols.

Marpurg, Friedrich Wilhelm. *Handbuch bey dem Generalbasse und der Composition mit zwey- drey- vier- fünf- sechs- seiben- acht und mehrern Stimmen.* Berlin: Johann Jacob Schützens Wittwe, 1755.

Massie, Joseph. *Farther Observations Concerning the Foundling-Hospital. Pointing Out the Ill Effects . . .* London: T. Payne, 1759.

[Mattheson, Johann]. *Abhandlung von den Pantomimen, historisch und critisch ausgeführt.* Hamburg: Geißler, 1749.

[May, Joseph]. *Erste Kenntnisse für Taubstumme. Zum Gebrauche by dem Unterrichte der Zöglinge des k. k. Taubstummen-Institutes zu Wien.* Vienna: Taubstummen-Instituts-Buchdruckerey, 1798.

Milchmeyer, P. J. *Kleine Pianoforte-Schule für Kinder, Anfänger und Liebhaber.* Dresden: Carl Christian Meinhold, 1801. 7[?] vols.

Mozart, Leopold. "Nachricht von dem gegenwärtigen Zustande der Musik Sr. Hochfürstl. Gnaden des Erzbischofs zu Salzburg im Jahre 1757." In *Historisch-Kritische Beyträge zur Aufnahme der Musik.* Ed. F. W. Marpurg, vol. 3, no. 3: 183–98. Berlin: Gottlieb August Lange, 1757.

————. *A Treatise on the Fundamental Principles of Violin Playing.* Trans. Editha Knocker. London: Oxford University Press, 1951.

————. *Versuch einer gründlichen Violinschule.* Augsburg: Johann Jacob Lotter, 1756.

Mozart, Wolfgang Amadeus. *Thematisches Verzeichniss sämmtlicher Kompositionen von W.A. Mozart, so wie er solches vom 9ten Februar 1784 an, bis zum 15ten November 1791 eigenhändig niedergeschrieben hat. Nach dem Original-Manuscripte.* Offenbach: André, 1805.

Müller, Johann Heinrich Friedrich. *Abschied von der k. k. Hof-Nationalbühne. Mit einer kurzen Biographie seines Lebens und einer gedrängten Geschichte des hiesigen Hoftheaters.* Vienna: Joh. Bapt. Wallishausser, 1802.

————. *Genaue Nachrichten von beyden kaiserl. königl. Schaubühnen und andern öffentlichen Ergötzlichkeiten in Wien.* Vienna: Kurzböck, 1772–1773. 2 vols.

————. *Theatererinnerungen eines alten Burgschauspielers* [1802]. Ed. Richard Daunicht. Berlin: Henschelverlag, 1958.

Musäus, J[ohann] C. [Karl]. *Moralische Kinderklapper für Kinder und Nichtkinder, Nach dem Französischen des Herrn Monget.* Gotha: Carl Wilhelm Ettinger, 1788. Rev. ed. 1794.

Nicolai, Friedrich. *Beschreibung einer Reise durch Deutschland und die Schweiz, im Jahre 1781.* Berlin and Stettin: n.p., 1783–1789. 12 vols.

Niemetschek, Franz Xaver. *Leben des K. K. Kapellmeisters Wolfgang Gottlieb Mozart.* Prague: Herrlischen Buchhandlung, 1798.

Nissen, Georg Nikolaus von. *Anhang zu Wolfgang Amadeus Mozart's Biographie . . .* Ed. Constanze Nissen. Leipzig: Breitkopf & Härtel, 1828.

————. *Biographie W. A. Mozart's . . .* Ed. Constanze Nissen. Leipzig: Breitkopf & Härtel, 1828.

Overbeck, Christian Adolf. *Frizchens Lieder.* Hamburg: Carl Ernst Bohn, 1781.

Pařízek, Aleš. *Ausführliche Beschreibung der am 15. November 1800 gehaltenen Jubelfeyer der k. k. Normalschule in Prag; nebst einer kurzen fünf und zwanzig jährigen Geschichte dieser Schule.* Prague: Kaspar Widtmann, 1801.

Pezzl, Johann. *Johann Pezzl's Chronik von Wien.* Rev. and updated by Franz Ziska. Vienna: Carl Armbruster, 1824.

———. *Skizze von Wien.* Vienna: Krauss, 1786–1790. 6 vols.

Plutarch. "De fraterno amore." In *Moralia.* Trans. W. C. Helmbold. Loeb Classical Library 6. Cambridge, MA: Harvard University Press, 1939.

Quantz, Johann Joachim. *On Playing the Flute.* Trans. Edward R. Reilly. London: Faber and Faber, 1966.

———. *Versuch einer Anweisung die Flöte traversiere zu spielen.* Berlin: Voß, 1752.

Richter, Joseph. *Warum wird Kaiser Joseph von seinem Volke nicht geliebt?* Vienna: Wucherers, 1787.

Ristelhueber, J. B. *Wegweiser zur Literatur der Waisenpflege, des Volks-Erziehungswesens, der Armenfürsorge, des Bettlerwesens und der Gefängnisskunde.* Cologne: Schmitz, 1831.

Rochow, Friedrich Eberhard von. *Der Kinderfreund: Ein Lesebuch zum Gebrauch in Landschulen.* Frankfurt: Eichenberg, 1776.

Rode, August. "Der Ausgang, oder Die Genesung." In *Kinderschauspiele.* [Leipzig: Crusius], 1777, 51–78.

Rousseau, Jean-Jacques. *The Confessions* [1782], *and Correspondence, Including the Letters to Malesherbes.* Trans. Christopher Kelly. Ed. Christopher Kelly, Roger D. Masters, and Peter G. Stillman. The Collected Writings of Rousseau 5. Hanover, NH: University Press of New England, 1995.

———. *Du contrat social; ou Principes du droit politique.* Amsterdam: Marc-Michel Rey, 1762.

———. *Emile or On Education.* Trans. and ed. Christopher Kelly and Allan Bloom. The Collected Writings of Rousseau 13. Hanover: University Press of New England, 2010.

———. *Émile, ou De l'éducation.* London, 1780. 2 vols.

———. *Émile, ou de l'éducation.* Amsterdam: Jean Néaulme, 1762. 2 vols.

Salzmann, Christian Gotthilf. *Ameisenbüchlein oder Anwendung zu einer vernünftigen Erziehung der Erzieher.* Schnepfenthal: Buchhandlung der Erziehungsanstalt, 1806.

———. *Ueber die heimlichen Sünden der Jugend.* Leipzig: Siegfried Lebrecht Crusius, 1785.

Schikaneder, Emanuel. *Die Zauberflöte: Eine Große Oper in Zwey Aufzügen* [libretto]. Vienna: Alberti, 1791.

Schiller, Friedrich. "On Naïve and Sentimental Poetry" [1795–1796]. In *Essays.* Ed. Walter Hinderer and Daniel O. Dahlstrom. The German Library 17. New York: Continuum, 1993.

Schlichtegroll, Friedrich. "Mozart." In *Nekrolog auf das Jahr 1791 . . . Zweyter Jahrgang, Zweyter Band.* Gotha: Justus Perthes, 1793.

Schmidt, C. F. *Lebensregeln für Jungfern nebst einem Pendant über das Heyrathen für alle Stände.* Vienna: Friedrich August Hartmann, 1783.

Schöneich, Christian von. *Merkwürdiges Ehren-Gedächtniß von dem Christlöblichen Leben und Tode des weyland klugen und gelehrten Lübeckischen Kindes, Christian Henrich Heineken.* Hamburg: Kißner, 1726.

Schubart, Christian Daniel Friedrich. *Gedichte aus der Gefangenschaft*. Ed. Karl-Maria Guth. Berlin: Hofenberg, 2013.

[Schummel, Johann Gottlieb]. *Fritzens Reise nach Dessau*. Leipzig: Siegfried Lebrecht Crusius, 1776.

Seibt, Karl Heinrich. *Von dem Einflusse der Erziehung auf die Glückseligkeit des Staats*. Prague: Mangold, 1771.

Siebigke, Christian. "Wolfgang Gottlieb Mozart. Nebst einer kurzen Darstellung seines Lebens und seiner Manier." In *Museum deutscher Gelehrten und Kuenstler in Kupfern und schriftlichen Abrissen*. Breslau: August Schall, 1800, 3–70.

Smith, Amand Wilhelm. *Philosophische Fragmente über die praktische Musik*. Vienna: Taubstummeninstitutsbuchdruck, 1787.

Smith, William, ed. *A Dictionary of Greek and Roman Antiquities*. 2nd ed. London: James Walton and John Murray, 1870.

Sonnenfels, Joseph von. *Grundsätzen der Polizei, Handlung und Finanzwissenschaft, Erster Theil, Dritte Auflage*. Vienna: Joseph Kurzböck, 1777 [1770].

Spiess, R. P. Meinrado. *Tractatus Musicus Compositorio-Practicus*. Augsburg: Johann Jacob Lotters seel. Erben, 1745.

Steinsky, Franz Anton. *Uiber die Pflicht der Anhänglichkeit junger Bürger der österreichischen Staaten an ihre Landesfürsten, aus dem Grunde der Schulverbesserungswohlthat* . . . Prague: Normalschulbuchdruckerey, 1799.

Sterne, Laurence. *The Life and Opinions of Tristram Shandy, Gentleman*. London: Becket and Dehont, 1759–1767. 9 vols.

Stork, Friedrich. *Anleitung zum Unterrichte der Taubstummen nach der Lehrart des Herrn Abbe de l'Epee in Paris, nebst einer Nachricht von dem kaiserl. königl. Taubstummeninstitute in Wien*. Vienna: Taubstummeninstitut, 1786.

Strutt, Joseph. *The Sports and Pastimes of the People of England* . . . London: J. White, 1801.

Sulzer, Johann George [*sic*]. *Allgemeine Theorie der schönen Künste in einzeln, nach alphabetischer Ordnung der Kunstwörter auf einander folgenden, Artikeln*. Leipzig: M. G. Weidemanns Erben und Reich, 1771–1774. 3 vols.

Tissot, Samuel-Auguste. *Avis aux gens de lettres et aux personnes sédentaires sur leur santé, traduit du Latin de M. Tissot, médecin*. Paris: J. Th. Herissant Fils, 1767.

———. *De la santé des gens de lettres*. Lausanne: François Grasset, 1766, rev. 1769.

Türk, Daniel Gottlob. *Klavierschule, oder Anweisung zum Klavierspielen für Lehrer und Lernende, mit kritischen Anmerkungen*. Leipzig and Halle: Schwickert, and Hemmerde and Schwetschke, 1789.

———. *Klavierschule, oder Anweisung zum Klavierspielen für Lehrer und Lernende, mit kritischen Anmerkungen. Neue vermehrte und verbesserte Ausgabe*. Leipzig and Halle: Schwickert, and Hemmerde and Schwetschke, 1802.

———. *School of Clavier Playing*. Trans. and ed. Raymond H. Haggh. Lincoln: University of Nebraska Press, 1982.

Uz, Johann Peter. *Sämtliche Poetische Werke*. Leipzig: Dyk, 1768.

Volkmann, Johann Jacob. *Historisch-kritische Nachrichten von Italien* . . . Leipzig: Caspar Fritsch, 1771. 3 vols.

Weschel, Leopold Matthias. *Die Leopoldstadt bey Wien*. Vienna: Anton Strauß, 1824.

Weisse, Christian Felix. *Kleine lyrische Gedichte*. Leipzig: Weidmanns Erben und Reich, 1772.

Whistling, C. F. *Handbuch der musikalischen Literatur, oder allgemeines systematisch geordnetes Verzeichniss gedruckter Musikalien.* Leipzig: C. F. Whistling, 1828.

———. *Handbuch der musikalischen Literatur* . . . Ed. Adolph Hofmeister. 3rd ed. Leipzig: Hofmeister, 1845.

Wimmer, Marian. *Sigismundus Hungariae rex: acta, amplissimis honoribus celsissimi ac reverendissimi domini domini Sigismundi Christophori . . . de Schrattenbach . . . consecrata a musis Benedictinis Salisburgi Kalendis, et III. Nonas Septembris M.DCC. LXI.* Salzburg: Johann Baptist Mayr, 1761.

Winckler, Théophile Frédéric. *Notice biographique sur Jean-Chrysostome-Wolfgang-Théophile Mozart.* Paris: J. J. Fuchs, 1801.

Young, Edward. *Conjectures on Original Composition. In a Letter to the Author of Sir Charles Grandison.* London: Millar and Dodsley, 1759.

Zedler, Johann Heinrich. *Grosses vollständiges Universal-Lexicon aller Wissenschaften und Künste.* Leipzig and Halle: Zedler, 1731–1754. 68 vols. http://www.zedler-lexikon.de.

Secondary and Post-1850 Sources

Abert, Hermann. *W. A. Mozart.* Trans. Stewart Spencer. Ed. Cliff Eisen. New Haven, CT: Yale University Press, 2007 [1919–1921].

Abrams, M. H. *The Mirror and the Lamp: Romantic Theory and the Critical Tradition.* Oxford: Oxford University Press, 1953.

Adelson, Robert, and Jacqueline Letzter. "*Mozart fille*: Lucile Grétry (1772–1790) and the Forgotten Tradition of Girl Musical Prodigies." In *Mozart aujourd'hui.* Ed. Brigitte van Wymeersch. Louvain-la-Neuve, Belgium: Presses Universitaires de Louvain, 2006.

Allanbrook, Wye J. "Human Nature in the Unnatural Garden: *Figaro* as Pastoral." *Current Musicology* 51 (1993): 82–93.

———. "Is the Sublime a Musical Topos?" *Eighteenth-Century Music* 7, no. 2 (2010): 263–79.

———. *Rhythmic Gesture in Mozart*: Le nozze di Figaro *and* Don Giovanni. Chicago: University of Chicago Press, 1983, repr. 2016.

———. *The Secular Commedia: Comic Mimesis in Late Eighteenth-Century Music.* Berkeley: University of California Press, 2014.

Alston, Robin. *Order and Connexion: Studies in Bibliography and Book History— Selected Papers from the Munby Seminar, Cambridge, July 1994.* Woodbridge, Suffolk: D. S. Brewer, 1997.

Angermüller, Rudolph. "Personae Musicae, Actores und Salii (Tänzer) des Schuldramas 'Sigismundus Hungariae Rex,' Salzburg, 1. September 1761." *Mitteilungen der Internationalen Stiftung Mozarteum* 50, no. 3–4 (2002): 1–11.

[Anonymous]. *Festschrift zum 175-Jährigen Bestande des Bundes-Taubstummeninstitutes in Wien.* Vienna: Bernhardt, 1964.

———. "Mozart and Dr. Tissot." *Notes* 8, no. 1 (1950): 40–64.

Archard, David. "John Locke's Children." In *The Philosopher's Child: Critical Perspectives in the Western Tradition.* Ed. Susan M. Turner and Gareth B. Matthews. Rochester, NY: University of Rochester Press, 1998, 85–103.

Ariès, Philippe. *Centuries of Childhood: A Social History of Family Life* [1960]. Trans.

Robert Baldick. New York: Knopf, 1962. Originally published as *L'enfant et la vie familiale sous l'ancien régime* [1960].

Austern, Linda. *Music in English Children's Drama of the Later Renaissance*. Philadelphia: Gordon and Breach, 1992.

Bachmann, Manfred. *Berchtesgadener Volkskunst: Geschichte, Tradition, Gegenwart*. Leipzig: Rosenheimer, 1985.

Baker, Nancy Kovaleff, and Thomas Christensen, eds. *Aesthetics and the Art of Musical Composition in the German Enlightenment: Selected Writings of Johann Georg Sulzer and Heinrich Christoph Koch*. Cambridge: Cambridge University Press, 1994.

Ballin, Ernst-August. *Das Wort-Ton-Verhältnis in den Klavierbegleiteten Liedern Mozarts*. Kassel: Bärenreiter, 1984.

———. "Zu Mozarts Liedschaffen: Die Lieder KV 149–51, KV 52 und Leopold Mozart." *Acta Mozartiana* 8, no. 1 (1961): 18–24.

Bander, Elaine. "Jane Austen and the Uses of Silence." In *Literature and Ethics: Essays Presented to A. E. Malloch*. Ed. Gary Wihl and David Williams. Kingston: McGill-Queen's University Press, 1988, 46–61.

Baragwanath, Nicholas. "Mozart's Early Chamber Music with Keyboard: Traditions of Performance, Composition and Commodification." In *Mozart's Chamber Music with Keyboard*. Ed. Martin Harlow. Cambridge: Cambridge University Press, 2012, 25–44.

Bastian, Hans Günther. "Wunderkinder." In *Die Musik in Geschichte und Gegenwart: Allgemeine Enzyklopädie der Musik*. Ed. Ludwig Finscher. Kassel: Bärenreiter, 1994–2007, 2nd ed. Sachteil 9 (Sy-Z) [1998], 2068–80.

Bauman, Thomas. "Becoming Original: Haydn and the Cult of Genius." *Musical Quarterly* 87, no. 2 (2004): 333–57.

———. *North German Opera in the Age of Goethe*. Cambridge: Cambridge University Press, 1985.

Beales, Derek. "Court, Government and Society in Vienna." In *Wolfgang Amadé Mozart: Essays on His Life and His Music*. Ed. Stanley Sadie. Oxford: Clarendon Press, 1996, 3–20.

———. *Enlightenment and Reform in Eighteenth-Century Europe*. London: I. B. Tauris, 2005.

———. *Joseph II, Volume 2: Against the World 1780–1790*. Cambridge: Cambridge University Press, 2009.

Beghin, Tom. *The Virtual Haydn: Paradox of a Twenty-First-Century Keyboardist*. Chicago: University of Chicago Press, 2015.

Bernstein, Jane. *Print Culture and Music in Sixteenth-Century Venice*. Oxford: Oxford University Press, 2001.

Betzwieser, Thomas. "Mozarts *Zaide* und *Das Serail* von Friebert. Genese und Datierung von Mozarts Singspiel im Licht neuer Quellen." *Mozart-Jahrbuch* (2006): 279–96.

———. "Zwischen Kinder- und Nationaltheater: Die Rezeption der Opéra-Comique in Deutschland (1760–1780)." In *Theater im Kulturwandel des 18. Jahrhunderts: Inszenierung und Wahrnehmung von Körper, Musik, Sprache*. Ed. Erika Fischer-Lichte and Jörg Schönert. Göttingen: Wallstein Verlag, 1999, 245–64.

Black, David. "Mozart and Musical Discipline at the *Waisenhaus*." *Mozart-Jahrbuch*

2006: Bericht über den Kongress "Der junge Mozart: 1756–1780." Ed. Henning Bey and Johanna Senigl. Kassel: Bärenreiter, 2008.

———. "Mozart and the Practice of Sacred Music, 1781–91." PhD thesis, Harvard, 2007.

Blackmer, Corinne E., and Patricia Juliana Smith, eds. *En Travesti: Women, Gender Subversion, Opera.* New York: Columbia University Press, 2005.

Blanning, T. C. W. *The Culture of Power and the Power of Culture: Old Regime Europe, 1660–1789.* Oxford: Oxford University Press, 2002.

———. *Joseph II.* Profiles in Power. London: Longman, 1994, repr. New York: Routledge, 2013.

———. *Joseph II and Enlightened Despotism.* London: Longman, 1970.

Blümml, Emil Karl, and Gustav Gugitz. *Alt-Wiener Thespiskarren: Die Frühzeit der Wiener Vorstadtbühnen.* Vienna: Anton Schroll & Co., 1925.

Boberski, Heiner. *Das Theater der Benediktiner an der alten Universität Salzburg (1617–1778).* Theatergeschichte Österreichs 6, Salzburg Heft 1. Vienna: Österreichischen Akademie der Wissenschaften, 1978.

Bodsch, Ingrid. "'Merckwürdige Nachricht von einem sehr frühzeitig gelehrten Kinde . . .': Von unvergleichlichen Begabungen und ihrer Rezeption in Literatur, Medien und Fachwelt." In *Beethoven und andere Wunderkinder.* Ed. Bodsch, with Otto Biba and Ingrid Fuchs. Bonn: Stadtmuseum, 2003, 103–35.

Boock, Barbara. *Kinderliederbücher 1770–2000: Eine annotierte, illustrierte Bibliographie.* Volksliedstudien 8. Münster: Waxmann, 2007.

Born, Georgina. "On Musical Mediation: Ontology, Technology and Creativity," *twentieth-century music* 2, no. 1 (2005): 7–36.

Bowers, Jane. "Mozart and the Flute." *Early Music* 20, no. 1 ("Performing Mozart's Music II," 1992): 31–42.

Breene, Samuel. "The Instrumental Body in the Age of Mozart: Science, Aesthetics and Performances of the Self." *Early Music* 42, no. 2 (2014): 231–47.

Brewer, Holly. *By Birth or Consent: Children, Law, and the Anglo-American Revolution in Authority.* Chapel Hill: University of North Carolina Press, 2005.

Brooks, Peter. *Reading for the Plot: Design and Intention in Narrative.* Cambridge, MA: Harvard University Press, 1992.

Brown, A. Peter. "Joseph Haydn and Leopold Hofmann's 'Street Songs.'" *Journal of the American Musicological Society* 33, no. 2 (1980): 356–83.

Brown, Maurice J. E. "Mozart's Songs for Voice and Piano." *Music Review* 17 (1956): 19–28.

Bruce, Emily. "Reading Agency: The Making of Modern German Childhoods in the Age of Revolutions." PhD thesis, University of Minnesota, 2015.

Bruckmüller, Ernst. *Sozialgeschichte Österreichs.* Vienna: Verlag für Geschichte und Politik, 2001.

Bruckner, Hans. "Die Pfeifenmacherei in Berchtesgaden," *Tibia: Magazin für Freunde alter und neuer Bläsermusik* 79, no. 2 (1979): 289–96.

Brüggemann, Theodor, and Hans-Heino Ewers, eds. *Handbuch zur Kinder- und Jugendliteratur: Von 1750 bis 1800.* Stuttgart: J. B. Metzlersche Verlagsbuchhandlung, 1982.

Buch, David. "Mozart's Bawdy Canons, Vulgarity and Debauchery at the Wiednertheater." *Eighteenth-Century Music* 13, no. 2 (2016): 283–308.

————. "Placidus Partsch, the *Liedersammlung für Kinder und Kinderfreunde* and Mozart's Last Three Songs." *Min-Ad: Israel Studies in Musicology Online* 11, no. 2 (2013): 61–79.

Burden, Michael. "'Divas and Arias': The Favourite Songs as Repositories for Promotion and Performance." Paper presented at the British Society for Eighteenth-Century Studies Annual Conference, Oxford, January 2013.

Butler, Judith. "Critically Queer." *GLQ* 1, no. 1 (1993): 17–32.

Caffiero, Marina. *Forced Baptisms: Histories of Jews, Christians, and Converts in Papal Rome.* Trans. Lydia G. Cochrane. Berkeley: University of California Press, [2005] 2012.

Cardi, Carola. *Das Kinderschauspiel der Aufklärungszeit: Eine Untersuchung der deutschsprachigen Kinderschauspiele von 1769–1800.* Europäische Hochschulschriften: Reihe 1: Deutsche Sprache und Literatur, 693. Frankfurt: Peter Lang, 1983.

Carew, Derek. "The Consumption of Music." In *The Cambridge History of Nineteenth-Century Music.* Ed. Jim Samson. Cambridge: Cambridge University Press, 2002, 237–58.

Carlson, David Moris. "The Vocal Music of Leopold Mozart (1719–1787): Authenticity, Chronology and Thematic Catalogue." PhD thesis, University of Michigan, 1976.

Carter, Tim. "Printing the 'New Music.'" In *Music and the Cultures of Print.* Ed. van Orden, 3–37.

Catanzaro, Christine D. de, and Werner Rainer. *Anton Cajetan Adlgasser (1729–1777): A Thematic Catalogue of His Works.* Thematic Catalogues No. 22. Hillsdale, NJ: Pendragon Press, 1995.

[Child Rights International Network]. "Minimum Ages of Criminal Responsibility Around the World," *Child Rights International Network,* https://archive.crin.org /en/home/ages.html, accessed September 21, 2019.

Chrissochoidis, Ilias. "London Mozartiana: Wolfgang's Disputed Age & Early Performances of Allegri's *Miserere*." *Musical Times* 151, no. 1911 (2010): 83–89.

Cipriani, Don. *Children's Rights and the Minimum Age of Criminal Responsibility: A Global Perspective.* London: Routledge, 2009.

Clark, Caryl. "Reading and Listening: Viennese *Frauenzimmer* Journals and the Sociocultural Context of Mozartean Opera Buffa." *Musical Quarterly* 87, no. 1 (2004): 140–75.

Clarke, Bruce Cooper. "The Annotated Schlichtegroll," *Apropos Mozart,* http://www .aproposmozart.com/Entire%20Schlichtegroll.pdf, accessed March 19, 2014. [note: website no longer published]

Coleman, Francis X. J. *Neither Angel nor Beast: The Life and Work of Blaise Pascal.* Routledge Library Editions: Philosophy of Religion. New York: Routledge & Kegan Paul, 1986.

Cook, Daniel. "On Genius and Authorship: Addison to Hazlitt." *Review of English Studies* 64, no. 266 (2012): 610–29.

Cook, Daniel Thomas. "Children as Consumers: History and Historiography." In *The Routledge History of Childhood in the Western World.* Ed. Paula S. Fass. London: Routledge, 2013, 283–95.

————. "Children's Consumption in History." In *The Oxford Handbook of the History of Consumption.* Ed. Frank Trentmann. Oxford: Oxford University Press, 2012, 585–600.

Cook, Daniel Thomas, ed. *Symbolic Childhood. Popular Culture and Everyday Life 5.* New York: Peter Lang, 2002.

Cooper, Barry. *Child Composers and Their Works: A Historical Survey.* Lanham, MD: Scarecrow Press, 2009.

Corneilson, Paul. "*Liedersammlung für Kinder und Kinderfreunde*: A Context for Mozart's Songs K. 596–98." *Mozart-Jahrbuch* (2011): 101–18.

Crofts, Thomas. *The Criminal Responsibility of Children and Young Persons: A Comparison of English and German Law.* Aldershot, Hampshire: Ashgate, 2002.

Croll, Gerhard, ed. *Musik mit Kinderinstrumenten aus dem Salzburger und Berchtesgadener Land.* Denkmäler der Musik in Salzburg 2. Münich and Salzburg: Musikverlag Emil Katzbichler, 1981.

Cuillé, Tili Boon. *Narrative Interludes: Musical Tableaux in Eighteenth-Century French Texts.* Toronto: University of Toronto Press, 2006.

Cunningham, Hugh. *Children and Childhood in Western Society since 1500.* Studies in Modern History. Harlow: Pearson Education Limited, 1995, rev. 2005.

———. *Children of the Poor: Representations of Childhood Since the Seventeenth Century.* Oxford: Blackwell, 1992.

———. "Histories of Childhood." *American Historical Review* 103, no. 4 (1998): 1195–1208.

———. "Introduction." In *Charity, Philanthropy and Reform from the 1690s to 1850.* Ed. Cunningham and Joanna Innes. Hampshire: Macmillan, 1998, 1–14.

———. *The Invention of Childhood.* London: BBC Books, 2006.

Cypess, Rebecca. "Duets in the Collection of Sara Levy and the Ideal of 'Unity in Multiplicity.'" In *Sara Levy's World: Gender, Judaism, and the Bach Tradition in Enlightenment Berlin.* Ed. Cypess and Nancy Sinkoff. Eastman Studies in Music. Rochester, NY: University of Rochester Press, 2018, 181–204.

———. "Keyboard-Duo Arrangements in Eighteenth-Century Musical Life." *Eighteenth-Century Music* 13, no. 2 (2017): 183–214.

Dahms, Sibylle. "Barockes Theatrum Mundi: Geistliches und weltliches Musiktheater im 17. Jahrhundert." In *Salzburger Musikgeschichte: Vom Mittelatler bis ins 21. Jahrhundert.* Ed. Jürg Stenzl, Ernst Hintermaier, and Gerhard Walterskirchen. Salzburg: Anton Pustet, 2005, 165–206.

Dahms, Sibylle, Michaela Cuvay Schneider, and Ernst Hintermaier. "Die Musikpflege an der Salzburger Universität im 17. Und 18. Jahrhundert." In *Universität Salzburg 1622–1962–1972: Festschrift.* Ed. Akademische Senat der Universität Salzburg. Salzburg: Anton Pustet, 1972, 193–219.

Daverio, John. "Mozart in the Nineteenth Century." In *The Cambridge Companion to Mozart.* Ed. Simon Keefe. Cambridge: Cambridge University Press, 2003, 171–84.

Davies, James. "Julia's Gift: The Social Life of Scores, c. 1830." *Journal of the Royal Musical Association* 131, no. 2 (2006): 287–309.

Davies, Steffan. *The Wallenstein Figure in German Literature and Historiography 1790–1920.* MHRA Texts and Dissertations 76, Bithell Series of Dissertations 36. London: Maney Publishing for the Modern Humanities Research Association, 2009.

Davis, Lennard J. *Enforcing Normalcy: Disability, Deafness, and the Body.* London: Verso, 1995.

Daw, S. F. "Age of Boys' Puberty in Leipzig, 1727–1749, as Indicated by Voice Breaking in J. S. Bach's Choir Members." *Human Biology* 42, no. 1 (1970): 87–89.

DeNora, Tia. *Beethoven and the Construction of Genius: Musical Politics in Vienna, 1792–1803.* Berkeley: University of California Press, 1995.

Derry, Siân. "Ludwig van Beethoven: An Understated Prodigy." In *Musical Prodigies: Interpretation from Psychology, Education, Musicology, and Ethnomusicology.* Ed. Gary McPherson. Oxford: Oxford University Press, 2016, 576–602.

Dettmar, Ute. *Das Drama der Familienkindheit: Der Anteil des Kinderschauspiels am Familiendrama des späten 18. und frühen 19. Jahrhunderts.* Munich: W. Fink, 2002.

Dieke, Gertraude. *Die Blutezeit des Kindertheaters: ein Beitrag zur Theatergeschichte des 18. und beginnenden 19. Jahrhunderts.* Emsdetten: Lechte, 1934.

Dopsch, Heinz, and Robert Hoffmann. *Geschichte der Stadt Salzburg.* Salzburg: Anton Pustet, 1996.

Douthwaite, Julia V. *The Wild Girl, Natural Man, and the Monster: Dangerous Experiments in the Age of Enlightenment.* Chicago: University of Chicago Press, 2002.

Drott, Eric. "Conlon Nancarrow and the Technological Sublime." *American Music* 22, no. 4 (2004): 533–63.

Dussinger, John A. *In the Pride of the Moment: Encounters in Jane Austen's World.* Columbus: The Ohio State University Press, 1990.

Edge, Dexter. "Mozart's Reception in Vienna, 1787–1791." In *Wolfgang Amadé Mozart: Essays on His Life and His Music.* Ed. Stanley Sadie. Oxford: Clarendon Press, 1996, 66–117.

Einstein, Alfred. "Die Text-Vorlage zu Mozarts 'Zaide.'" *Acta Musicologica* 8, vol. 1–2 (1936): 30–37.

Eisen, Cliff. "Mozart and the Four-Hand Sonata K. 19d." In *Haydn, Mozart, and Beethoven: Studies in the Music of the Classical Period—Essays in Honour of Alan Tyson.* Ed. Sieghard Brandenburg. Oxford: Clarendon Press, 1998, 91–99.

———. "The Old and New Mozart Editions." *Early Music* 19, no. 4, "Performing Mozart's Music I" (1991): 513–32.

Eisen, Cliff, and Simon P. Keefe, eds. *The Cambridge Mozart Encyclopedia.* Cambridge: Cambridge University Press, 2006.

Erickson, Wayne. "The Poet's Power and the Rhetoric of Humility in Spenser's Dedicatory Sonnets." *Studies in the Literary Imagination* 38, vol. 2 (2005): 91–118.

Erlin, Matt. "Book Fetish: Joachim Heinrich Campe and the Commodification of Literature." *Seminar: A Journal of Germanic Studies* 42, no. 4 (2006): 355–76.

Ewers, Hains-Heino, ed. *Kinder- und Jugendliteratur der Aufklärung: Eine Textsammlung.* Stuttgart: Reclam, 1980.

Ewers, Hains-Heino, and Annegret Völpel. "Kinder- und Jugendzeitschriften." In *Von Almanach bis Zeitung: Ein Handbuch der Medien in Deutschland 1700–1800.* Ed. Ernst Fischer, Wilhelm Haefs, and York-Gothart Mix. Munich: Beck, 1999, 137–156.

Fass, Paula S. "Is There a Story in the History of Childhood?" In *The Routledge History of Childhood in the Western World.* Ed. Paula S. Fass. London: Routledge, 2013, 1–14.

Fass, Paula S., ed. *Encyclopedia of Children and Childhood in History and Society.* New York: Macmillan, 2004. 3 vols.

Feigl, Susanne, and Christian Lunzer. *Das Mädchen-ballett des Fürsten Kaunitz. Kriminalfälle des Biedermeier.* Vienna: Österreichischen Staatsdruckerei, 1988.

Feldman, Martha. *Opera and Sovereignty: Transforming Myths in Eighteenth-Century Italy.* Chicago: University of Chicago Press, 2007.

Fischer, Friedrich Johann. "Das Salzburger Theater vom Barock zum Rokoko." *Mitteilungen der Gesellschaft für Salzburger Landeskunde* 95 (1955): 141–78.

Fischer, Renate. "Abbé de l'Epée and the Living Dictionary." In *Deaf History Unveiled: Interpretations from the New Scholarship.* Ed. John Vickrey Van Cleve. Washington, DC: Gallaudet University Press, 1993.

Flaherty, Gloria. "Mozart and the Mythologization of Genius." *Studies in Eighteenth-Century Culture* 18 (1988): 289–310.

Ford, Thomas. "Between *Aufklärung* and *Sturm und Drang*: Leopold and Wolfgang Mozart's View of the World." PhD thesis, University of Adelaide, 2010.

Forsaith, Peter S. "Pictorial Precocity: John Russell's Portraits of Charles and Samuel Wesley." *British Art Journal* 10, no. 3 (2009–2010): 98–103.

Freitag, Thomas. *Kinderlied: Von der Vielfalt einer musikalischen Liedgattung.* Frankfurt: Peter Lang, 2001.

Friedlaender, Max. *Das deutsche Lied im 18. Jahrhundert; Quellen und Studien.* Stuttgart: J. G. Gotta, 1902. 3 vols.

———. "Mozart's Wiegenlied" (1892). *Vierteljahrsschrift für Musikwissenschaft* 8 (1892): 275–85.

———. "Mozarts Wiegenlied" (1897). *Jahrbuch der Musik-Bibliothek Peters* 3 (1897): 69–71.

Fuhrich, Fritz. *Theatergeschichte Oberösterreichs im 18. Jahrhundert.* Theatergeschichte Österreichs, Band 1: Oberösterreich, Heft 2. Vienna: hermann Böhlaus Nachf., 1968.

Garrioch, David. "Making a Better World: Enlightenment and Philanthropy." In *The Enlightenment World.* Ed. Martin Fitzpatrick, Peter Jones, Christa Knellwolf, and Iain McCalman. London: Routledge, 2004, rev. 2008, 486–501.

Gelbart, Matthew. *The Invention of Folk Music and Art Music: Emerging Categories from Ossian to Wagner.* New Perspectives in Music History and Criticism. Cambridge: Cambridge University Press, 2007.

Gerlach, Sonja. "Textkritische Untersuchungen zur Autorschaft der 'Kindersinfonie' Hoboken II:47." In *Opera Incerta: Echtheitsfragen als Problem musikwissenschaftlicher Gesamtausgaben: Kolloquium Mainz 1988.* Ed. Hanspeter Bennwitz et al. Mainz: Akademie der Wissenschaften und der Literatur, 1991, 153–88.

Gerstner, Daniela. "Das Kinderballett von Friedrich Horschelt: ein Beitrag zur Wiener Ballettgeschichte des 19. Jahrhunderts." PhD thesis, Salzburg University, 1997.

Gétreau, Patrice. "Une harpiste au Concert spirituel, Mademoiselle Schencker." *Musique—Images—Instruments* 1 (1995): 178–81.

Gill, Natasha. *Educational Philosophy in the French Enlightenment: From Nature to Second Nature.* Farnham, Surrey: Ashgate, 2010.

Gramit, David. *Cultivating Music: The Aspirations, Interests, and Limits of German Musical Culture, 1770–1840.* Berkeley: University of California Press, 2002.

Grantzow, Hans. *Geschichte des Göttinger und des Vossischen Musenalmanachs* [1909]. Berliner Beiträge zur Germanischen und Romanischen Philologie 35, Germanische Abteilung No. 22. Bern: Herbert Lang, 1970.

Graubner, Hans. "'Sind Schuldramata möglich?' Epilog im 18. Jahrhundert auf deine auslaufende Gattung (Lindner, Abbt, Hamann, Herder)." In *Aspekte des politischen Theaters und Dramas von Calderón bis Georg Seidel: Deutsch-*

französische Perspektiven. Ed. Horst Turk and Jean-Marie Valentin. Jahrbuch für Internationale Germanistik A:40. Bern: Peter Lang, 1996, 93–130.

Grečenková, Martina Ondo. "Enlightened Absolutism and the Birth of a Modern State (1740–1792)." In *A History of the Czech Lands.* Ed. Jaroslav Pánek, Oldrich Tuma, et al. Prague: Charles University, Karolinum Press, 2009, 261–80.

Green, Emily. *Dedicating Music, 1785–1850.* Rochester, NY: University of Rochester Press, 2019.

Grosrichard, Alain. *The Sultan's Court: European Fantasies of the East* [1979]. Trans. Liz Heron. London: Verso, 1998.

Gruber, Gernot. *Mozart and Posterity.* Trans. R. S. Furness. London: Quartet Books, 1991 (orig. pub. 1985).

Gubar, Marah. *Artful Dodgers: Reconceiving the Golden Age of Children's Literature.* Oxford: Oxford University Press, 2009.

———. "The Drama of Precocity: Child Performers on the Victorian Stage." In *The Nineteenth-Century Child and Consumer Culture.* Ed. Dennis Denishoff. Aldershot: Ashgate, 2008, 63–78.

Gustafson, Susan E. *Absent Mothers and Orphaned Fathers: Narcissism and Abjection in Lessing's Aesthetic and Dramatic Production.* Detroit: Wayne State University Press, 1995.

Hadamowsky, Franz. *Wien Theater Geschichte: Von den Anfängen bis zum Ende des ersten Weltkriegs.* Geschichte der Stadt Wien 3. Vienna: Jugend und Volk, 1988.

Hall, Murray. "Schulverlagsanstalt für Böhmen und Mähren in Prag." In *Böhmische Verlagsgeschichte 1919–1945* (2016). http://www.boehmischeverlagsgeschichte .at/boehmische-verlage-1919-1945/schulverlagsanstalt-fuer-boehmen-und -maehren/. Accessed August 23, 2016.

Halliwell, Ruth. *The Mozart Family: Four Lives in a Social Context.* Oxford: Clarendon Press, 1998.

Hanslick, Eduard. *Geschichte des Concertwesens in Wien.* Vienna: Wilhelm Braumüller, 1869–1870. 2 vols.

Hausfater, Dominique. "Etre Mozart: Wolfgang et ses émules." In Sacquin and Ladurie, eds., *Le printemps des génies,* 73–86.

Hawkins, Ann R., and Maura Ives, eds. *Women Writers and the Artifacts of Celebrity in the Long Nineteenth Century.* Farnham: Ashgate, 2012.

Head, Matthew. "'If the Pretty Little Hand Won't Stretch': Music for the Fair Sex in Eighteenth-Century Germany." *Journal of the American Musicological Society* 52, no. 2 (1999): 203–54.

———. *Orientalism, Masquerade, and Mozart's Turkish Music.* Royal Musical Association Monographs 9. London: Royal Musical Association, 2000.

———. *Sovereign Feminine: Music and Gender in Eighteenth-Century Germany.* Berkeley: University of California Press, 2013.

Heartz, Daniel. "Coming of Age in Bohemia: The Musical Apprenticeships of Benda and Gluck." *Journal of Musicology* 6, no. 4 (1988): 510–27.

Heckle, Gerold. "'Ein lehrreiches und nützliches Vergnügen'—Das Kauf- und Lesepublikum der Kinderzeitschriften des 18. Jahrhunderts." In *Wege zur Kommunikationsgeschichte.* Ed. Manfred Bobrowsky and Wolfgang R. Langenbucher. Schriftenreihe der deutschen Gesellschaft für Publizistik- und Kommunikationswissenschaft 13. Munich: Ölschläger, 1987, 317–41.

Hedges, Stephen. "Dice Music in the Eighteenth Century." *Music & Letters* 59, no. 2 (1978): 180–87.

Helfert, Joseph Alexander Freiherr von. *Die Gründung der österreichischen Volksschule durch Maria Theresia*. Prague: Tempsky, 1860. 2 vols.

Herrmann-Schneider, Hildegard. "Edmund Angerer OSB (1740–1794) aus Stift Fiecht/Tirol. Der Komponist der 'Kindersinfonie'?" *Mozart-Jahrbuch 1996*. Salzburg: Internationale Stiftung Mozarteum, 1996, 23–38.

Heywood, Colin. "*Centuries of Childhood*: An Anniversary—and an Epitaph?" *Journal of the History of Childhood and Youth* 3, no. 3 (2010): 341–65.

———. *Growing Up in France: From the Ancien Régime to the Third Republic*. Cambridge: Cambridge University Press, 2007.

———. "Innocence and Experience: Sexuality among Young People in Modern France, c. 1750–1950." *French History* 21, no. 1 (2007): 44–64.

Highfill, Philip H. Jr., Kalman A. Burnim, and Edward A. Langhans. *A Biographical Dictionary of Actors, Actresses, Musicians, Dancers, Managers & Other Stage Personnel in London, 1660–1800*, vol. 2: Belfort to Byzand. Carbondale: Southern Illinois University Press, 1973.

Hinton, Thomas R. *Poetry and Song in the German Baroque: A Study of the Continuo Lied*. Oxford: Clarendon Press, 1963.

Hirsch, Marjorie. *Romantic Lieder and the Search for Lost Paradise*. Cambridge: Cambridge University Press, 2007.

Hoffmann, Freia. *Instrument und Körper: Die musizierende Frau in der bürgerlichen Kultur*. Frankfurt: Insel, 1991.

Hofmann, Regina. *Der kindliche Ich-Erzähler in der modernen Kinderliteratur: eine erzähltheoretische Analyse mit Blick auf aktuelle Kinderromane*. Frankfurt: Lang, 2010.

Huber, Nikolaus. *Die Literatur der Salzburger Mundart: Eine Bibliographische Skizze*. Salzburg: Anton Pustet, 1878.

Hüttler, Michael. "Hof- and Domkapellmeister Johann Joseph Friebert (1724–1799) and His Singspiele." In *Music Preferred: Essays in Musicology, Cultural History and Analysis in Honour of Harry White*. Ed. Lorraine Byrne Bodley. Vienna: Hollitzer, 2018, 393–408.

Huff, Steven. "Lotte's Klavier: A Resounding Symbol in Goethe's *Die Leiden des jungen Werthers*." *Germanic Review* 49 (1984): 43–48.

Hull, Isabel. *Sexuality, State, and Civil Society in Germany, 1700–1815*. Ithaca, NY: Cornell University Press, 1996.

Hunter, Mary. *The Culture of Opera Buffa in Mozart's Vienna: A Poetics of Entertainment*. Princeton Studies in Opera. Princeton, NJ: Princeton University Press, 1999.

Hurrelmann, Bettina. *Jugendliteratur und Bürgerlichkeit: Soziale Erziehung in der Jugendliteratur der Aufklärung am Beispiel von Christian Felix Weißes "Kinderfreund" 1776–1782*. Information zur Sprach- und Literaturdidaktik, 5. Paderborn: Ferdinand Schöningh, 1974.

Illing, Robert. *Berchtoldsgaden Musick: A Study of the Early Texts of the Piece Popularly Known in England as Haydn's Toy Symphony and in Germany as Haydns Kindersinfonie, and of a Cassation attributed to Leopold Mozart which embodies the Kindersinfonie*. Melbourne: Illing, 1994, Second Supplement.

Irvine, Thomas. "Der belesene Kapellmeister: Leopold Mozart und seine Bibliotheken." *Acta Mozartiana* 55, no. 1–2 (2008): 6–15.

Irving, John. *Mozart's Piano Sonatas: Contexts, Sources, Style*. Cambridge: Cambridge University Press, 1997.

———. "Performing Topics in Mozart's Chamber Music with Piano." In *Oxford Handbook of Topic Theory*. Ed. Danuta Mirka. Oxford: Oxford University Press, 2014, 539–50.

Isherwood, Robert M. *Farce and Fantasy: Popular Entertainment in Eighteenth-Century Paris*. New York: Oxford University Press, 1986.

Jackson, Barbara Garvey. "Musical Women of the Seventeenth and Eighteenth Centuries." In *Women and Music: A History*. Ed. Karin Pendle. Bloomington: Indiana University Press, 1991, rev. 2001.

Jacobs, Josef. "Der Waisenhausstreit: Ein Beitrag zur Geschichte der Pädagogik des 18. und 19. Jahrhunderts." PhD thesis, Albert-Ludwigs-Universität. Quakenbrück: Trute, 1931.

Jenks, Chris. *Childhood*. Key Ideas. London: Routledge, 1996, rev. 2005.

Joubert, Estelle. "Songs to Shape a German Nation: Hiller's Comic Operas and the Public Sphere." *Eighteenth-Century Music* 3, no. 2 (2006): 213–30.

Kaiser, Rainer. "Palschaus Bach-Spiel in London: Zur Bach-Pflege in England um 1750." *Bach-Jahrbuch* 79 (1993): 225–29.

Karniel, Josef. *Die Toleranzpolitik Kaiser Josephs II*. Trans. Leo Koppel. Schriftenreihe des Instituts für Deutsche Geschichte Universität Tel-Aviv 9. Gerlingen: Bleicher, 1985.

Keefe, Simon. *Mozart's Piano Concertos: Dramatic Dialogue in the Age of Enlightenment*. Woodbridge: Boydell Press, 2001.

Keefe, Simon, ed. *Mozart in Context*. Cambridge: Cambridge University Press, 2019.

Kendon, Adam. *Gesture: Visible Action as Utterance*. Cambridge: Cambridge University Press, 2004.

Kincaid, James. *Child-Loving: The Erotic Child and Victorian Culture*. New York: Routledge, 1992.

King, Alec Hyatt. *A Mozart Legacy: Aspects of the British Library Collections*. Seattle: University of Washington Press, 1984.

King, Margaret L. "Concepts of Childhood: What We Know and Where We Might Go." *Renaissance Quarterly* 60, no. 2 (2007): 371–407.

———. "The School of Infancy: The Emergence of Mother as Teacher in Early Modern Times." In *The Renaissance in the Streets, Schools, and Studies: Essays in Honour of Paul F. Grendler*. Ed. Konrad Eisenbichler and Nicholas Terpstra. Toronto: Centre for Reformation and Renaissance Studies, 2008.

Kivy, Peter. "Child Mozart as an Aesthetic Symbol." *Journal of the History of Ideas* 28, no. 2 (1967): 249–58.

———. "Mainwaring's *Handel*: Its Relation to English Aesthetics." *Journal of the American Musicological Society* 17, no. 2 (1964): 170–78.

———. *The Possessor and the Possessed: Handel, Mozart, Beethoven, and the Idea of Musical Genius*. New Haven, CT: Yale University Press, 2001.

Klorman, Edward. *Mozart's Music of Friends: Social Interplay in the Chamber Works*. Cambridge: Cambridge University Press, 2016.

Knutson, Roslyn L. "Falconer to the Little Eyases: A New Date and Commercial

Agenda for the 'Little Eyases' passage in *Hamlet.*" *Shakespeare Quarterly* 46, no. 1 (1995): 1–31.

Köberle, Sophie. *Jugendliteratur zur Zeit der Aufklärung: ein Beitrag zur Geschichte der Jugendschriftenkritik.* Weinheim: Beltz, 1972.

Köchel, Ludwig Ritter von. *Chronologisch-thematisches Verzeichnis sämtlicher Tonwerke Wolfgang Amadé Mozarts.* 6th ed. Ed. Franz Giegling, Alexander Weinmann, and Gerd Sievers. Wiesbaden: Breitkopf & Härtel, 1964 [1862].

Komorzynski, Egon. "Ist Papageno ein 'Hanswurst'?" *Österreichische Musikzeitschrift* 12, no. 6 (1957): 225–29.

Konrad, Ulrich, and Martin Staehelin. *"allzeit ein buch": Die Bibliothek Wolfgang Amadeus Mozarts.* Weinheim: VCH, Acta Humaniora, 1991.

Kopytoff, Igor. "The Cultural Biography of Things." In *The Social Life of Things: Commodities in Cultural Perspective.* Ed. Arjun Appadurai. Cambridge: Cambridge University Press, 1986, 64–91.

Kramer, Richard. "Diderot's *Paradoxe* and C. P. E. Bach's *Empfindungen.*" In *C. P. E. Bach Studies.* Ed. Annette Richards. Cambridge: Cambridge University Press, 2006, 6–24.

Kramml, Peter F., Sabine Veits-Falk, and Thomas Weidenholzer. *Stadt Salzburg: Geschichte in Bildern und Dokumenten. Kostbarkeiten aus dem Stadtarchiv.* Schriftenreihe des Archivs der Stadt Salzburg 16. Salzburg: Stadtgemeinde Salzburg, 2002.

Krause, Siegmund. *Kinderarbeit und Gesetzlicher Kinderschutz in Österreich.* Wiener Staatswissenschaftliche Studien, 5, no. 3. Vienna and Leipzig: Franz Deuticke, 1904.

Kroll, Mark. *Johann Nepomuk Hummel: A Musician's Life and World.* Lanham, MD: Scarecrow Press, 2007.

Krupp, Anthony. *Reason's Children: Childhood in Early Modern Philosophy.* Bucknell Studies in Eighteenth-Century Literature and Culture. Lewisburg, PA: Bucknell University Press, 2009.

Kümmerling-Melbauer, Bettina. *Kinderliteratur, Kanonbildung und literarische Wertung.* Stuttgart: J. B. Metzler, 2003.

Kutscher, Artur. *Das Salzburger Barocktheater.* Vienna: Rikola, 1924. Rev. as *Von Salzburger Barocktheater zu den Salzburger Festspielen.* Düsseldorf: Pflugschar-Verlag, 1939.

Lamb, Edel. *Performing Childhood in the Early Modern Theatre: The Children's Playing Companies (1599–1613).* Basingstoke: Palgrave Macmillan, 2009.

Lang, Helmut, Ladislaus Lang, with Wilma Buchinger, eds. *Bibliographie der Österreichischen Zeitschriften, 1704–1850.* Österreichische Retrospektive Bibliographie (ORBI), Reihe 3, Band 3. Berlin: De Gruyter, 2005–2006. 3 vols.

Langmuir, Erika. *Imagining Childhood.* New Haven, CT: Yale University Press, 2006.

Layer, Adolf. "Zasianellulus: Leopold Mozarts erster Auftritt auf der Schulbühne." *Acta Mozartiana* 18, no. 3–4 (1971): 71.

Leach, Elizabeth Eva. *Sung Birds: Music, Nature, and Poetry in the Late Middle Ages.* Ithaca, NY: Cornell University Press, 2007.

Leavis, Ralph. "Communications." *Notes* 43, no. 1 (1986): 216.

Lederer, Thomas. "The Clemency of Rufinus Widl: Text and Context of W. A. Mozart's First Opera." *Humanistica Lovaniensia* 58 (2009): 217–373.

Le Guin, Elisabeth. "A Visit to the Salon de Parnasse." In *Haydn and the Performance of Rhetoric*. Ed. Tom Beghin and Sander M. Goldberg. Chicago: University of Chicago Press, 2007, 14–38.

Leppert, Richard. *Music and Image: Domesticity, Ideology and Socio-Cultural Formation in Eighteenth-Century England*. Cambridge: Cambridge University Press, 1988.

Lerer, Seth. *Children's Literature: A Reader's History from Aesop to Harry Potter*. Chicago: University of Chicago Press, 2008.

Lippman, Edward. *A History of Western Musical Aesthetics*. Lincoln: University of Nebraska Press, 1992.

Lockwood, Lewis. "Beethoven before 1800: The Mozart Legacy." *Beethoven Forum* 3 (1994): 39–52.

Loewenberg, Alfred. "*Bastien und Bastienne* Once More." *Music and Letters* 25, no. 3 (1994): 176–81.

Lorenz, Michael. "New and Old Documents Concerning Mozart's Pupils Barbara Ployer and Josepha Auernhammer." *Eighteenth-Century Music* 3, no. 2 (2006): 311–22.

Loughnan, Arlie. *Manifest Madness: Mental Incapacity in Criminal Law*. Oxford: Oxford University Press, 2012.

Luehrs, Phoebe M. "Der Nordische Aufseher. Ein Beitrag zur Geschichte der moralischen Wochenschriften." PhD thesis, Ruprecht-Karls Universität Heidelberg. Heidelberg: Rössler and Herbert, 1909.

Macartney, C. A., ed. *The Habsburg and Hohenzollern Dynasties in the Seventeenth and Eighteenth Centuries*. Documentary History of Western Civilization. New York: Walker and Co., 1970.

Mályusz, Elemér. *Iratok a türelmi rendelet történetéhez* [Writings on the History of the Tolerance Edicts]. Magyar Protestantizmus Történetének Forrásai [Sources on the History of Protestantism in Hungary]. Budapest: Magyar Protestáns Irodalmi Társaság, 1940.

Marten, James. "Childhood Studies and History: Catching a Culture in High Relief." In *The Children's Table: Childhood Studies and the Humanities*. Ed. Anna Mae Duane. Athens: University of Georgia Press, 2013, 52–67.

Maunder, Richard. "Mozart's Keyboard Instruments." *Early Music* 20, no. 2, "Performing Mozart's Music III" (1992): 207–19.

Mayer, Christine. "Friedrich Eberhard von Rochow's Education of the Children in Rural Communities and Its Impact on Urban Educational Reforms in the Eighteenth Century." *Paedagogica Historica* 39, no. 1–2 (2003): 19–35.

McLamore, Alyson. "Mozart in the Middle: London's 'Musical Children.'" *Newsletter of the Mozart Society of America* 23, no. 1 (2019): 5–9.

McVeigh, Simon. *Concert Life in London from Mozart to Haydn*. Cambridge: Cambridge University Press, 1993.

Melton, James van Horn. *Absolutism and the Eighteenth-Century Origins of Compulsory Schooling in Prussia and Austria*. Cambridge: Cambridge University Press, 1988.

Miglio, Paula. "Le Magasin des enfants de Madame Leprince de Beaumont (1756): Lectures, réception et mise en valeur patrimoniale d'un livre pour la jeunesse." MA thesis, University of Lyon, 2018.

Miller, Naomi J., and Naomi Yavneh. "Introduction: Thicker Than Water: Evaluating

Sibling Relations in the Early Modern Period." In *Sibling Relations and Gender in the Early Modern World: Sisters, Brothers and Others*. Ed. Miller and Yavneh. Women and Gender in the Early Modern World. Aldershot: Ashgate, 2006.

Miller, Timothy S. *The Orphans of Byzantium: Child Welfare in the Christian Empire*. Washington, DC: Catholic University of America Press, 2003.

Mitchell, J. Allan. *Becoming Human: The Matter of the Medieval Child*. Minnesota: University of Minnesota Press, 2014.

Morrison, Heather. "Authorship in Transition: Enthusiasts and Malcontents on Press Freedoms, an Expanding Literary Market, and Vienna's Reading Public." *Central European History* 46 (2013): 1–27.

———. "Pursuing Enlightenment in Vienna, 1781–1790." PhD thesis, Louisiana State University, 2005.

Moseley, Roger. *Keys to Play: Music as a Ludic Medium from Apollo to Nintendo*. Berkeley: University of California Press, 2016.

Mueller, Adeline. "Learning and Teaching." In Keefe, ed., *Mozart in Context*, 10–18.

———. "Who Were the Drei Knaben?" *Opera Quarterly* 28, no. 1–2 (2012): 88–103.

———. "Youth, Captivity and Virtue in the Eighteenth-Century *Kindertruppen*." *Eighteenth-Century Music* 10, no. 1 (2013): 65–91.

Müller, Anja, ed. *Fashioning Childhood in the Eighteenth Century: Age and Identity*. Ashgate Studies in Childhood, 1700 to the Present. Aldershot: Ashgate, 2006.

Münster, Robert. "Aus Mozarts Freundeskreis: Johann Nepomuk und Elise Peyerl." *Acta Mozartiana* 20, no. 1 (1973): 27–37.

———. *"Ich bin hier sehr beliebt": Mozart und das kurfürstliche Bayern*. Tutzing: Hans Schneider, 1993.

———. "Neues zu Leopold Mozarts Augsburger Gymnasialjahren." *Acta Mozartiana* 12, no. 3 (1965): 57–60.

Murray, Joseph J. "Transnational Interconnections in Nineteenth-Century Western Deaf Communities." In *The Oxford Handbook of Disability History*. Ed. Michael Rembis, Catherine Kudlick, and Kim E. Nielsen. Oxford: Oxford University Press, 2018, 427–38.

Murray, Sterling. *The Career of an Eighteenth-Century Kapellmeister: The Life and Music of Antonio Rosetti*. Rochester, NY: University of Rochester Press, 2014.

Nedbal, Martin. *Morality and Viennese Opera in the Age of Mozart and Beethoven*. Abingdon: Routledge, 2017.

Nelson, Claudia. *Precocious Children and Childish Adults: Age Inversion in Victorian Literature*. Baltimore: Johns Hopkins University Press, 2012.

Nettl, Paul. "Prager Lieder aus der Mozart-Zeit." *Mozart-Jahrbuch 1953*. Salzburg: Internationalen Stiftung Mozarteum, 1954.

Neubacher, Jürgen. "Zwischen Auftrag und künstlerischem Anspruch—Zu Telemanns musikpädagogische Position als Kantor und Director chori musici in Hamburg." In *Das Kantorat des Ostseeraums: Bewahrung, Ausweitung und Auflösung eines kirchenmusikalischen Amtes*. Ed. Joachim Kremer and Walter Werbeck. Greifswalder Beiträge zur Musikwissenschaft 15. Berlin: Frank & Timme, 2007, 63–74.

Neuhouser, Frederick. *Rousseau's Theodicy of Self-Love: Evil, Rationality, and the Drive for Recognition*. Oxford: Oxford University Press, 2008.

Neumann, Friedrich-Heinrich. "Zur Vorgeschichte der Zaide." *Mozart-Jahrbuch* (1962/1963): 216–47.

Nierhaus, Gerhard. *Algorithmic Composition: Paradigms of Automated Music Genera-tion.* Vienna: Springer, 2009.

Nussbaum, Felicity. *Rival Queens: Actresses, Performance, and the Eighteenth-Century British Theater.* Philadelphia: University of Pennsylvania Press, 2010.

Ong, Ken, et al. "Timing of Voice Breaking in Males Associated with Growth and Weight Gain Across the Life Course." *Journal of Clinical Endocrinology and Metab-olism* 97, no. 8 (August 2012): 2844–52.

Outram, Dorinda. *Four Fools in the Age of Reason: Laughter, Cruelty, and Power in Early Modern Germany.* Studies in Early Modern German History. Charlottes-ville: University of Virginia Press, 2019.

Page, Janet K. *Convent Music and Politics in Eighteenth-Century Vienna.* Cambridge: Cambridge University Press, 2014.

Parsons, James. "The Eighteenth-Century Lied." In *The Cambridge Companion to the Lied.* Ed. Parsons. Cambridge: Cambridge University Press, 2004, 35–62.

Pesic, Peter. "The Child and the Daemon: Mozart and Deep Play." *19th-Century Music* 25, no. 2–3 (2001–2002): 91–107.

Picton, Howard. *The Life and Works of Joseph Anton Steffan (1726–1797): With Spe-cial Reference to His Keyboard Concertos.* Volume 1. Outstanding Dissertations in Music from British Universities. New York: Garland, 1989.

Pierre, Constant. *Histoire du Concert Spirituel 1725–1790.* Paris: Société Française de Musicologie, 1975.

Pimmer, Hans. *Würfelkomposition: Zeitgenössische Recherche mit Betrachtungen über die Musik 1799.* Munich: Akademischer Verlag, 1997.

Pirckmayer, Friedrich. *Ueber Musik und Theater am f[ürst] e[rzbischöflichen] salzbur-gischen Hofe 1762–1775.* Salzburg: Selbstverlage des Verfassers, 1886.

Plagnol-Diéval, Marie-Emmanuelle. *Madame de Genlis et le théâtre d'éducation au XVIIIe siècle.* Studies on Voltaire and the Eighteenth Century 350. Oxford: Vol-taire Foundation, 1997.

Polenghi, Simonetta. "'Militia est vita hominis': Die 'militärische' Erziehung des Jesuitenpaters Ignaz Parhamer im Zeitalter Maria Theresias." *History of Education & Children's Literature* 4, no. 1 (2009): 41–68.

Pollock, Linda. *Forgotten Children: Parent-Child Relations from 1500 to 1900.* Cam-bridge: Cambridge University Press, 1983.

Portowitz, Adena. "Mozart and Aristocratic Women Performers in Salzburg: A Study of the Piano Concertos K. 242 and K. 246." *Min-Ad: Israel Studies in Musicology Online* 2 (2002). https://www.biu.ac.il/hu/mu/min-ad02/portowiz_mozart.html, accessed March 2019.

Prince, Cashmann Kerr. "Ovid Metamorphosed: The Polymorphous Polyphony of Widl/Mozart's *Apollo et Hyacinthus*." *International Journal of the Classical Tradi-tion* 19 (2012): 211–39.

Pyatt, Janet Best. "Music and Society in Eighteenth-Century Germany: The Music Dramas of Johann Heinrich Rolle (1716–1785)." PhD thesis, Duke University, 1991.

Rainer, Werner. "Die Salzburger Szenare der studentischen Pantomimen und Ballette zur Mozartzeit." *Homo Ludens* 10 ("Musik und Spiel"), Internationale Beiträge des Institutes für Spielforschung und Spielpädagogik der Universität Mozarteum, Salzburg. Ed. Günther G. Bauer. Munich: B. Katzbichler, 2000, 187–243.

Rasch, Rudolf. "The Dutch Republic in the Eighteenth-Century as a Place of Publication for Travelling Musicians." In *Le musicien et ses voyages: Pratiques, Résaux et Représentations*. Ed. Christian Meyer. Musical Life in Europe 1600–1900: Circulation, Institutions, Representation. Berlin: Berliner Wissenschafts-Verlag, 2003, 95–112.

———. *The Music Publishing House of Estienne Roger: Facco-Fux*. Utrecht/Houten: Rudolf Rasch, 2018. https://roger.sites.uu.nl/wp-content/uploads/sites/416/2018/07/Facco-Fux.pdf.

———. *Muziek in de Republiek (Oude Versie): Hoofdstuk Dertien: Concerten*. Utrecht/Houten: Rudolf Rasch, 2018. https://muziekinderepubliek.sites.uu.nl/wp-content/uploads/sites/413/2018/12/MR-Oud-13-Concerten.pdf.

Ratner, Leonard. "*Ars Combinatoria*: Chance and Choice in Eighteenth-Century Music." In *Studies in Eighteenth-Century Music: A Tribute to Karl Geiringer on His Seventieth Birthday*. Ed. H. C. Robbins Landon. London: Allen and Unwin, 1970, 343–63.

Rensch, Roslyn. *Harps and Harpists*. Bloomington: Indiana University Press, 1989, rev. 2017.

Retford, Kate. "Philippe Ariès's 'Discovery of Childhood': Imagery and Historical Evidence." *Continuity and Change* 31, no. 3 (2016): 391–418.

Rice, John. "Adding Birds to Mozart's 'Sparrow Mass': An Arrangement with Children's Instruments by Paul Wranitzky." *Mozart Society of America Newsletter* 8, no. 2 (2004): 8–9.

———. *Empress Marie Therese and Music at the Viennese Court 1792–1807*. Cambridge: Cambridge University Press, 2003.

Richter, Simon. "Wet-Nursing, Onanism, and the Breast in Eighteenth-Century Germany." *Journal of the History of Sexuality* 7, no. 1 (1996): 1–22.

Ridgewell, Rupert. "Artaria Plate Numbers and the Publication Process, 1778–87." In *Music and the Book Trade from the Sixteenth to the Twentieth Century*. Ed. Robin Myers, Michael Harris, and Giles Mandelbrote. Publishing Pathways. New Castle, DE and London: Oak Knoll Press and British Library, 2008, 145–78.

———. "Mozart's Publishing Plans with Artaria in 1787: New Archival Evidence." *Music & Letters* 83, no. 1 (2002): 30–74.

Ridley, Glynis. *Clara's Grand Tour: Travels with a Rhinoceros in Eighteenth-Century Europe*. New York: Atlantic Monthly Press, 2004.

Rieder, Georg. *Ignaz Parhamer's und Franz Anton Marxer's Leben und Wirken*. Vienna: Mayer and Co., 1872.

Riggs, Robert. "Authenticity and Subjectivity in Mozart Performance: Türk on Character and Interpretation." *College Music Symposium* 36 (1996): 33–58.

Robertson, Ritchie. *Enlightenment and Religion in German and Austrian Literature*. Selected Essays 1. Cambridge: Legenda (Modern Humanities Research Association), 2017.

Roche, Maurice. *Exploring the Sociology of Europe: An Analysis of the European Complex*. Los Angeles: Sage, 2010.

Rommel, Otto. *Die alt-wiener Volkskomödie: Ihre Geschichte vom Barocken Welt-Theater bis zum Tode Nestroys*. Vienna: Anton Schroll, 1952.

Root-Bernstein, Michèle. *Boulevard Theater and Revolution in Eighteenth-Century Paris*. Ann Arbor, MI: UMI Research Press, 1984.

Rose, Jacqueline. *The Case of Peter Pan, or, The Impossibility of Children's Fiction*. London: Macmillan, 1984, rev. 1992.

Rose, Stephen. *The Musician in Literature in the Age of Bach*. Cambridge: Cambridge University Press, 2011.

Rowen, Ruth Halle. "Some 18th-Century Classifications of Musical Style." *Musical Quarterly* 33, no. 1 (1947): 90–101.

Sacquin, Michèle, and Emmanuel Le Roy Ladurie, eds. *Le printemps des génies: Les enfants prodiges*. Paris: Bibliothèque Nationale, Robert Laffont, 1993.

Safley, Thomas Max. "Introduction." In *The Reformation of Charity: The Secular and the Religious in Early Modern Poor Relief*. Ed. Safley. Boston: Brill, 2003, 1–14.

Schäffer, Gottfried. *Das fürstbischöfliche und königliche Theater zu Passau (1783–1883): Beiträge zur Theaterkultur in der fürstbischöflichen Residenzstadt Passau und deren Nachwirkung im 19. Jahrhundert*. Neue Veröffentlichungen des Instituts für Ostbairische Heimatforschung 33. Passau: Verlag des Vereins für Ostbairische Heimatforschung, 1973.

Scheutz, Martin. "Demand and Charitable Supply: Poverty and Poor Relief in Austria in the 18th and 19th Centuries." In *Health Care and Poor Relief in 18th and 19th Century Southern Europe*. Ed. Ole Peter Grell, Andrew Cunningham, and Bernd Roeck. Aldershot: Ashgate, 2005, 52–95.

———. "Pater Kindergeneral und Janitscharenmusik: Österreichische Waisenhäuser der Frühen Neuzeit im Spannungsfeld von Arbeit, Erziehung und Religion." *Österreichische Zeitschrift für Geschichtswissenschaft* 25, no. 1 ("Die Kinder des Staates," 2014): 41–81.

Schilling-Sandvoß, Katharina. "Kinderlieder des 18. Jahrhunderts als Ausdruck der Vorstellungen vom Kindsein." In *Geschlechtsspezifische Aspekte des Musiklernens*. Ed. Hermann J. Kaiser. Musikpädagogische Forschung 17. Essen: Die Blaue Eule, 1996.

Schleifer, Martha Furman, and Sylvia Glickman, eds. *Women Composers: Music Through the Ages, Volume 3: Composers Born 1700–1799, Keyboard Music*. New York: G. K. Hall, 1998.

Schmid, Manfred Hermann. *Mozart und die Salzburger Tradition*. Tutzing: Hans Schneider, 1976.

Schmidt, Matthias. "Den Zufall denken. Annähreungen an Mozarts Musikalisches Spiel KV 516f." *Mozart Studien* 12 (Tutzing: Hans Schneider, 2003): 189–216.

Schmitt, Peter. *Schauspieler und Theaterbetrieb: Studien zur Sozialgeschichte des Schauspielerstandes im deutschsprachigen Raum 1700–1900*. Theatron Studien zur Geschichte und Theorie der dramatischen Künste 5. Tübingen: Max Niemeyer Verlag, 1990.

Schönwald, L. F. "Kindertheater in Salzburg." *Salzburger Volksblatt* 66/62 (March 14–15, 1936): 5.

Schott, Walter. *Das k. k. Taubstummen-Institut in Wien 1779–1918: Dargestellt nach historischen Überlieferungen und Dokumenten mit einem Abriß der wichtigsten pädagogischen Strömungen aus der Geschichte der Gehörlosenbildung bis zum Ende der Habsburgermonarchie*. Vienna: Böhlau, 1995.

Schusky, Renate. "Illustrationen in deutschen Liederbüchern für Frauen und Kinder." In *Die Buchillustration im 18. Jahrhundert: Colloquium der Arbeitsstelle 18. Jahrhundert Gesamthochschule Wuppertal, Universität Münster*. Ed. Arbeitsstelle Achtzehntes Jahrhundert, Gesamthochschule Wuppertal. Beiträge zur Geschichte der Literatur und Kunst des 18. Jahrhunderts 4. Heidelberg: Universität Münster, 1980, 317–34.

Seebauer, Renate. *Kein Jahrhundert des Kindes: Kinderarbeit im Spannungsfeld von*

Schul- und Sozialgesetzgebung. Pädagogik und Gesellschaft 8. Vienna: Lit Verlag, 2010.

Semonin, Paul. "Monsters in the Marketplace: The Exhibition of Human Oddities in Early Modern England." In *Freakery: Cultural Spectacles of the Extraordinary Body.* Ed. Rosemarie Garland Thomson. New York: New York University Press, 1996, 69–81.

Senigl, Johanna. "Ignaz Alberti, privil. Buchdrucker, Buchhändler und akad. Kupferstecher. Samt Bibliographie seines Lebenswerkes." *Mitteilungen der Internationalen Stiftung Mozarteum* 49 (2001): 102–25.

Senn, Walter. "Mozarts 'Zaide' und der Verfasser der vermutlichen Textvorlage." In *Festschrift Alfred Orel zum 70. Geburtstag.* Ed. Hellmut Federhofer. Vienna: Rudolf M. Rohrer, 1960, 173–86.

———. "Zwei Schülerinnen Mozarts: Babette Natorp und Karoline Henikstein." *Österreichische Musikzeitschrift* 29 (1974): 346–49.

Shapiro, Michael. *Children of the Revels: The Boy Companies of Shakespeare's Time and Their Plays.* New York: Columbia University Press, 1977.

Sieveke, Franz Günter. "Johann Baptist Adolph: Studien zum spätbarocken wiener Jesuitendrama." PhD thesis, Universität Köln, 1964.

Silver, Larry. *Marketing Maximilian: The Visual Ideology of a Holy Roman Emperor.* Princeton, NJ: Princeton University Press, 2008.

Siskin, Clifford, and William Warner. "This Is Enlightenment: An Invitation in the Form of an Argument." In *This Is Enlightenment.* Ed. Siskin and Warner. Chicago: University of Chicago Press, 2010, 1–33.

Sisman, Elaine. "Haydn's Career and the Rise of the Multiple Audience." In *The Cambridge Companion to Haydn.* Ed. Caryl Clark. Cambridge: Cambridge University Press, 2005, 3–16.

———. "'The Spirit of Mozart from Haydn's Hands': Beethoven's Musical Inheritance." In *The Cambridge Companion to Beethoven.* Ed. Glenn Stanley. Cambridge: Cambridge University Press, 2011, 45–63.

Smeed, J. W. "Children's Songs in Germany from the Eighteenth to the Twentieth Centuries." *Forum for Modern Language Studies* 24, no. 3 (1988): 234–47.

Solomon, Maynard. "Mozart: The Myth of the Eternal Child." *19th-Century Music* 15, no. 2 ("Toward Mozart," 1991): 94–106.

Spielman, John Philip. *The City & The Crown: Vienna and the Imperial Court, 1600–1740.* West Lafayette, IN: Purdue University Press, 1993.

Spyrou, Spyros. *Disclosing Childhoods: Research and Knowledge Production for a Critical Childhood Studies.* Studies in Childhood and Youth. London: Palgrave Macmillan, 2018.

Staehelin, Lucas E. *Die Reise der Familie Mozart durch die Schweiz.* Berne: Francke, 1967.

Stevens, Gerd-Heinz. "Das Wunderkind in der Musikgeschichte." PhD thesis, Westfälische Wilhelms-Universität, 1982.

Stewart, Susan. "From the Museum of Touch." In *Material Memories.* Ed. Marius Kwint, Christopher Breward, and Jeremy Aynsley. Oxford: Berg, 1999, 17–36.

Stoelzel, Marianne. "Mozarts letzte vierhändige Sonate C-Dur KV 521, vollendet in Wien, 29. Mai 1787." In *Mozart-Jahrbuch 1991: Bericht über den Internationalen Mozart-Kongreß Salzburg 1991.* Ed. Rudolph Angermüller et al. Kassel: Bärenreiter, 1992, vol. 2: 716–23.

Straub, Kristina. *Sexual Suspects: Eighteenth-Century Players and Sexual Ideology.* Princeton, NJ: Princeton University Press, 1992.

Taddei, Ilaria. "*Puerizia, Adolescenza* and *Giovinezza*: Images and Conceptions of Youth in Florentine Society During the Renaissance." In *The Premodern Teenager: Youth in Society 1150–1650.* Ed. Konrad Eisenbichler. Toronto: Centre for Reformation and Renaissance Studies, 2002, 15–26.

Tar, Gabriella-Nóra, *Deutschsprachiges Kindertheater in Ungarn im 18. Jahrhundert.* Thalia Germanica 13. Berlin: W. Hopf, 2012.

———. *Gyermek a 18. és 19. századi magyarország és erdély színpadjain* [Child Actors in Hungary and Siebenbürgen in the Eighteenth and Nineteenth Centuries]. Kolozsvár: Erdélyi Múzeum-Egyesület Kiadása, 2004.

Taruskin, Richard. *Text and Act: Essays on Music and Performance.* New York: Oxford University Press, 1995.

Tenschert, Roland. *Mozart: Ein Leben für die Oper.* Vienna: Wilhelm Frick, 1941.

Teuber, Oscar. *Die Theater Wiens.* Vienna: Gesellschaft für Vervielfältigende Kunst, 1903. 2 vols.

Thayer, Alexander, et al. *Thayer's Life of Beethoven* [1866–1879]. Rev. and ed. Elliot Forbes. Princeton, NJ: Princeton University Press, 1967. 2 vols.

Thormählen, Wiebke. "Playing with Art: Musical Arrangements as Educational Tools in van Swieten's Vienna." *Journal of Musicology* 27, no. 3 (2010): 342–76.

Tommasi, Chiara Ombretta. "*De musica.*" In *The Oxford Guide to the Historical Reception of Augustine.* Editor-in-chief, Karla Pollmann, ed. Willemien Otten. Oxford: Oxford University Press, 2013. 3 vols.

Töpelmann, Viktor. "The Mozart Family and Empfindsamkeit: Enlightenment and Sensibility in Salzburg 1750–1790." PhD thesis, King's College London, 2016.

———. "Salzburg." In Keefe, ed., *Mozart in Context*, 81–88.

Traudes, Jonas. *Musizierende "Wunderkinder": Adoration und Observation in der Öffentlichkeit um 1800.* Vienna: Böhlau, 2018.

Turrentine, Herbert C. "The Prince de Conti: A Royal Patron of Music." *Musical Quarterly* 54, no. 3 (1968): 309–31.

Tyler, Linda. "*Bastien und Bastienne*: The Libretto, Its Derivation, and Mozart's Text-Setting." *Journal of Musicology* 8, no. 4 (1990): 520–52.

———. "'Zaide' in the Development of Mozart's Operatic Language." *Music & Letters* 72, no. 2 (1991): 214–35.

Tyson, Alan. "A Reconstruction of Nannerl Mozart's Music Book (Notenbuch)." *Music & Letters* 60, no. 4 (1979): 389–400.

Ulbricht, Günter. "Spielpädagogik des Philanthropismus." In *Europa in der Frühen Neuzeit: Festschrift für Günter Mühlpfordt, Band 6: Mittel-, Nord- und Osteuropa.* Ed. Erich Donnert. Cologne: Böhlau Verlag, 2002, 607–15.

Ulbricht, Otto. "The Debate about Foundling Hospitals in Enlightenment Germany: Infanticide, Illegitimacy, and Infant Mortality Rates." *Central European History* 18, no. 3–4 (1985): 211–56.

Uphaus-Wehmeier, Annette. *Zum Nutzen und Vergnügen—Jugendzeitschriften des 18. Jahrhunderts. Ein Beitrag zur Kommunikationsgeschichte.* Dortmunder Beiträge zur Zeitungsforschung 38. Munich: K. G. Saur, 1984.

Valentin, Hans E. "'Was die Bücher anlaget . . .': Leopold Mozarts literarische Interessen." In *Leopold Mozart, 1719–1787: Bild einer Persönlichkeit.* Ed. Ludwig Wegele. Augsburg: Verlag die Brigg, 1969, 102–10.

Vallini, Christina. "*Genius/ingenium*: derive semantiche." In *Ingenium propria hominis natura: Atti del Convengno Internazionale di Studi (Napoli, 22–24 maggio 1997)*. Ed. Stefano Gensini and Arturo Martone. Naples: Liguori, 2002, 3–26.

van Orden, Kate, ed. *Music and the Cultures of Print. Critical and Cultural Musicology*. New York: Garland, 2000.

Volek, Tomislav, and Ivan Bittner. *The Mozartiana of Czech and Moravian Archives*. Prague: Archives Department of the Czech Ministry of Interior, 1991.

Waldoff, Jessica. *Recognition in Mozart's Operas*. Oxford: Oxford University Press, 2006.

Wallace, Katherine. "Lessons in Music, Lessons in Love." In *Conjunctions of Mind, Soul and Body from Plato to the Enlightenment*. Ed. Danijela Kambaskovic. Studies in the History of Philosophy of Mind 15. Dordrecht: Springer, 2014, 155–72.

Wangermann, Ernst. *Aufklärung und staatsbürgerliche Erziehung: Gottfried van Swieten als Reformator des österreichischen Unterrichtswesens 1781–1791*. Schriftenreihe des Instituts für Österreichkunde. Vienna: Verlag für Geschichte und Politik, 1978.

———. *The Austrian Achievement 1700–1800*. London: Thames and Hudson, 1973.

———. *From Joseph II to the Jacobin Trials: Government Policy and Public Opinion in the Habsburg Dominions in the Period of the French Revolution*. London: Oxford University Press, 1959, rev. 1969.

Wasyliw, Patricia Healy. *Martyrdom, Murder, and Magic: Child Saints and Their Cults in Medieval Europe*. Studies in Church History 2. New York: Peter Lang, 2008.

Webster, James. "The Rhetoric of Improvisation in Haydn's Keyboard Music." In *Haydn and the Performance of Rhetoric*. Ed. Tom Beghin and Sander Goldberg. Chicago: University of Chicago Press, 2007, 172–212.

Weidenholzer, Thomas. "Bürgerliche Geselligkeit und Formen der Öffentlichkeit in Salzburg 1780–1820." In *Bürger zwischen Tradition und Modernität*. Ed. Robert Hoffmann. Bürgertum in der Habsburgermonarchie 6. Vienna: Böhlau, 1997, 53–82.

Weikle-Mills, Courtney. *Imaginary Citizens: Child Readers and the Limits of American Independence, 1640–1868*. Baltimore: Johns Hopkins University Press, 2013.

Weiss, Anton. *Geschichte der Theresianischen Schulreform in Böhmen: Zusammengestellt aus den halbjährigen Berichten der Schulen-Oberdirektion 17. September 1777—14. März 1792*. Beiträge zur Österreich. Erziehungs- und Schulgeschichte. Vienna and Leipzig: Carl Fromme, 1905. 2 vols.

Weiß, Karl. *Geschichte der öffentlichen Anstalten, Fonde und Stiftungen für die Armenversorgung in Wien*. Vienna: [Braumüller], 1865.

Werner, Anja. "*Why Give Him a Sign Which Hearing People Do Not Understand . . . ?* Public Discourses about Deafness, 1780–1914." In *In Our Own Hands: Essays on Deaf History, 1780–1970*. Ed. Brian H. Greenwald and Joseph J. Murray. Washington, DC: Gallaudet University Press, 2016, 1–17.

Wheatcroft, Andrew. *The Habsburgs: Embodying Empire*. London: Viking, 1985.

Wheelock, Gretchen. "Marriage à la Mode: Haydn's Instrumental Works 'Englished' for Voice and Piano." *Journal of Musicology* 8, no. 3 (1990): 357–97.

Witmore, Michael. *Pretty Creatures: Children and Fiction in the English Renaissance*. Ithaca, NY: Cornell University Press, 2007.

Wolf, Gerson. *Judentaufen in Österreich*. Vienna: Herzfeld & Bauer, 1863.

Woodmansee, Martha. "The Genius and the Copyright: Economic and Legal Conditions of the Emergence of the 'Author.'" *Eighteenth-Century Studies* 17, no. 4 (1984): 425–48.

Yolton, John W. "Locke: Education for Virtue." In *Philosophers on Education: Historical Perspectives*. Ed. Amélie Oksenberg Rorty. London: Routledge, 1998, 173–90.

Yolton, John W., and Jean S. Yolton. "Introduction." In Locke, *Some Thoughts concerning Education*, 1–78.

Yonan, Michael. *Empress Maria Theresa and the Politics of Habsburg Imperial Art*. University Park: University of Pennsylvania Press, 2011.

Zaslaw, Neal. "Communications." *Notes* 43, no. 1 (1986): 216–17.

———. "Mozart's Modular Minuet Machine." In *Essays in Honor of László Somfai on His 70th Birthday: Studies in the Sources and Interpretation of Music*. Ed. László Vikárius and Vera Lampert. Lanham, MD: Scarecrow Press, 2005, 219–35.

———. *Mozart's Symphonies: Context, Performance Practice, Reception*. Oxford: Clarendon Press, 1989.

———. "Wolfgang Amadeus Mozart. *Konzert für Flöte und Harfe* [review of NMA V/14/6]." *Notes* 42, no. 2 (1985): 387–88.

Zelizer, Viviana. *Pricing the Priceless Child: The Changing Social Value of Children*. New York: Basic Books, 1985.

Zohn, Steven. "Morality and the 'Fair-Sexing' of Telemann's Faithful Music Master." In *Consuming Music: Individuals, Institutions, Communities, 1730–1830*. Ed. Emily H. Green and Catherine Mayes. Eastman Studies in Music. Rochester, NY: University of Rochester Press, 2017, 65–101.

Index

Landlord of the Green Dog Inn)
(anonymous pantomime), 82

Yavneh, Naomi, 158
Young, Edward, 23–24
youth. *See* childhood; children

Zaide (Mozart, K. 344), 8, 80, 92, 101–3,
180. See also *Serail, Das*
Zaslaw, Neal, 189–90

"Zauberer, Der" (The Sorcerer)
(Mozart, K. 472), 130–31
Zauberflöte, Die (The Magic Flute)
(Mozart, K. 620), 61, 132, 177–78, 188,
191, 215n82
Zedler, Johann Heinrich, 37
Zelizer, Viviana, 40
Zohn, Steven, 112
Zurich, 90, 122